Spring 72

BODY AND SOUL

honoring Marion Woodman

A JOURNAL OF
ARCHETYPE
AND
CULTURE

Spring, 2005

SPRING JOURNAL
New Orleans, Louisiana

Dedication

This issue of Spring is dedicated to

MARION WOODMAN

in recognition of her profound contributions
to our understanding of
body, mind, and
soul.

Marion Woodman: A Brief Biography

Marion Woodman is an internationally-known Jungian analyst who has explored the relationship between psyche and soma through her work and teaching for over thirty years. Born and raised in Ontario, Canada, she was trained in Zurich, Switzerland, and subsequently practiced in Toronto and London, Ontario, where she now lives with her husband, Ross Woodman. She has traveled extensively, lecturing and conducting workshops for women in several countries around the world. In 2002, the Marion Woodman Foundation was established to honor Marion and to ensure that the work she started continues to flourish and expand its outreach.

She is the author or co-author of eleven books: *The Owl Was A Baker's Daughter: Obesity, Anorexia Nervosa, and the Repressed Feminine— A Psychological Study* (1980); *Addiction to Perfection: The Still Unravished Bride* (1982); *The Pregnant Virgin: A Process of Psychological Transformation* (1985); *The Ravaged Bridegroom: Masculinity in Women* (1990); *Leaving My Father's House: A Journey to Conscious Femininity* (1992); *Conscious Femininity: Interviews with Marion Woodman* (1993); *Dancing in the Flames: The Dark Goddess in the Transformation of Consciousness,* with Elinor Dickson (1997); *Coming Home to Myself: Daily Reflections for a Woman's Body and Soul* with Jill Mellick (1998), *The Forsaken Garden: Four Conversations on the Deep Meaning of Environmental Illness,* with Thomas Berry, Sir Laurens van der Post and Ross Woodman, interviewed by Nancy Ryley (1998), *The Maiden King: The Reunion of Masculine and Feminine,* with Robert Bly (1999), and *Bone: Dying Into Life* (2001).

For more information about her work and the BodySoul Rhythms intensives she has developed with her colleagues Mary Hamilton and Ann Skinner, visit her website, www.mwoodman.org, and the Marion Woodman Foundation website at www.mwoodmanfoundation.org.

Photograph by Candice Everett

CONTENTS

BOOK REVIEWS

CELLULAR RESONANCE AND THE SACRED FEMININE:
MARION WOODMAN'S STORY

TINA STROMSTED

> Body work is soul work. Imagination is the
> bridge between body and soul.
> —Marion Woodman

Background and Contributions

My first contact with Marion Woodman's work was in 1981, when I read *The Owl Was a Baker's Daughter: Obesity, Anorexia Nervosa, and the Repressed Feminine,* which, like a good deal of Marion's writing, draws its title from classical literature. Eight years later, I met Marion in person at a workshop she was leading through the San Francisco Jung Institute. Since then I have studied with her as often as possible, participating in the BodySoul Rhythms intensive retreats she leads for women. This article grew out of my

Tina Stromsted, Ph.D., ADTR, past co-founder and faculty of the Authentic Movement Institute in Berkeley, teaches at the Santa Barbara Graduate Institute, the Marion Woodman Foundation and other universities and healing centers internationally. With three decades of clinical experience, she is a Candidate at the C.G. Jung Institute of San Francisco.
This article was published originally in *Somatics: Journal of the Bodily Arts & Sciences XIII*(1) (2000-1, Fall/Winter), 4-11 & 51-54.

dissertation research, in which I interviewed Marion and other leaders in the field about their personal experiences and work with women in transformative movement practices.

Marion's early writings were followed by many other books, tracing the development of her work and ideas: *Addiction to Perfection: The Still Unravished Bride; The Pregnant Virgin: A Process of Psychological Transformation; The Ravaged Bridegroom: Masculinity in Women; Conscious Femininity; Bone: Dying into Life;* and five co-authored books: *Leaving My Father's House; Dancing in the Flames; Coming Home to Myself; The Forsaken Garden;* and *The Maiden King,* co-authored with poet and men's movement leader Robert Bly. A Jungian analyst and internationally acclaimed author, lecturer, and workshop leader, Marion retired from her private practice in Toronto, Canada some years ago in order to focus on her health, writing, and teaching.

Marion's work with the body is rooted in her own healing journey. A gifted high school English and drama teacher for 24 years, she struggled with anorexia and the kidney failure that ensued, a struggle that eventually led her to study analytic psychology at the C. G. Jung Institute in Zurich, Switzerland. There she analyzed her dreams with her analyst and continued her healing process by exploring experiential work at home. She had had a dream instructing her to place healing images from her dreams into afflicted areas of her body. There in her own room, she would stretch, breathe, and warm up her body, and then lie down on the floor. After taking time to open her body through relaxation, she would place healing images from her dreams into ailing parts of her body, allowing the images to move and change as they flowed naturally in the tissue and in the expressive movements that unfolded. Working alone, with herself as witness, she tape-recorded the stream of images, feelings, and associations that surfaced, working with them later through writing, drawing, dancing, and analysis.

These experiences provided the seed for her BodySoul Rhythms approach, which integrates analytical psychology, dreamwork, art, mask-making, voice, bodywork, structured dance explorations, inner-sourced movement, and improvisation. Assisted by colleagues with whom she has worked for decades, dancer and educator Mary Hamilton and vocal coach and mask maker Ann Skinner, she presents these explorations internationally in women's intensive retreats. Each is a *temenos* (sacred, protected space) in a natural setting.

At the heart of Marion's work is the development of "conscious femininity." The daughter of a minister, she sought her soul through dance. Marion's approach supports women in bringing conscious feminine energy into relationship with the Holy Spirit. Her lectures and experiential work bring consciousness to and activate healing in the body/psyche/soul split suffered by most modern women who have grown up in the context of "a cultural one-sidedness that favors patriarchal values—productivity, goal orientation, intellectual excellence, and spiritual perfection."[1] Marion values the earthy interpersonal values traditionally recognized as the heart of the feminine, and the inner spiritual light. The balance of matter and spirit is at the core of her work.

In her late seventies, Marion has a presence of casual elegance. Tall, with thick, rich, wavy, graying brown hair and sparkling blue eyes, she is energetic, vibrant, and articulate, packs a surprisingly wry sense of humor, and loves to dance. Marion's tone is informative, direct, forceful, dramatic, and warm, taking care to engage the audience—even in enormous lecture halls—in something experiential that will assist them in connecting with their bodies, and then drawing them out in relationship to the material she is presenting. Though the majority of her writing and teaching addresses women's experience, she is also sensitive to the wounded inner feminine in men. A true crone—experienced, unsentimental, forgiving, and conscious of life's many paradoxes[2]—she embodies androgynous qualities, weaving rigorous theoretical material with experiential work that awakens deep feeling, body awareness, and creativity. She speaks passionately about the sacredness of matter and sacredness of soul in Sophia (the feminine face of God), the relationship between the feminine individuation journey and bodily experience, and the value of dreams and intuition in guiding one's life from the depths of one's being.

Marion lives in London, Canada, with Ross, her husband of nearly five decades, who is an author and professor of the Romantic poets. Now retired, he sometimes accompanies Marion in her work, providing a warm and concentrated presence in the background. While we women are working in the studio, Ross is walking in nature and writing, later joining us for meals and offering a guest lecture on poetry that illuminates areas we are exploring. His humor, intelligence, and love for his subject are palpable and his presence brings the masculine principle alive in our gatherings.

Personal Background

Marion grew up in a small town in Southwestern Ontario, Canada, the only girl in the family, with two younger brothers. Her father and mother met when he was giving his ordination sermon and she was a soloist in the choir. Both placed a high value on their Christian beliefs and on a life of service. An important element in the transformative movement work is the concept of being able to contact the unconscious and move freely, bringing feelings, images, bodily sensations, and memories to consciousness in a safe container, in the presence of a nonjudgmental "witness." When I asked Marion about her mother as her first "witness," wondering how her influence may have informed Marion's life and work, she replied:

"She was a suffragette who was very much ahead of her time in conservative London. She drove her own car. She had very lovely clothes. She had a job, and she had her hair bobbed before anybody else in 1926. That was big in her life because she had magnificent hair, and she decided to have it bobbed. That was more than her family could deal with. I've still got her magnificent braid that was cut off. But she was not in her body. She was very proud of her body and she was a very good-looking woman, but she had no sense of herself as a woman, in terms of loving her menstrual cycle, or loving being a woman. She didn't like being a woman. Life would have been much easier for her in a man's body. I think that was one of the biggest things she had to deal with all her life: how to get along in a woman's body.

"In her day, she definitely suffered from being a woman. She was a very bright business woman—extremely clever. But because she was a woman, she had to fight her way. Then she married my father and moved to a village church. You can imagine a business woman marrying a minister. She was really put into a cage. The people of the church could not deal with this kind of person, especially since my father was the beloved of every girl in the congregation! And he went to the city and married a city girl and that did not sit well. By the time my mother arrived they were already against her. And so it was into that atmosphere that I was born."

Marion's independent-spirited mother felt sorry for Marion being a girl. In addition, these were Depression years, and she was aware of the added limitations that Marion would face. The family depended on farmers to bring them food. Her mother tried to provide for people who were coming in off the road hungry, and she couldn't afford to buy Marion even the simplest pretty clothes.

Then, when Marion was three years old, her mother became pregnant with her last child. She became seriously ill and was, for the most part, bed-ridden for several years. She had earlier contracted tuberculosis of the glands through contaminated milk from the town dairy. With no one to look after her at home, Marion had to accompany her father on his ministerial rounds. Relegated to the parlors of parishioners while her father performed his duties, Marion made blankets out of doilies, playing in the world of her imagination and "pretty things." "My mother was the organizer in our household, and my father was my witness," Marion reflected. Marion spent very little time with her mother during her mother's illness, and "didn't see much joy in the female body" during that time. "My mother hadn't been all that happy in her [female] body, and the illness took away what joy there was," she said sadly.

Marion's own body "shut down" during those years as she took on adult responsibilities that her mother wasn't able to fulfill. "All the spontaneous playfulness of a child was curbed by my feeling that I had to be quiet. I had to take responsibility beyond my years," she recalled. And this, she says, was a potent force behind her later putting on a great deal of weight, regardless of the number of calories she actually consumed. "The inner archetypal image was of the maternal body carrying the responsibilities," she said, and "matter follows image."

At the same time, Marion experienced her father as her friend. He would often say, "Leave the child to me," when she got into difficulties with other adults. Once they were in private, he would hear her out and empathize with her experience of the event. Reflecting on her development, Marion said, "I'm cut equally from the cloth of both parents." True enough, her mother's down-to-earth, Irish-Canadian pragmatism and humor is reflected in Marion's sense of irony, which moves easily from speaking of matters of the spirit to the direct and practical experience of the body. Her father's dedication and sense of ministry have always been important to her, as has his profound connection with nature. Having grown up in the "bush," on land cleared by his Scottish parents, he was a natural gardener and a lover of animals. He took Marion fishing and hay-baling with him. The inner feminine was more accessible to him than it was to Marion's mother, who strove to overcome being a woman and all that womanhood meant in her day. As a man and minister, Marion's father was sensitive to the feelings of the people in his parish and concerned for the welfare of the Native Americans on the nearby reservation, who were always ready to offer him a chair at their table whenever he came around.

Marion's father began teaching her to read at a young age. By the time she was six, she was looking forward to going to school, expecting to be able to immerse herself further in books. Instead, "public school was a horror for me," she said. The teacher had the children continually making "windmills," an activity Marion hated, and she told the teacher so. The teacher developed a "negative thing" for Marion, told her father she was rude, and hit her fingers with the pointer. Marion survived through the power of her will, deciding to sit at the back of the classroom, as far away from the teacher as possible, or perched atop a ladder, cleaning the blinds, in the home economics class. "I was out of my body by the age of six because of my anguish at school, though paradoxically I was never more aware of my body," she said. The life of the body was cut off again when she went to university, where she spent hour after hour looking into a microscope. "Again a paradox," she said, "as I was mesmerized in the biology lab."

Books and their authors were her constant companions during those difficult school years, as they continue to be now: Emily Dickinson, Shakespeare, the Bible, C. G. Jung, T. S. Eliot, William Blake, Marie-Louise von Franz, Rilke, Berdyaev, and others. Her brothers, too, offered support. As "the preacher's kids" they didn't fit into any of the social cliques, but were in a different category, with other children cleaning up their language around them.

As a little girl, Marion talked to God continually. She also carried a picture of the courageous young Joan of Arc in her apron pocket as a source of companionship—not the soldier Joan, but the girl in a simple mauve dress with bare feet, surrounded by the angel choir to whom she talked. "Wherever I went, I would put this picture down, put two stones on it, and she would take care of me. As long as she was there, I was safe," Marion recalled.

Marion, too, saw angels as a child. "Because my father was a minister I was with death all the time, and tried to tell my mother about the angels that I was watching when my father would be at a funeral and I was waiting for the soul to take off through the sky. I would sit at the window and explain to her what I was seeing, and she would come over and say, 'Marion, I tell you there are no angels.'"

Though her mother encouraged her to be more down-to-earth and practical, Marion's belief in angels was fine with her father. But it was her faith in God that ultimately made it possible for her to carry on. "I would not say that it was faith in myself," she reflected. "I thought that God gave me the angels, and God told me to follow the images in my dreams." Here, God functioned as her ultimate, larger witness and her father as her personal witness. Marion's mother possessed a no-nonsense, practical style, a tough love that came from a "huge heart that refused to be sentimental." She was concerned that Marion did not have a strong enough hold on reality and gave her a grounding in this world, for which Marion now feels grateful, though it was difficult at the time. Not only was her mother a good business woman, but she was a wonderful cook as well. Marion remembers how, as a small girl, she would put on an apron and join her mother in the kitchen, standing on a chair to roll cookies on the counter. At the same time, her mother clearly conveyed the message, "I'm not raising a crybaby." Marion soon learned to hide her tears under her blankets when she encountered a heart-breaking experience, such as hearing the story of 'The Little Match Girl." Though her mother was capable of projecting a public persona of practicality and strength in a crisis—wrapping the gangrenous legs of poor parishioners in newspaper, for example—she could experience feelings of vulnerability only in private.

At twenty-two, Marion became anorexic, believing that she "had to be thin to *live*," as dictated by the images of women at that time. She remembers feeling "beautiful and extremely feminine" during her years of anorexia. Being able to "touch my hip bones gave me a sense of security"; their presence "assured me that I was the 'right size.'" She had always been admired for her scholarship, yet nobody had ever said she was beautiful or attractive. Suddenly she found herself in a situation where "nobody cared a hoot about what was in my head." How "high" she felt dancing, and how "out of prison," allowing herself to enter into "a paradisal state" as she "disappeared into the music"! Riveting energy accompanied her then, so much so that on one occasion, at the end of a polka, the man she was dancing with asked her politely, "Marion, would you mind putting me down?"

"There was a huge creativity in that space," she noted as she pointed out the discrepancy in her life then: she felt happy staying up much of the night dancing—waltzes, polkas, and ethnic dances with the Croatians, Finns, and Swedes in Northern Ontario—and then, though exhausted, turning around and doing a good job teaching at 9 o'clock the next morning. Determined to be thin and closer to spirit, she starved her body. "But I was on a straight rampage and I was being driven by forces that were killing my femininity. I had to change," she said. There came a day when she could no longer keep both worlds going: she collapsed on the floor while teaching. Unable to sustain her hectic lifestyle, she left for London, England, her "spiritual home," where she felt "free of the old images of responsibility for being a 'good upstanding citizen' in a 'good conservative town.'" There she danced "wonderful nights of intricate Scottish toe dancing!"

When the time came to head back home to her teaching job, Marion found that "the old heavy images of responsibility and perfection were still waiting" for her. This time she stayed, however, and married Ross Woodman. After recovering from a near-fatal car accident ten years later, she traveled to India in 1968. It was there that surrender began to play a significant role in her life, something that later profoundly informed her practice and teaching of inner-sourced movement. A severe case of dysentery led her to an out-of-body experience (described below). Summing up her experiences, Marion said, "That was the thing that broke my relationship with the school. I did go back to the school, but I knew after I came back from India that there was a new life ahead somewhere." It was also in India that Marion discovered Sophia, the feminine face of God. She had gone there fed up with being a good "father's daughter" (a woman whose sense of identity is more closely affiliated with the father than with the mother), needing to "find out who I was when all my support systems were taken away." She describes walking home alone through the snow in Canada one night, lacking the courage, without her husband, to summon up the strength to stretch out her arm and hail a cab. It was at that moment that her inner rumblings grew into a volcano.

"I knew I would buy a ticket to India and I hoped I might encounter God in an ashram in Pondicherry. Six months later I arrived in New Delhi. God was with me all right, but His ideas were somewhat different from mine. 'He' turned out to be 'She' in India, a She that I never imagined existed in the narrow confines of my Protestant Christian tradition, a She that reached out to me not in the protective walls of an ashram, but in the streets seething with poverty, disease and love."[3]

There, Marion underwent a number of transformative experiences that changed her life.

Personal Transformative Experiences—India

During her severe bout with dysentery in India, Marion had an experience that turned her life around. Too weak to stand, she fell on the tile floor of her bathroom.

"How long I was there I do not know. I came to consciousness on the ceiling, my spirit looking down at my body caked in dry vomit and excrement. I saw it lying there helpless, still, and then I saw it take in a breath. 'Poor dummy,' I thought. 'Don't you know you're dead?' And mentally gave it a kick. Suddenly I remembered my little Cairn terrier. 'I wouldn't treat Gyronne that way,' I thought. [In fact, she'd saved his life not long before by doing CPR on him all night to revive him after he'd been hit by a car.] 'I wouldn't treat a dog the way I'm treating my own body. I wonder what will become of it if I leave it here? Will they burn it? Will they send it home?'"[4]

She wondered why her body wouldn't stop breathing, why her spirit was not taking advantage of this opportunity to finally free itself: "I've been wanting to get out all my life. And here I'm out. All I have to do is take off," she thought.

"Paralyzed by the immensity of my decision—either to leave my body there or go back into it—I saw it take another breath. I was overcome with compassion for this dear creature lying on the floor faithfully waiting for me to return, faithfully taking in one breath after another, confident that I would not forsake it, more faithful to me than I to it.

"All my life I had hated my body. It was not beautiful enough. It was not thin enough. I had driven it, starved it, stuffed it, cursed it, and even now kicked it, and there it still was, trying to breathe, convinced that I would come back and take it with me, too dumb to die. And I knew the choice was mine. Most of my life I had lived outside my body, my energy disconnected from my feelings, except when I danced. Now it was my choice—either to move into my body and live my life as a human being, or to move out into what I imagined would be freedom. I also thought of what a blow it would be to Ross, not to know what had happened to me, and did not want my body to be burned on the ghats in India. A profound shift took place: an overwhelming sweetness and love came into me for this poor thing on the floor.

"I saw it take another breath and there was something so infinitely innocent and trusting, so exquisitely familiar, in that movement that I chose to come down from the ceiling and move in. Together we dragged ourselves to the little bed. I did my best to take care of it. It was as if I could hear it whispering, 'Rest, perturbed spirit, rest.' For days, perhaps nine days, I stayed in the womb of the Ashoka [Hotel]."[5]

Through this experience Marion was able to see her body as "separate" but not as a thing to be controlled. She forged a new awareness of her body/psyche connection, and, for the first time, was filled with good feelings and love toward her body. "She seemed so sweet," she said, recollecting the image of her body on the floor, "and like my beloved dog who was so loyal and dependent on me, I felt a loyalty in this creature. And I felt I didn't really know her at all, but I wanted to get to know her." Two weeks later she was still too weak to leave her hotel and negotiate the chaos of the streets of India. Providentially, one of the guests at the hotel sensed her weakened state and sent his wife to help her.

"I was sitting at the end of the couch, writing my letter, frightened to death, because I had to go back out on the street again. Then I realized that I was terrified because now I wanted to live. Before I was able to go around because I did not care as much. But this woman came and pushed her way right up against me. And she had this fat arm, soft, black, black. And she pushed right up against me so I couldn't really read or write. Every time I moved, she moved. She knew her purpose, and we eventually got down to the other end of the couch. She knew no English at all and just kept smiling at me. But she was warm and I can remember relaxing *into* her a little. And that went on for a whole week.

"And one day her husband came and said, 'You're all right now.' 'What do you mean?' I asked, startled at his intimacy. 'You were dying,' he said. 'You had the aloneness of the dying. I sent my wife to sit with you. I knew the warmth of her body would bring you back to life. She won't need to come again.' I thanked him. I thanked her. They disappeared through the door—two total strangers who intuitively heard my soul when I was unable to reach out my arms. Their love brought me back into the world. Having claimed my body and at the same time having surrendered myself to my destiny, I was undergoing both the joy and the pain of experiencing life in the flesh. ... I was no longer the victim, however. I no longer felt physically raped or in danger of death. I was participating in life with an open heart, ravished by the sights and sounds and smells of that extraordinarily paradoxical world. ... I knew something was being burned away that had to be burned away if I was going to live my life. I knew the pain was my pain. I had no idea what it meant, but I knew it had to be. I knew I was living my destiny."[6]

Upon returning to Canada, Marion taught at the university for two years and then took a sabbatical in England with her husband. There she began working on her dreams with Dr. Bennet, a wise old Irishman and Jungian analyst, whose compassion and directness helped her to get started on the task of identifying her true feelings and setting a direction for her life.

When Marion returned to her teaching job at South Secondary School, her work took on new life. "I couldn't stand the fact that the kids were bored with poetry. And I thought if I could just get these images into their bodies we wouldn't be able to stay in the room with them! And that's what happened," she said. Mary Hamilton was teaching there, too, and the two began to collaborate. Marion would take the teenagers from the English Department on the top floor down to the theater on the second floor; Mary would bring them up from the gym.

"Every afternoon at 3:00 we would start the rehearsals. We would do an hour of yoga and then start working with the poetry and imagery. ... They lay on the floor and breathed in the breath of life until their rigid bodies were relaxed. Often we did simple yoga asanas until the energy that was focused in their heads was more balanced throughout their bodies. We did obscene tongue, lip, and jaw exercises until they could open their mouths. Then we brought the 'm' and 'n' sounds resonating into their skulls, and the 'o' and 'a' vowels resonating into whatever dark corners opened.

"[Mary] encouraged them to concentrate inside, to breathe into their solar plexus, and allow the emotions to connect with the breath until the frozen organs felt the vibration of the genuine feeling, and then in its own time, to allow that emotion, always connected to the breath, to express itself wherever it moved in the body. Over a period of weeks, rigid, mechanical movements became fluid expression of whatever feelings wanted to be expressed through movement. When the joy and suffering in those young bodies was unfettered, the release of energy through their dance was almost uncontrollable.

"… Mary and I began to understand what we were, in fact, activating. Her dance training gave me insight into the unconscious blocks in the body and how to breathe and move in order to release them. My understanding of metaphor and sound and the release of energy through implanting an image in the body brought new insights to her. Body and soul came together in the programs that we and the students created in that space mid-way between the gym and the top floor."[7]

"And you know I'm going to go back to that, Tina, because I'm convinced now that if we did microbiology tests on people that we would be able to scientifically test how the cells of the body change when they read poetry. … I know from my own experience that poetry can change the metabolism of the cells," she said.

It was during this time that Marion also perceived more clearly the power of the "witness." Through careful attending, she noticed that when her attention wavered during rehearsals, "… something went wrong on the floor. The energy became lax, muffled, attenuated, an edge of fear crept in, the courageous spontaneity was lost. I suddenly understood that perceiver and perceived were one: my perception of a block in a body influenced the energy in the perceived block without one word spoken. Similarly, my lack of perception (while I thought about softening the spotlight) resulted in unconscious whorls on the stage. …

"However chaotic the theater became as the students dropped into their musculature to discover who was there, the witness was one hundred percent concentrated on what was happening, holding the conscious container. Sometimes the students witnessed each other; always [Mary or I was] witnessing the group."[8]

Eventually, Marion developed a severe kidney disorder. After 24 years of teaching English literature and directing theater productions in high school, her body once again forced her to reexamine her life. Since there were no Jungian analysts in Canada at the time, and Dr. Bennet was getting very old, he advised her to go to Zurich to work with an analyst there. Her conscious work in integrating imagery and movement with Mary and the students, following on the heels of her dreamwork with Dr. Bennet, prepared her for the deep transformative work that she would later undergo on her own.

Partnering: Body and Analysis

Hoping to find healing, Marion moved to Zurich. Now she wanted to live, but *not* on a dialysis machine for the rest of her life. She studied depth psychology and dreams at the C. G. Jung Institute in Zurich, and eventually became an analyst.

"When I arrived, there was nobody doing body work at the time. But my dream told me to take the images from my dreams and put them in my body, saying, 'Don't ask any questions, because it won't make any sense!' So many weekends I spent, maybe ten hours Saturday and Sunday, lying on the floor on a woolen blanket with another woolen blanket over me. I was in a womb, and I worked with the imagery from the dream and allowed the energy of the dream to go into my body. Over the period of four years a very severe kidney condition was healed.

"[Yes,] I was in analysis, but my analyst was outraged at the thought of body movement. So he didn't want to know anything about what was going on. His attitude was, 'If you can't transform through your dreams there's something wrong with the way you're handling your dreams.' I knew that I could have a wonderful time with my dreams because I had been through two years of that, but it didn't change my body. In fact, I got higher and higher into spirit, so my body became more and more exhausted.

"[But] there was a great pact between me and God doing this work. It's like the container in analysis. ... If it's held absolutely sealed, it's much stronger than if there's a leak. So ... I had no leaks, because I didn't have anyone to talk to. I didn't have anybody that was remotely interested in what I was doing. But my relationship with Sophia and God was sufficiently deep that I didn't have any fear. I trusted the dreams and I believed that the dreams were given by God. And I simply did what the dreams told me to do. And, of course, I was studying, so I was able to work with my studies, further amplifying and integrating my experience."

When I reflected back to Marion how amazed I felt at her ability to persevere under the circumstances, without a human witness and with so little support, she responded, "It was fear, Tina. I had to heal that kidney! I didn't go to Zurich to be an analyst. I went to Zurich to try to get this terrible problem healed. So I was profoundly faithful, simply because I wanted to live." Thus, her healing commenced through a profoundly integrative and transformative process, which was eventually to become her life's work.

The Development of Marion's Work

Marion has had to contend with several life-and-death struggles through the course of her life: with her anorexia, her severe kidney condition in Zurich, her illness and out-of-body experience in India, and her ongoing healing from the cancer diagnosis and treatment she received more recently. Marion described the importance of a lot of "good mothering" in the transformative process, and the paradox inherent in the inner-sourced movement and analytic work: in the process one must build up the strength and flexibility of the body ego, while simultaneously dismantling the defenses.

"[Women] have to be patient and build their ego until they are strong enough to dialogue with the unconscious energies that are pushing them into new territory. The ego is the filter between conscious and unconscious. The sorting process goes on in the ego. If the ego is not strong enough to dialogue with the unconscious, then it collapses under the power of complexes and addictions."[9]

"... This kind of aligning is an essential part of the healing process in which the movement from the psychic pole to the somatic pole is met by a countermovement from the somatic to the psychic. The body comes forward to meet the psychic process on the assumption that no matter how much work is done on the psyche, the body cannot absorb it unless it has been prepared."[10]

Marion describes how the work can transform the effects of the negative mother complex—the Medusa whose gaze turns the life impulse to stone—which afflicts a majority of women (and men) in patriarchal culture.

"The head recognizes; the body experiences ... [and] nature presents her bill if we do not obey our instincts. ... Whereas Medusa wants everything permanent and perfect, engraved in stone, Sophia wants things moving, breathing, creating.

"Once the body is relaxed and [following breathwork] the creative spirit is flowing between head and body, our workshops concentrate on the symbols that have been given in the dreams. Individuals work with their own energy circuits, attempting to recognize where the body is conscious and where it is unconscious, differentiating between habitual reactions and conscious body responses. Where a woman finds the body is 'black'—that is, the energy refuses to move into that area— she experiments by taking a positive healing symbol from one of her own dreams, putting it into that area and concentrating until the energy begins to move and transform. This is a very different process from concretizing the symbol, for the symbol brings together body, mind and soul, through the creative imagination, constantly transforming."[11]

"Here, too, is the real mystery of the body in movement. Each instant of movement is the instant of creation. To touch that instant is to bring consciousness into that movement, is to strike home to the very core of Being and to know it simultaneously in a gesture that is Being itself. Being resonates with YES to the Goddess."[12]

"The work is to let the ego go and *become* the music. So that you are *being* danced. Many people can't sustain that kind of surrender. Their ego becomes inflated with the archetype; they begin to identify with the archetypal energy. The result is an inflated ego, functioning out of will-power. Instead of surrendering their ego to the Self, they cling to their will-power in their own ego. It's a failed spiritual journey. We can do all we want to try to change something with our will, but Jung says it's the archetypal energy that heals, and anything else is Band-Aid. In my experience that is true. It is the essence of the feminine experience. It's the secret of great lovemaking."

Body Integrity and Surrender

For Marion, each important experience of being touched by spirit, or "broken open," has been accompanied by some kind of trauma to her body that has profoundly changed her relationship to it.

Marion acknowledges the importance of strength and the integrity of the woman's body structure as a ground for opening to consciousness, agreeing that some background in dance and/or other body disciplines can be of help with this. In fact, she feels that if it had not been for her

"Scotch-peasant body" her story would have ended in tragedy. "It kept me walking on the ground, humble, and compassionate," she said. Marion realized in her own early crisis that the path to healing lay in surrender to what she "had no will power over"—in this case, her body weight. Paradoxically, this surrender was exactly what she needed in order to grow. At that point she had lost all faith in God and her will to live. "It was in the breaking of my health that the transcendent came through from the other side," she said. "And because of the anguish in my own soul I have been totally in communication with the anguish in others." She pointed out that this is where the love comes in: "Until your heart breaks open, you don't know what love is about." Marion reminded me that it is the archetypal energy that heals. Since the turning point with the car accident and the brush with death in India, her life path has been one of "deeper and deeper surrender."

As Marion spoke with me during our interviews, paradox was ever-present in many of her life's transformative experiences. For example, during her anorexic years she felt, on the one hand, that she was living life "with the intensity, and the joy, and the rapture" that she had never had before, while at the same time "there was a death wish at the center of it" that she had not yet brought to consciousness. "I didn't care if I lived or died, so long as I was 'happy,'" she remarked with irony.

Loved Body: Living Body

Given the negative, distorted, limiting images that have been passed down in the projections of the patriarchy through the mother and father lines, learning to love our bodies plays an important role in Marion's work. Body image is a mysterious phenomenon about which we still have much to learn. However, in listening to Marion, I began to have a sense that body parts that are loved and valued in early life often continue to carry their aliveness into adulthood. For example, though Marion's mother felt sorry for Marion for being a girl, she was nevertheless able to "witness" her daughter's hair, skin, and hands, parts of Marion's body that are still vibrant and expressive today. Marion's mother was adept with her hands. "The consciousness that I have developed in my hands came through from a very early age," says Marion. Since those were the days of the Depression, when Marion's mother could not afford to buy her daughter even the most basic skirts and sweaters, she "didn't know what to do."

"But she knew how to fix my hair. ... As far as she was concerned, I had a head and hands. And if you know how I teach, and you do, I have a head and hands. I know when the kids used to parody me in high school, whoever was playing me would put on a long gown, which simply covered the body, and this extremely beautiful dance would go on with the head and the hands."

Creating the Container

Marion passes this "good mothering" and body witnessing down to her workshop participants in an evening partner exercise (modeled with Mary Hamilton) in which mother (Marion) cradles and rocks her daughter (Mary), singing and telling her stories as she brushes her hair. In this way the daughter feels held, nurtured, and accepted in the cells of her feminine body, and is able to release any excess bodily tension to this containing feminine presence. Marion also guides participants in giving each other hand and foot massages, loving the skin and easing the muscular constrictions that accompany a "lifetime of holding oneself up, holding oneself together." Marion feels strongly that even women who have never had that loving touch or sense of being contained—"and many have not"—can "experience in their body the loving arms around them, which, in turn, gradually helps them to experience their own female body as a loving container for the soul." Working in pairs also helps women experience inner "self-holding" and relaxation, in contrast to the "drivenness" that characterizes most "father's daughters." This facilitates an opening up to the vulnerability of the wounded inner child, in place of the compensatory stance that many women adopt with the use of various guises—tough Amazon, helpless little girl, seductress—or with the anesthetizing effect of various addictions, strategies that further alienate them from the source of their pain and thus from the potential for healing.[13] In the process, women begin to learn to soften their defenses, trusting that their bodies, inner life, and the firm container created within the workshop can hold them.

Marion works to create the container not only at a physical and interpersonal level, but at an archetypal level as well, using ritual elements throughout her workshops.

"I build a container at the altar so that Sophia is present. That's very important. And in analysis I always say, if you have to [telephone me in-between sessions], do so, so they know that the container has to hold. And they've got to take responsibility for holding it because, in my experience, the transcendent will come of its own accord when the container is strong enough. So I'm trying to build it with them so that when the transcendent does arrive, they'll be ready."

Marion begins each day of her workshops with a prayer at the altar. This often takes the form of asking for Sophia's guidance in assisting the group in working through specific emotional issues, as well as acknowledging important related events that are going on in the world at that time, linking inner and outer realities. From the altar, the group moves to experiential work: a group member volunteers to lead a warm-up or guided meditation to open the participants' bodies, in preparation for the day's work.

A Student's Transformative Story

Here Marion reflects on her experience with a woman in one of her workshops. This example illustrates the importance of the container provided by the feeling in the other group members. Their concentration played an essential role in the healing that was able to occur.

"I've been in workshops where the tears run down my face, because I can see pain in somebody's body. The pain starts to come out in a shriek and I can see how the body is writhing. I'm describing a mask workshop that I was working in. All the members of the workshop were working with their clay to make the masks; they had their eyes shut. I was working with one woman who had broken on the floor. The other women just kept going with their masks. They all knew she had to go through it. Not one of them opened their eyes. They sent their love over to us in the corner—I could feel their love pouring in. And that little body writhed, and pulled, and pushed, and did its best to get born. And did. In that situation love is born in the whole group. There's positive mother in the group. Nothing else will go through that wall [of the embodied negative mother] but that kind of love. If you confront the wall you come against it, but love melts it. And when you come through the wounding to the suffering, you see what the matter [the body] has endured."[14]

Integrating the Shadow

M arion's work emphasizes the importance of acknowledging and experiencing the energies of the Shadow. "Where perfection is worshipped in consciousness, imperfection is magnetic in the unconscious. Splitting light from dark denies human wholeness," she says.[15] And "as the struggle for survival intensifies, so do the forces ranged against it."[16] For this reason, Marion feels it is crucial to keep a creative outlet open in the analytic process.

"[If the woman can be encouraged] to play with the imagery, allowing it to take whatever form it happens to come up with, the energy locked in the Shadow will emerge, bringing with it the buried creative fire. In that new integration, the Self brings healing for the soul and energy for the art. The soul blossoms in the mystery connecting it to the Self."[17]

Making faces, conscious breathwork, odd sounds, awkward or funny dances, masks that can be gorgeous, terrifying, ugly, or sympathetic—all help to break down the stereotypical body image of perfect beauty that patriarchal culture sets for women. Marion says of this integrative process:

"For me, body work is soul work, and the imagination is the key to connecting both. Most of us keep our breath as shallow as possible because the eruption of feeling is too intense if we inhale deeply. Breathing is very important because it is a matter of receiving, and that is the feminine principle incarnate. [Fear of rejection is related to our breathing.] If, for example, a person has an intense negative mother complex, this often manifests in a plugged throat, plugged nose, sinus trouble, asthma, and all kinds of difficulties.

"Sometimes in body work, the mucus starts to pour out—it oozes out in ropes, out of the eyes, the nose and the mouth—when the complex is releasing! This often signals the end of asthma and related diseases. Such people often cannot give you their chest if you offer to hold them. They will arch. But when they start to trust, their body will begin to free itself and they will be capable of a full embrace.

"However, as you solve these problems, you often encounter new ones. The whole vaginal area is related to the throat and the breath. So if you release something here, you also release energy at the other end. Then you're dealing with a problem that is sexual."[18]

Finding Authentic Voice

O pening to one's voice is another essential part of Marion's
BodySoul intensives, often facilitated by vocal coach Ann Skinner.
Marion points out that often a woman's voice is pushed up into the
higher range by her negative animus, which squeezes her throat with
inner criticisms such as, "You're worthless. You don't have anything to
say. You don't expect anyone to take you seriously, do you? Who gave
you permission to take up space? Anything you have to say has been
said much better by somebody else!" Developing the capacity to stand
to one's beliefs is another element of this work. Marion tells the story
about holding her ground with a man who wanted to borrow money.
The tension between them grew so strong that the glass in a picture
frame snapped spontaneously. "Better that, than your body!" I
remarked, marveling at how she was able to develop a body that was
strong enough to contain a remarkably high level of energy without
snapping or becoming ill (UCSC Intensive, February, 1995).

Movement and vocal exercises are often followed by drawing or
painting a "body map," in which women trace each other's bodies and
then fill in the tracings of their own bodies with colors and/or other
media in response to how they perceive their bodies, and how they are
experiencing themselves at the physical, emotional, and energetic levels
at that time.

Once the participants' bodies are attuned and alive, Marion guides
them in using their dreams to facilitate healing by placing positive
dream images in "dark" parts of the body, much as she did to cure her
own kidney condition. She allows the image to move and transform as
it wishes. She also uses inner-sourced and structured, directive
movement work guided by Mary Hamilton, and often refers analysands
in her private practice for sensitive and professional touch/bodywork
when appropriate. These methods help the body open, release the
grip of the complexes, attend to the woman's wounded child, and
help the traumatized body catch up with the ego, which otherwise
often tries to move ahead too swiftly in the analysis.[19] Working with
the unconscious through the use of dreams, active imagination,
imagery, dance, art, music, voice, mask-making, and improvisational
theater, Marion's work assists women in building stronger, more flexible
and feelingful bodies—vessels for feminine consciousness.

Addictions

Integrating shadow elements and working through addictions play a large role in Marion's work.

"The trouble is that we lack basic respect for our bodies. There's a complete denial of the sacredness of matter. And that is very much connected to any addiction. That's certainly true of eating in our culture. It's true of workaholics, too, because they don't pay any attention to what they're doing to their bodies so long as they can keep working eighteen, nineteen, twenty hours a day. ... I think many of us cannot face the pain of our lives. So work is an escape, or compulsive relationship is an escape, or eating is an escape, until we weep when we look in a mirror."[20]

In working with addictions, Marion attends to the metaphor in the behaviors, holding a larger frame of reference in helping the addict understand the meaning of the patterns that accompany the illness.

"I always try to grasp the metaphor at the root of an addiction. That varies. With food, it can be mother; with alcohol, spirit; with cocaine, light; with sex, union. Mother, spirit, light, union—these can be archetypal images of the soul's search for what it needs. If we fail to understand the soul's yearning, then we concretize and become compulsively driven toward an object that cannot satisfy the soul's longing."[21]

Marion feels that it is through contacting this deep soul longing and bringing it to consciousness, rather than simply treating the external symptoms, that our culture may be healed of the addictions that exist on such a massive scale. Her style in working with people is honest, direct, forceful, respectful, humorous, sometimes confrontational, and deeply supportive. Though Marion's mother "had no sense of loving being a woman," and Marion feels sad because she herself had no child, the mother archetype has been generously expressed through her work with thousands of students, workshop participants, and analysands—"un-mothered women" and father's daughters who have benefited a great deal from the healing her work has provided them. Her own struggle with the death wish in anorexia is a testament to the work, which she models for women who wish to recognize and value their feminine being. Marion also models a feminine mode of leadership, working collaboratively with Mary Hamilton and Ann

Skinner. Their styles weave together naturally, as each takes turns leading elements of the work as well as supporting one another in the process, seeming like mother and daughters in one moment, while at other times like sister muses as they integrate their gifts.

Developing the Masculine Principle

For Marion, masculinity is "the assertive energy, the energy of discretion, discernment, clarity, the clarity that moves toward a goal. And it exists in women as well as in men. Some women call it the 'feminine yang.' I don't care what the words are. But for me, the masculine principle is parodied in the patriarchy as we have it now. It has become a despicable power principle. Our society functions through power—controlling other people, our bodies, nature—for the sake of controlling. I don't call that masculinity."[22] Paradoxically, developing a healthier relationship to the masculine principle—what Marion calls the woman's "inner Bridegroom"—is essential to feminine development.[23]

"[The] covenant to the inner masculine establishes a firm feminine standpoint: outwardly it gives a woman the ego strength to act from her own lunar consciousness grounded in her own feelings and musculature; inwardly, the masculine spirit guides her to cherish the images that alone can reveal to her who she is. Ultimately it is the unifying energy between outer and inner worlds. Her covenant with her inner Bridegroom releases her from unconscious nature, from the natural, incestuous, rigid world of her parental complexes."[24]

The animus expresses itself not only in projections onto men and in dreams, but on a body level, where it can be worked with directly. Mary Hamilton, who has often been guided in her inner work by Marion, describes the development of her animus during a movement session in which an inner Warrior figure came to her:

"I practice visualizing the Warrior's spear in my spine. After many careful observations I learn to sense the difference between being supported by the inner masculine as compared to being defeated before I even get started by the fierce negative animus. When the negative animus controls my body, my insecure and performing persona has to hold me up. It is the distinction among three postures: proper alignment with my positive masculine; a collapsed upper body with my negative masculine; an assumed rigid and inflated posture with my persona."[25]

"So how did the minister's daughter find dance?" I asked Marion. Smiling, she told me that when she returned from England with Scottish dancing records she was surprised to learn from her father's sister that she had probably inherited her Scottish Highland dance ability from her father. He had never revealed to her that he had won a number of gold medals before giving up his dancing to join the ministry! True enough, the steps had been easy for her to learn, and she had been in "heaven" on the dance floor.

Cellular Resonance

Marion described an "overwhelming sense of sweetness and love" that has come over her, sometimes accompanied by the scent of orange blossoms, in moments when Sophia is present. She also spoke of the change in the metabolism of the cells that comes about through metaphor—how when she reads Shakespeare, "the person that starts reading and the person that ends an hour later are two different people in the cells of the body." A "shimmer" comes in, a higher metabolism, something that she likens to the old feeling she had when she was anorexic, only now she has a ground for it, a "body that is strong enough to take the intensity of what's coming through. And when the metabolism, the shimmer, gets to a certain stage, the transcendent comes in."

When I shared with Marion my longing to let go of some of my current work responsibilities, and how at times when my schedule gets too busy my body sometimes feels as if it would burst in the presence of beauty or poetic metaphor (tearful with gratitude, and resonating with energy that feels big enough to burst the tension in my tissues), she urged me to pay attention. "It's the edge, Tina. The very edge. The bursting is to be touched by God," she said, "and to deny that is to block energy. Repressed energy can kill. The experience needs to be brought to consciousness, through writing, making a poem." Here she reflected again on how the bodies had changed in the high school students whom she'd invited to read and embody poetry. "It's the metaphorical body we're building. It's that place between spirit and matter."

Marion's current questions are bringing her full circle to her early days as a teacher as she pursues research in psychoneuroimmunology to discover what it is that takes place at the biological level—how *does* poetry change cell structure? Having sensed something of this in my own experiences in inner-sourced movement, I asked Marion to elaborate further.

"When I read a poem aloud and let it resonate through my body, if I love the poem, if I am really resonating with it, I get a 'shimmering' sensation. The resonators are open. They are really working. So that by the end of the poem I feel a real difference—you know, emotion, imagination, intellect, all come together—and it's as if psyche and body are whole. The only way I could describe that would be as an inner marriage where body and psyche are one."

"And does your subjective experience of yourself and your world change?" I wondered.

"Well," she responded, "if I don't read poetry every day and don't listen to music, I tend to get mired in mud. I fall into body and feel slow. I put on weight. My eating patterns don't change, but there's a slowness in the metabolism and everything is 'matter.' Whereas when I read poetry aloud, when I listen to music, especially if I dance to it, my body is alive. Every cell is full of spirit."

"You're also really speaking about this as a 'living,' daily practice, as a way of life," I noted. "As, for example, differentiated from other images of 'enlightenment,' where people assume an 'end point' or something that you achieve—images that seem to be more characteristic of the masculine perspective."

"That's right," said Marion. "I don't see an end point to that, except death. And I've had a pretty good look at that one with this cancer, because with that in the wings you don't fool around."

About ten years ago, Marion was diagnosed with cancer at the base of her spine. Since then she has been in a healing process, combining Western medical, homeopathic, and movement and dreamwork practices, outliving all of her doctor's predictions. In 2000, she completed a book articulating her experience living with and recovering from cancer, entitled *Bone: Dying into Life* (2000). Integrating findings from quantum physics and information from current psychoneurological research, she remains passionate in deepening her understanding of the relationship between spirit and matter.

Personal Practices: Integration into Daily Life

Marion reflects that it took her sixteen years "to understand why I went to India" and to integrate the transformative experiences that she had there. When I point out that I rarely hear about the integrative aspects of the transformative process—it's usually the "peak experiences"[26] that people focus on—Marion underscores how essential this is, and how "useless it is if you leave it [the transformative experience] alone."

"How do you integrate these experiences into your daily life?" I asked her, to which she responded, "It's challenging to live in the body, and all of the things I do now—dancing, drawing, holding people, writing—are all part of my effort to continue to integrate and live this."

Though she has become much more receptive to her body sensations and "allows intuition to flow through her body," she states that she still has to discipline her body, since "periodically it's like a wild race horse. There's still a teenager in me. That energy [which would have her up dancing all night long, and then teaching school at 9 a.m.] is still in me periodically, but now my body and I are friends," she said. One of her daily personal practices is to put on music and "lie on the floor and spend half an hour letting my body do anything it wants to do." In this safe and free space, she often speaks as she moves, tape recording the movement patterns and images that emerge, or journaling following her movement experience to understand better what was going on, "because I believe that you have to bring [the material] to consciousness." Over years of this practice Marion has developed a sensitive and refined "inner witness," capable of maintaining a conscious awareness as she allows herself to be moved by unconscious material.

After moving, she often draws the images that have come to her, working with them in the same way that she would analyze a dream, tracking the sequence of images "to see where the energy wants to go," as the imagery "has the transformation right in it." During this integrative phase of the work she first brings her own personal associations to the images, and then uses a dictionary of imagery and symbols and other relevant texts to amplify them further, historically and mythologically.

Marion also takes daily hour-long walks to the river in London, Ontario, keeps a daily journal, carries on research for her books, listens to music, and shares long conversations with Ross. The two work on their dreams together, as well. "I lost my daily six hours of imagery when I retired from my teaching job because I didn't sit down and read Shakespeare every day!" Now that she's realized how deep her need for poetry is—"it's food for the soul"—she and Ross read poetry aloud to each other. "The older you get, the more you understand it," she said, again describing the "shimmer" that runs through her when she reads Shakespeare, a shimmer that found a pathway through her work with inner-directed movement.

Now when she dances, her body comes alive. "Every cell fills with spirit, so that I no longer feel weighted down and mired in the mud of matter." Having come to know the sacredness in matter, Marion takes time to "tune her body/instrument, as if preparing for Mozart." Her senses are now considerably more heightened and intensified, and she experiences the same electric "shimmer" when she sees beauty in nature, such as the red tulips that create a "little epiphany" that stays with her. After decades of work with the body, Marion finds that her intuition has also grown keener as she picks up things going on with other people at greater distances. "When you've got more ground, the intuition can fly higher or more broadly," she said, referring to her psychic experiences. Marion's teaching combines a practical, grounded, sensation-specific use of language with profoundly metaphoric, symbolic, aesthetic, and spiritual images, grounding the latter with the former in daily life. The effect is often surprising, humorous, and powerfully integrative.

Sophia's Perfume

As our conversations came to a close, Marion reflected on another transformative experience she'd had, which, like the others, engaged her directly at a body level. In this instance, she had been driven nearly crazy by the tinnitus that had been ringing loudly in her ear ever since her car accident, "to the point where I nearly didn't care if I lived or died," she said.

"But the tinnitus in my ear was the opening to Sophia, because I had a dream, filled with the scent of an orange blossom bush, in which I heard a clear voice ask, "How does it feel on the eve of becoming everything you've fought against all your life?" And I thought, "For heaven's sake, what does that mean?" Well, I found out, in a vision that immediately followed. I'd fought the feminine all my life, but I didn't know it. And, again, it was the love that healed me ... this overwhelming sense of love, and the perfume ... I could feel it, just cell by cell by cell. [Marion vibrated her fingers to demonstrate the shimmering sensation that grew from the ground up, traveling up her legs and through her whole body.] My body became limp with the beauty of the perfume. And I'd never known this kind of love before—pure, transcendent—feminine transcendence from below."

"How did you identify it as 'feminine' energy?" I asked. "Remember the song you sang at the end of that workshop, Tina, with the words that were given to you from your dream? How did that go?"

Recalling the lyrics from years ago, still resonant within me, I sang to the tune of "Motherless Child":

> *I used to feel like a*
> > *mother-less child,*
> *Now I know that I'm*
> > *really wild,*
> *Right now I'm finding my*
> > *personal style,*
> *Deep, down*
> > *in my bones.*
> *Last night I dreamed of*
> > *dance and perfume,*
> *Crazies and red wine filled the*
> > *upstairs rooms.*
> *Downstairs the choir sang,*
> > *"Sophia blooms!"*
> *Deep, down*
> > *in my bones.*
> *There, I'm not alone.*
> *She gives us our Home.*

"What a beautiful expression of feminine energy, Tina!" Marion responded. "And I want to connect this with your story. The love I experienced was soft. It was warm ... like the lady in India. I could relax into it like those little Japanese dolls ... they can hardly hold their heads up. It was sinuous, it was flexible, it was total surrender. One hundred percent surrender. Yet I was totally immersed. And the healing would not have happened without that—I became totally concentrated on *being* the orange bush. The energy leapt beyond simile, 'like an orange bush'; it *became* the orange bush. That's metaphor.

"This is the secret of the transformation: when I see an orange bush in my meditation, I *become* the orange bush. I become the perfume. So the ego is not present, ... there is union. My being is permeated; it is total intercourse with the Divine. And it feels like an orgasm, yes, it does. ... And there's nothing new about that."

Movement created an opening, India cradled the initiate, and Sophia responded. Of her experience she said:

"Vulnerable and alone, infinitely at the mercy of whatever was to happen, I knew it was not my will, not my love, but Her will, Her love, that there was some meaning to my life infinitely beyond anything I had ever imagined, and that my delicate body—in all its ugliness and all its beauty—was the temple through which I had come to know Her on this earth."[27]

Years of work with body and psyche, integrating dreams and inner-sourced movement, have provided a tremendous healing and guide for Marion. Today, she invites women she works with to find the discipline and surrender that can allow them to open to Sophia's gifts.

> The feminine
> has slower rhythms
> meanders,
> moves in spirals,
> turns back on herself,
> finds what is meaningful to her,
> and plays.
> This is your body,
> your greatest gift,
> pregnant with wisdom you
> do not hear,
> grief you thought was forgotten,
> and joy you have never known.[28]

NOTES

1. Marion Woodman, *Addiction to Perfection: The Still Unravished Bride* (Toronto: Inner City Books, 1982), back cover.

2. Marion Woodman, Kate Dansen, Mary Hamilton, and Rita Greer Allen, *Leaving My Father's House: A Journey to Conscious Femininity* (Boston: Shambhala Publications, Inc., 1992), 202.

3. Marion Woodman, *The Pregnant Virgin: A Process of Psychological Transformation* (Toronto: Inner City Books, 1985), 176.

4. *Ibid.*, 178.

5. *Ibid.*

6. *Ibid.*, 179-81.

7. Woodman, *et al.*, *Leaving My Father's House*, 120-21.

8. *Ibid.*, 123.

9. *Ibid.*, 205.

10. Woodman, *Pregnant Virgin*, 57.

11. *Ibid.*, 88.

12. *Ibid.*, 111-12.

13. Linda Leonard, *The Wounded Woman: Healing the Father-Daughter Relationship* (Chicago: Swallow Press, 1982); Linda Leonard, *On the Way to the Wedding: Transforming the Love Relationship* (Boston: Shambhala Publications, Inc., 1986); Linda Leonard, *Witness to the Fire: Creativity and the Veil of Addiction* (Boston: Shambhala Publications, Inc., 1989); Marion Woodman, *The Owl was a Baker's Daughter: Obesity, Anorexia Nervosa, and the Repressed Feminine* (Toronto: Inner City Books, 1980); Woodman, *Addiction*; Woodman, *Pregnant Virgin*; Marion Woodman, *The Ravaged Bridegroom: Masculinity in Women* (Toronto: Inner City Books, 1990); Marion Woodman, *Conscious Femininity: Interviews with Marion Woodman* (Toronto: Inner City Books, 1993); Marion Woodman, "Conscious femininity, Part One," in *Sitting by the Well: Bringing the Feminine to Consciousness through Language, Dreams, and Metaphor* [Cassette Recorded at the conference "Care of the Soul," presented by Carol Susan Roth, June 4-5, 1993] (Boulder, CO: Sounds True Recording, 1993); Marion Woodman and Robert Bly, *The Maiden King: The Reunion of Masculine and Feminine* (New York: Henry Holt & Company, 1998); Marion Woodman and Elinor Dickson, *Dancing in the Flames: The Dark Goddess in the Transformation of Consciousness* (Boston: Shambhala Publications, 1996).

14. Woodman, "Conscious Femininity, Part One," tape 5.

15. Woodman, *Ravaged Bridegroom*, 143.

16. Woodman, *Conscious Femininity*, 86.

17. *Ibid.*, 100-101.

18. *Ibid.*, 16-17.

19. Woodman, *Pregnant Virgin*, 55.

20. Nancy Ryley, *The Forsaken Garden: Four Conversations on the Deep Meaning of Environmental Illness* (Wheaton, IL: Quest Books, 1998), 83.

21. Woodman, *Conscious Femininity*, 124.

22. Ryley, 66.

23. Woodman, *Ravaged Bridegroom*.

24. Woodman, *et al.*, *Leaving My Father's House*, 206-207.

25. *Ibid.*, 149.

26. Abraham Maslow, *Toward a Psychology of Being* (New York: D. Van Nostrand, 1968); Abraham Maslow, *The Farther Reaches of Human Nature* (New York: Viking Press, 1971).

27. Woodman, *Pregnant Virgin*, 181.

28. Marion Woodman and Jill Mellick, *Coming Home to Myself: Reflections for Nurturing a Woman's Body and Soul* (Berkeley, CA: Conari Press, 1998), 147-149.

THE EYE THAT CANNOT SEE

MARION WOODMAN

For thirty years, I have been grappling with, "What is conscious femininity?" Recently that question has dropped to a deeper level of my spiral as I ask myself, "What is the death mother?" The question is an electric shock through my body as I work with young women diagnosed with breast cancer or older women who, having worked for years holding the connection between psyche and soma (initially perhaps as opposites), are suddenly faced with treacherous autoimmune break down. What is this unconscious pull out of life? What is this unconscious acceptance of death? What is this sudden reversal from a strong forward thrust into life to a life-threatening struggle? A dark, archetypal energy emerges.

This death goddess is not the Indian goddess Kali, she who apparels herself with sword and skulls. Kali is death in the service of life. She appears in dreams when the dreamer is clinging too long to outworn patterns of thinking and behaviour, infantile attitudes long since deserted, new energies ravaged by empty rituals. Kali cleans with an

Marion Woodman, to whom this issue is dedicated, is an internationally-known Jungian analyst and lecturer, a pioneer in women's psychology, and the author or co-author of eleven books, including *The Pregnant Virgin: A Process of Psychological Transformation*, *The Ravaged Bridegroom: Masculinity in Women*, and *Bone*. For more information about her work, see www.mwoodman.org and www.mwoodmanfoundation.org.

exacting sword, making room for fresh green sprouts to shoot into life
with all the energy of new thoughts, new loves.

Nor is this death goddess the negative mother, who controls her
child with unconscious power and judgment. Negative mother is the
voice that rules in many households, whether it comes from mother or
father. Her message is, "If you love me, you will do as I say. Be who I
want you to be. I know you better than you know yourself; I know
what is best for you." Men and women attempting to live their freed
vitality in a workshop often crumble to the floor. "I heard the old
voice," they say. "Who do you think you are? When all this artsy-
fartsy flakiness is over, you'll be mine." While that voice can keep its
victim imprisoned, struggling for breath and light, scratching psoriasis,
or some other torn-between-the-opposites illness, the level beneath
may contain what feels like unnegotiable despair.

Despair is death mother, unnegotiable because looking her in the
eye is turning to stone, being literally unable to move—what I have
called "possum psychology." "If a person is doing his or her best to
establish a standpoint based on authentic feeling values," I wrote,

> then the body must reinforce the stand. What I have discovered
> in many of my analysands, however, is what I call "possum
> psychology," where the body either cannot or will not reinforce
> the feeling value. It experiences life as a magical minefield in
> which it alone is knocked down by inaudible explosions. If
> there is unconscious hostility in the environment, the inner
> body, acting autonomously, falls over "dead." Having experienced
> this inner collapse all their lives, these people have learned to
> keep up the social chatter and use the polite persona as a decoy
> to beguile danger away from the fallen ego. When the crisis
> subsides, the ego attempts to stand up, but if it senses an unseen
> enemy, it automatically falls "dead" again.
>
> When the body is so intuitive and so unconscious, the ego
> has never functioned properly because, in any threatening
> situation, the autonomic nervous system has said *No*, and the
> ego has withdrawn. Until the body responses are brought to
> consciousness so that the individual can recognize what is
> happening both internally and in the environment, one cannot
> act with normal aggression, cannot respond to everyday
> challenges, and the ego cannot mature through normal
> interchange. The sensitive body sets up a defense mechanism

that may manifest in fat, in swelling, in blushing, in vomiting; it will do what it can to keep poison out. If the individual lives close to the unconscious—e.g. is a psychic or an artist—then the body responses require acute observation and must be dealt with consciously [art, for example, as the conscious or "subtle" body]. Otherwise, the isolated ego will seek some soporific to escape the unfocused dread.[1]

The ego can become conscious enough to hear the possum's warning, "Mines here somewhere!" If it is strong enough to fend off the invisible threat, it will decide whether to withdraw or stand firm. Even the standing still may release psychic poison (terror, rage) into the physical body. That encapsulated poison requires an appropriate outlet. Dancing in one's room, for example, allows the body to recreate its own rhythms rather than dismember itself in chocolate, alcohol, or satin pajamas. Otherwise, it moves into unconscious, compulsive action.

Within the traumatic structure, the trauma itself protects the victim from destruction. There is no place in this psyche that allows abandonment; abandonment and rejection are too death-dealing to be accommodated because they are coming from such a primordial, prenatal place. When the archetype of the death mother is at the core of the mother complex, then the body, as the primal scene of the unconscious, carries the psychosis. Body acts as what Donald Kalsched calls a "Protector/Persecutor"[2]: whenever danger of rejection or abandonment occurs, the blinkers are in place to blind the ego to the actual situation. (In extreme cases, actual blindness may occur.) Possum drops "dead." Life energy drains out of the cells. Trauma protects from actuality. Idealization is the compensating situation that will block the recurrence of abandonment.

Examining a dream may clarify the theory.

> I am living in a refurbished attic. I am seated on the Victorian settee I inherited from my maternal grandmother. A majestic golden-white lion is living with me. He is sitting under the small window.
>
> My male analyst is coming for a session because I am too weak to go to his office. We hear a footstep on the stair. Instantly, the lion stands up, sashays around the back of the settee, swirling its tail in my face. He comes around to the front of the settee,

looks straight into my eyes, and decides to sit in front of the
door, blocking the only entrance.

Here we have a sealed-off trauma. The dreamer, who was anorexic,
lives in her head, in a refurbished world, cut off from reality, sitting on
the idealized heritage of her maternal line. Her guardian is a golden-
white lion, suggesting strong spirit in her emaciated animal body. He
will protect her from any new life coming into this stagnant attic
world. With the arrogance, assurance, and jealous affection of a master,
he *protects* her from the blistering pain of life and at the same time
persecutes her by refusing to share her with anyone, especially one who
might awaken her to her own life. Her stripped anorexic body is carrying
the trauma.

Here, too, we can sense the idealization of the compensating
structure that will block the recurrence of sheer naked abandonment.
She writes that the lion was golden-white, a special, even sacred, animal,
white shining with gold. For her, he seems to embody majesty, strength,
fun, companionship, even cherishing. Her description of his audacious
behaviour does not suggest that she feels imprisoned by him. She
blandly accepts that the one who could help to awaken her does not
gain entrance. She as yet has no awareness that the lion may be carrying
her idealized father-god projection and he might devour anyone who
attempts to change their relationship, especially an analyst whose
mission on this visit may be to one day release her from her persecutor,
the father-god who has cast his deathlike spell upon her. The lion is
her demon lover who holds her in the embracing arms of the trauma,
keeps her in it under the illusion that he is protecting her psyche from
it. He holds her in an embrace of death. Her erotic idealization of the
trauma keeps her under the spell of the illusion. This is all happening
in the depths of her psyche.

Great artists work from these depths, which Jung characterizes as
the collective unconscious. They articulate the archetypal field that
other mortals drop into in deep sleep. William Blake was mapping
the unconscious a hundred years before depth psychology was named.
In his poem, "The Little Girl Lost," from *Songs of Experience*, he
describes this analysand's dream-situation in the figure of the naked
Lyca, locked by her guardian animals in the "caverns deep" of trauma.
"Sleeping Lyca lay," writes Blake,

> While the beasts of prey,
> Come from caverns deep,
> View'd the maid asleep
>
> The kingly lion stood
> And the virgin view'd,
> Then he gambold round
> O'er the hallowd ground;
>
> Leopards, tygers play,
> Round her as she lay;
> While the lion old,
> Bow'd his mane of gold.
>
> And her bosom lick,
> And upon her neck,
> From his eyes of flame,
> Ruby tears there came;
>
> While the lioness
> Loos'd her slender dress,
> And naked they convey'd
> To caves the sleeping maid.[3]

The spell of trauma can become the fantasized penetration of the lion taking her into rapturous death. "Now more than ever seems it rich to die," writes Keats of the spell of trauma (the nightingale's song), a trauma that, facing his own imminent death following fast upon his brother's death, Keats compares to a "drowsy numbness" in which, having drunk hemlock or some "dull opiate," he sinks "Lethe-wards."[4]

Culturally, the Romantic poets were the harbingers who were taken into the depths of the collective unconscious where they were compelled to face the anguish of the repressed feminine. (The nightingale of Keats's ode is archetypally Philomel, who is raped by her suitor. To silence her, he cuts out her tongue and, as lyric poet, assumes it as his own.) In the embrace of the silenced feminine, many of the Romantics died before the age of thirty. The Victorians too, even the Edwardians, were in the grip of disillusionment, doubt, undercurrents that "bring the eternal note of sadness in."[5] Prestige, power, fame, and fortune— all in the ranks of two world wars drove the feminine deeper underground, rendering the lyric voice of the male poet more and more tortured. Now the ranks are being filled again. Is the feminine still locked in trauma both culturally and individually? Can the male singer survive his song? Or can the emergence of the conscious feminine redeem him?

Take, for example, the magnificent opening of the Olympic games in Athens, 2005. Television at its best! The majestic lion swishing its tail! Perfect vignettes of ancient Greece, bringing up exact memories of pictures in our history books: Athens as the seed bed of government, law, religion, medicine, theatre, spirit descending in full flight. Then a small glitch seemed to happen. A teenage girl, her back to the camera, her long hair decorated with a flower or two, her dress a flimsy see-through affair, stumbled across a web of television wires. The contrast between perfection and accident was totally incongruous. She went resolutely on and, to my knowledge, not one commentator took any notice. Then she turned, and before us was a modern Primavera, her arm curved around her large pregnant belly—pregnant with luminous light. She wandered down into the crowd and finally into the centre of the stadium. The lights went down. Her brilliant belly was the only light in the darkness—this young feminine carrying the light that can change the world. The female creator of this extraordinary piece, like all great artists, connected the end to the beginning. Then we saw the tiny children from several lands receive in their hands light to carry home. With millions of eyes around the world spellbound by this spectacle, Plato's cave, to my knowledge not one commentator could see the pregnant feminine carrying in her womb the new life that could change the world. Another victory for "caverns deep"?

Emily Dickinson knew only too well the anguish of the inner marriage between death mother and demon lover. "The difference between Despair / And fear," she writes,

> is like the One
> Between the instant of a Wreck—
> And when the Wreck has been—
>
> The Mind is smooth—no Motion—
> Contented as the Eye
> Upon the Forehead of a Bust—
> That knows—it cannot see—[6]

The falling into stone (the Eye that cannot see) recalls the story of Medusa, the most beautiful of the three Gorgon sisters, she who dared to make love with Poseidon, Lord of the Sea, in the temple of Athena. Outraged, Athena punished her for the sacrilege by transforming her beauty into ugliness and her beautiful hair into ever-writhing snakes demanding more, more, more of anything, so long as it was more. Medusa's ugliness turned anyone who looked directly at her into stone. A supersaturated solution (more, more, more) crystallizes.

Ugliness or anguish? Here was a full-hearted, passionate woman who gave her love to a god in a temple on an island. That passion— that projection onto a handsome god—was cut off by a shadow sister who was known for her wisdom, her bounty of spirit to Athenian sailors and warriors, the soul of Athens itself, Leo-born, fully matured from the forehead of Zeus. Did Medusa embody a feminine passion Athena yearned for? On her shield, the goddess of wisdom had engraved the head of a Gorgon, knowing Medusa embodied an energy she needed, knowing too that no one dared look into the eyes of Medusa.

In pondering this story, I think of Mary Magdalene, the shadow sister of the Virgin Mary through hundreds of years of Christianity. The Church Fathers dared not look into her eyes, nor did they allow the parishioners to look, in spite of her closeness to Christ throughout the Gospels. (Nor did they dare allow themselves or their parishioners to contemplate the Virgin Mother's ascent to the wedding chamber of her Son until Pope Pius XII dogmatically proclaimed it in 1950.) Modern research is opening abundant insight into the humanity of Mary Magdalene as the closest friend of Christ, his beloved wife, the mother of his child. Even *Time* dared very recently to put her on the cover.

So what has this to do with not looking the Medusa in the eye? If we dare to look, what do we see? A woman whose life was not lived. Perhaps she was a woman who began with a vision, a woman who loved beauty, whose soul sang with love and sexual laughter, her spirit fired with creativity, a woman who dared to love the god. Her feminine light was snuffed out.

The eyes I am describing are the eyes we see in photographs of our great grandmothers and grandmothers, generations of women who struggled to walk life through. Perhaps their dream carried them to a distant shore, where they learned that sharing their life with their god-husband was ceaseless drudgery—building a log house, hand-washing clothes, scrubbing bare planks, feeding six children, with another in the belly and two already in the grave, belly and grave now closely intertwined. The carved hope chests, full of linens brought from home, were never opened, but always present. To look into their eyes is too often a plunge into a pool of grief and disbelief. "Who am I?" they ask. "Whatever happened? What is it all about?" They did the very best they could and went to church in their worn-out satin shawls on Sunday. They carried a load of imprisoning responsibility with a sense of loss of their own freedom, the anguish of hope crushed in a life unlived.

The shadow side of disappointment can jump out: "I have no life, but my children will live what I worked so hard to achieve. My work swallowed achievement. They will live what I died for." With that load on their shoulders, children attempt to speak their own truth and find themselves looking into the anguished eyes of Medusa, while hearing the insatiable cries of the snakes, "More, more, more!" More of what?" they ask. "Life I never had," comes the answer. There is the paralysis of the trauma. If this child knew in the womb that it was not the gender the parents longed for, or there was no money for another child, or timing in the marriage was bad, or it barely escaped abortion, this child knows it is not welcomed into life. It carries a skeletal fear of death. *Not Wanted.* Is there anything worse for a helpless infant to experience in its bones? It looks into the anguished eyes of its mother and sees itself as the cause. If this realization hits in the very early years, the central nervous system is ready at any moment as if under the spell of a curse to experience obliteration and death and the shock of finding itself alive.

Living in a culture where the feminine is constantly mocked, marauded, or raped, the darkness of that shadow surreptitiously sneaks into everyday living like the serpent in the dank garden of Eden. We read the newspaper, listen to the news. Environmentalists are warning us that our greed—our more, more, more—must stop if we are to survive. Mother Nature rebels in tidal waves, cyclones, volcanoes. We try to dismiss it as superstition. Monsanto is stripping our farmers from their land: they cannot compete with the corporate pig farms, chicken farms—hell holes where the powerless animals never see the sun and we, sun-dependent beings, are expected to thrive on the sunless ravaged protein, as if not to thrive is to become the victims of wanton superstition, victims of the irrational, hysterical feminine. Yes, personal despair can quickly escalate into archetypal despair, despair that escalates into death mother. "What's the use?"

Or perhaps despair escalates into addiction—more, more, more driven energy that has no satiation point because concrete and symbolic are confused. If, for example, the soul is starving for sweetness, nourishment, love, no amount of honey, granola or chocolate is going to satisfy the yearning. Moreover, if the soul connection is projected onto the food (the sweetness that symbolizes the loving mother), the addict becomes bonded to the surrogate. She knows her soul is at ransom, so is her body. "Of course I prayed—," writes Emily Dickinson,

> And did God Care?
> He cared as much as on the Air
> A Bird—had stamped her foot—
> And cried "Give Me"—
> My Reason—Life—
> I had not had—but for Yourself—
> 'Twere better Charity
> To leave me in the Atom's Tomb—
> Merry, and Nought, and gay, and numb—
> Than this smart Misery.[7]

The path of addiction leads to death. Does that matter? Does she care? Was she ever living her own life? Was she always pleasing someone else, speaking with someone else's voice? Would death be an escape from this charade?

That's the question in the eye of Medusa. The snakes cannot go on writhing forever. Food, alcohol, drugs, work, shopping are ultimately no escape from that eye. Men and women who are unconsciously carrying that shadow gaze at it in their own mirror and experience it in their own body.

A deep irony is at the core of addictive behaviour. When the death mother is strong, the child has to go into life with pretended verve. For his survival, he has to put extra will power into almost everything he attempts, often with astonishing results that even he believes in. His ego may become stronger, his depressed energy released into creative outlets that flower into real happiness. Then his ego may be called upon to sacrifice some of its desire to Destiny's desire, beginning the journey from 'my will be done' to 'thine be done.' A crisis will almost surely erupt. He has survived by driving his will power to believe in anything, to try to do anything, to try to survive. He has carried his ego to its human breaking point. Survival, he realizes, is not enough. The more, more, more becomes suddenly less and less until it is finally, and dangerously, nothing at all. To give up his will power is surely to choose death. Will he ever get out of bed? Will he ever try again? The plan that worked for the ego is being dismantled for what? Why do so many successful people die of autoimmune breakdown when they retire from their life's work? Was it, in reality, their death work?

This watershed is crucial where a death mother is at work in the body and certainly in the psyche. The possum is that moment of blank when the frail ego's hold on life is wiped out by a comment that violates all the soul knows. In its past, the battling soul unknowingly settled into its own defeat. It first retreated into its own collapse and then, unconscious of what it had done, forged unknowingly the protective armour of death. In this protective armour, the death mother assumes the guise of the demon lover, a deadly hermaphroditic union that is, in psychic reality, the demonic parody of the *hieros gamos* or inner marriage. If in this sepulchre the soul can transform the energy harnessed against it, the energy of the lion who guards the tomb—the stone of Medusa—may become the energy that releases the soul into life.

This resurrection is not the work of the ego. Its energy does not issue from the will ("So free we seem, so fettered fast we are!"[8] writes Browning.) It comes from a far deeper place, free of the ego, where the death mother is released from the curse that Athena imposed upon Medusa, so that her love is free once again to participate in the ceaseless flow of Poseidon's power. It comes from the collective unconscious, which is, for Jung, the realm of the gods in the infinite variety of their human constellations. Issuing from Medusa's impregnation are the two winged horses, the white Pegasus, charged with limitless vision, and the black Chrysaor, armed with the golden sword of discrimination, the one necessary to the other. "Lest from this flying steed unreined," writes Milton,

> Dismounted, on th' Aleian field I fall,
> Erroneous there to wander and forlorn.[9]

This archetypal drama enacted again and again in the soul's mythopoeic life is the birthright of every soul born into the world. In poetry and the other arts, in religion, dream, synchronicity, the passions, the soul has access to the infinite resources of the collective unconscious, which is ultimately on the side of the ongoing process of life. If only by the skin of its teeth, humanity has long survived and still continues to survive.

But there are no short cuts. The patterns of survival run deep. No resurrection can skip a crucifixion, a descent into hell, without being denied the consciousness upon which the soul finally depends for what Jung calls God's incarnation in "creaturely man."[10]

The following two dreams enact the necessary shift (transformation) in the dreamer's consciousness. In the first the dreamer is a priestess in a temple arranging a bouquet of flowers for a ritual. She cannot fit the centerpiece of white and red flowers into it. Light from a hole in the shape of a cross shines directly onto the point where the centerpiece is to be placed. A voice tells her that her hymns cannot reach heaven until she cleans up her mess in the basement, which she did not know was there. She finds her way down a staircase into it and there in a dark, stagnant pool she sees a black, writhing snake trying in vain to get its head onto an eight-spoked wheel. The snake's task is to keep the wheel turning so that water will flow freely through the temple. The dreamer (who suffered from acute edema) tries to help the snake by bringing the wheel (of life) closer to it. The snake strikes at her. Her analyst pulls her quickly out of the way.

In the second dream, the same woman is wandering through a wasteland. She sees a green and brown snake coming toward her, not on its belly, but rising from the earth to propel itself forward, its golden eye crowning its head as it moves merrily along. She follows it to a cave where in a niche are two immense books. She reaches for the first, *The Seven Chronicles of the Western World*. The snake strikes her hand, insisting that it is not for her. The other book has a golden eye on its cover, the same golden eye that crowns the snake. She opens it. Inside there are no words. She feels only an unrestricted love pouring into her from the living golden eye on the cover of the book. "This is your task," says the snake.

The snake, as a symbol of a newly released consciousness (biblically associated with forbidden knowledge), is, in the first dream, a consciousness for which she is as yet unprepared. She is not yet ready to embrace it. In the second dream she is ready. Though she reaches first for a consciousness that has collectively completed its work, she is told by the snake that her task lies with a new consciousness arising out of the collective unconscious of which there is as yet no written record. This is the work of the conscious feminine. This new feminine is the centre of the bouquet, the red and the white as complements, a paradox that she has yet to comprehend. This paradox consciously held is the inner marriage, the eternal object of the soul's earthly task.

As the pendulum swings, the intensity of darkness is balanced by the intensity of light. When the Death Mother is depotentiated, her gift is life lived with the discrimination of the golden sword and the creativity of the winged horse.

NOTES

1. Marion Woodman, *The Pregnant Virgin* (Toronto: Inner City Books, 1985), 61.

2. Donald Kalsched, *The Inner World of Trauma* (New York: Routledge, 1986), 45.

3. William Blake, *The Complete Poetry & Prose of William Blake,* ed. David. V. Erdman, commentary Harold Bloom (New York: Doubleday, 1988), 20–21.

4. John Keats, "Ode to a Nightingale," in *The Norton Anthology of English Literature*, ed. M. H. Abrams (New York: W. W. Norton & Co., 1975), 1853.

5. Matthew Arnold, "Dover Beach," in *The Norton Anthology of English Literature,* ed. M. H. Abrams (New York: W. W. Norton, 1975), 2183.

6. Emily Dickinson, *The Complete Poems of Emily Dickinson,* ed. Thomas H. Johnson (Boston: Little Brown & Co., 1960), 144.

7. *Ibid.,* 179.

8. Robert Browning, "Andrea del Sarto," in *The Norton Anthology of English Literature,* ed. M. H. Abrams (New York: W. W. Norton & Co., 1975), 2116.

9. John Milton, *Paradise Lost,* ed. Scott Elledge (New York: W. W. Norton & Co., 1975), 7.17–20.

10. C. G. Jung, "Answer to Job," *Collected Works* 11 § 743.

Marion Woodman's
"Vale of Soul-Making"

ROSS WOODMAN

Oddly enough, the problem is still the same 2,000-year-old one:
How does one get from Three to Four?
— Jung, letter to Pauli, October 24, 1953

"There is no linear evolution; there is only a circumambulation of the self" in which all human experience "points toward a centre,"[1] Jung writes, describing his use of the mandala in a series of meditations figuratively enacting the surrender of the ego to the self. Symbolizing a fourfold wholeness, Jung's mandalas consist of greatly elaborated internally squared circles or internally circled squares. That which, as without beginning or end (circle), transcends the *mythos* (archetypal narrative) of human consciousness nevertheless remains for Jung bound to it.

Ross Woodman is a Professor Emeritus of English at the University of Western Ontario and author of *The Apocalyptic Vision in the Poetry of Shelley* (University of Toronto Press), *Sanity, Madness, Transformation: The Psyche in Romanticism* (University of Toronto Press, forthcoming), and numerous articles on Romantic literature and contemporary art. He is also the recipient of the Distinguished Scholar Award (1993) from the Keats-Shelley Association of America. He has been married to Marion Woodman for nearly fifty years.

Psychologically understood in its Jungian perspective, *mythos* is the
linear logic or causality which, as a natural supernatural narrative,
shapes the subjective variety of individual life into a fourfold (squared)
consciousness of its wholeness. This consciousness, which Jung calls
the Self, is the fourfold representation of an "irrepresentable" circle
whose centre is nowhere and whose circumference is everywhere. Jung
describes this nowhere centre, hypothetically uniting into one circle
and square, as a "real zero point"[2](without extension), which, he
suggests, is spiritually present as its virtual physical absence, the
physical defined as measurable extension in space and time. In a
characteristically Romantic way, William Blake describes this absent
spiritual presence in terms of his fleeting contact with the Christian
source of his poetic vision, a contact which, he writes, takes place in
"Every Time less than a pulsation of the artery."[3] Rejecting the
materialism of his age, Blake insists that every "pulsation of the artery"
is the living presence of spirit. He identifies what he calls his divine
inspiration with a sudden overpowering consciousness springing from
the unconsciousness of his body, a consciousness often instigated and
propelled by illness, in which time as eternity becomes "Every Time,"
his body poetically assuming its fourfold visionary or resurrected form.
"The Sexual is Threefold: the Human is Fourfold,"[4] he explains.
Psychology, for Marion, is the knowledge of this metaphorical body
grounded in the conscious making (incarnation) of it.

    This article will explore four circumambulations around this "real
zero point" (all-too-regularly described as the cessation of life rather
than its endless extension) in the unfolding life of Marion Woodman.
Drawing upon her Christian background, Marion identifies the "zero
point" with the Holy Spirit psychologically imaged, which is to say,
dynamically represented or extended, as the Self understood as a
masculine/feminine soul-making process from the unconscious One
to the fully conscious Four.[5] Immediately present as embodiment in
this soul-making process is the life force as every "pulsation of [her]
artery." The body as the pulsating presence of the life force is what,
with reference to her workshops, she calls the bodysoul. The awakening
to it is the soul understood as the incarnate body's consciousness of
itself. "Man," writes Blake, "has no Body distinct from his Soul."
"Energy," he explains, "is the only life, and is from the Body."[6] The
origin of what later, working with Mary Hamilton and Ann Skinner,

became the BodySoul Workshops lay in her English classes, in which, returning from a sabbatical year in London at the *Central School of Drama and Speech,* she taught, and her students bodily enacted, Blake's *Marriage of Heaven and Hell.*

Within the psychological framework of Marion's project, the mandala as the paradoxical identity of circle and square is the life sustaining notion of the unity of the inner masculine as *theoria* with the inner feminine as *praxis.* Theory and practice, the one dependent upon the other, cannot be separated without dangerously distorting both. In the Semitic tradition this increasingly catastrophic separation must be healed, the inner masculine having for more than six thousand years assumed the incarnate or closed form of patriarchy, which Marion describes as the tyrannical or absolute form[7] of the masculine. By opening the inner masculine as a closed patriarchal system to the long suppressed creative presence of the inner feminine in both men and women (which Marion describes as their ceaseless interpenetration), her project seeks to establish a thoroughly differentiated union of the inner feminine and masculine by raising to a fourfold consciousness the unconscious, undifferentiated One, which, in prehistoric times, was archetypally imaged as a primordial divine being who is both male and female. In Jung's psychological terms, this inner differentiation constitutes the mythical transformation of the unconscious (undifferentiated) hermaphrodite into the conscious (differentiated) androgyne.

In *Answer to Job,* which for a number of years Marion taught in her high school World Literature class, Jung psychologically interprets the jealous, vengeful figure of Yahweh as his division into two in which a limited consciousness emerges from the primordial abyss of unconsciousness, turning it into a *deus absconditus,* a dark unconscious shadow split off from the emerging consciousness he is dogmatically struggling to maintain. The one-sided masculine resolution of this struggle lay, for Jung, in the Christian dogma of the Holy Trinity, in which, in the sacrifice of the *deus absconditus* in the guise of the crucified Son, Yahweh is consciously re-united with himself, the divided Two transmuted into the unity of the patriarchal Three: Father, Son, and Holy Spirit. As a result of his self-crucifixion, the Christian Threefold God is reunited with his divided self. Christ henceforth rules in the name of the patriarchal Father, a rule which, as the crucified Son, cuts him off from the Great Mother whose primaeval Son he also is. The patriarchal Father, that is, is haunted by the *Pièta*, the dead Son in the arms of what Marion calls the Death Mother, beautiful as she may (must) be.[8] In the arms of the Great Mother, the patriarchal God confronts his own death. Describing this death in its larger context of resurrection, Shelley, in *Prometheus Unbound*, describes death as the marriage bed uniting the Earth Mother with her son in a ceaseless fourfold process of eternal becoming: "And death shall be the last embrace of her / Who takes the life she gave, even as a mother / Folding her child, says, 'Leave me not again!'" (111. iii, 105-07).

Absent from the Three, as the absence of the good (*privatio boni*), lay the feminine as a forbidden covenant with the serpent later identified as Satan, which Marion describes as the *dea abscondita*. This absence, Jung argues, has left evil at large to its own autonomous designs, evil residing outside the closed system of Three-in-One Godhead. And since, he argues, in the twentieth century it has brought humanity to the point of self-destruction by placing in its hands the means to achieve it, God, if humanity is to survive, must assume responsibility for a reality which God has rejected as totally alien to himself. He must, that is, at a new level of consciousness already destructively manifest in the weapons of mass destruction, confront in and as the human condition his own imminent destruction described by Nietzsche in 1894 as the death of God. He must, Jung insists, confront again his primeval, undifferentiated male/female oneness and bring it to a new level of consciousness, described by Jung as his progressively continuing incarnation. He must, that is, reunite at a conscious level with his rejected feminine if humankind, confronted by the danger of its extinction, is now to find an answer to the "2,000-year-old" question: "How does one get from Three to Four?"[9] Jung's bold answer, easier heretically said than actually done, is by raising the God within to a consciousness of himself/herself as human. Psychologically understood, the *mythos* of creation is the dialectical process by which God gradually becomes human. For Jung, as for Marion, this is what archetypal psychology is.

Responding in part to the mounting collective danger of human extinction, which as its *Weltanschuung* haunts the atomic age, the Catholic Church, anagogically understood as the divine Mother of God united with her Son, the Seven Sacraments serving as the marriage vows bringing humanity into the marriage chamber, decided in 1950 to make dogmatically explicit what for centuries had remained implicit. The Papal Bull of Pius XII, *Munificentissimus Deus,* formally promulgated the physical Assumption of the Blessed Virgin Mary to the heavenly bridal chamber of her Son where, as Sophia (Wisdom), she is united with the Godhead, thereby bringing the feminine into the masculine Trinity as the Fourth person of the Godhead. Astonished by Jung's contextual account of the *Munificentissimus Deus* in terms of the collective unconscious in his *Answer to Job,* the quantum physicist, Wolfgang Pauli, saw in the physical ascent of the Virgin Mother to the marriage chamber in heaven an archetypal model of the quantum ascent of matter to spirit. For some twenty years, Pauli, working with Jung, had, in the interpretation of his dreams, explored alchemy in depth, both men finding in the alchemical *vas,* or retort, an unconscious or archetypal model of the ascent of matter to spirit. This ascent dogmatically promulgated by Pius XII in 1950 had its counterparts both in Jung's psychology and in quantum physics. By means of the pure mathematical logic of archetypal numbers, Pauli was struggling to understand the subatomic behaviour of matter as it was being experimentally observed in quantum physics, an understanding that had to take fully into account the unconscious operations of the psyche as the subatomic observer of matter that influences (interrupts) its still largely underdetermined operations. "I very much welcome the fact that you generally give credit to the archetype of the feminine for influencing psychology and physics and—last but not least—the pope himself," Jung writes to Pauli in reply to Pauli's long, essay-length letter dealing with *Answer to Job.*[10]

    Pauli dealt with his response to *Answer to Job* by describing a dream in which he gets off the train at the wrong station, where a dark woman and strangers are waiting for him. "Apparently," writes Jung, "your initial reaction to *Hiob,* as the dream indicates, did not contain or make conscious everything that might have arisen to consciousness through the reading. Consequently, in the dream you unintentionally end up in an insignificant (inappropriate) place (Esslingen), but that is where you find what was missing in your reaction—namely, the *dark anima* and the *strangers.*" "[I]t goes even further than that," Jung continues, "and includes the physical backside [the cabbalistic *posteriora Dei* seen by Moses] of the *Assumpta,*" which, as a lapsed Catholic, Pauli consciously rejected.

What he rejected, however, was what Jung psychologically considered the cornerstone of the fourfold edifice that, as a quantum physicist, Pauli was attempting to construct, though largely in vain because his mathematical consciousness rejected, rather than supported, the operations of the collective unconscious. "The dark anima," Jung rather ambivalently explains, "has a direct connection with the dogma of the Assumption in that the Madonna is a one-sided light goddess, whose body (womb) seems to have been miraculously spiritualized. *The strong emphasis placed in such a figure brings about a constellation of the dark Opposite* [Satan] *in the unconscious,*" a constellation which led Pauli, as it led many others, to dismiss the dogma as "a *political maneuver,*" which is to say a Catholic response to the Marxist dogma of dialectical materialism. "In my view," Jung nevertheless insists, "it is not a political trick but a genuine phenomenon, i.e., the manifestation of the archetype that much earlier on had occasioned the assumption of Semele by her son Dionysus."

"But the dogma of the Assumption is *implicitly* a concession to the Devil," Jung then continues, dealing more minutely with Pauli's negative response as a way of partially resolving his own, "first because it exalts the feminine, which is related to the Devil (as *binarius*), and second because the assumption of the body signifies the assumption of Matter. It is true that the feminine is virginal, and the material is spiritualized, which you justly criticize, but *the eternally renewed virginity, on the other hand, is an attribute of the goddess of love,* whereas [whereby] the material is endowed with a living soul." The endowment of matter with "a living soul" is, as Pauli recognized, precisely what confronted him in matter when its apparently contradictory (i.e., feminine) operations are perceived at a subatomic level. What horrified both Jung and Pauli was the manifestation of the "living soul" of matter as the atomic bomb. (Pauli, at Princeton, refused to participate in the Manhattan Project.) For Jung in particular this horror arose directly from the inherited notion of the feminine as the *privatio boni*, a notion which, by 1945, left it at large to destroy humankind. The feminine as the Dark Mother, the *femme fatale.*

Jung's psychological account of the *Munificentissimus Deus* in *Answer to Job*—Marion and I conducting our courtship by reading Jung's *Job* together—brought to consciousness what at an unconscious level she had instinctively known since early childhood. Jung's interpretation of the physical ascent of the Virgin Mother to the wedding chamber of her Son provided Marion with a psychological account of the *hieros gamos:* the inner marriage of the masculine and feminine understood as *"the eternally renewed virginity"* of the feminine as *praxis,* which the masculine logocentrically transforms into *theoria,* while yet as soul-making remaining embedded in *praxis.* If this introduction to Marion's project focuses on *theoria,* my masculine focus, I suggest, remains thoroughly embedded in her feminine *praxis,* the marriage between them acting in our relationship as the working out in *praxis* of a theoretical model understood as a new constellation of the "transcendental," in themselves "irrepresentable," operations of the Holy Spirit,[11] a mystery with which Marion is more at ease than I.

As a "2,000-year-old" quest "from Three to Four," Jung, it will be noted, tended narratively to relocate the center of the mandala outside of itself in an historical or linear process toward which the soul is logocentrically progressing. "I knew," Jung continues, "that in finding the mandala as an expression of the self I had attained what was for me the ultimate. Perhaps someone else knows more, but not I." Rather than imaging the soul in terms of its logocentric, centrifugal attainment of "the ultimate," Marion locates the soul in a centripetal, living, pulsating present, which, as presence,[12] is always now, Blake's "Every Time less than a pulsation of the artery." Rather than a goal logocentrically to be achieved, it is the inner reality of the here and now which is always already present. The knowledge of it lies not in a system or an external organization mentally embraced as product (*theoria*). It lies, rather, in a method or inner dynamic pulsatingly experienced as process (*praxis*) in which everything as it appears external to it (masculine) is restored to its internal source (feminine). The ceaseless immersion of organization or product in its inner process of formation constitutes a difficult union that requires careful differentiation for a conscious awareness of it. The masculine and feminine are the other of each (each other), which is essential to a conscious recognition of their identity. The conscious feminine thus resides in its masculine other, even as the conscious masculine resides in its feminine other. The BodySoul Workshops are devoted to the conscious shaping of their identity. The self as consciousness (self-consciousness), writes Coleridge, "is a subject which becomes a subject by the act of constructing itself objectively [as other] to itself; but never is an object [other] except for itself, and only so far as by the very same act it becomes a subject."[13]

Born and raised in a parsonage, Marion early recognized that religious faith, left to its unknown, hidden resources (the transcendental operations of the Holy Spirit), is a form of blindness which isolates the soul from what Keats calls "a world like this," a world which, he insists, is the necessary condition of the "*Soul-making*" process. Blind faith, Marion early realized, her reading of the Bible assuming in her an active imaginal life, can in undetected ways rot the soul. Equally, in its arrested form as the tyranny of the masculine (which Marion, drawing upon her parsonage life as well as her life with me, would later call the wounded masculine), Jung's fourfold system may enclose (square) the feminine as that which, as temptress, might otherwise subvert the masculine attainment of the "ultimate." Her relationship to what she recognized as a lingering patriarchal prejudice at work in Jungian psychology, a prejudice that Jung, at least theoretically, sought to overcome in his relations with Pauli, constitutes her feminine quarrel with it. It lies more immediately or personally in her repeated, hard-won release from the squared circle which threatens to contain her, even as the radiation chamber described in the fourth circumambulation threatened to contain her. In this quarrel, increasingly apparent in what she has written and how she has lived, Marion's chief support has been the Romantic poets, whose works largely shaped the literature courses she taught for 24 years, as well as, in certain essential respects, her relationship to me. While, for Marion, psychology is the inner masculine knowledge of the inner feminine process, *praxis* (particularly in the soul-making labors of the Romantics) continues, in her experimental work, to subvert a *theoria* that seeks to comprehend it, comprehension too often, for her, reifying the process into a product. The consciousness-making gap between them remains for Marion the empirical/experimental ground of knowing.[14] "There may be intelligences or sparks of divinity in millions," Keats writes in his letter on "*Soul-making,*" noting the way a poem can be consumed by the very energy which originally nourished it,

> —but they are not Souls till they acquire identities, till each one is personally itself. I[n]telligences are atoms of perception—they know and they see and they are pure, in short they are God— how then are Souls to be made? How then are these sparks

which are God to have identity given to them[15]—so as ever to possess a bliss peculiar to each ones individual existence? How, but in a medium of a world like this? This point I sincerely wish to consider because I think it a grander scheme of salvation than the chrystean religion.[16]

In order to bring her early religious faith into some sort of relationship with "a world like this," a world which it had unknowingly rejected, Marion had actively to appraise the blindness of her idealized childhood religion. "In energetic minds," writes Coleridge as a Romantic precursor of Jung, "truth soon changes by domestication into power; and, from directing in the discrimination and appraisal of the product, becomes influencive in the production." Marion's critical appraisal of her religion, that is, became productive of her psychology. "To admire on principle," Coleridge insists, aptly describing Marion's principled admiration of Keats and other poets, "is the only way to imitate without the loss of originality."[17] In his letter, Keats goes on to describe the original "domestication " of truth into "*Soul-making*" power as "effected by three grand materials acting the one upon the other for a series of years." "These three Materials," he writes, "are the *Intelligence*—the *human heart* (as distinguished from intelligence or Mind) and the *World* or *Elemental space* suited for the proper action of *Mind and Heart* on each other for the purpose of forming the *Soul* or *Intelligence destined to possess the sense of identity.*"

Finding these "grand materials" too abstract for his own image-making, sense-engendered mind, Keats renders his conception answerable to perception. "I can scarcely express what I but dimly perceive—and yet I think I perceive it," he writes. Addressing himself as much as his brother and sister-in-law, to whom he wrote the letter, Keats continues: "[T]hat you may judge the more clearly I will put it in the most homely form possible—I will call *the world* a School instituted for the purpose of teaching little children to read—I will call the Child *able to read,* the Soul made from that *school* and its *hornbook.*" A hornbook was a sheet of paper inscribed with the letters of the alphabet and a short prayer covered over with a layer of translucent horn and mounted on a wooden frame with a handle. To copy the letters onto the horn, sounding them aloud into words (as Shakespeare probably did as a child) was, Keats suggests, to learn by heart, the hornbook serving for Keats as a metaphor of the heart. To

learn by hornbook (heart) was internally to absorb what is copied so
that the letters and words became, as "*Soul-making*," not simply signs
for external things, but symbols of an identity "peculiar to each ones
individual existence." As signs of external things, the mechanical
copying of letters and words reduces them to "a World of Pains and
troubles," which must, as signs, be transformed into symbols if
copying is "to school an Intelligence and make it a soul." One's
identity, that is, resides in the embodiment of soul, symbolized by
the hornbook. Elaborating on his metaphor of the hornbook as the
heart, Keats turns it into an allegory of salvation. "Not merely is the
Heart a Hornbook," he explains. "It is the Minds Bible, it is the
Minds experience; it is the teat from which the Mind or intelligence
sucks its identity.—As various as the Lives of Men are—so various
become their souls, and thus does God make individual beings ... of
the sparks of his own essence—This appears to me a faint sketch of
a system of Salvation which does not affront our reason and
humanity—I am convinced that many difficulties which christians
labour under would vanish before it."[18]

By the time she was three, Marion's father had taught her to read
and write by heart. Her hornbook was her tracing paper and, as an
extension of it, her blackboard in her father's study. On them she
copied the letters and words from the primers her father gave her,
sounding each letter so that gradually, carrying her hornbook (her
primer), she was able to accompany her father wherever he went, reading
the words by sounding aloud the letters. The ceaseless sounding of
letters into words, which is the way she learned to read, became in her
early childhood what Coleridge calls "a repetition in the finite mind
of the eternal act of creation in the infinite I AM."[19] It became *in
potentia* "a system of Salvation which does not affront our reason and
humanity." Literacy, for Marion, is an incarnation: the making of soul
through its bodily engagement with the Word. A second birth.

Marion's project as a Jungian analyst found its origin in the soul-
making process of learning to read and write. The poets whom she
read "by heart" assume in the eleven books she has written (five co-
authored) an importance shared only by the works of Jung. What she
found in Jung was a psychological account of her unconscious experience
of the child's divine act of creation, which, as a soul-making process,
constitutes for her the poetry of life. (Marion's initial interest in Jung

lay in the realm of mythopoeia.) "To carry on the feelings of childhood into the powers of manhood, to combine the child's sense of wonder and novelty with the appearances, which every day for perhaps forty years had rendered familiar," writes Coleridge, "... this is the character and privilege of genius. ... And therefore it is the prime merit of genius ... so to represent familiar objects as to awaken the minds of others to a kindred feeling concerning them and that freshness of sensation which is the constant accompaniment of *mental, no less than bodily* convalescence."[20] The "freshness of sensation" that awakens the mind to its "bodily" presence constitutes as embodiment what, for Coleridge (and for Marion), poetry is.

Coleridge is here describing the genius of Wordsworth. In the larger context of his *Biographia Literaria,* however, his notion of genius becomes his dialectical account of the soul-making process, which must now be raised to a consciousness of its own psychosomatic operations. Genius as Coleridge describes it is not the "character and privilege" of the few. It is the unconscious nature of every human being. It is the poetry of life rendered, as the soul's embodiment, conscious of its own making, of its own "bodysoul rhythms." The poetry of life is what the soul is. In a manner prefigured by Coleridge, Jung describes the unconscious human state as the soul's unconscious identification with matter. The Christian religion, Jung suggests, here departing from Coleridge, mythically rather than rationally attributes the soul's separation from matter to a primordial crime, which left the soul alienated from matter, while yet, in defiance of the divine judgment upon it, longing to return to it as to a realm forbidden. This soul-longing for the forbidden, he argues, psychologically manifests itself as the longing of the masculine to unite with the feminine, a longing which is morally, as matter, bound to the notion of the feminine as evil, an evil mythically configured as the identification of Eve with Satan. For Jung, the history of the Christian West largely resides in its struggle with matter as both forbidden and desired. This struggle, he believed, had now come to a head with the release of atomic energy, which engages as matter the highest earthly hopes and the greatest earthly fears. "Physics," Jung writes, "... is in a position to detonate mathematical formulae—the product of pure psychic activity—and kill seventy-eight thousand persons at a blow."[21] Working with Pauli, Jung, particularly after Hiroshima, was persuaded (as was Pauli) that the future of humankind now depended upon a successful resolution of the Christian soul's struggle with matter. For Jung, as for Pauli, this successful resolution lay in releasing the soul from its unconscious fear of matter as its unconscious fear of itself into an entirely new consciousness of matter as the soul's conscious affirmation of itself. Matter as the enemy of soul is matter as the precision weapons of mass destruction. Matter as the other of soul, essential to soul's consciousness of its own operations, is the release of the unlimited creative power of the soul's matter, the Alma Mater, the feminine in its primal, unconscious state as the First Mother.

"Psyche," Jung explained in a letter to Pauli, "could be placed parallel to the physical term of *matter* (corpuscle + wave). Like matter, psyche is also a *matrix* based on the mother archetype. Spirit, in contrast, is *masculine* and is based on the *Father archetype,* in consequence of which, favoured by the fact that we are living in a patriarchal age, it claims precedence over both the psyche and matter." Rejecting this patriarchal precedence of spirit over psyche and matter, Jung turns to the Biblical figure of Sophia as the Wisdom of God, which, since the Reformation, has remained too long buried in the fear of God. "But with *Sophia* as his consort," he explains, "he also has a feminine aspect, which emerges more clearly the closer one gets to the unconscious. ["Eros is a *kosmogonos*, a creator and father-mother of all higher consciousness," Jung writes in *Memories, Dreams, Reflections.*[22]] In this *matriarchal* sphere, the spirit is ... the 'primeval son of the mother.'" Jung then goes on to argue that the Christian "elevation of the spirit to a divinity" radically distorted the role of the soul as mediator ("*ligamentum*") binding together "*corporis et spirtus*" (matter and spirit). "A further complication," he argues, "was caused by the identification of the pneumatic divinity with the *summum bonum,* [supreme good] which forcibly led to matter slipping into the vicinity of the *malum* [evil]." "These theological entanglements," he concludes, "must [in analytical psychology as in quantum physics] be avoided ... and the psyche be given a middle or superior position." "Psyche and matter, as a 'matrix,'" he then repeats, describing the psychoid archetype, "are both an X—i.e., a transcendental unknown quantity and thus indistinguishable in conceptual terms, which makes them *virtually identical*; only on a secondary level are they different, as different aspects of Being."[23]

While, like Keats in his letter, Jung here gives the soul a human position superior to that of spirit (Keats's "intelligences or sparks of divinity"), Keats's interest in *"Soul-making,"* unlike Jung's, is directly, though not solely, concerned with the life of the imagination in the making of art. As an end in itself (art for art's sake), Jung considered the making of art an arrested form of soul-making which released the soul from its larger social responsibility. "If I had taken these fantasies of the unconscious as art," Jung writes of the fantasies recorded in the Black Book, which he later transferred to the Red Book, embellishing them with mandala drawings, "they would have carried no more conviction than visual perceptions, as if I were watching a movie. I would have felt no moral obligation toward them. The anima might then have easily seduced me into believing that I was a misunderstood artist, and that my so-called artistic nature gave me the right to neglect reality."[24]

In his two failed attempts to write an epic on the fall of Hyperion, modelled on Milton's and Dante's epics, Keats, like Jung after him, voiced his fear of being psychically seduced by the anima. ("'Beauty is truth, true beauty,' that is all / Ye know on earth, and all ye need to know" [49-50], Keats concludes in his "Ode on a Grecian Urn.") In his second attempt, which he recast as a dream in order to internalize the action, Moneta,[25] the death goddess who presides over the ruined temple of the fallen Saturn, confronts the poet who, a victim of the anima, has entered the ruin (the archetypal site of Romanticism) as "a dreaming thing / A fever to thyself."[26] Keats concludes the introduction of his theme by addressing a posthumous reader: "Whether the dream now purposed to rehearse / Be poet's or fanatic's will be known / When this warm scribe, my hand, is in the grave."[27] The fragment was published after Keats's death. What he attempted and could not complete (as other than a ruin) was an epic in which the fall of the Greek gods becomes their dying as psychology into human life. Marion's subtitle for *Bone: Dying into Life*, is taken from Keats. Psychology, Jung argues, was born from the death of the gods. And, it may be argued, from the death of poets. Marion in *Bone* confronts this death as a dimension of life which cancer propelled her to explore. "Coming at the very end [of the transition from nature to spirit in Hegel's corpus]," Tilottama Rajan argues, "illness stands as an inassimilable oversight in Idealism, a confession that compromises the alchemizing of nature as spirit."[28] Marion's project, it may be argued, attempts to assimilate this "inassimilable oversight" in her notion of soul as mediating the otherwise unknowable relations between nature and spirit ("*ligamentum corporis et spiritus*"). The scene of her BodySoul workshops is the alchemical retort.

In Jung's acknowledged distrust of the anima, particularly as the anima relates to the arts, Marion recognized a patriarchal fear of the feminine (dying into life) which unconsciously stood in the way of the work he set out to accomplish, particularly with Pauli after he returned to Zurich in 1946, deeply disturbed by what he considered the perversion of quantum physics as it manifested itself in the building and detonation of the atomic bomb. In her work, the inner feminine in both women and men, as personified by Sophia, is what Jung calls the "consort" of the "*Father archetype.*" As the "consort" or bride, Sophia releases in *praxis* the *theoria* of their *hieros gamos*, or inner marriage, understood as the union of the differentiated masculine and feminine within the individual. This inner marriage presides over Marion's BodySoul workshops much as, for Jung, "an X—i.e., a transcendental unknown quantity [of energy]" presides over psyche and matter, making them "*virtually identical.*" Marion's BodySoul workshops, conducted in a variety of ways over a period of more than thirty years, are, in her growing understanding of them, a working out in practice of Jung's hypothetical conception of the *hieros gamos,* which constitutes his notion of the psychoid archetype. In this practical working out lies, for her, the kind of healing upon which, as Jung never ceased to argue, the future survival of humanity depends. For this reason, therefore, the four circumambulations of the self, which are the subject of this paper, must be seen in the larger framework of the *hieros gamos* as it becomes the informing energy of Marion's work, an energy which, focusing more on the long suppressed feminine, corrects by subversion the Jungian emphasis upon the logocentric role of the masculine.

While, as we shall see, this work has its unconscious origins in a psychic disposition manifesting itself in early childhood, it became in Zurich, against the advice of her supervisors, the subject of her dissertation. For her thesis, Marion turned to Jung's difficult notion of the psychoid archetype, which he had developed with the assistance of Wolfgang Pauli in his 1946 paper "On the Nature of the Psyche." "If these reflections are justified," Jung concludes his paper as a supplement to it, "they must have weighty consequences with regard to the nature of the psyche, since as an objective fact it would then be intimately connected not only with physiological and biological phenomena but with physical events too—and, so it would appear, most intimately of all with those pertaining to the realm of atomic physics."[29] In *The Owl Was A Baker's Daughter*, Marion makes considerable use of Jung's proposed intimate connection between the unconscious psyche and "physiological and biological phenomena," particularly, though not directly, in relation to her own experience of obesity, which, in *Addiction to Perfection*, she extends, by indirection, to an analysis of her own experience of *anorexia nervosa*. Matter as embodied soul is crucial to any understanding of her work. Pauli, it should be noted, describes Jung's analytical psychology as "unconscious" or "background" physics.[30] The larger area of quantum physics to which Marion tentatively turned in *Dancing in the Flames* (216-221) is one that casts its now powerful shadow upon her work without as yet being fully absorbed into it. Its absorption is, in part, the subject of what she conceives as her final book, which, now in its planning stage, she intends to write with me.

First Circumambulation

Marion's inner world, which in childhood she shared only with her father, found its initial reality in her father's church and the nearby graveyard. Assured by her father that God's home was in his church, Marion, who had daily access to it through the back door, would hide under a pew or under the pulpit and wait for him to come. The sun streaming through the windows in the late afternoon would cause the wooden pews to creak, a creaking that Marion heard as the footsteps of God, whom she both longed and feared to see. His footsteps sounding through the pews were the footsteps of a giant large enough to fill the church. If she could not see him, it was because he was too big to be seen as other than his Biblical reflection pouring through a multicoloured, stained-glass narrative. His nowhere was everywhere, which only her imagination could fill. And fill it it did. Every sight and sound were the sights and sounds of God, which she, with her father's help, secretly understood. God spoke to her through her eyes and ears. He was present even in the beating of her heart and the sound of her breathing. There was nowhere where he was not. Except, perhaps, in her mother.

When, shortly after her marriage, Marion's mother, an early suffragette, found herself pregnant, she, unable to cope with the isolation of a village parsonage and a small congregation who rejected her bobbed-hair city ways, returned to her parents' home and remained there until after the birth of her daughter. With her return, her unconscious rejection of her female child was sufficiently severe that Marion's father did his best to protect her from her mother's unrecognized hostility, Marion herself unconsciously assuming the protection of her own imagined invisibility only slightly betrayed in her mother's presence by the sound of her own breathing. In the presence of her mother she settled into a state of impenetrable silence, which her mother interpreted as rejection. She projected, that is, her unconscious rejection of her child onto her child's assumed rejection of her. The result was a silence so profoundly disturbing that Marion's mother would go to Marion's infant bed, where Marion lay for hours absolutely still, to see if she was dead.

As a result of the impasse constellated by the unconsciousness operative in their relationship (partly shaped by her mother's parsonage despair at her loss of freedom), Marion's father took considerable care to keep them apart as much as possible, Marion in *Leaving My Father's House* describing the care as psychic incest. Daily he would take her with him on his pastoral rounds, which included, among other things, visits to the funeral home to make arrangements for a funeral. On one such visit, Marion, left at the age of four to her own already developed inner resources, found her way into a parlour where she saw a small cradle about the size of the bed her father had made for her doll, a big doll that Marion treated not as her baby but as her student. Intrigued by the cradle just beyond her reach, she climbed up on a chair to look more closely at it. Astonished by what she found, she leaned over and picked it up and held it in her arms. To her bewilderment, she recognized that what she held in her arms was not a doll. Nor was it an infant. It was Death, which her father had tried to explain, but couldn't. The grieving parents entered the room and discovered, to their horror, their dead infant in the arms of a child standing on a chair unable to get down. Alarmed by the sound of their frantic cries, her father hurried into the room. Fearing that his young daughter might drop the dead infant, he immediately, as on other not entirely dissimilar occasions, took charge. "Leave the child to me," he said to the parents, who were now quite out of control. Quietly, he relieved her of her charge as, on so many occasions, he relieved her of her mother's presence.

In this incident, Marion enacted the trauma that unconsciously defined her early relationship to her mother, a relationship that would continue to haunt her through much of her adult life. Her unconscious image of herself was that of a frightened child tightly holding her dead self in her arms. A *Pietà* of sorts. This image of death (the Medusa), which, in ways she could not fathom, became, as trauma, her own frozen state, a fearful immortality not unlike the monumental brasses which, as an adult, she would, on her brass-rubbing expeditions, spend an entire summer restoring to life in much the same way as children were once taught to write by means of a hornbook. (In a short story published in *Alphabet*,[31] Marion describes a monumental brass uncannily coming to life as its face emerges on the paper from the rubbing of her heelball.) In the traumatic figuration of herself standing on a chair, cradling a dead infant and unable to move, the child Marion may be psychologically described as giving birth to herself as dead. In this iconic configuration, death, that is, became the unconscious condition of her being alive.

The next day, Marion knelt at the kitchen window watching in the sky for the baby to be taken to heaven in a golden chariot accompanied by angels, pictures of which she had seen in the books her father had given her. While her father had told her not to cut the pictures out, nor touch his sharp shaving razor, Marion could not resist a picture of Joan of Arc standing in a dress and apron not unlike her own, arms outstretched, looking up at the branches of an oak tree filled with angels. Using her father's forbidden razor, she carefully cut it out and placed it in the pocket of the apron she always wore. When later her mother washed the apron with the picture in it, she knew that her mother had not known what she had done, and, because she had not known, Marion still had her Joan of Arc and the angels within her.

Wondering what her child was now up to, Marion's mother, standing at the ironing board, finally dared to ask. When Marion unthinkingly told her, her mother panicked. The behaviour of her daughter was becoming increasingly disturbing. Marion appeared in her silence to be living in another world, a secret one she shared with her father, a world that clearly excluded her. She saw in Marion everything she had come to fear in her husband, a world that in courtship she had conditionally embraced, only, in marriage, to find herself trapped. She feared for her child's sanity. Suddenly, unthinkingly, she swatted Marion across the head. Marion fell to the floor, her mother towering over her shouting that there were no such things as angels and she was never to speak of them again. Marion settled back into her silence. She shed no tears. She saw that, for whatever reason, her mother could not understand what she and her father knew to be true.

While all this was going on, Marion's father was next door in the church, conducting, in tears, the funeral of his closest friend. The friend would be buried in the nearby graveyard, which, as Marion's own backyard, was where she daily played with her many invisible friends, all of whom were her students, whom she was teaching to read, carefully explaining the meaning of what miraculously emerged from the assembled letters on the page. Marion got up from the floor where she had fallen, concerned only to find her father. He would tell her if the baby had been taken to heaven in her own chariot, or if she had gone in the chariot of her father's friend. He would certainly know. Recalling the experience, Marion remarked that the baby, with its pink bow, had the sweetest face she had ever seen. Death, which for the child was angelic, was for her mother, as for the grieving parents, a terror. This terror was unknowingly lodged in her soul as trauma, as the dark side of the God she otherwise dearly loved, the *deus absconditus* of Jung's *Answer to Job*. Which is to say, the God who needed her adult consciousness as much as he needed the infantine unconsciousness of the child if he was ever to be humanly and immediately known.

Second Circumambulation

Hanging over the sideboard in the dining room of the parsonage was a picture of Jesus inscribed with the words: "Christ is the head of this house, the unseen guest at every meal." What went on in the parsonage should, Marion's father insisted, be shared with Christ alone. It was no one else's business. Indeed, on some level, it was not even the business of the members of the family who might reasonably claim it as their own. It was ultimately perhaps not even Christ's business. Christ, after all, was about his heavenly Father's business. So far as the outside world was concerned, life in the parsonage was a secret, so secret that it became a secret even to those who in the parsonage shared it. The Christ who was the head of the parsonage in which Marion and her two brothers grew up presided over it in ways that made the life of its inhabitants so essentially secret that it remained consciously unknown even to them. The secret life of the parsonage was its unconsciousness of what, as other than Christ, it was. And what Christ was was finally unknown, a reality seen through a glass darkly until his return in the glory of his heavenly Father. The real Father who would eventually come.

Out of the depths of this unconsciousness over which Christ presided would emerge in the fullness of time the shaping spirit of Marion's life and work. Its dark side, best understood as the secret life of repression, was first found by Marion in her mother's anguish. Identified in Jung's archetypal psychology as Eve in her alignment with the Devil as the *deus absconditus* (or what Marion calls the *dea abscondita),* Jung associates the figure of the death mother (the *pietà*) with the transcendent feminine. Her release from the tyranny of the Trinity, from which she is excluded as evil, constitutes a new birth of consciousness over which presides the *hieros gamos.* Marion's Sophia psychologically emerges from her unconscious relationship to her mother as the energy of the creative anima which her mother had to repress in order to remain in the essentially Trinitarian realm of the parsonage. Viewed in this limited personal perspective, Marion's life and work enacts the release of her mother from her imprisonment in the parsonage. (When Marion decided to go to Zurich, she sought her mother's blessing. "If you can be free, go," her mother had said.) The secret life of the parsonage that was ruled by Christ became in Marion's mature consciousness of it the release of the creative feminine into a new healing alignment with a severely wounded masculine. The process of this release is the subject of *Leaving My Father's House.* The "unseen guest" at the table in the parsonage was the feminine Christ. In the absence of her true mother, the role of the feminine Christ was assumed by her father. The disentangling of this contrasexual constellation into its true form as the *hieros gamos* is the unconscious process that, as Marion consciously discovered it, inhabited the parsonage's secret life. Archetypally understood, her mother's despair lay in the repression of Sophia, which, in Marion's unconscious childhood, was present in Marion as the Joan of Arc whom her mother figuratively drowned in the roar of the washing machine.

When finally at the age of six Marion went to the public school, she found to her horror that, instead of reading new books, the students did not read at all. Instead, they folded sheets of paper, making them into tiny windmills. Supporting the windmills on thin sticks supplied by the teacher, they set the windmills spinning by running in circles around the room. When it was decided to promote her to the third grade, they still were not reading what she had long since read, including some of Dickens's novels. What was worse, her teacher also taught home economics, in which Marion had to cut out and sew a slip from material her mother had hesitated to purchase, figuring, as she had to, the cost. Marion cut it so badly that when she sewed it up, the slip didn't fit. Her mother refused to risk another purchase. New material, pink flannelette for a nightgown, was cut by her mother's dressmaker. The teacher objected, treating this as an act of defiance on Marion's and her mother's part. Marion found a desk at the back of the room. For the rest of the year, she laid her head in her folded arms and pretended to sleep. In the home economics class, she was told to sit on the top of a ladder and clean the Venetian blinds. This she did.

Something, however, was seriously wrong. Marion at school was sleeping, not pretending, most of the time. She became increasingly obese. Finally, her mother could endure it no longer. She took her to the doctor, who discovered that her metabolism was alarmingly low. He prescribed thyroxin, which she has had to depend upon ever since. Her mother then attempted to hide the obesity by fitting her into a corset, which she wore for years. She felt as if her body were a dead child that, unknown to others, haunted her as a ghost. She had become the very personification of her mother's despair. Crawling as silently as possible from grade to grade, she suddenly awakened in the twelfth grade by projecting onto a handsome blond classmate the creative masculine that she had buried. The result was that along with her back-row classmate, she moved literally to the front of the class, received the highest grades, and became the president of the student body. Perhaps best of all, her weight fell away. She returned to her body.

Joan of Arc had found her Dauphin. Unlike Joan and the Dauphin, however, Marion and her fellow student together became leaders in the school, as, in almost every respect, her projection onto him began to mirror an inner transformation in her. The school became their royal kingdom, until, that is, the coronation: the annual school dance. Marion supervised the arrangements, helped decorate the auditorium, only to discover when the work was done that she had not been invited. Her young prince and heir-apparent had invited somebody else. Marion sat out the gala in the parsonage, listening to Kate Smith on the radio, singing all those songs, which, in some unknown, mysterious way, were a celebration rather than a denial of the singer's impressive weight.

The following year, the students in the graduating class were told they would be released from their obligation to write the departmental exams if they were willing to work on a farm instead, since, on account of the war, farms were desperately in need of help. They had to agree to work for thirteen weeks, from the beginning of May until the end of July. For Marion, who chose the farm option, this meant the end of her high school years. It meant transferring the enormous creative energy that had been released to farm labor. Her two major tasks were to plough the fields on a tractor and plant trees. Grieving for what she had lost, day after day under a hot sun she sat on her tractor ploughing. Finally, one day the farmer took her out to show her what she had done. To her amazement, Marion saw stretching before her long curving furrows which seemed to be turning in upon themselves toward a center that was not there. The next day, determined to follow a straight line, she realized she was losing consciousness. Shutting down the engine, she managed to stagger back to the farmer's house, where her parents came to fetch her. By nightfall, her face had begun to swell, and by morning she could no longer see. Swollen flesh covered her eyes and mouth. She had suffered a sunstroke. She had been exposed too long to the relentless heat of the sun.

Back in the parsonage, her mother, in vain, did what she could to bring the swelling down. The doctor feared that her brain might have been damaged. For one whole night, he sat with her, fearing the worst, sharing his fears with her parents, and praying with them for divine help. Marion, in her semicomatose state, could hear them. Not quite unconscious, she thought of *A Stairway to Heaven*, a film she had loved. In it was a palatial staircase, which airmen were called upon to climb. At the top, as if among the clouds, was a signal board that kept flashing numbers. If an airman's number came up, he knew his time had come. As she heard, without quite understanding, what was being said by her parents and the doctor, Marion felt herself climbing the staircase. As she approached the top, a number flashed 4424. It was not her number. Her number was 4444. She had still more climbing to do. She knew she was not going to die.

Some years later, on Christmas Eve in Finland, she found herself on a *gilka*, a Finnish combination of scooter and sled, looking down toward the village where she had been staying. Before her in the graveyard outside the church lay lines of lighted candles burning brightly in the snow, its whiteness strangely luminous in the midst of the enveloping dark. She felt overwhelmingly empty, as if the silence that she had inhabited since childhood was suddenly being heard. Everything she had projected outward had withdrawn back into herself, as if it had all been an illusion, as if it had been nothing at all. She was filled with its nothingness, and she knew in that nothingness that in an unknown world on Christmas Eve she was suddenly, unexpectedly, not lonely, but free. There was now, in this moment, no one else but herself. She was full and free to begin her life. In the twinkling of an eye, in a foreign graveyard, the dead had been released, a child had been born. It had everything and nothing to do with herself.

Third Circumambulation

My third choice to describe Marion's circumambulations around the self involves me, upon whom she projected her own creative masculine, a projection that, however desirable, I was at the time in no position to receive. We met in the context of the parsonage where, after the failure of a marriage, I unconsciously sought and consciously found what I experienced as a refuge. The refuge lay not in the unburdening of myself around a kitchen table, but in the gradual realization that in this household, whatever the evidence to the contrary, all burdens had been assumed by Christ, who took them to his Father, where, no longer burdens, they became our place in heaven. In some curiously blinded way that perfectly suited my needs, I found myself in the parsonage in a Heaven in which, at least for a time, I was more than willing to suspend my disbelief. I embraced the irreality by supposing it real. I inhabited a fiction which I knew to be a fiction in much the same way that I knew any literary work, however true, to be a fiction. I entered the parsonage as a stranger and, so long as I knew myself to be a stranger and was satisfied to remain one, I was welcome. I knew I was not to intrude upon its secret life in an effort to unveil it. It was as restricted to my intrusion as was my own sense of failure, which, at least for now, I could not explore. My sense of the parsonage as well as of myself was one of virtual reality, which, in my suspended state, was the only reality I could safely inhabit. Here, beyond the classroom, I could read and enter a Romantic poem knowing it to be a poem, which, in the parsonage, was also my life. I embraced myself as a Romantic fiction, and it was as a Romantic fiction that Marion and I together in the parsonage conceived my long postponed Ph.D. thesis on Shelley as what was now for me in the parsonage the fiction of my life toward which, as a fiction, I had no moral responsibility. I could watch it as I watched a movie.

My psychic situation might be compared to that of Coleridge in his composition of *The Rime of the Ancient Mariner.* Unlike Wordsworth, he had chosen a subject "in part at least supernatural" as opposed to natural. His task was to treat the subject, which was himself, as if it were natural, though knowing it was not. "[T]he excellence aimed at," he explains, "was to consist in the interesting of the affections [including his own] by the dramatic truth of such emotions, supposing them real. And real in *this* sense that they have been to every human being [including himself] who, from whatever source of delusion, has at any time believed himself under supernatural agency."[32] I was, in truth (as distinct from the Romantic fiction of it), a very sick man.

Marion received my fiction as my truth. In that reception, what Jung called psychic reality was born between us. We were henceforth bound together, and we knew it. There was, for both of us, no way out, and a deep way in. Among other things, we read *The Tempest* together. "And deeper than did ever plummet sound / I'll drown my book," declares Prospero as the spell of his "rough magic" finally achieves its object, allowing him to return to the world he had lost, though not as he had lost it, but as he now knows it to be: a genuinely mortal world, free of the magic which makes it imaginally appear as more than it is, a world in which, for all his dukedom, his "[e]very third thought shall be [his] grave." To describe this world, something more than his "so potent art" is required. What he requires is "some heavenly music" which, as prayer, "pierces so that it assaults / Mercy itself and frees all faults." In asking the audience to "release him from [his] bands / With the help of [their] good hands," Prospero, in Shakespeare's Epilogue, is asking them for the "indulgence" which, were Shakespeare still a Catholic in Protestant England, would set him free from the "crimes" which he, as magician, has performed upon them. Shakespeare, it would appear, no longer had direct access to the "indulgence" of the Roman Church which the Christian reformers rejected. He writes his plays in the absence of a Catholic truth, which now by magic he must by indirection rediscover in the new forms and the new ways that his dramatic imagination provides (Coleridge's "dramatic truth"). By the indirection of magic, he must find his new Christian direction out. In what was born as psychic reality between Marion and me lay a larger reality which presided over it, which Jung called the *hieros gamos.*

In the final book of the Bible, the *hieros gamos* as its total form is celebrated as the return of Christ. In my Ph.D. thesis on the apocalyptic vision in the poetry of Shelley, the *hieros gamos* as an encompassing Romantic theme was my subject. Marion and I explored it together in the parsonage until finally I was in a position to go to Toronto and write it. And I did. But now that it had achieved the end it was unconsciously meant to perform, I had to drown it, release it into the unconscious from which it emerged, so as to be free at last of the "rough magic" that is the Romantic vision, a vision whose dangers can mount, the longer it is sustained. Burial by water involves a consciousness that is other than drowning, a consciousness that, as I gradually realized, Shelley had struggled in vain to shape. He was only 28. Keats was dead at 25. "Born 28 Nov 1757 in London & has died Several Times Since," writes Blake.

With the publication of my thesis, my tenured security at the University was achieved. Marion and I, now married, were in a position to settle into it, a task both of us, in vain, attempted to do. The rewards of what had been accomplished became, particularly for Marion, a demonic parody of them. Success carried within it a fundamental sense of betrayal. It was as if my achievement, such as it was, were radically undermined by what now appeared as success to have been the hidden motive of it. Two martinis before dinner served nightly to drown my book, the book which was, for Marion, the unveiled truth of my psychic life. For Marion and me, this unveiled truth was, as we explored it together, Keats's understanding of the world as a "Vale of *Soul-making*" which I, in the name of art, was now reducing to a fiction whose chief aim was pleasure. I was acting as if what I had written were nothing more than a tedious rerun of a movie I had watched over and over again. I was acting as if I had no moral responsibility toward it.

I had turned the writing into a crime that lacked any indulgence that might set me free. I became for Marion what she would later describe as the demon lover, upon whom, as the feminine projection of the creative masculine, her own energies were, in the false name of love, dangerously wasted. Suffering from acute edema, Marion appeared to be drowning in the waters of her own despair. Finally hospitalized, she was reduced to a condition as severe in its own way as her high school sunstroke. The truth of my psychic reality had unveiled its shadow side, perhaps best epitomized in Shelley's visionary nightmare, *The Triumph of Life*, found after his prophesied drowning in written fragments on scattered sheets of paper partially filled with other things. In my book I had argued that Shelley's poetry contained as its hidden agenda a metaphysical defence of suicide, which he finally acted out. I had projected onto Shelley's poetry the *deus absconditus* in myself. It was, in part, from this that Marion would seek release. Describing his boyhood passion for nature, Wordsworth explains that he was "more like a man /Flying from something that he dreads than one / Who sought the thing he loved."[33]

Confronted by the mounting evidence of a collapsing marriage over which we had apparently no control, both of us took refuge in our teaching of literature, particularly, in both our cases, the literature of the Romantics. I immersed myself with increasing intensity in my apocalyptic reading of its major texts, finding in them the making of what Wallace Stevens called a "supreme fiction," a myth which, in the absence of another kind of truth, would now have to suffice. Literature had become for me an end in itself. The subject of a Romantic poem became the making of it. I willingly submitted to its spell. Several of my students—the Romantic version of Milton's "fit audience ... though few"—submitted with me. "The way up is the way down" was the Romantic way to the discovery of the fictional self, who, as the hidden author, performed as text the disrobing dance of seven veils. "Veil after veil may be undrawn, and the inmost naked beauty of the meaning never exposed,"[34] writes Shelley in his *Defence of Poetry.*

Marion followed a radically different path. Withdrawing the projection of her creative masculine from me, she received permission from her school principal to tear down a wall and join together two adjacent classrooms, which, with the eager help of her students, she converted into what she named the Tostal, the Celtic word for a place of coming together in a joyous, participatory celebration of poetry, dance, and music. Here she created what was essentially a theatre in the round, in which her students could not only read poems but perform them. Taking the poetry into their bodies, tossing the words back and forth as if playing catch (the students used a ball), the students discovered that the poems began to assume new embodiments of themselves, which, as Wordsworth describes it in "Tintern Abbey," were "felt in the blood, and felt along the heart," before they finally passed into the "purer mind, / With tranquil restoration."[35] Students at the age of sixteen, Marion realized, were not prepared to receive a poem directly into the "purer mind" unless they had first experienced it in the "blood" and in the "heart," heart and blood serving, in the exercise of them, as the purifiers of the mind.

What was true for the student was equally true for the poet. Only to the degree that what the poet wrote was felt in the blood and heart was it alive as a poem in the mind. The students in the Tostal were directly entering the poet's creative process. They did not, because they could not, stand outside the process, analysing with their disembodied minds what they had been told was the poem's meaning. In the Tostal, poems rose from their graves as if newly released from the abstractions they had for most students become. Marion's work in the Tostal with her students became the basis of her future BodySoul workshops.

Literature, for Marion, was not, as I had introvertedly insisted, trapped in the ceaseless making of itself. It was for her extroverted mind actively mirroring the ongoing process of life, an ongoing process that had in me come to a halt as other than a fiction. "We want the generous impulse to act that which we imagine; we want the poetry of life,"[36] Shelley declares in his *Defence of Poetry* only months before he wrote his elegy on what, as an enactment, amounts to its death, Shelley not realizing that whatever is living contains its death as the mysterious renewal of it. While I had read Jung (and introduced Marion to him) for his major contribution to a mythological understanding of literature, Marion clearly found in him a psychology far more directly related to life. With this in mind, she entered Jungian analysis. After a year of analysis, she knew from a powerful dream, in which she was told to turn her face toward Jerusalem and not turn back, that she wanted to (had to) give up (willingly sacrifice) her high-school teaching career, which embraced a now richly fulfilled stage of her life, and go to Zurich. I did my best to persuade her not to go, only slowly to realize that my persuasions, the more urgent they became, were, in reality, the tolling of a powerful bell summoning us both toward a death by drowning.

Once again, Marion psychically experienced herself as standing as if helpless on a chair holding a dead infant in her arms, which was now in essence what her relationship to me had become. It was not a case of my letting her go. It was a case of restoring the infant to life. Marion knew if she was going to live, she would have to go. She left, neither of us knowing whether the marriage, if not already dead, could in fact survive. She did in her marriage what her mother could not do in hers. And she did it more with her mother's blessing than with mine. The creative animus in her mother, which she was never able to express sufficiently to appease her profound despair, found in her daughter an outlet by means of that conscious indirection which in the unconscious finds its direction out.

Fourth Circumambulation

On March 3, 1994, Marion writes in her journal: "As I come out of the anesthetic, words are sobbing out of my mouth. 'What happened? Whatever happened?' I am writhing in my abdomen, and my genitals feel as if I've been raped by an elephant. 'What's wrong?' the nurse asks. 'You have to do something. Now!' I say. 'Take it out.' 'Pain anesthetizes itself,' she says. 'Try to hold it for two hours.'" Two hours later, the journal continues: "No relief. The nurses stay for 45 seconds for fear of their own reproductive systems being radiated. They are doing what they can but nobody can come close enough to help me. They've placed lead shields around the bed and they don't dare step beyond them. I can't reach the phone. Anyway, it's broken." At 6:10 p.m., a new entry: "Can endure no longer. Ask the nurse if many people can take these nodes. 'Most people have no problem,' she says. 'There's something wrong with the way mine are in,' I say. 'I hope not,' she says, swinging out of the room after forty seconds. The little girl who brings my supper literally shoves it through the screen and runs. I don't blame her, but I can't reach it. Don't want it anyway." At 7:00 p.m., Marion asks the nurse to phone the doctor to come and take the nodes out. The nurse says, "I can't do that." "Then I'll pull them out. This is not endurable for forty-eight hours." "You *cannot* do that," the nurse says. "I have orders to give you Demerol." "Do," says Marion. At 12 noon the next day, the journal continues: "Twenty-four hours complete, twenty-four hours to go. I keep praying to Sophia to shield me from these hideous rays, but I cannot concentrate on the prayers. The pain is beyond anything I have ever known. Comes in bolts. If I could concentrate maybe I could stop the pain. I deep breathe, try to remain motionless. That works best." At 6:00 p.m., the journal reads: "I tell the nurse I can't go on. 'You can't stop now,' she says. More Demerol." At 10 p.m., it continues: "I'm a bit crazy. I signal the nurse to come. Lovely woman. She says she's had her kids, so she'll try to help me for a few minutes. She finds the bed soaked. … I only know it's got to end, got to end, end, end. NOW. She throws a new sheet over the shield and pulls the old one while I gently lift up. It is soaked with blood. She cannot figure out what is happening. She's sorry she can't stay. I tell her please to get out and care for herself." March 5, 1994, 2:00 a.m.: "I read from my little red Keats book. Writing these great odes while he coughed his lungs out. They're different when Death is real, just at my fingertips." At 7:15 a.m. the journal reads: "Mercifully a woman doctor whom I have never seen before comes early to take out the nodes. 'What's happened here?' she says as soon as she looks. 'What do you think happened?' I ask, hoping to find out something. 'Far too much packing,' she says, muttering other things as she pulls packing upon packing out of my vagina, every piece a torment. 'This catheter is going to hurt,' she says. 'You're raw.' As she pulls, I scream. OVER, THANK GOD. AND ROMEO NOT DEAD AND ME READY TO GO FREE OF MY VAULT."[37]

Marion "READY TO GO FREE OF [HER] VAULT" is a readiness that constellates the "all" of the self. What in Marion's case it took to constellate it is brutally described in these journal entries, first spoken into the tape recorder which, for forty-eight hours, she had with her in the radiation vault along with her New Testament, Shakespeare's sonnets and a small volume of Keats. In those forty-eight hours she experienced in her flesh the "no less than everything." In some still inexplicable way, this "all" is the crucifixion price that, it would appear, must be paid for the ongoing life of the creation. Creation as a crucifixion that as creation includes a resurrection enacts for Marion the reality of the soul as she herself has experienced it. I, like many others, still find that these journal entries verge upon the unreadable. They confront us with a darkness that cannot comprehend the Word descending into it as the oppositional condition of their both becoming known as the two sides of a single psychic reality. The soul-making dynamics of this oppositional condition is, for Marion, what psychology is. "I said to my soul, be still" are the lines from *East Coker* with which Marion concludes most of her lectures and workshops,

> and wait without hope
> For hope would be hope for the wrong thing; wait without love
> For love would be love of the wrong thing; there is yet faith
> But the faith and the love and the hope are all in the waiting.
> Wait without thought, for you are not ready for thought:
> So the darkness shall be the light, and the stillness the dancing.[38]

It was I who persuaded her to publish the cancer portion of her journal. Marion had kept a journal since the age of twelve. I had never read any of it, nor had she wanted me to. Her journal was between her and God. I knew that place at a distance from it, where it was safely lodged as a fiction, a prescribed body of literature called a canon, which I had been secularly trained to read as part of what was fondly called a liberal education. In the presence of Marion as I had come to know her, this would no longer suffice. When she had every reason to fear that she might be dying, her fear was less in the dying than in the possibility that it would remain beyond my knowing, that when and if she died I would somehow not be there. She feared that the long journey that had taken her from her death-in-life into our marriage and on to Zurich to the life-in-death that now confronted her would end without our shared recognition of the *hieros gamos,* which for both of us had been its secret life. It was this fear that led her one Sunday morning to bring out her journal and read to me her account of the lead chamber. I was stunned. I had, in listening, entered a place that I had never been in, a place that somehow became, as I listened, a veritable Holocaust that seemed to contain not simply the terrible fate of the Jews, but in some inexplicable way the fate of a humankind that, whether it knew it or not, could collude with a world in which the Holocaust could consciously occur. It was a reality I had to know if I was ever in the twentieth century to be alive in the fullest dimension of death, explored painfully in Marion's journal, which appeared to be what the century required. The assumption of a human consciousness that has within its power the means to obliterate itself entirely is a responsibility ("To be or not to be") that had now collectively been imposed upon it as the condition of its continuing life. To confront Nietzsche's death of God as the killing of the "chosen seed" was collectively to confront a Western consciousness within the psychotic framework of its boldly attempted extinction, an extinction making use of precision weapons engaging the most enlightened operations of the quantum-inspired mathematical mind.

Marion, as a child, carried a picture of Joan of Arc in her apron until the apron was put in the wash and the picture disappeared. So long as she had the picture upon her, Marion, when she went to the woods, felt safe; and after the picture was lost in the wash, she still felt safe because she now held it in her heart. Thinking of the role that Joan of Arc played in Marion's inner life, I think of Marion's horrendous experience in the lead vault as Joan of Arc's being consigned to the flames, no longer as a fiction, which is the way it is culturally absorbed, but as a raw reality out of which our present civilization assumes its all-too-human shape. I think of Marion as a hero who learned to dance in the flames a dance of life that includes in its intricate figuration the footsteps of death. "And still her feet," writes Shelley in *The Triumph of Life*, describing the muse who inspires his song,

> no less than the sweet tune
> To which they moved, seemed as they moved, to blot
> The thoughts of him who gazed on them, and soon

> All that was seemed as if it had been not,
> As if the gazer's mind was strewn beneath
> Her feet like ambers, and she, thought by thought,
> Trampled its fires into the dust of death. [39]

Marion's account of her experience in the lead vault, the barbarity of which is no longer practised, even in the most extreme cases of cancer, is not a poem written, like Shelley's *Triumph of Life,* in the highly disciplined *terza rima,* with its interlocking rhyme, used by Dante in *The Divine Comedy.* It is the raw stuff of Shelley's final hours out of which as out of a fire the poem as a fragment of itself emerged, for all its beauty, as "the dust of death." The fragment as it stands is essentially an allegorical account of the decaying condition of Shelley's corpse which was burned on the shore after Shelley's boat capsized and he drowned off the coast of Lerici. "The defaced body," writes Paul de Man in "Shelley Disfigured," "is present in the margin of the last manuscript page and has become an inseparable part of the poem,"[40] in something of the same way that the corpse of Nazi Germany has become an inseparable part of a dying Western culture. Romanticism, in its perverse excess, turns upon itself to give birth to death. Marion, in her quintessentially human life, should not, however, become identified with an archetypal one. Such an identification would declare her insane, thereby excluding her from the world in which she so eagerly participates. Marion is herself. She is not Joan of Arc. This is not to say that she, in all her declining strength, could not dance in the flames. The hysteria waiting in the wings to claim her enters as an ever-advancing consciousness psychologically informing the actions of her ongoing daily life.

Marion concludes her account in *Bone* of "dying into life" with her experience at the birthday party of a fifty-year-old Dutch friend who invited us not only as personal friends but as a token of his gratitude for the role that Canadian soldiers had played in the liberation of Holland. Marion begins her final journal entry (April 1, 1995) with a poem by Emily Dickinson:

> Between the form of Life and Life
> The difference is as big
> As Liquor at the Lip between
> And Liquor in the Jug.
>
> The latter—excellent to keep—
> But for ecstatic need
> The corkless is superior—
> I know for I have tried.

"We talk quietly to everyone," her journal records. "Don't move from the safety of the couch. Very tired. At 10:30 we are about to leave." Greeting us at the front door was a Dutchman playing a tuba as he entered, followed by twelve more Dutchmen all playing brass instruments. "I haven't dared to dance for three years," the journal goes on. "Ross and I returned to the couch. I can barely endure listening. 'Come on, Ross,' I finally say. 'Let's dance.' 'Oh, Marion,' he says, 'you know you can't dance. You could break your back.'" "I sit out the polka, can't keep my feet still," the journal continues. "They remember—oh how they remember tapping it out in South Porcupine, Timmins, Schumacher, Heidelberg, Rüdesheim, Grinzing, yes, even Old London. Then my hands are clapping like a child's. The energy builds, becomes so fierce I feel like a puppet with hands and feet tapping syncopated rhythms, feet doubling in toe and heel. Puppet becomes young woman, vibrant with animal energy. A voice comes up from my perineum, 'Marion, you can sit on this couch until you rot, but I am going to dance. I don't care what Ross thinks. ... I don't care if you break your back. I don't care if you drop dead. I am going to dance! I am going to live!'"[41]

And she did. When she stood up to dance, I wanted to grab her, but before I could, one of the Dutchmen who arrived just as we were leaving grabbed her instead, and I, unable to stop them, watched in some horror (fearing the worst), as they swung in circles through the room and through the house until at last Marion was returned to where I was seated. "Happy 50th, Henrikus," the journal entry ends. "I'll never forget this birthday. Thank you, dear Sophia. From every cell in my broken body, my radiant body, I thank you. I am alive. I am free ... to live ... or to die."[42]

The night before she had her cancer operation, Marion dreamt that at sunset a purpled ship is coming into shore bearing two pearls which she cannot see, though she knows they are on the boat. A five-year-old girl, barefoot, with a simple dress and a mop of curls, stands on the deck watching. Behind her, a woman, young, gypsy-like, barefoot, hair flowing, is also watching. After the operation, the gypsy figure with flowing hair became the object of her daily meditations, in which she directed the gypsy's energy into her body, and then, with the radiation that followed the operation, into the cells of her body. Her imaged desire was to restore her severely wounded body to the healthy condition of a five-year-old. Describing in *Bone: Dying into Life* her "initiatory" dream, Marion in the text made her marginal comment upon it by quoting two lines from an Emily Dickinson poem: "Ourself behind ourself, conceal-ed—/Should startle most."

Beginning her account of what she described in *The Pregnant Virgin* as, at the age of three, "the most important psycho-logical discovery of my life," Marion comments upon the discovery by again locating it within the larger context of an Emily Dickinson poem:

Marion, the five-year-old girl with a simple dress and a mop of curls standing on the deck

"Then Sunrise kissed my Chrysalis—/ And I stood up—and lived." "One day," she begins her account,

> I was smoking my corncob bubble-pipe helping my father in the garden. I always enjoyed helping him because he understood bugs, and flowers, and where the wind came from. I found a lump stuck to a branch, and Father explained that Catherine Caterpillar had made a chrysalis for herself. We would take it inside and pin it up on the kitchen curtain. One day a butterfly would emerge from that lump.[43]

The butterfly that did emerge from the chrysalis pinned on the kitchen curtain became at the age of four the angels which outside the kitchen window would take her dead infant in a chariot to heaven.

For six months, confined to a wheelchair, Marion meditated on these natural miracles, imaging her way back into her father's garden with her corncob bubble pipe and the life of discovery she experienced there. Particularly, she meditated on the gypsy who accompanied the five-year-old to shore. Had she not daily imaged her as the sexually mature, fully energized woman shaping within the chrysalis of a five-year-old, Marion believes, she would herself have remained too deeply buried in the unconscious chrysalis to respond to the trumpeting of the resurrection which she heard in the brass band of the twelve Dutchmen as she was about to leave the house. "Ourself behind ourself concealed— / Should startle most." "The Sunrise kissed my Chrysalis— / And I stood up—and lived."

Marion's first total experience of standing up and living as a fully embodied soul was on the dance floor in Timmins in northern Ontario where on Friday and Saturday nights from midnight until dawn she danced on a sprung wooden floor that warmly embraced her dancing feet. Her partners were Germans, Slavs, Finns, Czechs, Russians, Scots, and Croatians, men inwardly still fighting a war in a bleak, exiled land, their troops a thousand miners who spent their days five hundred feet below ground, whose children Marion taught in a classroom above, hoping their bodies might pick up and dance to the rhythm of a Shakespearean line.

Conclusion

In each of these four circumambulations around the self, the self is closely associated with death. The circumambulations around the self are, in each of them, a circumambulation around death: a dead infant, a sunstroke, a drowning (edema), cancer. In the first two circumambulations, the circling takes place largely at an unconscious level; in the last two, the circling takes place at an ever-increasing level of consciousness, in which death finds its place in the dance of life in which Marion is finally "free ... to live ... or to die." A crucial difference between the realm of the ego and the realm of the self is that the realm of the ego rejects death as an intruder, while in the realm of the self death becomes the condition of its archetypal realization. The danger, as Marion understands it, resides in the unconscious identification with the personification of the archetype as the demon lover whose embrace is "the stroke of death ... / Which hurts and is desired."[44] A psychology of the self, she insists, must, in the name of the ego, confront the danger rather than embrace it. The *hieros gamos* is, for Marion, an inner marriage of equals in which neither is subordinated (or sacrificed) to the other. Bound to the *Liebestod,* Romanticism had not taught her this truth, any more than it had taught me.

A perennial symbol of the feminine is the Tree of Life, with its blossoms, fruits, and spreading branches. Marion concludes the published version of her Zurich thesis, *The Owl Was A Baker's Daughter,* by quoting the closing stanza of Yeats's "Among School Children." In her study of obesity, she symbolically identifies the obese woman with the Ophelia of Shakespeare's *Hamlet,* who drowns because she is not "capable of her own distress." She drowns in her own repressed tears, as Marion nearly drowned in her edema. In her mad song, Ophelia describes herself as the baker's daughter who turned into an owl, the bird of night, because, obeying her father, she turned the beggar, who is Christ, from her door. On Christmas Eve, she and her father had no room for him. The daughter's body immediately began to swell, turning finally into the puffed-up body of an owl. In the legend to which Shakespeare refers in his presentation of Ophelia's madness, the bread is the body of Christ, which, in its suffering and death as well as in its resurrection, the baker's daughter rejects. "In the course of this study," Marion concludes her book,

> one resolution of obesity has become clear. If the little owl, bewildered and bewitched, rejects her role as the baker's daughter, she can throw off her cloak of many feathers and become 'capable of her own distress.' Then she can come out from behind the patriarchal eyes and recognize the beggar at her own back door. In that stranger she may discover her own psychological identity with Eve and the Virgin Mary. Her emancipation lies in the psychic enactment of her own physical resurrection – her conscious release from the tomb to which her heritage has unconsciously assigned her, and her entrance into her eternal and divine seed-bearing body. [45]

It is as the embodied soul that Marion, quoting Yeats, describes the dancing Tree of Life. "Labour," writes Yeats,

> is blossoming or dancing where
> The body is not bruised to pleasure soul,
> Nor beauty born out of its own despair,
> Nor blear-eyed wisdom out of midnight oil.
> O chestnut-tree, great rooted blossomer,
> Are you the leaf, the blossom or the bole?

> O body swayed to music, O brightening glance,
> How can we know the dancer from the dance?[46]

Yeats, in the poem, is a "sixty-year-old smiling public man" who is
inspecting a school where the children are taught by a "kind old nun
in a white hood" to "study reading books and history, / To cut and
sew, be neat in everything, / In the best modern way." In the midst of
his inspecting, he daydreams of Leda, who was caught up in the air
and ravished by Zeus in the form of a swan, the ravishment giving
birth to Helen and the tragedy of the Trojan War. Is, he wonders, all
this buried somewhere in these children learning to "cut and sew, be
neat in everything." Is there, as there was in Marion, a wild child
buried in the third grade? In Quattrocento sculpture, Leda now keeps
"a marble or a bronze repose" as, for Marion, the monumental brasses
in English country churches do. Marion in her rubbing restored them
to life, as Yeats in "Among School Children" restores Leda to life. He
sees the children in the schoolroom no longer subjected to the "blear-
eyed wisdom" born from "despair," but suddenly released into the
dance of life, like the angels in the oak tree toward which, in Marion's
picture, Joan of Arc's outstretched arms are reaching. "For too long,"
Marion concludes her first book, which announces all the others,

> the body has been 'bruised to pleasure soul,' the feminine
> nature denied to feed the rational mind. The one-sidedness of
> extreme spiritualization has produced only a 'blear-eyed wisdom'
> born of 'midnight oil.' The tree of life does not unfold towards
> the fruit of individuation in this manner. Consciousness must
> share in the organic nature of the tree itself. The 'brightening
> glance' of the Eighth Eye, of the eye of the healing serpent [a
> reference to one of her recorded dreams] whose feminine power
> Christianity has largely ignored, must be allowed to penetrate
> to its darkest depths. Only then can the 'great-rooted blossomer'
> stretch to its true height, sway to its true music, dance to the
> One dance.[47]

In Marion's life and work, *theoria* is answerable to the subversion
of *praxis*. Coleridge compares the soul-making path to "the motion of
a serpent, which the Egyptians made the emblem of intellectual power."
"[A]t every step," he writes, "he pauses and half recedes, and from the
retrogressive movement collects the force which again carries him
forward."[48] In Marion's dream of the healing serpent crowned with

the Eighth Eye of God (recorded in *The Owl Was A Baker's Daughter),* the dancing serpent leads her to a stone chamber, where he points to two books. As she is about to open the first book, entitled *The Seven Chronicles of the Western World,* the serpent interferes, pointing to the second. On its brightly engraved cover is the Eighth Eye of God, whose fiery gaze penetrates her body with its heat. When Marion told me her dream, I read to her Blake's account, in the concluding plates of *Milton,* of the feminine Christ descending "[i]nto the Fires of [his] Intellect" as the "Starry Eight." What emerges as Blake's epic from "the Fires of [Blake's] Intellect" is "the Divine Revelation in the Litteral expression" which is "[w]ritten within & without in woven letters."[49] For Blake, "Divine Revelation" is "the Litteral expression" of the soul understood as the subversion of what "Priesthood" is presumed to know. In analysis, the presumption as projection is gradually withdrawn, the knower becoming the endless mortal deferral of the unknown known. Marion's life and work, which is her project, resides, not in the construction of a masculine system, but in the feminine deferral of it, a deferral which, as process rather than product, is the enlivening condition which releases the masculine from its logocentrically-wounded state. "How," finally, she never ceases to ask, "can we know the dancer from the dance?" "For the truth is," I once heard her say, "the beginning is where we always are, acknowledging as silence (presence) the end that it is."

NOTES

1. C. G. Jung, *Memories, Dreams, Reflections,* ed. Aniela Jaffé, trans. Richard and Clara Winston (New York: Random House, 1963), 196-97. (Hereafter abbreviated to *MDR.*)

2. C. G. Jung, *The Collected Works of C. G. Jung,* trans. R. F. C. Hull (London; Routledge & Kegan Paul, 1960), 8 § 418. (Hereafter abbreviated as *CW.*)

3. William Blake, *The Complete Poetry of William Blake,* ed. David V. Erdman, commentary Harold Bloom, rev. ed. (Berkeley: U of California P, 1982), *Milton,* 28[30].62. In the composition of *Memories, Dreams, Reflections,* Jung, as he explains in his Prologue, was primarily interested in the primal point as the transcendental source of his

autobiographical narrative. Only at the end, which he realized was without closure ("On Life after Death," "Late Thoughts," "Retrospect"), autobiographical narrative dissolving into "an unexpected unfamiliarity with myself" (359), did he go back and construct a narrative grounded a "uniform development" ("First Years," "School Years," "Student Years").

4. *Ibid.*, 4.5.

5. Jung treated numbers as archetypes rather than as counters. "My dreams and my intuition have both referred me to natural numbers," Jung writes to Wolfgang Pauli. "These seem to be the simplest and most elementary of all archetypes." As a result, "one can never make out whether they have been *devised* or *discovered;* as numbers they are *inside,* as a quantity they are *outside.*" Because they are both, "the possibility can be predicted that equations can be devised from purely mathematical prerequisites and that later they will turn out to be formulations of physical processes." Equations as the logic of the soul, that is, are "formulations of physical processes." Soul and matter are two manifestations of the same archetypal reality which, as number, binds Jung's psychology to Pauli's physics. One, Jung explains, is "the absolute, non-divisible ... and the unconscious, the beginning, God, etc." Two "is the division of the One, the pair, the connection, the difference." Three is "the renaissance of the One from the Two, the son, the first masculine number." Four is "*Unus Mundus,* the *one* world, a Platonic prior or primeval world [the unconscious One] that is also the future of the *eternal world* [the fourfold consciousness of the One]" (*Atom and Archetype,* 127-29). Zero, for Jung, is the "ineffable" Absolute that is without beginning or end as distinct from the One in which beginning is always already joined to its end.

6. *The Marriage of Heaven and Hell,* 14.

7. In his review of *Memories, Dreams, Reflections* in the *International Journal of Psycho-Analysis* 45 (1964), Donald Winnicott argues that the mandala as used by Jung "is a truly frightening thing for me because of its absolute failure to come to terms with destructiveness, and with chaos, disintegration and other madnesses. It is an obsessional flight from disintegration." "What is more important," he continues, "is to reach to the basic forces of individual living, and to me it is certain that if the real basis is creativeness the very next thing is destruction." Marion's understanding of the "creativeness" of the feminine,

particularly in her encounters with death, takes, as we shall see, fully into account the necessity of what an inadequate notion of the masculine considers its destructiveness. She directly confronts in her own project the Biblical myth of original sin (disintegration and chaos) identified with Eve's relationship to the serpent.

8. In a favourite *Liebestod* passage, Jung quotes St. Augustine's account of the cross as Christ's "marriage bed" in which "there, in mounting it, he consummated his marriage." "And when he perceived the sighs of the creature," Augustine continues, "he lovingly gave himself up in the place of the bride, and he joined himself to the woman forever" (*CW* 5 § 411).

9. C. G. Jung and Wolfgang Pauli, *Atom and Archetype: The Pauli/ Jung Letters 1932-1958,* ed. C.A. Meier, intro. Beverley Zabriskie (Princeton: Princeton University Press, 2001), 129.

10. *Atom and Archetype,* 97-98. All italics added.

11. Invoking as Muse the Holy Spirit, Milton in *Paradise Lost* describes it as both male and female. "[T]hou from the first/Was present," he writes,

> and with mighty wings outspread
> Dove-like sat'st brooding on the vast abyss
> And madst it pregnant. (1.19-22)

In this same metaphor of the dove, the Holy Spirit impregnates the Virgin Mary. In *The Dove in the Consulting Room: Hysteria and the Anima in Bollas and Jung (*Brunner-Routledge, 2003), Greg Mogenson invokes it as the presiding spirit in analysis.

12. What Marion calls presence, Coleridge calls the immediate. "On the IMMEDIATE, which dwells in every man," he writes, "and on the original intuition, or absolute affirmation of it, (which is likewise in every man, but does not in every man rise into consciousness) all the *certainty* of our knowledge depends; and this becomes intelligible to no man by the ministry of mere worlds from without" (*Biographia Literaria,* 1.243-44).

13. Samuel T. Coleridge, *Biographia Literaria,* ed. James Engell and W. Jackson Bate (Princeton: Princeton University Press, 1984), 1.273.

14. Over a period of more than thirty years, the BodySoul workshops have evolved from within themselves to become what may now be called a human laboratory in which, by a series of carefully designed

experiments, all of which directly engage the operations of the unconscious manifest in the body and in dream, the *hieros gamos* as *praxis* is gradually becoming as a psychic reality psychologically known. What in itself as spirit and as nature the *hieros gamos* is remains a mystery mediated as soul, psychology becoming the soul's knowledge of itself. "[N]o explanation of the psychic," Jung insists, "can be anything other than the living process of the psyche itself." Because, unlike science, it has no "outside," psychology, he explains, "is doomed to cancel itself out as a science." And yet, precisely by cancelling itself out, "it reaches its scientific goal," the "object" of psychology being "the inside subject of all science" (*CW* 8 § 429). In this paradoxical sense—psychology reaching its scientific goal by cancelling itself out—psychology embraces, for Marion, the abiding methodology of the inner feminine, a methodology which, to the patriarchal despair of the logocentric masculine, pervades her work as its *raison d'être.*

15. Drawing upon the alchemy of Paracelsus, Jung calls these "sparks of divinity" the "*scintillae*" or "*lumen naturae*" which, as the "*sol invisibilis*" or "*imago Dei,*" constitute the unconscious *plenum* which as soul must be consciously (*opus contra naturam*) individuated to form a human identity (*CW* 8 § 388-96).

16. John Keats, *Letters of John Keats,* ed. Robert Gittings (New York: Oxford University Press, 1975), 250.

17. *Biographia Literaria,* 1.84.

18. *Letters,* 250.

19. *Biographia Literaria*, 1.304. Mythically perceived, Coleridge's "eternal act" is the "infinite I Am" forming man from "the dust of the ground," breathing into his nostrils "the breath of life," man becoming "a living soul" (Genesis 2:9). This "breath of life" becomes in the New Testament the *pneuma* of the Holy Spirit impregnating the Virgin Mother. Its "finite repetition" in Marion's case is the making of words by tracing in early childhood the soundings of her breath onto a blackboard, the soundings becoming as words what she would later identify with her "living soul." The rhythmical sound of poetry as the poet's "living soul" is, for Marion, a foundational notion informing her BodySoul workshops, particularly in the voice work developed by Ann Skinner, whose professional training and coaching preceded her work with Marion.

20. *Ibid.,* 1.80-81, italics added.

21. *CW* 8 § 421.

22. P. 353.

23. *Atom and Archetype,* 126.

24. *MDR,* 187.

25. Moneta is the Roman name for Mnemosyne, the Greek goddess of memory. She is an epithet for Juno, in whose temple coins were struck, giving us the English word "money." In giving a new coinage to the succession of Greek gods as their progressive dying (decaying) into life (human consciousness), Keats is attempting psychologically (metaphorically) to re-embody them. "English ought to be kept up," Keats writes, rejecting the high rhetoric of the gods borrowed from Milton, Milton's mannered style producing in Keats a "false beauty proceeding from art." "Miltonic verse cannot be written but in an artful or rather artist's humour," he explains. "I wish to give myself up to other sensations" (*Letters,* 292). The "other sensations" are the bodily sensations which literally bind him in the act of composition to the death of the gods. With each stroke of the pen ("one minute before death"), he feels "a palsied chill ... ascending quick to put cold grasp / Upon those streams that pulse beside the throat" (1.124-32). Confronting as death what, in the now false guise of an epic, he is struggling to achieve, he experiences the movements of his pen as "deathwards progressing / To no death" (1.260-61). The life into which the gods are dying is his own tubercular body. As a memorial (Mnemosyne), his fragment is, at best, a false coinage, offering a pseudo-immortality which, as a wish-fulfilling fantasy, would seductively provide both poet and reader with a "paradise for a sect" (1.2).

Like Keats before him, Jung also feared that in writing down his fantasies after his break with Freud, inscribing them in a high Gothic script further embellished with his own painted mandalas, he was merely creating "a paradise for a sect." "Archetypes," he explains, "speak the language of high rhetoric, even of bombast. It is a style I find embarrassing; it grates on my nerves" (*MDR,* 178). Like Keats and his fellow Romantics, Jung recognized the necessity of sublating the operations of the creative imagination into a consciousness of what, however unknown, they metaphorically represent. Because, like the Romantics, Jung considered this reality "irrepresentable" (*CW,* 8 § 418), he remained mythically bound to a ceaseless process of dying and rising.

As embodied soul, Marion's work also remains metaphorically bound. Far from resting in the metaphorical body, however, Marion continues to interrogate the meanings temporarily assigned to the ceaselessly shifting patterns into which the metaphorical appears to assemble. Above all, she continues to struggle with the demon lover, who, in the name of romantic love, would, by identification, erotically slay her. "Now more than ever seems it rich to die" (54), declares Keats as, lured by the spell of the ode he is writing, he sinks "Lethe-wards" (4). "Was it a vision or a waking dream?" he asks as the spell dissolves. "Fled is that music:—Do I wake or sleep?" (*Ode to a Nightingale,* l. 79-80).

26. John Keats, "The Fall of Hyperion: A Dream" in *The Poems of John Keats,* ed. Jack Stillinger (Cambridge: Harvard University Press, 1978), l. 168-69.

27. *Ibid.,* l. 17-18.

28. "Philosophy as Encyclopedia: Hegel, Schelling, and the Organization of Knowledge," *The Wordsworth Circle* (Winter, 2004): 9.

29. *CW,* 8 § 442.

30. *Atom and Archetype,* 56.

31. "Chrita Mente Maria," *Alphabet* (December, 1965-March, 1966): 45-62. In the story, the exhausted brass-rubber confronts two piercing eyes "fixing her as if to a stake." "You are the devil," she cries, the "flames licking her whole body, stifling her breath." Gradually as she keeps rubbing the brass effigy with her heelball, the flames become the loving embrace of Thomas Neland, whose effigy it is. As what Jung calls "active imagination," Marion in writing the story brought her childhood identification with Joan of Arc to its spiritual consummation, which is the subject of *Dancing in the Flames,* as well as of *Bone, Dying into Life.*

32. *Biographia Literaria,* 2.6.

33. "Tintern Abbey" in *Poetical Works,* ed. Thomas Hutchinson, rev.ed. Ernest de Selincourt (Oxford: Oxford University Press, 1988), 70-72.

34. Percy Bysshe Shelley, *Shelley's Poetry and Prose,* ed. Donald H. Reiman and Sharon B. Powers (New York: W. W. Norton, 1977), 500.

35. *Poetical Works,* 28-30.

36. *Shelley's Poetry and Prose,* 502.

37. Marion Woodman, *Bone: Dying Into Life* (New York: Penguin Putnam Inc., 2000), 127-31.

38. T. S. Eliot, *Four Quartets* (London: Faber and Faber, 1952), 19.

39. *Shelley's Poetry and Prose*, 382-88.

40. *Deconstruction and Criticism: Harold Bloom, Paul De Man, Jacques Derrida, Geoffrey H. Hartman, J. Hillis Miller* (New York: Continuum, 1979), 66-67.

41. *Bone: Dying Into Life*, 240-41. Commenting on a draft of my article, my colleague, Balachandra Rajan, wrote to me about Marion dancing: "The dance for an Indian is inevitably Siva's dance where something must die for something to be created."

42. *Ibid.*, 241.

43. *The Pregnant Virgin: A Process of Psychological Transformation* (Toronto: Inner City Books, 1985), 13.

44. Shakespeare, *Antony and Cleopatra*, V. ii. 298-99.

45. *The Owl Was a Baker's Daughter: Obesity, Anorexia Nervosa, and the Repressed Feminine* (Toronto: Inner City Books, 1980), 122.

46. William Butler Yeats, *The Collected Poems of W.B. Yeats* (New York: Macmillan Co., 1952), 214.

47. *The Owl Was a Baker's Daughter*, 123.

48. *Biographia Literaria*, 2.14.

49. *The Complete Poetry of William Blake*, *Milton* 42[49] 9-14.

IN APPRECIATION OF MARION

STEPHEN AIZENSTAT

P acifica Graduate Institute, of which I am the founding President, was born of a dream, and Marion Woodman was one of the chief midwives who lovingly tended Pacifica through gestation, delivery, and infancy. Her devotion to the eternal wisdom of dream sustains the Pacifica vision even to this day, all these years later.

Marion's keen interest in the conversations between mind and body, between spirit and matter, and most importantly between the authentic masculine and the authentic feminine gives value to Pacifica, and in turn, asks that Pacifica value not only the many demands of institutional and corporate life, but the stirrings of the deep psyche as well. Her call for knowing the inner reaches of a deeper logos (masculine principle) and the expansive breath of a full-bodied Eros (feminine principle) offers guidance to an institution that is dedicated to sustaining itself as soul-centered in a culture dominated by corporate values.

Stephen Aizenstat, Ph.D., is the founding president of Pacifica Graduate Institute, a private graduate school offering M.A. and Ph.D. programs in depth psychology and mythological studies. A clinical psychologist, Dr. Aizenstat has conducted dreamwork seminars for over 25 years throughout the United States, Europe, and Asia.

These elemental forces of the authentic masculine and the authentic feminine transcend the exclusivity of gender and inform everything, from curriculum development and classroom teaching to decision-making and financial planning. In all areas of institutional life, giving value to the conversations between these two voices requires vigilance and interest. In today's world, this is not an easy thing to do, and Pacifica is no exception. The many demands for productivity at all levels, fed by the manic pace of academic life, make it difficult to find time to listen. To interrupt business-as-usual, to pause, and to listen deeply to the unspoken is often painful or threatening. Without the presence and support of an experienced elder, paying heed to what is easily marginalized can sometimes lead to a breakdown in the system. In a world lacking in the wisdom of elders, Marion is a notable exception. Her teachings infuse Pacifica with the values of patience and of being still. She reminds us to make the space to experience just what is so, to hear what is alive, what is known, what is perceived through the deep male and female wisdom of the body.

What is true for Pacifica is true, in a very personal way, for me as well. As a tender of dreams, both my own and those of the people with whom I work, I find these weavings of the deep psyche essential. In fact, more than essential—these elemental ideas of the masculine and feminine are at the very center of my existence and survival. Not too long ago, my relationship to these living figures helped in substantial ways to save my life and all that I have worked for at Pacifica. This was a time when I felt most lost—a time of hitting bottom, of being crashed and shattered on the rocks of life. It was a time in which all external support eroded, the familiar gave way to the uncertain, and the light leeched away into darkness. Externally, the Pacifica campus was being attacked by developers who were looking to expel us from our land. It was a time of litigation, endless struggle, and threat. On the internal front, the springs of my creative life had dried up. My health turned bad, and my body was depleted. Though friends and family lent support, I felt more alone than at any other time that I can recall. I had lost connection to my soul life. It felt like a wasteland.

Worst of all was my separation from dreams. Things had been so hectic for so long that I had, little by little, cut back on my dream work—the very thing that gave me ground, balance, and peace in life. Sustaining relationship to the figures of imagination and dream, experiencing them as embodied entities intimately connected to our actual emotional and physical body is one of the foundational teachings of Marion. As I drifted further and further from people in waking life, I was increasingly distancing myself as well from the figures of the dream time.

There is hardly a lecture, seminar, article, or book in which Marion does not assert as primary the necessity for an active cultivation of ongoing relationship with the animated figures of dream. They are the psychic medicine for the soul, she asserts, and without their presence, we are left without the healing resources so vital in maintaining wellbeing. That is exactly what happened to me. I was no longer spending time with my tribe of inner figures. Primitive cultures describe this disconnected state as a kind of soul loss. It is the worst thing that can happen to a person. To lose one's inner connection is to lose all purpose and meaning. Neither sick, nor crazy, such a person is nonetheless in danger of total collapse and may even die.

My companions were gone. I was alienated from the embodied figures of dream as well as from everyone else in my life. No longer did I spend time with the visitations of the night. My dream journal dialogs with great-grandfather, with coyote, with the ten-year-old boy, with the woman with turquoise eyes, with goanna, forest, ocean, mountain, and even with the often scary tyrant and harpy were now only faint memories of a time moving farther into the past. Gone now were their support, warnings, and guidance. Every day I felt more and more helpless and alone. I felt consumed by anxiety, which was spiraling out of control into obsessive tendencies. I felt numb and spiritually bankrupt, lost, and without hope—exactly the dangerous position the native peoples describe. The external and internal pressures threatened to push my whole life—already at the breaking point— over the edge. I couldn't hang on any longer. I was going down.

On the rocks, and literally wasting away, since I had not eaten much of anything for many weeks, I found myself in the home of a longtime friend. She took one look at me, and without any further discussion, placed a bowl of soup and a sandwich in front of me and insisted that I eat. She is one of many people whose lives have been deeply touched by the work of Marion Woodman. She looked me straight in the eye and told me firmly that I had to make time to return to the figures of my dreams.

In a way, I had no other choice. There was nowhere else to turn. Not at the depth that was now required. I had tended the dreams of so many other people in their time of need, people whose condition had been far worse than mine was. If my life's work had any meaning at all, then a return to embodied dream figures should be of some assistance to me now. Out of familiar options, emotionally exhausted, and skeptical, I returned—without real trust or hope—to my dream companions. It was time to find out the hard way just how real, how valid, how useful these image bodies of the deep psyche actually are. I heard Marion's voice of encouragement. Just as she had helped hold Pacifica in its time of gestation, believing in the eternal images that inform and give form to its purpose, now I felt her presence in supporting my search for an embodied soul that was, at the time, nowhere to be found.

Some friends of mine made a cottage available to me. I arranged to take a retreat there, completely cut off from communication or interruption. For five days and four nights, I would follow the path of dream. I had no idea what would happen. I was (like the man in the title of the book by Jung) a man in search of a soul. I prayed that I would be found. And I hoped more than anything that the figures and the landscapes of dream, which had always been there for me in the past, would again reappear. It was time to take the leap of faith.

Once at the cottage, I set about creating the retreat for myself. Because I had little energy or belief left in me, this was hard to do. But gradually I put together a program. In honor of my friend's helpful gesture, I decided I would try to eat as well as possible. My appetite had vanished with my spirits. How many times I had heard Marion talk about the relationship between food and soul! Her work on anorexia now had immediate and personal meaning. I would take long walks. I would swim in the ocean nearby. Most of all, I would pay attention to dreams, do my best to remember them, tend to them as thoroughly as possible, and engage them in a focused way.

Getting started was a struggle. I knew that I would have to write down my dreams in a journal. Although I had kept dream records for many years, I had abandoned this practice in the past months. To push myself back into the practice took an enormous effort of will. But after so many years, I knew some surefire tricks to make it a little easier. One was to endow the dream journal with personal value. I covered mine with beautiful leaves and shells I found on my walks, and kept it beneath my pillow. I also stated aloud my intention of remembering my dreams each night, and made sure to allow myself time in the morning to do this. And lastly, I wrote a letter to my dreaming psyche, in an effort to open a dialog with her. I have found that dreams like to be befriended: they yearn for attention, and respond positively to gestures of greeting. Having emptied out my bag of tricks, I went to bed on the first night of my retreat, wondering if anything would happen at all.

That night there was a visitor to my dream life. I felt it as more of a presence really, not yet a full-bodied image. I had the sense of a woman watching over me. I woke up in the morning and decided to make pictures of this "felt-sense." And, as I did so, one of the most important journeys of my life began.

I must admit that I am not an artist—certainly not one who has been blessed with the talent to create images that have any resemblance to actual figures or landscapes. Even my attempts at abstract art fail the test of "abstraction"! Having said this, I should hasten to add that I am quite good at what I call primitive "expressive art." That is, when I feel things deeply I can let go and give my hands permission to make bold or subtle lines and blotches of paint on paper. I can also collect things like shells, bottle caps, stones, feathers and the like and arrange them in relation to one another in such a way that they represent what I see so vividly in my imagination. In both instances, with paint on paper or objects on the floor, I can express from the inside out the exquisite and remarkably detailed artistry of my dream life. I have found that once this creative explosion starts, I become free of the constriction of self-conscious judgment and paralysis. If art is in the eye of the beholder, then there is at least one person who finds what I do artistic—me. And see it and treasure it I do!

The first morning at the cottage, I laid out the stacks of butcher paper and mixed the bright powdered watercolors in plastic cups, carefully, just as we are instructed to do in kindergarten. I placed my three brushes of different sizes near the paints and even had half of a sponge available for "special effects." Now, all was in order to give visual expression to the woman figure that was pressing so mightily the night before.

The first paintings were simple strokes of paint swirled in forms that carried a sense of her feminine presence. A certain momentum began to build and a push from inside started to take over. After putting dark green tones and curved lines on one page, I filled a second sheet with bright red and yellow. This was quickly followed by more distinct outlines on a third sheet, and her form began to emerge. A woman came forward, a woman with blue eyes. I recognized her immediately. She had visited before. The montage of colors and forms on the paper brought to life an inner beloved companion, a soul mate, who lives and thrives in the realms of my dreaming psyche. Oh yes, sometimes I encounter her semblance in waking life. I see her across the aisle at the market, or walking down the street in town. Sometimes she is bigger than life and I get a glimpse of her on the screen at the movies or in an image in a magazine. But where she exists most profoundly is in my inner life, in my soul experience. And here, alive and embodied, she is as real as any living woman that I know or have ever been partnered with. She has a name, but I keep that to myself.

What was so utterly surprising to me that first morning in the cottage was the fact that she was still alive and active in my life. For months, I had lost all connection to the familiars of dream. Something else surprised me that morning, an occurrence that I would never have imagined, nor thought possible. When I looked more closely into her blue eyes, I noticed something different. She had grown older. No longer a maiden, she now appeared to be nearer to my age, perhaps in her late forties or early fifties. There were fine lines around her radiant turquoise blue eyes. They were clearer now, yet spotted with specks of cobalt blue and titanium grey. They had earned the linkage to the eternal, like the crystal clear, aqua blue, spring-fed waters of the deepest alpine lakes.

She was beautiful in her age and in her wisdom. I felt met by an inner feminine presence that I had never before known at this depth. In turn, my heart opened in ways that had long been stilled. This was different from my deep love for my wife or for my children. The level of intimacy was so personal, and now that both of us had grown older, so richly textured with the knowledge that only times of anguish, disappointment, loneliness, joy, love, and loss can bring. Here now, her eyes open and available, I looked inside her. What I saw was the maturity of enduring care. I wept, my tears a mixture of deep belonging, homecoming, relief, surprise, and gratitude. Still feeling raw and isolated in waking life, I found that her presence made that first day at the cottage more tolerable. In her company, even for a little while, the tightness of despair gave way to the softness of vulnerability.

As I moved through my day, I realized that I had encountered a figure that Marion has spoken of many times. This wise woman of psyche was an embodiment of the authentic feminine. She was not simply an "anima figure," a stand-in for a long-lost lover or a fulfillment of a romantic ideal. As Marion has taught time after time, the authentic feminine is not necessarily a real woman. She is that elemental quality, beyond gender, that brings body to spirit, soul to matter. She is born from nature and inheres in our true and authentic nature. It is she who matters most.

That night I went to sleep a lot less lonely, feeling more whole, and looking forward to the fruits of my re-engagement. I placed my dream journal next to my bed and with hopeful intent eagerly approached visions of the night.

Unfortunately, the night was not at all simple or joyous. The promise of another encounter with the accepting feminine quickly turned to something altogether different. Filled with currents of anxiety and torment, I was visited by dreams that came and went, like bats criss-crossing at lightning speed in the darkness. I felt helpless and victimized, assaulted by terrors from all sides. Unable to defend against this aggression, I clenched my jaws, tightened my stomach, curled into a groaning ball, and held on for life's sake. Just before I reached the point of yielding to the certainty of my imagined annihilation, something new occurred. From some unfamiliar place, an emotion arose: the feeling of volcanic rage.

This upsurge of fire was new to me in this circumstance. Drenched with sweat, eyes wild, fists pounding, I required an answer. Who is visiting? What force is here now, in the room, moving through me? Words did not come—gestures did, and so did a few startling dream images.

He entered my dream life that night with considerable potency. At first, in a dream appeared an image of a tenacious dachshund dog who was determined to break away from his leash and attack the intruders who were trying to kill me. Then, even more graphic, an image of a phallus appeared. It lay on a marble table, being readied for the meat cutter's knife. I woke up abruptly both times, distressed and tense. The significance of these images of being utterly cut off did not escape me—castration at every level.

At 4:30 a.m. I got up and started putting colors on paper. Scarlet reds, bright yellows, obsidian black filled the pages. At first no real form, just an explosion of expression. Then, as the dawn came, a phallus-shaped figure emerged. He made his presence known: the one who was compromised, sacrificed, emasculated long ago. His form was, of course, a familiar one, but his presence was different. There was a figure behind the image, a masculine entity that spoke with authority and conviction. This dream figure was both powerful and generative—not only a destroyer, but also a creator.

I then turned to working with clay, forming this figure over and over, each time getting more in touch with the essential drive that sparked this presence. I was filled with a feeling of something very deep, something rooted in the ground of instinct and necessity. He, who lives beyond patriarchy, beyond my personal father and my high school coach, had entered the room. I did not have a reference for him. He was unlike any warrior hero figure that I had encountered in movies, literature, or mythology. He was different from the version of the almighty God that I had grown up with, the creator of Adam and Eve. He was someone else. His name I also keep to myself.

In a workshop not too long ago, I heard Marion talk about the authentic masculine, a male figure who knows body, mind, and spirit—a male force that is rooted deeply in the human experience. Not necessarily "belonging" to any one gender, this figure understands the generative drive from the "masculine" point of view. Of course, I had read classical Jung, and had understood intellectually the attributes of the male archetype: those of differentiation, delineation, separation, rational analysis, and above all discernment. All these features were apparent in the dream figure, whose visitation was now quite visceral. Yet, when one engages a figure in immediate experience, descriptions give way to something far more actual.

That morning, He returned. His presence affected every cell of my being. I felt rearranged from the inside out. My legs grew stronger, my feet came awake, my hands vibrated with an energy that originated in my chest. My entire body was shaken by his power. Astonished at these new developments, I could do only one thing other than explode or wield a sword, and that was to "ride the wave" and to give concrete expression to the continuing currents of felt experience. In addition to painting and sculpting, I went down to the beach and made noise. I pounded sticks on logs, struck rocks on boulders, and made guttural sounds and primal gestures. In other words, I engaged in something like tribal enactment. Psychologically correct or not, appropriately Jungian or not, I just carried on. My experiences at the beach were more like being in an extended Marion Woodman body seminar where most anything goes and embodied expression is valued and supported.

Days went by at the cottage, and with each passing day the figures became more active, taking center stage, and asserting themselves in vivid, yet unexpected, ways. Lest this sound too simple or obvious, let me say that taking the time to consciously live in a field of essential images that become primary orchestrators, movers, architects of everyday life, is not an everyday occurrence. During these days and nights at the cottage, my primary role of being in control of life's circumstances gave way to a new position. I was no longer in the driver's seat. I felt more like a passenger looking out the window of a vehicle driven by the vivified figures of the dreaming psyche. I was still interactively helping to guide my experience, and yet, in many ways, I was just along for the ride, and had virtually no idea where "we" were going.

This is not a mental exercise (interpretive/rational modes thinking), but rather an experiential interaction with the figures of dream. From their life force, rooted in the depths of their essential nature, comes an intelligence that informs my own. What is important is the direct experience of how these forces come to life both internally and externally. What is of lesser value here is attributing symbolic meaning or applying conceptual theory. Ideas like the conjunction of the masculine/feminine, or yin/yang, or lunar/solar are recognized and regarded principles of explanation. Yet these images exist on behalf of themselves with an embodied life of their own, and do not require our interpretations to wield their life-enriching power.

Marion Woodman knows a lot about the sacred marriage of inner life. This is not only because she studied and explored these archetypal themes in classical literature, mythology, theatre, and music. (She is, of course, an accomplished Jungian analyst, scholar, and author). In addition, Marion took the time to explore her own direct experience, a deep listening to dreams and the subtle voices of body. She discovered the profundity of the one and the necessity of the two.

In time I discovered for myself more and more of what Marion was teaching. It is not only that the authentic feminine and masculine become a union of opposites, and thus a potent singular force—it is that each in his or her own depth occasions the other into the deeper resources of its unique intelligence. Each is a life force that flows up from the eternal wellsprings like a fountain, forever offering itself to imagination and wellbeing. The vitality of the authentic masculine and feminine informs personal life in very direct ways.

I have mentioned how my role as President of Pacifica is informed by these wisdom figures. In my personal life as well, particularly in intimate relationships, I am shaped by my relationship with these embodied soul-beings. The intimacy I experience with them directly affects the intimacy I share with the primary persons in my life. My vows of friendship and marriage include a commitment to be with the persons of both inner and outer life. Deep intimacy with soul liberates deep care for others. Feelings of hurt, rage, and love, as well as physical body expressions of pain, illness, anxiety and wellness are rooted in my relationships to inner figures as well as in my relationships to actual persons. The capacity to be in relationship on the one level opens the way to the other.

The gift that Marion Woodman continues to offer me, both personally and professionally, is her articulated exploration of the many relationships we have with the embodied soul. Images have body, she says, and our body creates images. She maintains that our dream images come with breath, blood, bones, and knowledge. And the wisdom of our body animates the images that inspire magnificent works of literature, poetry, and scientific discovery. For me, the gift of Marion's work is the process of giving body to image in order to give these back to the yearnings and the afflictions of our physical as well as planetary body. In this way, healing extends beyond the personal and moves into the psychic body of family, community, and world. Marion's work is both a psychological and spiritual practice that opened for me the way to embodied dream tending and to the life of the soul. I am forever grateful.

WHAT MATTERS FLUTTERS STILL:
A TRIBUTE TO THE TRANSFORMATIONAL WORK OF BODYSOUL RHYTHMS

NINA MAHAFFEY

> Since psyche and matter are contained in one and the same world; and moreover are in continuous contact with one another and ultimately rest on irrepresentable, transcendental factors, it is not only possible but fairly probable, even, that psyche and matter are two different aspects of one and the same thing.
>
> —C. G. Jung

hat is it like to take image into the body? Answering a question of this kind invites one into the intricacies of Marion Woodman's work of the past two decades. Since 1995, it has been my great fortune to participate in ten BodySoul Rhythms Intensives and to complete the three-year BodySoul Rhythms Leadership Training Program with Marion, her magnificent colleagues, and an exquisite circle of women, our cherished bodysoul sisters.[1] Some would say that we were called from our parts of the world—Canada, the United States, England, Ireland, Mexico, and Brazil—like a reunion of the lights. Surely our psyches, souls and bodies share common ground. Through these years, we have studied, experimented, danced, sounded, prayed, laughed, and wept together; we have shared dreams and symbols in the most poignant and intimate ways imaginable. We

Nina Mahaffey is a Marriage and Family Therapist and a Registered Nurse. She currently works at Santa Barbara City College in the Learning Resources Center.

have courageously bared our souls to one another and dared to be seen, heard, and held in awe.

By now I have come to understand, on a more intellectual plane, some of the underpinnings of this work and its rootedness in the ideas of Jung. Yet, my deeper appreciation for these roots has come, not through rigorous academic study, but through visual and poetic distillations of essence.[2] As a participant, I routinely took to wandering the workshop grounds with my camera, attempting to process the experience of each provocative session. These images still resonate and deliver me directly to the felt experience of each intensive. Looking back, I can see that my very first intensive contained the seeds for all that followed. I have lived the work—or to be truer to the heart of it—the work has been *living me*—ever since.

For many women, reading the work of Marion Woodman in the early 1980s was the beginning of hope. This has been beautifully articulated by Marlene Schiwy:

> At first it seemed I had stumbled across a new language and syntax, one which my mind was not sure it understood. My body, on the other hand, prickled with excitement. It reverberated to the tuning fork of her words and recognized them as shockingly true, even familiar. Reading on, I felt comforted and nourished, as if some hidden hunger were at long last being satisfied. More mysteriously, my body felt accepted and loved as I continued, page after page. Here were words that burned through to my soul. Here was my life inscribed on every page, my anguish illuminated with such compassion that I could see past the neurotic subterfuges of my ego to the authentic suffering they attempted to suppress.[3]

When I first read *Addiction to Perfection*, I was a deeply anguished young woman and what Marion would describe as a "serious eater" with "unquenchable cravings for something" unknown.[4] I learned of Marion's intensives at one of her public lectures. After expressing interest by letter via her publisher, I was surprised to receive a personal acknowledgment from her despite the fact that she was in poor health at the time (June 1994). The significance of this gesture was profound. Marion Woodman had thrown me a lifeline. From that moment, certain forces seemed set in motion, leading me into the mystery of the work.

When I arrived that September night at Abraxas Retreat Center near Toronto, I was entrenched in my own neurotic suffering. I scanned the faces of thirty unfamiliar women who had come to participate in a week-long intensive workshop with Marion, Ann Skinner, Mary Hamilton, and Paula Reeves. I took in each one's individual beauty, her expressive affect, and intensity of speech. I was overcome by their power and terrified of being found out:

I'm not a real woman, I'll be humiliated; their lives are so full, they are so experienced, so worldly, so accomplished, so smart; they are high-powered women and I am not. How did I get here? Who do I think I am?

Some of them had been participating in the work for years. Surrounded by this throng of bright and soulful women, I imploded into a state of dread so profound I could not speak.

I sat through the morning lecture on Jung and dreams and the place where psyche and soma "meet and don't meet"; the art of "conscious self-soothing"; the difference between conscious and unconscious surrendering to archetypal energy; and the nature of metaphor. *"What does it mean,"* asked Marion, *"to live the wisdom in the body?"*

At the first opportunity, I drew Marion aside and earnestly confessed what I thought—that somehow a mistake had been made in the participant selection process. Marion explained that all women are in different places relative to the safety and strength of their personal "containers" and she graciously suggested that I stay and explore what had brought me here. "You've got power in that body of yours you don't even know you've got," she said.

This was my introduction to the fundamental concept of the *container* in the work of BodySoul Rhythms. Although it is only one element among many in the complex design of an intensive, it is critical. In my experience, it is the exquisite quality of the containing in BodySoul Rhythms that is its trademark.

To contain is to hold together, to hold in, to have within, to include, to bound. Glass bowls nesting one inside the other, ceramic pots filled with earth or rainwater, the pregnant womb—such images of the feminine container abound in nature. In the work of BodySoul Rhythms, the container is carefully configured from the moment of arrival, like concentric rings in water moving gently outward from the dropped

stone at their center. At the core of each intensive is Sophia—described
by many as "the feminine aspect of God"—whose presence is invoked
each morning by Marion's prayer and whose intention is revealed in
the opening petals of the lilies on the group's collective altar. Nature is
also a great container and the beauty of each workshop site, from the
mystical meadowland of Abraxas—its pathway lined with Queen Anne's
lace, cool grass, and spider weavings—to the fierce and windy shoreline
of Lake Huron near Oakwood Inn, serves to calm the ego and reassure
the bodymind. If the feminine principle is about holding the
environment in love, then what happens so effortlessly in the outdoors
can be the template of possibility in one's inner landscape. The
structure, scheduling, and pacing of the week-long intensive also
concentrate focus. Morning, afternoon, and evening sessions, eight
hours a day for a week, keep the heat up in the alchemical process and
help to hold the container.

In the afternoon sessions, we did movement and voice work, guided
by Mary and Ann, to ground the morning lectures in the body. Through
expressive and explorative movement, breath work and soundings, we
began to strengthen the container of our individual bodies by loosening
the joints and musculature, freeing the voice and attending to its subtle
inner impulses with patience, tenderness, and love. Meanwhile, Paula,
the fourth member of the team, scanned the room with "soft eyes" and
offered the abiding presence which contained the entire process. As Paula
has said, "I look for the one odd thing which might be happening in the
room—what Jung says to do with the dream." Because of their
unwavering concentration, it became clear early on that there was a
conscious presence in the room that you knew you could trust. Hovering
outside were the soothing pastels of the meadow.

The "mothering exercise" on the first night was the next
reverberating ring in the holding structure. Every exercise builds on
all the others. Here the conscious mother is the container, who provides
the longed-for cherishing to her child. As Marion has said, "If you
have not had a positive mother or mirror who could hold you in an
atmosphere of non-judgment, you end up with death mother in your
cells." Here the body attempts to trust the arms of another woman to
hold her in love, despite its fear and vulnerability. If one can allow
oneself to trust this first night, the next experience, mask-making, can
unfold the following evening.

It was after this "cherishing exercise" that I dared to break out of my anguished silence by disclosing to my partner the shameful dread and alienation I had experienced the first twenty-four hours. She mirrored my experience exactly! How convenient it is, we laughed, to indulge one's fantasy of separation from the others! It had become clear in one day, as the group and individual work deepened, that, regardless of life experience—we were in good company here among professional dancers, concert-level pianists, painters, writers, doctors, analysts, executives—we had all come to address our wounded feminine, a wounding we shared as individuals and as women in the culture. The feeling was one of reunion. I was still very afraid, but I began to consider the possibility that I had traveled all this way to enter a *temenos* where it was safe to break through old patterns of psychic distress and come to understand the meaning of authentic suffering.

The next evening was dedicated to the mask-making process, another activity which involves positive mothering and helps people delve even further into the place of soul, where psychic treasures dwell. In making masks, regressive ego energy emerges. A lot of creative energy gets released and it is a sensitive moment when we see, in Marion's words, "what negative mother has done to your creativity." In dyads, we grant trusting permission to the other woman as she strokes our face with petroleum jelly and places plaster strips on its contours, temporarily covering our eyes and mouths. In this way, we create a whitened canvas on which to transfer the raw energies stirring within.

In subsequent bodywork sessions, we began working in pairs, attuning to a place in the body that called out for attention and tenderly placing our partner's hand there in order to learn what it means to enter another's energetic field, to touch and be touched with patience and genuine interest. We then moved into the "dance of three," building further trust in preparation for the descent to come. We practiced a subtle and profound process of energy somatization. In this practice, intense concentration on a dream image or symbol, a line of color, or even a word draws you into relationship with it such that the body and voice surrender constraint and deeply repressed material is released. Rather than dancing with an image or interpreting or reacting to it, one's body actually experiences the impetus and is *danced*. This is the transformative process and one of the intended purposes of the week's work: to bring shadow energy out of the unconscious and make it available to the ego as creative impulse.

In my first experience of this practice, a tiny impulse, carefully tended, developed something like this:

Afternoon warm-up—repetitive vocalization of the AHHH sound— begins on a high pitch, drops in level and intensity—voice rising up and down, AHHH-YEEEE, AHHH-YEEE, ahhh-yeee ahhhyeee ahhhyeee, forlorn sounds, wild dog in the night sounds—higher pitch, dropping low, over and over—peak and trough, up then down, rising falling rising falling rise fall—body mimics sound—undulating motion—sounding moving— crayons on paper—peaking and falling—colored peaks on paper—flames—flame shapes—licks of flame—fire—on fire—burning— burned out—flame went out—no spark—no more spark ...

How to move this process onto the mask? With natural materials I had collected from the meadow, the process continued:

Up and down strokes of paint—pinks, reds and golds on the right side of the mask—a motion like the rising up to be seen and the falling away invisible—rising, falling, giving up, giving up, I've given up, I'm falling into flames—orange, yellow, red, blue, gold glitter—flame-like, burning, burned—scorched, singed—shading into browns and blacks on the left side, blackness on the lower left jaw, blackness spreading over my mouth— black lips—no lips—no mouth—black bark for lips—how can I speak?—dead leaves in the left eye socket—dry, dead leafs—leaves—what leaves—what has left?—what has been lost?—black eyes—blackened eyes— how can I see?—can't see the right side's color—can't see—can't see right—nothing but black—piece of bone stuck on the left cheek—stuck bones—stuck—I'm stuck dead bones, dead leaves—dead or alive?

I had no rational concept of what was being created. It was a direct translation of the energy evoked in the bodywork onto the mask's blank surface.

Now we come to the wearing of the mask, first engaging it at a distance, touching it, smelling it, placing it on parts of the body—the hip, the belly, the knee, then placing it over the face and breathing in its energy, attempting to engage, bit by bit, the repressed energy which has been held down in fear. From inside the mask, I felt that I moved with the physical strength and grace of a dancer. I tried to experience the split between the energetic right side of the mask and the deadened left. After a while, I began to sound and scream inside this mouthless mask, screaming into my own ears, crying with the realization, both literal and metaphorical, that *I will suffocate if I do not find a way to speak*! In that moment, the symbolism in the mask was working as healer on three levels: emotional, imaginative, and cognitive. The energy played itself out, then calmed and shifted. This is how the wisdom in the body moves. Now what energy chooses you in the mask?

> *On the lectern—an object attractive to the eye—colored wings, stuffed toy—butterfly?—now we are butterfly-in-motion, shimmering, pulsing, undulating, afloat, flitting towards this one in the cold, white mask to another masked form who lies stiff and still on the floor—won't play— won't see—won't move, damn them!—Hide, I'll hide, stuff the wings in my shirt, they'll never know what's there—covering my chest—no one can see, no one will know (I'm not a woman, I don't have breasts). You can't see what I have under my shirt, I'm hiding—in the black ... still ... CHRYSALIS.*

In that moment, the image and the energy of my body were one. Metaphor, the bridge between body and soul, brought me back to a memory of wholeness and the truth of my experience in the flesh: *I am not dying! I have been here in the chrysalis, waiting, waiting still ... I am alive!*

My original dread at the start of the intensive manifested in death-like imagery on the mask's surface. What actually occurred that week was the opposite of what I imagined upon arrival. Rather than dying into silence, with the life force and brilliant colors of the right side of the mask degenerating into blindness, blackened bones and bark, I recognized that I was in fact moving *into* life, as one emerging from the cocoon. In the final exercise of the intensive, we were asked to integrate the energy of the mask into ourselves, to translate the experienced motions and energies into sounds, and to distill the weeklong process into words:

> *What Matters*
> *Flutters*
> *Still*

How essential is the sweet poetry of the body! And how very critical for the culture is the work of BodySoul Rhythms. It is a unique depth psychological process solidly grounded in the ideas of Jung and comprised of intricately interrelated forms of containment, mirroring, movement, sound, mask-making, dream-work, reflection, and love. It provides women an opportunity to realize the conscious feminine in their lives by releasing the creative energy and wisdom stored in the body. The body is matter and is inseparable from soul. I know it because I have lived it in this work.

NOTES

1. Marion Woodman developed BodySoul Rhythms in collaboration with two colleagues: Mary Hamilton, a graduate of the National Ballet School of Canada and former professor of dance technique and improvisation at the University of Western Ontario for 20 years, and Ann Skinner, former head of Voice at both Canada's Stratford Shakespearean Festival and the National Theater School of Canada. Paula Reeves, a psychotherapist in private practice in Atlanta, Georgia, an author and leader of workshops teaching women to recognize the healing wisdom of the body as it relates to illness, emotions, dreams, and creativity, later joined them as facilitator.

2. To my knowledge, a detailed description of BodySoul Rhythms work has not yet been published. For the theoretical context for this work, see Marion Woodman's primary writings such as *The Owl Was a Baker's Daughter* (Toronto: Inner City Books, 1980), *Addiction to Perfection* (Toronto: Inner City Books, 1982), *The Pregnant Virgin* (Toronto: Inner City Books, 1985), *The Ravaged Bridegroom* (Toronto: Inner City Books, 1990); and *Leaving My Father's House* (Boston: Shambhala, 1993), a work co-authored with Kate Danson, Mary Hamilton, and Rita Greer Allen.

3. Marlene Schiwy, "Saturating Language with Love: Variations on a Dream," in *Wise Women: Reflections of Teachers at Midlife*, eds. Phillis R. Freeman and Jan Zlotnik Schmidt (New York: Routledge Press, 2000), 31.

4. Woodman, *Addiction to Perfection*, 11.

IN MARION WOODMAN'S CAMP

JOEL FAFLAK

> I am neither a philosopher nor a theologian. I am a woman searching
> for the meaning of my life, and my dreams are filling in the feminine
> gaps left by my Christian heritage.
> —Marion Woodman, *Addiction to Perfection*

This article is a testament, not a homage, to MarionWoodman's life and work. "Homage" suggests doors closed rather than wings unfurled to new exhilarations of the soul, and Woodman is, to borrow the title of one of Lillian Hellman's memoirs, profoundly, beautifully, an unfinished woman. Rather than summarize her mind through the body of her work, I want to glimpse that mind's body in mid-flight. What follows is misrepresentative and revisionist because I cannot know Woodman's radically singular psychic space. For me this not-knowing reveals the uncanny reflection of who Woodman might possibly be. In that ambivalence I can only witness, never prove.

Joel Faflak is Assistant Professor in the Department of English at the University of Western Ontario, where he teaches Theory and Criticism, British Romantic and Nineteenth-Century Literature, and Popular Culture. He has co-edited *Nervous Reactions: Victorian Recollections of Romantic Literature* (SUNY Press), *Cultural Subjects: A Popular Culture Reader* (Thomson-Nelson), and is editing Thomas De Quincey's *Confessions of an English Opium-Eater* for Broadview Press.

Moreover, I have no firsthand knowledge of what happens in her analytical office or BodySoul workshops, where her work *matters* most. Yet this ignorance feels right to me, because in Woodman's work mind and body meet in a strange-making and transformative—transformative *because* strange-making—interdependence that constitutes the soul's counter-valent activity. Perhaps now more than ever this process is necessary to redeem what it means to be human, a meaning that can come only when the Self recognizes that it is entirely strange to itself. So here is my strange testament to the counter-valence of Woodman's soul-making.[1]

Embodying the Mind

In this essay I have chosen sometimes to invoke my own life and work as a critical analogue, a strategy of self-reflection that seems, well, all too 'Jungian.' I want to examine this misconception, because Woodman's work is fundamentally constituted by self-critique and self-articulation, a performative psychoanalysis that brings to consciousness the embodied experience of our humanity. Eventually, I want to consider this process as camp and thus as the camp soul of Woodman's work. Camp is, among other things, the enraptured performance of the self that is at once off the mark, a little ironic and deadly serious. In her 1964 "Notes on 'Camp'," Susan Sontag defines camp as part of the indefinable "sensibility" of modern consciousness, the "sensibility of an era" being "not only its most decisive, but also its most perishable, aspect."[2] Camp "converts the serious into the frivolous,"[3] and so it also speaks to what we now call *post*modern consciousness. But whereas Sontag asks that we share with camp a "deep sympathy ... modified by revulsion,"[4] I see in its play of appearances a release of psychic energy bordering on the spiritual. Camp greets the world on its own terms, yet performs those terms back to the world as rote familiarity. It parodies the world's lifeless and stereotypical imposition on our bodies, but only in order to release us into the profoundly human nature of who we are. This performance is both healing and redemptive, mediating the traumatic encounter with our unfamiliar natures, the selves we set aside to be ourselves, or rather, the psychic energy of being our self that gets necessarily but nonetheless repressively harnessed for the ego to cohere.

Let me first elaborate on my understanding of this process by way of explaining the psychodynamics of Woodman's analytic phenomenology—as I understand them. In Jungian terms, the process of identity formation, through which we come to be and know who we are, is silently directed by the Self, which Woodman describes as "the ordering center of the personality" (160). The Self is the sphere of the ego's possible re-acquaintance with the psychic stages or *dramatis personae* of its past and future experience. This experience is continually set aside by the ego in order for us to conform to the dull routine of daily existence that is the ego's quotidian sphere of action. Put another way, the ego is but one performance of the Self as the script or matrix of the ineffable and endless potentiality of what the ego has been and might become. The Self is the as-yet undrawn map of the ego's archetypal proportions (the absolute dimensions of which can never be fully charted) should the ego choose to surrender itself to the soul's expansion into this psychic territory. Camp transformations are implicitly archetypal in this regard, and the ego's performance that taps into the Selfhood that is its potential archetypal home *is* camp. Venturing upon the psychic territory that the camp ego claims for the Self is a dangerous journey. Undertaking all the multiple performances demanded of this potentiality would be like playing the sound of countless frequencies simultaneously: the ego would be obliterated in the face of its own white noise. Rather, the ego must bring its self-performance to a heightened state of consciousness, yet it must do so with a sense of Nietzschean tragic awareness that both mourns and celebrates the fact that the Self can never be known fully in its archetypal dimension.

The ego's presumption to reach the ideal of its potentiality would be what Woodman calls an "addiction to perfection." Only when we surrender to our limitations can the ego achieve a fuller experience of this possible energy. Camp taps into the pathos of this addiction, makes self-reflexive both the absurdity of and the necessary desire for striving after the ideal. Woodman's psychology rests upon an understanding of the inherent risks involved in this undertaking: dangerous if not pursued, equally dangerous in the pursuit. The Self "presents the ego with the challenge to move to a new level of consciousness."[5] Breaking through to the ego's potentiality is at first a traumatic encounter with the unconscious, an encounter that threatens to overwhelm the ego. One must let go of the fear of this encounter in order to reach an awareness of the archetypal dimension of what it means to be human:

> If the ego is afraid to make the passover, preferring to clutch at what it has always known, then psychological and physiological symptoms break out. These the ego has to deal with, for learning the meaning of these symptoms and situations is what leads to the new level of awareness and a new harmonious balance between consciousness and the unconscious. So long as consciousness is afraid to open itself to "the otherness" of the unconscious, it experiences itself as the victim. Once it is able to open itself to the new life flowing through, it becomes the beloved. To be a victim is to be raped; to be the beloved is to be ravished.
>
> Ravishment, unlike rape, involves the integration of unconscious contents so that instead of being overpowered by "higher" or "greater" forces (i.e., archetypal contents), one enters into a loving relationship with them. Ravishment can only be experienced when the ego is a sufficiently strong container to receive the dynamic energy bursting through. Paradoxically, that point can only be reached when the ego is strong enough to be vulnerable enough to surrender.[6]

The embodied practice already at work in Woodman's theory centers around the crucible of the ego's unharnessed energy in the unconscious of the body. The process here is paradoxical, as Schopenhauer realized only too well, for the path to enlightenment that comes with the necessarily embodied perception of thought is also the impediment we, at least in Western culture, strive to leave behind in the name of intellectual superiority. Woodman seeks to undo this persistent Cartesianism, not out of any blindness to the fact that mind and body are distinct from one another, but precisely to bring this distinction to consciousness. Only through the body can the Self begin to emerge to itself, and Woodman's metaphors of rape and ravishment are particularly telling in this regard. The body bears the often painful inscription, the cardinal libidinal imprint, of how we come to be human, absorbing every shock of the new that is the ongoing experience of (a) life. Yet it carries this experience as the aftershocks of what cannot at every turn be brought to consciousness through this experience. To read the afterlife of this bodily trauma is to comprehend the soul's logical life as Woodman understands it, yet it is also to encounter the body as alien to human consciousness because to know the body one must confront the double structure of trauma itself. Cathy Caruth argues that we comprehend trauma only through its repeated 'possession' of us.[7] Because trauma can never be taken in at one go, we experience it as the aftereffects of an original experience, almost a non-experience. But this traumatic knowing is even more fundamental. Constituted by an interplay of psychic forces that we cannot in the first instance fully comprehend (but which determine our ability *to* know), consciousness itself is always traumatically belated insofar as its making sense of experience always comes after the fact.

We are, then, always having to play catch-up with what the world is telling us through the body, victims of a fundamental lag in existence that profoundly affects how we speak back to the world through our bodies. Put another way, there is in our experience of the world a psychic energy always being set aside by the body *as* it experiences (perceives, feels) the world, yet retained in its psychosomatic musculature. To release this buried and untapped energy is thus itself traumatic—traumatic because often the result of trauma itself, but also because so deeply buried and forgotten—and this is why Woodman speaks of turning rape into ravishment. This time warp of trauma that characterizes tapping into an energy always set aside is the Self's constitutive matrix in which the ego loses itself in order to find itself, and rape and ravishment stand as particularly stark signifiers for the traumatic psychology of embodiment through which we come to know ourselves. They are further apt because the body's forgotten identity can never be fully reclaimed. And here Woodman is as un-illusioned about any myth of the fully resurrected body as she is about any myth of full enlightenment. Rather, the mind must be placed in dialogue with the body, not by reading the body's symptomatology in order to produce a cure for the mind, but by reading the body as a site of agency separate from, yet working parallel to, the mind. The body reminds the mind of what it cannot know, the space of a possible knowledge concealed in the body yet available to the mind that would surrender what it already thinks it knows. What the body carries in its cells, both genetically or biologically, and culturally and psychically— both personally and transpersonally—is the language of the Self, a language we have profoundly neglected for fear of discovering who we might really be and having to give up our most cherished notions of who we think we are.

Woodman first tackled the symptoms of this neglect through an examination of obesity (in *The Owl Was a Baker's Daughter*) and anorexia nervosa (in *Addiction to Perfection*). Her personal history dictated these topics, and Jungian psychology offered one of the few modes through which she could transform their painful resonance.[8] Within this exploration of her body's personal feminine, however, she recognized a transpersonal cultural dictate as powerfully deterministic as patriarchy itself in shaping women's lives and bodies. It needs to be noted that this recognition came as a result of never treating symptoms as pathologies to be cured. Treating them as such would be merely to reinscribe the categories of "feminine" or "masculine," "patriarchy" or "matriarchy," and thus re-imprison the body in the very social terms that gave rise to the symptoms in the first place. Instead, Woodman reads in the bodily phenomena of illness a powerfully transformative energy by which these distinctions begin to realize their potentiality as through a creative marriage, what Jung calls the *hieros gamos*. This alchemy amalgamates opposites without erasing the difference between them, transforming the categories without forgetting the categorical imperative that got the feminine, like the masculine, in trouble to begin with.

In this respect, the "feminine" posits an archetypal rather than an essential dimension of soul, yet an archetypal *energy* essential*ized* through women's radically embodied experiences *as* women, a psychic space that they can *potentially* inhabit and through which this embodiment *might* be brought to consciousness. Key here is the feminine's release from the codification of its psychic energy as it is stifled by social and cultural iteration and reiteration. The poststructuralist theorist Judith Butler argues that our subjection to a "regulatory power … producing and exploiting the demand for continuity, visibility, and place"[9] constitutes our subject-*ion*: the process by which we become subjects in the first place. Our psychic life is determined by power's "iterability," the inbred effects of its social regulation. This iterability, paradoxically, constitutes our agency, the way in which power acclimatizes us to its arbitrary nature by repeating itself in order to appear *natural* or *given*. However, Butler continues, agency also "consist[s] in opposing and transforming the social terms by which it was spawned."[10] The repetition of power's effects offers us the possibility of transforming them, not as transcendence, but as our chance productively to alter, recreate, or transgress these effects—to *de*naturalize and *de*familiarize them.

The difference between Butler and the post-Jungian Woodman might seem profound, but like Butler, Woodman would not think to question the *determinism* of this positing power of subjectivity. Her own experience of obesity and anorexia betrayed culture's all-too-real imprint upon the body in a way that made it seem autonomously alien. Yet she further recognized within this autonomy the possiblity of transformation: the body's turn against the Self holds a reminder to the Self about what the ego does not know. Excessive fatness or excessive thinness are mirror images uncannily reflecting a Self both too much and too little with itself; yet this radical imbalance, played out through the ego's neurotic battles with itself and with the world, contains a profound potentiality, the libidinal matrix that is the Self's sphere of becoming. The ego must initially surrender to this process by abandoning itself to the body, first as repressed or unknown energy— hence the ego's initial sense of this surrender as traumatic and fearful—then as an overflow or excess of energy—hence the ego's experience of its own radical otherness through what Woodman calls love or *eros*. It is in this sphere of attachment between analyst and analysand that I want next to consider Woodman's practice. This practice is informed profoundly by a therapeutic *eros* that grows out of the rigorous discipline of Woodman's exacting and exhaustive analytical training, as it is for any analyst worth his or her salt. But it has been the cause of anxiety for some, both professionals and lay-people, where Woodman's therapy is concerned.

Minding the Body: Four Charges

As long as theories remain theories, they do not matter much, and are not a cause for much alarm. Where Woodman's theory matters most, and starts to make people most uneasy, however, is where it gets embodied as a groundbreaking practice. Here I can think of four distinct but interrelated ways in which people mind the body that Woodman talks about transforming. While one cannot question her commitment to the care of the Self in her practice, the methods she uses open her in the first instance to the charge of sentimentality. Woodman's work is "woman's work": too "touchy-feely," evoking the worst aspects of analytical practice combined with feel-good therapy. Where is the scientific and rational objectivity? the professional distance? That this charge tacitly presumes to question Woodman's profound concern for personal and professional boundaries is itself grounds for its immediate dismissal, but her illustrious and unimpeachable record also speaks for itself. Nevertheless, the charge is worth pursuing for other, not a little ironic, reasons. The concept of sentimentality originated in a middle- to late-eighteenth-century concern with sentiment and sensibility, notions that suggested that one can feel strongly for others by turning one's passionate reflection about one's own inner feelings into outward sympathy for one's fellow human beings and thereby add to the cohesive force that holds all individuals together in the social sphere. As the Enlightenment shades into Romanticism at the end of the eighteenth century and into the early nineteenth century, however, too much feeling becomes a problem. That is, too much meditation came to be seen as a sign of melancholy and morbidity rather than as a necessary step in the individual's progress towards proper public and civic action. And so, too much feeling, at first heroized and idealized through the forceful self-expressiveness of the eighteenth-century "man of sentiment" and later the vatic Romantic artist or genius, becomes pathologized as a bodily predisposition in need of properly reflective self-containment. To be described as sensible was to be accused implicitly of relying too much on one's feelings, of being too tied to one's body, and (to invoke a stereotype that would last well past the nineteenth-century constitution of the separate spheres of private female domestic activity and public male social action) too feminine. Mary Wollstonecraft, generally thought of as the first modern feminist, was widely vilified in the early nineteenth century for daring to address the issue of women being always caught in the complex vagaries of body and mind, and, more than that, for daring in turn to use this analysis as a call to political action. As a female Romantic writer she was not alone, although the many who looked to her as an example were matched by an equal number who denounced her. Such were the times, we could say.

I invoke the long chronicle of civilization's discontent with feminism (the prolonged vilification of Wollstonecraft serving as but one symptom of this discontent), by way of exploring a second resistance to Woodman's work: that of institutional and institutionalized resistance to Jung himself in academic circles. I now realize that I have in many ways been a closet Jungian for most of my life, but certainly for that part of my life spent in academia. I am here confessing what have been my own suspicions about Jung and Jungianism. These relate directly, I now realize, to my doubts about the possibility, practicability, and authenticity of the kind of transformations Woodman explores, but more particularly to my conditioning by the academy. It occurs to me that the very attitude that prompts criticism of Woodman's thinking is at play in the dismissing of Jung, wherever that occurs, and it still does, often vehemently, under the aegis of academia's institutional authority. Here I take Eric Savoy's powerful statement, paraphrasing Eve Sedgwick, that "ignorance circulates institutionally as powerfully as knowledge; indeed, it is a form of knowledge, reducible to the automatic, 'we-know-what-that-means'."[11]

Let me explain. My work in my primary fields of research—literary studies, theory and criticism, popular culture—is informed by my interest in psychoanalysis. Criticism in these fields, when it addresses psychoanalysis, usually does so in the language of Freudian and post-Freudian theory. The latter treats the psyche with skepticism because, it argues, Freud himself, on account of his theory of the unconscious, saw the psyche this way. This skepticism extends to Freud's theories, the scientific authority of which (despite Freud's desire for scientific respectability) is turned over to fantasy and to the parapsychic staging of the conscious mind by the unconscious. Freud's theories are thus open to multiple interpretations. Like the unconscious, they articulate themselves beyond our power to control them: behind their manifest content are the latent dream thoughts of psychoanalysis that never get spoken. And Freud, supposedly, knew this. As a modernist, he exposed, beneath the veneer of civilization's fundamental values and truths, its instinctual half life. As a *post*modernist, he taught us that all truth—if there is any such thing at all—is relative. He taught us to be suspicious of the given, the natural, the normal within any utterance, inscription, or representation, which thus become chimerical significations, the sign of a false consciousness masking the traumatic renunciation of the truth, or its absence altogether. He practiced what poststructural literary criticism calls a "hermeneutics of suspicion."

Jung rarely makes an appearance in these discussions, despite his profound and often equally skeptical attitude toward the fantasy structure of myth and the mythopoeic. We can trace this dismissal back to Freud and his heirs who, after Jung and Freud 'parted ways,'[12] pathologized Jung as a religion-crazed narcissist threatening the supposedly pristine scientific objectivity of Freud's metapsychology. Jung felt Freud's theory of sexuality represented a return to the dark ignorances of what, writing to Karl Abraham about *Totem and Taboo*, he called "'Aryan religiosity'."[13] In *Memories, Dreams, Reflections*, Jung recounts how he resisted what Freud called the "'dogma'" and "'unshakeable bulwark'" of his "'sexual theory'."[14] Jung felt Freud's sexual theory would "lead to an annihilating judgment upon culture," and that "[c]ulture would then appear as a mere farce, the morbid consequence of repressed sexuality"; Freud saw in Jung's rejection the drowning of his hard-won scientific enlightenment about psychoanalysis in the "'black tide of mud'," "'of occultism'."[15] Jung's dismissal created a psychoanalytical version of the separate spheres and in many ways inaugurated a persistent intellectual profiling, and implicit feminization and racialization, of the Jungian "type."[16] Certainly Jung's subsequent interest in alchemy, parapsychology, and flying saucers did not help the cause, and must have struck Freud and his allies as a symptom of the worst excesses of the imagination of psychoanalysis deluded by its own metaphors of the unconscious. Jung has thus become too easily popularized as godfather of the New Age, of a facile return to spiritualism, of a pseudo-psychological mapping of the soul's logic too easily confused with Tolkienesque fantasies about the daimon world of guardian angels, evil fairies, or archetypes materialized as talking china in Disney's *Beauty and the Beast*. At the very least, then, Jung is un-academic; at the worst, he's a charlatan.

Time does not permit an examination of the precise differences between Freud and Jung, but I am concerned to note that a difference *does* persists as natural law in our critical and popular imaginaries. That this difference has become the fate rather than the destiny of psychoanalysis, something it must grimly accept rather than productively engage with, speaks to why Jung far more than Freud is the scapegoat for the credibility gap of psychoanalysis: Jung's desire to compromise psychoanalysis as a legitimate science was somehow too wanton, which is why the Freudians had to get him out. Jung, that is, did not seem to care that, like quantum physics, mesmerism, or alchemy, psychoanalysis by its very nature trades in the empirically absent and so must, to sustain its theoretical authority, repress its very existence as a kind of anti- or non-science. In that empirical absence, Jung can be and has been blamed for inventing all types of metaphorical intrusions. The further charge here is that Jung was himself misled about the psyche and that post-Freudianism proceeds by the assumed and unassailable obligation to demystify the psyche, as if on Jung's behalf, but really by not considering him at all. In this regard, to resist being a Jungian is to resist mythologizing the psyche, to dissociate the psyche from its own mystifications, a kind of negative enlightenment that poststructuralism frequently turns into a sign of its own positive value, quite against the skeptical outcome of its own dialectic.[17] We must see through the myths of the modern soul that Jung has supposedly reinscribed in the place of a religion that was for Freud the opium of the psyche as it was for Marx the opium of the masses. God forbid we ever go back that way, one hears this critical voice say. But God, as Marion Woodman knows all too well, is precisely the issue, more than we realize when we go about stripping emperors of their clothes. Religion's persistence in our global community cannot be only a dream from which we have yet to awaken. And if I understand him correctly, Jung never understood God to be anything other than our fantasy of what God means through our willing suspension of disbelief in the idea *of* God. Rather, he was led to interrogate the psychological imperative *to* suspend our disbelief, not only, but especially, when we know this suspension is a feint, as Jung powerfully explores in his *Answer to Job*.

What is at stake, that is, in *our* dreaming of God such that it becomes God's dreaming of *us*? Jung suggests that culture's power comes as much from its repeated turn to myth as it does from our breaking of the vessels, the breaking constituting one of this return's most potent symptoms. Put another way, the forms of myth might change, but the symptom of change is rather startlingly consistent. Myths are not necessarily sites of repression or sublimation, of a missed encounter with a possible enlightenment of the species, a forgetting that, once remembered, would make myth itself vanish. Instead, they might constitute a *necessarily* missed encounter with truth, without which transforming the energy of this repression would be impossible. So, by what deep psychological need do we repair to myth, as if compelled to return to the repressed? Humankind's glacial ignorance cannot be the only explanation for *Star Wars* or *The Lord of the Rings*, the virtual mythologies of Gameboys and video games, the resilient half-lives of the gothic or science fiction, the belief in other worlds and other dimensions. Perhaps this ignorance is our destiny as much as it is our fate. Are we merely unable to accept change, despite our global mind's hourly modulations? Or does change come with a return to the still center that repeats what we already know, but in a finer tone, when we are ready to hear it, like Nietzsche's eternal recurrence?

This, by way of considering the interrelationship between my previous three points, brings me to my fourth and final sense of what might trouble people about Woodman's work. My education very often denies the transformation that comes when we are stunned by the completely unexpected moment of encountering our own psyches as places we have been before but never knew. More precisely, the academy seems to diminish our *feeling* what this encounter means. Our waking, rational intellects are unprepared for this moment, which we ignore at our peril, although one would have thought it was the particular relevance of the university *to* startle us out of our intellectual complacencies. We have, I wonder, forgotten that the intellect can be a feeling instrument capable of an embodied rationality that refuses to cut the mind off from the body and heart. The academy tolerates bodies and hearts as mental constructs so that it can both analyze them, skeptically, as constructions of consciousness somehow dissociated from the construction of consciousness itself. I have been trained to accept this reticence toward the body and heart as a critical agnosticism, my ascetic superiority, one of the many advantages of higher education in our culture. This gives me the privilege to speak my mind in order to discriminate acceptable ideas from those less acceptable, to participate in civilization's progressive revelation, *especially* when I am most demystified about it.

What I find still surprising, and not a little ironic, however, is the affective *strength* of reactions against the kinds of affect Woodman asks us to address, a reaction that I have frequently shared in the past. I am not questioning the fact that to respond with careful and skeptical scrutiny is the whole point of a higher learning that functions at arm's length from the public sphere that would legislate the kinds and methods of scrutiny that can take place. I *am* skeptical about the intensity of this scrutiny when it shades over into a seemingly tacit desire to occult certain fields of inquiry to which, one presumes, the university would remain receptive as part of its epistemological mandate. As I describe above, Woodman explores the embodied soul as the staging of the absent psychosomatic body's traumatic consciousness of itself in the irrational. She writes, "If we allow ourselves to receive, to be ravished by the irrational, we are compelled to face our own evil. Trust takes on a new dimension, for in knowing our own darkness, we know only too well what another's darkness can release."[18] She follows Jung in this regard, for in ways Freud was unable to broach, Jung was able to hear the sounds of the subject's absent psychosomatic body, which it is the particular crucible of psychoanalysis to apprehend. In the "clinical" setting of the analyst's office, this body resonates through listening to the other voices of consciousness as they articulate themselves through the body's symptomatology, the place where the mind expresses itself through the body, but also where the body has a mind of its own.[19] This is not merely to accept the mortal coil of our biological heredity, like Freud's *Triebe*. At this level, as Jung knew, culture was a demonic parody of man's deluded aspirations beyond this biology, some divine joke played on man for thinking he could escape the body. Refusing to play along with this joke, Jung at some level rejected the body's dark materiality.

Julia Kristeva calls this site of indeterminate articulation the "semiotic," which is her way of speaking of how the subject emerges into being at the most fundamental level of the body's dark materiality. Kristeva speaks of the semiotic *chora,* an "essentially mobile and extremely provisional articulation constituted by movements and their ephemeral stases" not unlike Freud's *Triebe*. The *chora* functions like the primary processes in Freud's dreamwork and registers the drives as "'energy' charges as well as 'psychical' marks."[20] As the psychic 'binding' of the subject's instinctual and libidinal motility, the semiotic is associated with the infant's biological attachment to the mother, but also with the intersubjective relationship between them, and thus is the primal matrix of biological *and* cultural regulation from which the subject emerges—the site of the *semiosis* of the subject, the marking of the meaning of the body as a body of meaning. This (m)other is both material and psychic, both semiotic and symbolic, a process Kristeva calls *poetic* for, as she argues, the drives evoke a kind of fundamental and constitutive "dramaturgy."[21]

We can relate this dramaturgy to the performance of the Self via the body that Woodman's analytical practice undertakes. As we have seen, for Woodman the physiological geography of trauma that is the body's articulation of experience marks a creative imprint, the possibility for a transformation of self which leaves it better prepared to understand, accept, and revise its place in the world. Kristeva refuses to identify this absent psychosomatic body with the 'feminine' in order to resist the kinds of gender essentialism historically associated with the mother or with the female body. She does so to mark within this restrictive symbolic economy its systemic instability, its vulnerability to critique. Woodman *does* call it 'feminine' in order to address the fear of confronting the body as a rejection of its genesis in the mother's body— fearful *because* it has been rarely confronted or because it has been so routinely set aside as the feminized and irrational other to a more sane, healthy, normative subjectivity. Because the body constitutes psychic reality at some fundamental level, this bodily feminine is the inescapable matrix from which we emerge to experience and thus understand the world.

The fact that this bodily unconscious, like Kristeva's semiotic, is profoundly pre-verbal comes as an affront to the fixedly verbal and thus supposedly highly rational sphere of action that defines something like the university. Also, what is "pre-verbal," like the origins of symptoms (the reading of which is at the core of the modern founding of psychoanalysis in Freud and Breuer's early work on hysteria), is fundamentally resistant to what became the hallmark of psychoanalytic therapy: the talking cure. To 'speak one's mind' became imperative in Freud's practice, especially as he realized early on that hypnotism and other cathartic interventions betrayed the residue of occultism that had haunted psychoanalysis ever since the days of Mesmerism. More than that, any therapeutic practice that focused on powers at the subject's disposal *other than* intellectual ones left him open to certain ethical charges—like the time a female patient, under the effect of hypnotic suggestion, threw her arms around Freud's neck. A mind out of control was one thing; a body that was psychosomatically wayward was altogether too messy. The talking cure, Freud's eventual therapy of choice, then, spoke to a confirmed rationality, and thus to a certain scientific objectivity (i.e., a location of the mind objectively from the body) that would make psychoanalysis respectable once and for all.

It makes a certain kind of 'common sense,' then, that the university would use the skeptical methodology that informs its civilized and civilizing influence as a bulwark against having to examine the pre-verbal and chaotic provenance of its academic sanity. This is also, I would guess, where many Jungians and non-Jungians alike start to get uncomfortable with Woodman's BodySoul workshops, which reconstitute the body's performance to itself as the radically performative analytical space where the body revisits its silent, forgotten vignettes for the mind's startled audience. Participants confront how trauma works in and through the body, and thus how the power of psychic belatedness can be brought to consciousness as the soul's unfolding through the body. I would guess that for many this bodily therapy—despite the fact that Woodman and her co-practitioners bring to these workshops a lifetime of clinical and institutional training and practice to hear the body's pre-verbal resonances—is more *acting out* than *acting for*. Behind this unease are also suspicions about Jung's attempt to embody the psyche as empirical truth and thus to essentialize its mythography of the subject's unconscious life. Moreover, these workshops appear to turn the serious work of clinical practice into performance art, a move that smacks of self-indulgence, even charlatanism. To reintroduce the body into the equation is to regress to the very stage of occultism that provoked Freud's break with Jung in the first place. Furthermore, the performance takes place with other workshoppers present. In these presumably unbridled, unrehearsed public dramatizations, bodies betray their secret traumas as part of social theater: trauma as group therapy. One imagines the Mesmeric crisis rooms of late eighteenth-century France, where primarily affluent female clients joined in hysterical group "crises" or catharses, or the spiritualist sessions that Henry James satirizes as such trivial women's work in *The Bostonians*. In both, the feeling subject is feeling too much.

Yet isn't the uncomfortableness with this performance of the body Woodman's point? First, there is the specter of a New Age, "touchy-feely" psychologism or too overt sentimentalism that I have touched upon above. If the gaze turned upon bodies in this situation is not medical, clinical, or scientific on the one hand, or purely aesthetic on the other, or is not prescribed by a carefully legitimated and supposedly healthy skepticism about the psyche, it cannot be authentic. This is to miss the deadly serious care of the soul that, coming from her profoundly intimate knowledge of trauma in the body, has informed Woodman's work as a practicing analyst. More telling, then, is the trauma that comes with society's discomfort with the body, its sense of the sheer difficulty of reading the complex language of that which is our most native habitat: the chiaroscuro of movement and affect that is both the inscription of experience upon us and our experience of this inscription in turn. Woodman does not read this language at the level of the archetypes as essential or transcendental forms. Instead, she reads in the materialization of certain bodily schemas and rhythms the pattern recognitions of a buried but not forgotten experience that is essential or archetypal *for that person*. These patterns can often be recognized by others in the group, not as universal or fixed, but as recurring with a kind of psychological regularity. This insistent re-cognition produces a transpersonal group memory, suggesting a common, even archetypal human legacy. However, the process cannot stop here, for this experience of what egos have forgotten about themselves is idiosyncratic for each person, a singularity that points to the rule only by naming exceptions to it. That the experience of our human legacy through the body is at once profoundly therapeutic and profoundly alienating is, perhaps, Woodman's most difficult lesson. In this singularity without rule exists a kind of existential performativity that keeps trauma as its fundamental matrix of development while at the same time witnessing in the passover to this profound absence of ego the chance for personal transformation. In this singular space, the empty center that is the absent container of the Self is filled with the Self's performance as a presence, staged on the abyss of its own absence to itself. For me this defines the experience of the closet, camp being the saving gesture of inhabiting this space. Let this return to my opening point about camp also be my endpoint.

Camping with Marion Woodman

In her article "Emily Dickinson and the Daimon Lover" (*Spring* 2004), Marion Woodman writes that Dickinson throughout her "whole life ... defended her private room—her place of freedom—where she scrutinized her life under a microscope in tiniest particles and dared to articulate her honest observations in a poem."[22] I want finally to speak as a gay man who finds this statement incredibly moving, not because it speaks to the fact of being gay but because it exemplifies for me what is most movingly exemplary about Woodman's work. I normally resist calling myself "gay." I am a person like and not so like other people, the way we are and are not ourselves. I am, that is, in the process of searching for the meaning of my life. So, I am still (certainly naively) amazed that anyone should care so much about my desires or sleeping habits. Yet "gay" often necessarily distinguishes my identity from "the norm." "Normality," although an essentially nineteenth-century invention, persists now more than ever in an increasingly global world order bent on reducing us to a common democratic currency. I have only to recall the image of Matthew Shepard tied to a fencepost to remind myself of the always darker side of what it means to be part of a blindingly self-making universal citizenry—the norm's horrifying ability to annihilate by intolerance and fear what threatens it. Even when culture appears to recognize difference, I always worry whether this acceptance isn't really just the norm's ability to silence difference by absorbing it into the norm's larger sphere of influence. And so, much as I resist speaking the language of the other and of otherness that culture would impose upon me, I know that at some level I ignore this imposition and its bodily effects at my own peril. Like Woodman, I am necessarily, vitally "forced" to listen to the terms of this embodiment, to turn its rape into ravishment.

This turns me to my other sense of being "gay," which is to signify difference transgressively, productively—to dissent from the accepted, the given, the deadeningly insistent ground of common sense. In the opening chapter of *Symbols of Transformation*, "Two Kinds of Thinking," Jung veers away from "directed thinking" toward one that "lacks all leading ideas and the sense of direction emanating from them," one in which "[w]e no longer compel our thoughts along a definite track, but let them float, sink or rise according to their specific gravity."[23] In other critical parlance this is called "queer" thinking. To 'queer' the norm means to confront the blindnesses of normality, its expulsion of fundamental otherness by which, through the expulsion, it constitutes itself. To 'queer' the norm also reminds the norm that what it expels, by its expulsion, becomes fundamental *to* its identity. The body, always the fundamental marker of what being human means in the world, is also the world's reminder of what it risks by re-inventing itself in ways that preclude this bodily humanity. Mary Shelley knew this when she wrote *Frankenstein* in 1818. Woodman's dramaturgy of the embodied soul signifies how a return to the body queers the given, the rational, the hegemonic, the norm and the normative. The body reminds culture of its oppressive positing power. Talking back through the trauma of its soul-language, the body releases this trauma through the profound orchestration of its inherent logic. In this logic one can hear the rustling of angels' wings.

Perhaps what makes us uncomfortable about the kinds of transformations of the body that Woodman invites us to undertake is the idea of transformation itself, which is more often than not a transformation of common sense. As she notes in *Addiction to Perfection*, our culture is so resolutely wedded to the material and the concrete (while, paradoxically, so profoundly ignoring the materialities of the body in other ways—by ignoring the body's death, for instance) that any opportunity for psychic transformation appears like a parapsychological phenomenon. When the psyche hears the echo of its own traumatically forgotten embodiment deeply buried in the labour of the five senses that the body perpetually performs, it manifests itself as the extraterrestrial epiphenomenon of this labour's cultural effect. Here the psyche reads back the impression of the external world upon it as the radical pathologizing of this impression in the bowels of the psyche's furnace, which always forges new forms from old types. James Hillman speaks of the fundamental psychological reality in and through which we all find our being as humans as an essentially pathologizing function.[24] But we can read before Hillman the influence of William Blake, in whose work we find the radical defamiliarization of the given terms of the psyche's impressive life through which the Self comes to know itself.[25] Ross Woodman has explored this defamiliarization as the madness of the *cogito* in the Romantic psyche's encounter with itself.[26] Marion Woodman brings this madness home to roost in the body, where it exerts its most chaotic and most profoundly productive human response.

A friend and colleague, skeptical of the kind of theory-in-practice that Woodman's work evokes, once said to me, "What bothers me most about Jung is that he gives the subject a hell of a lot of agency." Certainly we need to suspect too much agency for we risk forgetting how we are interminably and acutely restrained by the world. This is implicitly to make a feminist argument, with which I don't think Woodman would disagree. Yet Woodman's BodySoul work does not make the subject a free agent. Quite the opposite: it begins with a sense of the subject's acute limitations *as* a bodily and embodied subject in the world. Woodman is nowhere more clear on this point than in her cancer memoir, *Bone: Dying Into Life*. *Bone* recounts in stark, visceral terms at its dark climax in the lead-lined radiation room how the body must fight the rape perpetrated against it by both its own biology and by the cultural forces that would contain this body's chaos as if it didn't have a life of its own. How to turn this rape into ravishment? Woodman was brought to the absolutely still and deadly center of her lifelong dedication to the body's transformation of the soul. In the brutal fact of the body's frail resiliency, what kind of transformation could be possible past the annihilation of both the body and its psychic life?

Woodman survived cancer only by remaining true to the body's language as it was forcing itself, with unimaginable ferocity, to consciousness in her mind. Cancer put her theory of the body to the test as nothing else had ever done in her professional or personal life. It demonstrated that spirit must be radically earthbound for its moment of bodily transformation to have any saving resonance within the human. Only once Woodman confronted the specter of transformation's virtual impossibility, in the Dantesque Hell of her imprisonment in the simulacrum of the medical system's rhetoric of cancer and its treatment, could transformation itself take place. Only then does the importance of the suspension of our disbelief about the possibility of transformation make itself felt, potently, tragically, in an ecstasy of suffering, and thus offering the only real breakthrough into the human dimension of living our lives. This used to be called the martyrology of the saints, and while I do not write this to canonize Woodman or her cancer experience, something of the suffering of martyrs informs this experience, which demonstrates that much more profoundly the logic of soul that she helps her analysands to understand. I would not confuse the agony of Woodman's cancer with my being gay, although I would parallel the cancerous effects of her medical treatment to those of Matthew Shepard's victimization and to other equally violent forms of cultural embodiment and inscription.

So, what is finally most moving for me about *Bone*, and about Woodman's life and work in total to this point, is her ability to dance, to continue with the performance *because of* her life, not *in spite of* it. This takes me back to her statement about Dickinson. When speaking about what he calls the "chiaroscuro of queerness," Skye Gilbert, one of Canada's most prominent dramatists, says that camp, perennially associated with the gay and the queer, is a "metaphysical statement about life itself, a protection from the pain of life and its living."[27] For Gilbert the term "protection" does not signify defense, repression, or remedy. Rather, it signifies the necessary gesture by which life, through which we find ourselves otherwise alienated from ourselves, from our *Self*, also allows us a measure of profound release into the experience of life armed with a deeper consciousness of it, of our role within it, of the necessary performance by which we bring our souls to some kind of fruition.

For me this statement speaks directly of Marion Woodman's life and work. Richard Dyer argues that camp is "the reality of the pretence of illusion,"[28] meaning that its strident articulation figures the real as a complete façade, as something both larger-than-life, but is also ironic and parodic about the kinds of generalizations this excess implies and takes for granted. Camp, then, points with great *élan* to the singular performativeness of everyday life, which is, by virtue of its performativeness, deadly serious. When Judy Garland sings "The Man That Got Away" in George Cukor's 1954 *A Star is Born*, the staging, the lighting, the quavering inflection in Garland's voice, all suggest not that Garland *is* camp, which would be to reduce her to some cultural stereotype of the Garland persona, but that she "expresses camp attitudes,"[29] a knowing awareness of the pain of life that transforms its own stereotypical understanding of this pain into a far deeper experience. Camp is where, as William Butler Yeats writes in "Sailing to Byzantium," soul can "clap its hands and sing, and louder sing / For every tatter in its mortal dress."[30] Camp, the work of the drag queen, for instance, is where stereotypes about the feminine are performed to indicate their stereotypical imposition on both male and female bodies. Camp evokes a certain tacit misogyny, one of the more persistent of culture's dirty little secrets. Yet it makes no bones about this misogyny, and in this cynical confrontation also redeems the misogyny for what it doesn't have to be: a profound and often violent dis-ease about those parts of the soul's experience that, because they incite dis-ease in us, have been called "the feminine." At its core, camp expresses the deepest anger and pain that we were in the first instance helpless in determining how we became embodied. Camp is the body's outrage with culture.

The expression of the psyche as the imagination of the body has this camp quality. It speaks to the body's dramaturgy as a metaphorical gaiety transfiguring all that physiological and biological dread. In her Dickinson article, Woodman figures the space of this transfiguration as a room or closet in which the denial of self-expression, the turning over of who we think we are to who we might become, produces the highest poetry. Here the soul's reduction to the body produces from its raw materials the soul's artistry, one that is born from the impossibility of transformation in the brute, radical limitations of the body. In this moment of trauma where we confront in the body its inability ever to know itself definitively, a painfully ecstatic transformation takes place. This is the sensibility of camp as a gaiety, once again to paraphrase Yeats, transfiguring the dread of living.

In our own time, perhaps no work speaks to the vital necessity of camp more than Tony Kushner's two-part meta-drama, *Angels in America*. In Kushner's plays, AIDS is a vast, over-arching metaphor for how, like Walter Benjamin's angel, life proceeds by rising from the ashes of its own death-like history. The play stages the apocalyptic transformations of trauma, loss, and memory which constitute the American psyche and its impossible dream of democracy. At the work's center is the volatile relationship between Belize, a black nurse and former drag queen, and Roy Cohn, who embodies the amoral and acquisitive underbelly of America's ideal of freedom, democracy's exploitation of personal power. But, Cohn's own body, ravaged by AIDS, is also failing him—fast. Cohn is camp's Stalinist reincarnation, a viciously closeted homosexual who would sooner kill Belize than admit to being a homosexual himself. Yet Cohn's reliance on Belize, despite a rabid denial of what his own body is feeling, coupled with Belize's reluctant but unwavering care for her patient, constitutes the darkly uncompromising, yet ultimately redemptive heart of the play's morality. Despite Cohn's vicious racialization and feminization of Belize, Belize, as nurse practitioner and caretaker, must always see beyond cultural boundaries to the care of Cohn's body, and thus of Cohn's soul. At this fundamental level, all divisions necessarily disappear. That Belize will still wipe Cohn's ass when Cohn is no longer able to do so, Kushner seems to say, indicates the most profound level of humanity at which point all ideological or intellectual distinctions and boundaries become irrelevant. To care for one's most hateful enemy is to share a camp understanding of one another, more than likely born of cynicism, loathing, and self-loathing, but pointing precisely to its own intrinsic humanity.

Kushner's term for this articulation of camp is "theatre of the fabulous." He means "fabulous" in two senses: "an evolutionary advance over the notion of the being ridiculous," which redeems in the ridiculous its transforming quality that is camp's province; and "the sense of being fabled, having a history."[31] The history that kills us is the only one that can save us: there is no other way to be human. The fabulous transfigures history's dread weight with gaiety: "As Walter Benjamin wrote, you have to be constantly looking back at the rubble of history. The most dangerous thing is to become set upon some notion of the future that isn't rooted in the bleakest, most terrifying idea of what's piled up behind you."

Kushner goes on to argue that in America "lives are in fact shaped by trauma and loss," which leaves us wondering, "how does one progress in the face of that?"[32]

In *The American Religion*, Harold Bloom keeps referring to this country as the evening land, where the promise of Utopia is so impossibly remote that it brings one almost to grieving and despair: seeing what heaven looks like from the depths of hell. It is the most excruciating pain, and even as one is murdering and rampaging and slashing and burning to achieve Utopia, one is aware that our chances of attaining Utopia are being irreparably damaged. People in this country once knew somewhere within themselves what they were doing, but as we moved into this century, we began to develop a mechanism for repressing that knowledge. There's a sense of progress, but at tremendous cost. What will never be.[33]

Marion Woodman understands all too well how a utopia that works by its own self-repressions wounds the world's body. For her, anorexia was one form of this wound, the traumatic de-materialization of a childhood idealism that never existed to begin with, yet which nonetheless oppresses our bodies, first through our parents, then through society and culture. Cancer was another. Through the de-materializations of radiation Woodman confronted at the most fundamental level of the history carried in the body's cells the ruins of history's devastating effect, a ruin in history's body that plays itself out repeatedly on the world stage, each time against seemingly irredeemable odds. How to carry on? How to remain fabulous, to transform the absurd script of our embodied lives into the story of a transformative suffering? Woodman almost died suspended by those questions. Fearless enough in her fear, she recognized that where we are most profoundly alone, left with the genetic makeup of bone and heart, the closet where Emily Dickinson let a thousand midnight swallows sing away her pain, is the only place where we are able to return to ourselves—if we are ever to make a go of the larger sphere that is life on this planet. It is a perilously lonely path. But like Emily, like Marion, we can put on our makeup, strike a pose, and with the sterling resolve that carries the transfiguring power of camp attitude, sing "The Man That Got Away" as though it were the one thing left worth doing—fabulously.

NOTES

1. I understand "soul" in both Woodman's and its more general Jungian use to stem from Keats's use of the word. See note 4. Soul is the matrix of mind and body, struggling both with and against each other in the world of circumstance, that gives the powerful illusion of identity for which we suspend our disbelief. This body constitutes the sphere of experience that defines the fundamental starting point for how we exist as humans in the world, the creative psychological matrix of an embodied experience from which our entire affective, cultural, social, political, economic, sexual beings emerge and find their being.

2. Susan Sontag, "Notes on 'Camp'," *Against Interpretation* (New York: Farrar Straus Giroux, 1966), 276n.

3. *Ibid.*, 276.

4. *Ibid.*, 276.

5. Marion Woodman, *Addiction to Perfection: The Still Unravished Bride* (Toronto: Inner City Books, 1982), 160.

6. *Ibid.*, 160.

7. See Cathy Caruth, *Unclaimed Experience: Trauma, Narrative, and History* (Baltimore: The Johns Hopkins University Press, 1996), 1-24.

8. This returns me to another sense of my title. I am sometimes aware that the word "Jungian," when applied to practitioners such as Woodman, connotes an overweening self-concern associated with the

Me Decade in which she came to prominence, also the time of second-wave Feminism, of women reclaiming their bodies as their own. But this is to confine Woodman to camps she never chose in the first place. Certainly her work speaks volumes about how both women and men in the seventies and afterward needed to reclaim a lost sense of Self and soul, as much as it does to impressing upon the age the arduous and often tortuous effort required to take this reclamation seriously, a caution even now rarely honored. The impetus for Woodman's pioneering writing and analytical practice was a reconsideration of the creative feminine *and* its relationship to the creative masculine. That is, that Jungian psychology, along with the rest of the world, often distorted the feminine signaled something wrong with our understanding of the feminine *and* the masculine.

9. Judith Butler, *The Psychic Life of Power: Theories in Subjection* (Stanford, CA: Stanford University Press, 1997), 29.

10. *Ibid.*, 29.

11. Eric Savoy, "Restraining Order," *English Studies in Canada*, 29 (March/June 2003): 81.

12. See Ross Woodman, "Freud and Jung: The Parting of Ways," *Queen's Quarterly* 85 (1978): 93-108.

13. Cited in Ernest Jones, *The Life and Work of Sigmund Freud*, ed. Lionel Trilling and Steven Marcus (New York: Basic Books, 1961), 288.

14. C. G. Jung, *Memories, Dreams, Reflections*, ed. Aniela Jaffé, trans. Richard and Clara Winston (New York: Vintage Books, 1965), 150.

15. *Ibid.*, 150.

16. This profiling is not a little ironic, given that Jung, very early on attracted to the transformational capabilities of the *ubermensch* in Nietzsche's writings, afterward vehemently rejected the inflation that came with this transformation, especially once he came to see to what ends the National Socialists would use this power in 1930s Germany.

17. Put another way: a common charge is that Jung essentializes the psyche. From the work that announces his break from Freud, *Symbols of Transformation*, Jung seems to talk about the psyche, and about the collective unconscious of the archetypes which is always dreaming the psyche, as if it had a positive or essential content amenable (some might say reducible) to analysis. The archetypes are equally troubling because they suggest a universal or transcendental realm of

truth that Freud, right from his earliest work on hysteria, suggests can never be at one with itself. More sophisticated developments in post-Jungian psychology, as in the work of Wolfgang Giegerich or Greg Mogenson, certainly indicate otherwise in this regard. Nonetheless, how Freud and Jung parted ways speaks to a kind of essentialized scientific determinism guiding the history of ideas that post-Freudians often unwittingly construct in the name of a hermeneutics of suspicion, as much as it does to any essential theoretical difference between the two figures who dreamed our modern psyches for us.

18. *Addiction to Perfection*, 187.

19. This psychoanalytical body emerges before Freud or Jung in post-Enlightenment thought as it struggled to delineate the contours of a post-Cartesian subject split between psyche and soma and in radical doubt about her existence. Descartes crystallizes this doubt as the *cogito* contemplating its own psychological functioning. Here it both finds and loses itself, and the mind's supposed clarity is bewildered by the blindness of its physical manifestations. This struggle produces the psychiatric clinic on the one hand (see Michel Foucault's *The Birth of the Clinic*); but on the other hand it expresses itself through this clinic's parapsychological form in Mesmerism, hypnotism, and the later nineteenth-century work of alienists and spiritualists. Psychoanalysis emerges at this intersection between the rational and the irrational, the scientifically legitimate and the culturally arcane. I explore this genealogy in terms of Romanticism's role in inventing psychoanalysis in an unpublished manuscript entitled "Romantic Psychoanalysis and the Burden of the Mystery." See also my "Schopenhauer's Telling Body of Philosophy," *Idealism without Absolutes*, ed. Tilottama Rajan and Arkady Plotnitsky (Albany, NY: State University of New York Press, 2004), 161-180.

20. Julia Kristeva, *Revolution in Poetic Language*, trans. Margaret Waller (New York: Columbia University Press, 1984), 25.

21. Julia Kristeva, "Psychoanalysis in Times of Distress," *Speculations After Freud: Psychoanalysis, Philosophy, and Culture*, ed. Sonu Shamdasani and Michael Münchow (New York: Routledge, 1994), 16.

22. Marion Woodman, "Emily Dickinson and the Daimon Lover," *Spring* 70 (2004): 54.

23. C. G. Jung, *Symbols of Transformation: An Analysis of the Prelude to a Case of Schizophrenia*, 2nd ed., Bollingen Series XX, trans. R. F. C.

Hull (Princeton: Princeton University Press, 1956), 17 § 18.

24. See James Hillman, *Revisioning Psychology* (New York: Harper & Row, 1975), especially Chapters 2 and 4.

25. I borrow the term "defamiliarization" as Julia Wright uses it (via the Russian Formalist thinker Viktor Shklovsky) in thinking about how Blake's works defamiliarize the familiar. Wright notes that the translation of the Russian word *ostraneniye* is "usually translated as 'the device of making strange,' while its shorter version is variously translated as 'estrangement,' 'making strange,' 'alienation,' and, most commonly, as 'defamiliarization'" (*Blake, Nationalism, and the Politics of Alienation* [Athens, OH: Ohio University Press, 2004], xix). Wright's analysis of Blake veers more toward the political, but I take her point that the process of defamiliarization "disrupts the interpellative effect, separating subjects from the comfortable familiarity of cultural codes and so making obedience to their injunction seem less inevitable" (xx).

26. In a book entitled *Madness, Sanity, Transformation: The Psyche in Romanticism*, forthcoming from University of Toronto Press (August 2005).

27. Gilbert made this statement in a colloquium paper entitled "Noel Coward and the Queer Feminine," presented at Wilfrid Laurier University March 5, 2004.

28. Richard Dyer, "Judy Garland and Camp," *Hollywood Musicals, The Film Reader*, ed. Steven Cohan (London and New York: Routledge, 2002), 112.

29. *Ibid.*, 107.

30. William Butler Yeats, "Sailing to Byzantium," ll. 11-12.

31. David Savran, "The Theatre of the Fabulous: An Interview with Tony Kushner," *Essays on Kushner's Angels* (Winnipeg: Blizzard Publishing, 1993), 140.

32. *Ibid.*, 149-50.

33. *Ibid.*, 144-45.

THE LAST TEMPTATION OF MARION WOODMAN: THE ANOREXIC REMAINDER IN BONE: DYING INTO LIFE

DAVID L. CLARK

> Following the eternal act of self-revelation, the world as we now behold it is all rule, order, and form; but the unruly lies ever in the depths as though it might again break through, and order and form nowhere appear to have been original, but it seems as though what had initially been unruly had been brought to order. This is the incomprehensible basis of reality in things, the irreducible remainder ...
>
> —Friedrich Schelling, *Philosophical Inquiries into the Nature of Human Freedom*

I

F ive years after its publication, we have only begun the task of reading Marion Woodman's cancer narrative, *Bone: Dying into Life*. The fact that a fuller understanding of the journal selections

David L. Clark is Professor in the Department of English and Associate Member of the Health Studies Program at McMaster University, where he teaches critical theory, Continental philosophy, and courses on the discourses of HIV/AIDS. Recent publications include: *Regarding Sedgwick: Essays on Queer Culture and Critical Theory* (Routledge 2002), co-edited with Stephen M. Barber; and *Bodies and Pleasures in Late Kant* (forthcoming, Stanford University Press).

collected under that vivid title is still in its infancy should perhaps
come as no surprise, since Woodman herself opens the book by warning
against reading it too quickly. What risk is evoked here? When time is
of the essence, as it surely is amid the experience of the mortal illness
that the book chronicles, why is "speed" necessarily the enemy of
consciousness?[1] Among many other things, *Bone* is a labor of love—
both an account of Woodman's profound love for her husband, Ross,
whose Afterword graces the book, and a memory of her struggle to
"surrender" to the amorous embrace of Sophia, the demanding but
finally benevolent goddess of consciousness who forms "the still point"
(ix) of her life and work. But the book *is* a labor, the first-hand record
of an agonistic subject-in-process, the outcome of which is unknown
and unknowable—even if there are voices in *Bone*, as I want to argue,
that suggest otherwise and that clamor for knowledge, or for a punctual
form of knowledge, where none may be had. All that is certain is that
today, happily, in the shadow of her cancer, Marion Woodman thrives—
not in spite, but because of the travail of soul and body that she
describes in *Bone*. She often characterizes this labor as a form of
parturition or giving birth to herself, although these metaphors of
reproduction vie uneasily in the text with figures of disavowal, loss,
and emaciation. This ambivalently executed work includes the creation
of *Bone* itself, whose pangs of remembrance and imagination are enacted
on every page. Like its author, the text is a case of dying into a life that
is marked in advance by the violence and conflict of its origins.

   We need to trace these mortal and mortifying marks if we are to
understand the book at all; to read *Bone* closely and slowly, just as
Woodman bids us in her prefatory remarks, will mean first of all
resisting the temptation to erase these signs of struggle and
incompleteness in the name of what is perhaps too quickly or too
triumphantly called "life." Woodman is dying into *life* ... but nothing
could be less certain, less available to thought than the nature of this
newly won existence. To this day, Woodman loves, teaches, and writes.
She is alive, but as the title of her book suggests, that quickened
condition remains complexly interwoven with death and with forms
of irreducible loss for which there may be no recompense. *Bone* is
difficult to read, or rather, it should be difficult to read because the
radically reconfigured life that it describes and incarnates—the flesh
made word, so to speak—is arduous: at its most far-reaching and self-

searching moments, and there are many of these, *Bone* evokes a form of living that is not a thing or a substance that can be touched or brought to the light of consciousness but a way of being-in-the-world (or arriving "here onto Earth" as Woodman puts it [xi]), a resoluteness towards an ungraspable future that the mortally ill subject endures at the moment that it is summoned to keep watch over death. The vigilant "life" into which Woodman dies, or rather, is "dying," is not so much a place or destination as it is a time, or a timeliness, which she repeatedly captures in the words of Hamlet: "the readiness is all."

Ready for what? That may well be the wrong question, since it threatens to make the uniqueness of the moment of sheer facility that thrives at the heart of *Bone* answerable to something particular, as if one knew with a kind of visionary illumination and spiritual certainty not only *that* which was coming but also the clear direction of the path leading towards it. We might remember that Hamlet's phrase, "the readiness is all," does not mean that he moves from indecision to decision; it is rather a question of progressing *from* the abstention from decision (which is just as much a decision) *to* the more radical condition of in-decision through which all new decisions must pass if they are genuinely to be new. It would be fairer to the nuances of Woodman's text to say, not "ready for something," but more starkly, "being-*ready*," dwelling in a state of tensed anticipation, by turns joyous and fearful, for the *arrivant*, for the *coming* of who knows what. Precisely what one must be ready for is not a query that needs to be answered in advance: the readiness is *all*. Somehow the experience of cancer induces this productively unstable condition in Woodman, even if there are moments in *Bone*—to which I want to draw the reader's attention— in which metaphors and myths of certitude threaten to tempt her away from the wisdom of Hamlet. The most difficult thing of all, it turns out, is not the cancer that attacks Woodman's uterus or the treatment that ravages her body, but choosing in freedom to live without absolute surety—which is to say, in the book's Keatsian idiom, *dying into life*. As she argues, sounding a great deal like Søren Kierkegaard, cancer opens the way for her "to be strong enough to surrender certainty. To leap into the mystery" (233).[2] Readiness is therefore not passivity, but rather an agile alertness, an active reluctance either to reach anxiously after the facts or to consent to the assurance of the given; it is not a state of self-possession so much as a species of willing dis-possession, a relinquishing of the need always to possess oneself and thus to know ahead of time what one's future and what one's future self will look like. This explains the uncanny rightness of the scene with which *Bone* concludes: Woodman is swept away by the irrepressible sound of the Dutchmen's tubas, and although her heart pounds and her spine cracks and her husband looks on in astonished horror, she casts herself into the unknown, at once unsure *and* preternaturally calm—as if coming to the realization that the jump is not the means by which to get from one place to the next but is itself the destination. As Kierkegaard's Johannes de Silentio says, true faith amounts to a "leap into life."[3]

If Woodman's mortal illness is a "gift" (xv), it is a gift of honoring radical uncertainty; it is a gathering up of the courage to reject the consolations to be found in the idealizations, abstractions, and projections that in effect relieve the subject of the agony (but also the pleasure) of its responsibilities and decisions. A great part of *Bone*, especially its most pressingly affective moments, come in the form of a prayer to Sophia—and we now see why. For prayer can only authentically *be* prayer if it is made in the midst of incertitude, in the profound openness to the unknown. As the French philosopher Jacques Derrida argues, "This suspension of certainty is part of prayer. ... If I knew or were simply expecting an answer, that would be the end of prayer. That would be an order .... No, I expect nothing like that. I assume that I must give up any expectation, any certainty, as the one, or the more than one, to whom I address my prayer, if this is still a prayer."[4] The subtlest form of the Demon Lover with whom Woodman must wrestle in *Bone* is the trickster who would transform prayer into its stiffened likeness—"an order," a determinate plan or myth or even metaphor, in which Woodman had surrendered not certainty but her freedom to decide either for certainty or uncertainty, death or life. At the point where *Bone* becomes programmatic, at the point that it declares itself most sure, it threatens to become nothing more than an elaborate version of "A Patient's Guide to Radiation Therapy" (100)— the withered and withering instruction manual that Woodman indeed folds into the narrative of her book, as if inoculating *Bone* against its parodic semblance. Her book is also a "patient's guide," but one that must resist the temptation to idealize and simplify the experience of illness in the manner of the patient's pamphlet.

A particular determinable faith in a particular determinate promise: that is the danger of religiosity with which *Bone* flirts, and at those points, I want to suggest, it is half in love not with dying into life but with its unsafe mimic—with easeful death, and thus with living *for* death. "With cancer," Woodman says in the book's opening sentences, "I discovered how much dying it takes to get here" (xi)—*here* being that no man's land of decision and responsibility where, precisely, there are no absolutely obvious instructions, no assured path or "patient's guide" leading one safely or predictably from *here* to *there*, from the sorrow of the actual to the reassurances of what Woodman calls the "archetypal dimensions" (113) of existence. It is instead a state of radical freedom: "I am alive," Woodman announces at the book's conclusion. "I am free ... to live ... to die" (241), she says, pacing her declaration with ellipses that figure forth the blank contingency of decision, the momentary absence of all plans, programs, and metaphors that lies at the heart of every determination that makes a claim to freedom.

With Woodman the stakes are typically high, and because of that the book in which they are raised obliges its most attentive readers to proceed with caution. For various reasons, however, not everyone is or can be so circumspect. Not everyone is willing or able to follow the winding path that is Woodman's ongoing journey of consciousness and something other than consciousness. Yet this is not the difficulty to which Woodman first draws our attention in the book. When she characterizes *Bone* as taxing on the reader in her Foreword, she does not do so on account of the wrenching scenes that are to follow—some of which even her husband Ross finds impossible to read—or on account of the sobering realization that death is not opposed to life but the very matrix in which life and freedom have meaning. The problem that initially concerns Woodman is that her readers will find it difficult to make sense of the book's idiosyncratic narrative form, and in particular the peculiar co-existence of different verbal and visual languages in one textual space. To be sure, the body of *Bone* is itself already a heterogeneous text, its sometimes wild excursions into the psyche's undiscovered countries barely kept in check by the journal entry dates that implacably sound off through the narrative. These dates are the chronological stitching-points that knit the fabric of this story together, and in effect prevent it from pulling itself into pieces,

so ferocious is the mortal struggle at its core. But this is only part of
what makes the volume "complex" (xii), as Woodman says. For the
journal entries comprising the bulk of the narrative compete and
cooperate with an elaborate out-work: photographs, illustrations, and
images, as well as fragments drawn from poems and scattered
psychological and philosophical writings in various hands. All of these
materials function as a gloss on the text and form its elaborate "margin"
(xii)—or rather one of its margins. What worries Woodman is how her
readers will negotiate both these borders and the emotional and
intellectual hinterlands that they mark. And with good reason. We are
never sure if these extra-textual voices and perspectives are avatars of
the author, externalizations of her inner life, or whether in their
otherness they speak for and out of spaces of alterity by which
Woodman is herself haunted—"new images," as she says, "that I don't
yet comprehend" (xii). Do the marginal remarks confirm and amplify
what is being said in the body of the narrative, distilling what is being
experienced into memorable epigrams and summaries? Or do they
allegorize that body, spiriting away its complex local densities with
answers and lessons that are *grafted* onto the book's central narrative
from a wholly different place?

"If the rumblings in the margins seem disruptive to the text, then
you, as reader, need not be slowed down," Woodman counsels: "Skip
them" (xii). Why dwell at all on this question of haste—and in a text
that elsewhere avows an ambiguous faith in "the speed of bone" (221)?
Why suggest to readers that the gloss itself should be glossed? I think
that this is Woodman's quiet way of calling attention to the fact that
the book is replete with borders, and that a great part of reading her
work involves the question of how to traverse its verges of thought and
feeling. That the material on the margins is more significant than
Woodman at first seems willing to admit is evident in her quick change
of heart about the matter. Contradicting her initial advice to her readers,
she tells us that by passing over the text's margins too quickly we risk
repudiating *Bone*'s most urgent details. "We are now moving at a pace
that is dissolving the world into an abstraction before *we can take it
in*," Woodman writes, her buried metaphor of ingestion reminding us
of the connections that obtain between slow reading and eating slowly,
on the one hand, and the fast life and an indifference to sustenance,
on the other. "If the marginalia slows you down, it is doing what I

intended, knowing what it has done for me" (xii; emphasis mine). This is a book with which to tarry, then, and not one whose insights can be taken up or cast off without remainder.

As if to ensure that we work hard at reading *Bone*, it is a text that is replete with margins, many more than the already complicated partitions dividing Woodman's journal entries from their glosses. Literary criticism in the shadow of deconstruction has taught us that the difference *between* the body of a work and its glosses almost always repeats and reproduces differences *within* each field. It is those interior partitions, perhaps less legible than the boundaries dividing Woodman's autobiographical voice from the voices of the others that she draws into her circle, to which I want principally to attend. It may be that Woodman's focus on the text's obvious formal divisions displaces—hides, but also remembers—the analogous strata unsettling the integrity of the body of the book, throwing into question some of its more strident claims for wholeness. In other words, the formal split between *Bone*'s body and marginalia is expected to bear away evidence of more substantial self-divisions rippling through the text. To say the least, these differences call for a *slow reading*. Friedrich Nietzsche demanded such deliberation when it came to reading writing that mattered—not the only point in *Bone* in which Woodman's work resonates with that of the German philosopher, whom she otherwise derides as ushering in a world without god and without sacred books.[5]

This is the sort of interpretation that I want to bring to bear here, making tentative steps towards parsing the intricacies of Woodman's illness narrative, this, by dwelling less on its large features—its insistent arc from disaster to triumph, crucifixion to resurrection, or death to life, for example—and more on what William Blake would call its "minute particulars."[6] For as Blake might also have said, the devil— here, a metaphor for the book's unruly energies—is in the details. If we read *Bone* entirely from Sophia's perspective, everything about Woodman's psychic life is answerable to the lucidity of consciousness. But what would it mean to reverse the perspective—turn the telescope around, as it were—and to see Sophia from the point of view of the localized eddies that swirl inside *Bone*'s overall narrative and that trouble the Apollonian surety about its author's metamorphosis that is evoked by its very subtitle? What mutinous remnants haunt this extraordinary story of health and illness, loss and recompense, mortality and divinity, disrupting the economies of spirit that reconcile these terms in elegant dialectical "spirals" around Sophia's "still point"?[7] What "irreducible remainders"—to recall a phrase from the great German philosopher and critic of idealism, Friedrich Schelling[8]—trouble the book's claims for wholeness and oneness? A slow reading is a way of being in the world that ratifies the presence of these leavings in our lives, and affirms their productive and restless place amid our tempting dreams of untrammeled integrity and purposiveness. These are dreams that Woodman's book pursues, but not without a palpable degree of ambivalence. Far from being a well-wrought urn, unequivocally confident in its findings, *Bone* is a text that is riven with self-differences—and in this way it earns the right to say, as it does in its opening sentence, that it is a "book about living, not dying" (xi). I hasten to add that this is not to fault Woodman's narrative, even if it is sometimes to read it against the grain. Rather, such a reading finds that the text is never more productive, never more searchingly difficult or provocative, than when it offers up contending visions of its author's life and work. We have only begun to read Marion Woodman's *Bone: Dying into Life.*

II

> When he opened his lips to greet me, I half expected the answer—
> a newly coined proverb, an aphorism so apt as to seem even obvious.
> I looked for a radiance to rise from his flesh, I put my ear to the shell
> of his hollowed body as one listens to the murmur of a conch,
> waiting for the stage whisper. Could this pain be with a program?
> Can a man emaciate without meaning?
> —Anatole Broyard, *Intoxicated By My Illness*

Sophia is the name that Woodman uses to describe the dissenting work that she conducts on behalf of the "feminine," which is the wisdom of the ages that she marshals to resist the predations of abstraction and idealization—the seductive yet suicidally destructive impulses that she identifies with the "masculine" and for which she blames modernity's sorrowful inability to bring living and dying into a meaningful convocation. These impulses, she has observed throughout her writings, form and deform the culture at large, but *Bone* is unique for exploring the extraordinary degree to which they have continued to shape her own psychic life. Among other things, Sophia means authentically *embodied* life, life lived in a manner that apprehends and prizes the subtle knot of spirit and flesh that is, as Woodman says, every person's "birthright" (168). How does one come to see and grasp this "patrimony" and make it one's own? The body-soul work that is a mainstay of Woodman's practice as an analyst and as a teacher has been largely devoted to nurturing this ennobling and healing task in others. The objective is not so much a decisive breakout to a wholly different universe—for where or what could that transcendent place be?—as a circuitous *return* to that universe's otherwise obscured and wounded heart. To dedicate and to re-dedicate oneself to the labor of consciousness *is* this movement of circling recollection; Sophia is therefore not a single location towards which all consciousnesses move (this would make her indistinguishable from the Christian God Woodman abandoned in childhood) but, as it were, the curvature of psychic space in which the soul is given the opportunity to fashion itself.

Bone is a testament to the project of Marion Woodman's own soul-making. This is a project that was of course always already under way in her life, but it takes the trauma of her cancer and the imminent prospect of her death to give its centrality to her life a new imperative—as if she were confronting its demands and intuiting its significances for the first time. This is the "gift" of her experience with illness, the rich but unhappy endowment that comes her way unexpectedly and without declaring itself as such. As Plato teaches, resolute attention to and concern with death (*melete thanatou*) is what awakens the self to itself and to the need to gather up its parts into a meaningful whole. He suggests that true thinking is in essence nothing more than this act of vital self-possession before the prospect of one's death. In the words of the Czech philosopher and human rights activist, Jan Patočka (whose work Jacques Derrida reads so closely in his book, *The Gift of Death*), "the concern of the soul is inseparable from the concern for death which becomes authentic concern for life; … life is born from this event of looking death in the face."[9] Looking back at Woodman's *oeuvre* from the vantage point of *Bone*, I am not sure whether all of her work isn't *mortified* in this way, a testimony to the possibilities of dying into life whose antecedents can be traced to Socrates' argument in the *Phaedo*. What makes *Bone* stand out among Woodman's other published writings, however, is the frankness with which it admits to the need for her to pursue this reparative and constitutive work in her own life—and thus for the healer to heal herself. As she confides in her journal entries, helping others recognize their "covenant with Sophia" (14)—and thus to live a more fully realized life—had somehow led her to disregard the importance of reaffirming the same compact in herself. This irresponsible distraction from what Woodman calls her "own truth" (17) is counted as one of the causes of her cancer, and so the difficult path back to consciousness begins there, in her sacrum, where the disease appears literally and metaphorically. Like Apollo in Keats's *Hyperion*, the process of dying into life is characterized as the advent of a new dawn. The dense opacity of her tumor forms the dark background against which Woodman sets the clarifying powers of her evolving consciousness. Under the blaze of its allegedly incontestable light, she comes to discern the patterns that organize her existence and that give meaning to the anguish of her illness.

Woodman is the first to admit that a great part of herself resisted this illumination, but the overall psychological momentum of *Bone* is irrefutably one from unconsciousness to consciousness, repression to self-transparency. Like the acids with which William Blake etched his copper plates, consciousness is what burns away apparent surfaces to reveal the infinite which was hid. It is the light that enables her to parse the obscurities of the world and therefore to make it a truly liveable place; "consciousness makes the difference," as she says, between being an ego that submits to fate, and an ego that cooperates with destiny (12). Step by step, Woodman brings into view not only the inner significance of her cancer but also, more powerfully, the ways in which her illness forms a part—indeed a crucially important part—of a larger voyage of consciousness begun when she was a child. "I am seeing the archetypal dimensions that have forced me towards wholeness against my will," Woodman observes; "I see the progression of spirals through which I have moved upward and downward, higher into spirit, deeper into grounding. ... What an incredible map I seem to have followed! I am silenced by its intricacies" (113). In her account of the radiation chamber, Woodman affords us a glimpse of what it means to dwell within the darkest depths of the vale of soul-making; but *Bone* does not find its center there. Instead, in moments that surprise Woodman as much as they offer profound reassurance, she finds herself occupying a vantage point on her own life that is nothing if not divine—a placeless place from which Woodman glimpses both the center and the circumference, the local details and the large design, the still point and the spirals around which the widening gyres of her life are oriented.

It is only because of the incandescent light of consciousness that Woodman is able to apprehend her experience with cancer not only as the traumatic destruction of the body but as the prelude towards a subtler and more fully realized mode of embodied life: as Woodman says in the opening words of *Bone*, the "shattering" effect of her illness is the means by which she assumes a path to "wholeness." There are many moments in *Bone* in which this unity is not a state to be desired but a deed to be celebrated; indeed, the book *as* a book, as a crafted story that gathers together the strands of Woodman's life and weaves them into a meaningful whole, stands as both a figure for and testament to this accomplishment. Its elegant and articulate achievement contrasts with the ragged cry of pain that it also subsumes within its covers. In the details of the narrative, we see how the light of consciousness brings important clearness to being-ill, this, primarily, by locating Woodman's experience with cancer amid a larger significance that would be all but invisible to ordinary sight. Going into her surgery, Woodman has the first intimations of this design: "[M]aybe this is the sacrifice of my feminine organs to prepare me for the next step—to release me from all physical mothering," she muses, "to release me into a new vibration in my body" (17). Through cognate narratives of purposiveness, the senselessness of disease is compelled to yield sense: the cancer is "a lesson to be learned" (5); it is the means by which her body makes itself into an "instrument" (105) that forces her to come to consciousness. For a month after the radiation treatment, there is nothing—the blank space in Woodman's diary entries speaks volumes. Then the narrative of the book starts up again, and even in her disoriented state—"still not sure who has emerged," she confides to her journal—Woodman finds much needed consolation in the outlines of an archetypal "map" of the territory ahead: "felt the crucifixion this year, and the tomb, and Easter Sunday" (132), she writes, transforming bare survival into redemption and resurrection. In a testament that makes the highest possible claims for the powers of metaphor (for Woodman, they are in the end responsible for healing what the physicians could not cure), we are invited to take these consolatory figures seriously.

The self-achieving consciousness is monumentalized in *Bone* as a courageous convocation with Sophia. Under these mythic conditions, the remnants which resist consciousness or inhibit the apprehension of the divine marriage of soul and body can be figured as perverse. Indeed, not to accede to Sophia's light is experienced as a form of weakness, even cowardliness. When Woodman balks at giving herself wholly over to alternative therapies that have been urged upon her by others, for example, she feels answerable to Sophia's all-seeing eyes. "I need to acknowledge that in my December 12 session with Jean I could not get by the *ifs*, and therefore could not surrender to the wisdom of the limbic system, as Jean encouraged me to do. ... Fear is still stronger than faith. Forgive me, Sophia" (82). Here and elsewhere in *Bone* Woodman describes her continuing attachment to conventional medicine in terms of cowardliness, irresponsibility and apostasy—as faults requiring a kind of confession to a superior power. It is in moments like these that we see that the incandescence of consciousness not only positively illuminates the ultimate purposiveness of the nature of things; it also negatively brings a normative gaze to bear on the heart's reluctance to give itself too quickly over to that design. The aura of impotence and failure that attends Woodman's self-castigations reminds us that the claims *Bone* makes for light and clarity in the face of death are not only Apollonian but also residually masculinist inasmuch as they associate perfectly understandable hesitations with "fear," and strength with acts of heroic self-possession. But facing death need not necessarily be described in these judgmental terms as a test of the psyche's willingness and ability to triumph over doubt and self-difference. As the cultural theorist Gillian Rose wrote prior to her own cancer death, it was philosophers like Martin Heidegger who taught us to believe that "being-toward-death" was properly a matter of attaining "'a supreme lucidity and hence a supreme virility.'" Against Heidegger, and, indeed, against a tradition of life-writing going back to Plato, Rose opposes the very different thought of Immanuel Levinas, for whom the proximity of death is "'foreign to all light'" and "'absolutely unknowable.'"[10] Levinas is not interested in the subject who comes into a form of stringent clarity by steeling itself for death; it is the mortality and suffering of the *other*—and this includes the other that is also oneself—which has precedence in human life, and which deprives the self of its pretensions to mastery.[11]

Levinas invites us to revalue the alterities that lie beyond and before consciousness, and to treasure their traces as evidence of our radical singularity, mortality, and unknowability. For him, we are never more ourselves than when we are most vulnerable, and thus calling out to the other for justice and responsibility. In Heidegger, by contrast, the potent philosophical subject seeks total self-sufficiency through heroic self-assertion and the disavowal of the other. In a way that has complex resonances with Woodman's project, Levinas characterizes this ascetic way of being-in-the-world as a refusal either to eat or to demonstrate a need to eat: "*Dasein* in Heidegger is never hungry," he writes.[12] Committed to the radiance of Sophia and the labor of consciousness, however, Woodman's book approaches Levinas's insight into the anorexic remainder haunting philosophical idealisms about facing death with caution. In her hands, what refuses to be brought into the light of day is more often banished to a deeper darkness; hence the degree to which *Bone*'s narrative is moved along not only by inclusive affirmations but also by sharp disavowals. For example, Woodman characterizes her surgery as "the letting go of something that is finished in order to move into new life" (58). Moving forward, her primary task is to make sure that this disavowal penetrates to the profoundest part of herself; as she adds: "How then to let go? How to be sure at the unconscious level that I am letting go?" (58), as if the searchlight of consciousness could sweep into the farthest corners of the psyche. On the eve of entering the radiation chamber, Woodman's resoluteness is again expressed in the form of disavowals: "Your task right now is to let the old thinking go, flush the toilet, accept the love, walk free" (124). On the Christmas Eve following her radiation therapy, she revels in a vision of the wholeness of the nature of things: "God/Goddess in every living thing—the totality of the universe" (218). But in the next sentence, we see that this totality is at best a qualified one, for it is constituted by the refusal of part of itself: "The old questions won't matter; the old answers will be obsolete" (218). When Woodman receives the diagnosis of a metastasized cancer from Dr. Thomas, she prays to Sophia for, among other things, "the steadfastness to reject sentimentality" (184). As Woodman repeatedly says, the voyage of consciousness is for her a voyage of ongoing reduction, of bravely purging what is deemed to be inessential and burdensome. "Simplify. Get rid of all conflict" (205): these are the categorical imperatives of her newly embodied life, a life of light, orderliness, transparency ... and above all, *evacuation*: "the letting go—the clearing" (28).

But is this sort of voiding simplification possible, or, for that matter, self-evidently desirable? In one of the book's most affecting moments, Woodman recalls how her mother, on the threshold of her death, lets go of her beloved daughter. Unable to say goodbye to Woodman in person, she leaves a fragment from Shakespeare to speak on her behalf. Written out in her "beautiful handwriting," the scene her mother chooses is from *Julius Caesar*: "If we do meet again, why, we shall smile," Brutus says, bidding farewell to Cassius; "If not, why then, this parting was well made" (58). Does it matter that Woodman's mother casts their separation as one between two virile but imaginary men? In the world of actual mothers and daughters, are partings ever "well made"? Through Woodman's eyes we see what it feels like to be the remnant, the one who is let go, and from that reversed perspective it is obvious that the cut, as "beautiful" as it is, and perhaps precisely because it is so "well made," is dissatisfying because it unfolds with otherworldly perfection. Compelled to play the role of the remainder, Woodman objects and pushes back: "I wanted you to die my way," she recalls; "God had another way" (58). So much is said in this cry from the heart: to be sure, there is anger at losing control over her mother's life, a sense of being pre-empted both by her death and by the way in which she said goodbye; but there is inconsolable grief too, not only for the loss but also for the incalculability and inaccessibility of that loss, the sorrowful realization that the mother's departure from Woodman's life cannot be economized into something that is "well-made." For can the psyche ever "simply" have done with any part of itself, much less a part of itself to which it is so deeply attached that only the extremity of a mortal illness can loosen those bonds? Perhaps it is the prospect of death that prompts these fantasies of cleanly perfect divisions and reorganizations of life. Or is this faith in the purgative powers of renunciation itself an idealism of the sort that Judith Butler, Jacques Derrida, and others have associated with fantasies of achieved mourning work—work in which the psyche imagines that it can, through the heroic effort of repudiation, part with its losses without ever looking back? Is it the case that all partings are melancholically incomplete, but some forget this messy and discomforting fact, and become triumphantly mournful?[13] These questions seem worth asking of a text which is so palpably haunted by what *remains*—beginning with the book itself, whose effect is vividly, permanently, and publicly to *remember* what its author deems worthy of being abandoned and forgotten. That the book was written at all puts to us that at the very least Woodman is unwilling to disavow her disavowals, the result being that she remains connected, psychically speaking, to the very things that she has given up. She avows them, but in the negative form of renouncing them. The look forward to what she calls her "new life" is literally written in the form of a sustained look back at the "old."

Many other leftovers trouble the book's strident demands to let go: the marginal materials that Woodman at first disdains ("Skip them," she says, as if they were a meal that she could avoid), but then acknowledges as a part, and an important part of the body of her book; the physical and psychic spaces from which Woodman's cancer was cut and burned, all absent presences forming and deforming her life; the lingering effects of the radiation on her body and spirit, including the literal and metaphorical scars she bears; the memories of her dead friend Mary, whose anguish at being alone before death Woodman remembers in order to forget (67); the sounds of the "groaning" and "weeping" patients and family members that waft unbidden and unstoppably into her head as she lies in her "radiation tank" (131), all the intimations of otherness haunting the edges of her consciousness; the loss of her beloved brother, Fraser Boa, the grief for whom, as Woodman herself admits, lies locked up in her own flesh and thus the object of a melancholic return rather than a mournful having-done-with (7). Consider too the break with the oncologist, Dr. Thomas, which happens at a crucial turning point in the course of the recovery from her illness. Of that split Woodman tells us emphatically that she "hold[s] no resentment, no anger" (205). Yet she chooses to reproduce her formal letter of discharge to Thomas in its entirety; the physician is renounced, but the *renunciation* of the physician, the act of his being cast off, is carefully preserved as part of the archive of *Bone*'s narrative. And then there is the striking image of herself as her own remains, her "body going back to dust." "Think of our compost heap in which earth does go back to earth" (184), she writes in her journal, folding metaphors drawn from the burial service into more familial and domestic terms. Up until this point in the book, the move to the beautiful new house on Sydenham Street in

London, Ontario has figured forth the birth of Woodman's embodied psyche; not surprisingly, given the logic of sacrifice that governs the book's narrative, this move is accompanied by a decisive disavowal: "only essentials going to the new house," she insists: "Move into the new life. That is where it is to happen. High ceilings, light, a garden, fresh air, fresh sunlight, new hope" (28-9). But Sydenham, like the psyche for which it is a metaphor, is not only this scene of space and illumination, for we learn that out back, away from the light, the home's cast-offs ferment in the darkness and also make their claims on Woodman's thoughts. For a strange moment, Woodman allows that the protected home is also a kind of cemetery or bone-yard, exposed to an otherness for which there is no conscious apprehension: "This is not metaphor," Woodman flatly says; "so be it" (184). Although untranslatable into the idiom of the archetype, the "compost" nevertheless asserts its rightful place in the nature of things.

The tensions surrounding the irreducible remainder that limns consciousness without necessarily being drawn into its light become perhaps most apparent around Woodman's characterization of the surgery to remove her "carcinoma of the endometrium"(15). "My baby was born by Caesarean section and disposed of," she writes, self-consciously rejecting the diagnostic terminology of the physicians, "—but a baby, nonetheless, that forever changed my life" (167). Woodman has just told us that the "metaphorical connection between birth and death is very strong in [her] ... psyche" (167), perhaps to prepare us for this strange way to imagine the nature and fate of her cancer. But it is worth noting here how even Woodman's language strains to accommodate what it has been asked to explain metaphorically: the growth in her uterus must be cut away, all traces annihilated if she is to survive her illness. But at the same moment as Woodman speaks of "disposing" of the cancer, it is refashioned as a spectral "baby" who is figuratively speaking dead to the precise extent that it remains alive to Woodman's memory. The literal act of having-done with the tumor competes with the figural translation of that act into a violent giving-birth; yet the cancer remains, to the extent that it resists its too easy sublimation into the form of a "baby," even one that is stillborn. Nothing could more powerfully call for being eliminated than the cancer, yet Woodman experiences that saving rejection as an abortion that allows her to recuperate her loss as a loss of life—albeit a monstrous and fatally parasitic life, without coherence and quite possibly at the far side of the recuperative powers of metaphor. In the end, the cancer surgery that forms the literal ground for these elaborate figures insists itself, this, by throwing into relief the macabre over-reaching of Woodman's metaphors. Bordering on the hallucinatory, these figures possess consolatory power for Woodman, but from the reader's perspective they call attention to the hyperbolic demands that Woodman's archetypal understanding places on her illness—and to the ways in which her illness can resist those demands, bringing the edifice of metaphor crashing down to earth. Of the cancer we might indeed also say, "This is not metaphor. So be it."

Woodman often characterizes her disavowals as a stripping down, "letting irrelevant matter go. Lightening up, simplifying in order to concentrate on essentials" (112). Fleshless "bone" is the book's metaphor *par excellence* for this emaciated purity. But one cannot read these figures of refinement and deprivation (and refinement *as* deprivation) and not also see the striking similarity between the principal means by which Woodman renews her covenant with Sophia and much less felicitous forms of renunciation that are explored in the text. For isn't the psyche that takes pride and pleasure in "lightening up" and "letting go" not also in some spectral sense an anorexic psyche? Does the fiercely reiterated desire to buoy herself up through a process of divestiture not mimic a more archaic lust operating in Woodman's psyche, the thing of darkness that she struggles to acknowledge as her own? Is the path of unburdening simplification—a path that is undertaken, precisely, in the name of turning from "old eating patterns, old patterns of relationship"(40)—not evidence of the survival of these patterns, a repetition of the addiction to perfection, albeit in a finer tone? "When I *was* anorexic," Woodman tells us, "I always felt that starvation brought me close to God. It brought me close to death, a Demon Lover, whose radiance lured my senses into a life so exquisite I yearned to escape gross matter" (62; emphasis mine). By safely locating this condition of disavowal in the past, Woodman repudiates the will to repudiate, lightening herself of the burden of the craving for lightness that once controlled her life. But is the irrefutable lucidity of consciousness, the clarity that it offers to Woodman in her darkest hour, not itself a form of this seductive "radiance"? As she puts it, "Starvation is a metaphor for getting out of an impossible situation—death to the old and maybe hope for the new" (81). In its local context, Woodman is thinking of both herself as a younger woman and that aspect of her present self which, in agreeing to undergo the killingly destructive radiation treatment, "colludes" with the desire to withdraw from life. But does this account of starvation not also exactly describe the process of dying *into* life—the move from the "impossible situation" of the cancer diagnosis and treatment, through a period punctuated by increasingly demanding renunciations ("death to the old"), all in expectation of or "hope for the new"?

This is a difficult and unexpected thought, to be sure, but provoked by a book that brims with such possibilities and that does nothing but encourage them in its readers. An anorexic remainder haunts Woodman's myth of feminine consciousness as its dark semblance. We see this most clearly near the book's conclusion. On New Year's Day, 1995, Woodman feels "caught between two worlds, trying to move into new imagery, still not knowing what's in the bones in my back" (221). Then, a flash of certainty and a flood of images: "One thing I do know: I am no longer ashamed of having been anorexic. I yearned for lightness; I still yearn for lightness. Lightness is freedom—freedom from the heaviness of too much stuff, too many words, too heavy a pull toward inertia. ... I yearned for bone—the lightness of bone, the stark reality of bone, the speed of bone, the beauty of bone" (221-2). It would take a great deal to unpack properly the complexities of this admission, but for the purposes of this argument it is important to emphasize not only Woodman's unexpected turn towards embracing— rather than forsaking—her anorexic impulses, but also the unblushing surefootedness with which she makes this turn. With respect to her anorexic desires, she is here more like a woman who seeks the thing she loves, than one who flees from something she dreads. Elsewhere in the book, Woodman prides herself in the hard-won consciousness that anorexia means falling prey to the seductions of the Demon Lover, "the pathological idealism" that "continues to murder the feminine that cherishes life" (216). But on New Year's Day comes a clarity about the nature of that clarity, a consciousness not about the seductive powers of the Demon Lover but about the consciousness that makes those powers visible. "[B]one ... bone ... bone ... bone:" the self-conscious tolling of the title of the book puts to us how Woodman herself grasps the uncanny resemblance between the yearning for lightness that is anorexia and the cherishing of the feminine that is the covenant with Sophia. As Woodman tells us in the next sentence, honouring the "feminine, right here and now in my body, my bone" is inevitably caught up in the labor of "letting the weight of possessions go" (222). The greatest threat to consciousness is that in its ferocious quest to unburden itself it falls over into the idealization and wasting abstraction that it abhors. For the dark side of taking on the beauty and speed and lightness of bone in the name of escaping what feels like inertia can also mean the *skeletization* of the psyche. The very title of Woodman's book inadvertently remembers that discomforting possibility.

"Let your last remnants of your yearning for God-like perfection go," Woodman notes towards the end of her book, calling for a final and therefore monumentally decisive act of renunciation. Does a fully-embodied life lie on the other side of that perfect release ... or does death? In the name of what, if not another kind of ascetic purity, is this summons made? What but another way of being in the world whose rarity and worth is predicated on the disavowal of those elements that are deemed to be a contagion? All disavowals in *Bone* have in a sense been a prelude to the casting off of these "last remnants," the disposal of all that remains—or is imagined to remain—between Woodman's partly unconscious earlier life and the authentically realized existence that awaits her in the face of death. "Cherish your imperfect humanity," she continues: "Die into life" (207-8). Insofar as the call to consciousness is also an expression of this "yearning" for "perfection," Woodman here finds herself at a profound limit. *For the very act of disavowing the seductive desire for flawlessness re-inscribes the arc of that desire anew.* The "last remnant" is last in the sense of being irreducible because it is produced and reproduced by Woodman's impulse to lighten herself of its weight.

Perhaps it is no accident that this is the moment when Woodman most pointedly recalls the origins of her book's subtitle in Keats's fragment, *Hyperion*. As she says, "I hope I can 'with fierce convulse / Die into life'" (207). We should recall that in the third, uncompleted book of *Hyperion*, Apollo, the young sun god, attempts, like Woodman, to come into consciousness with the assistance of the goddess of memory, Mnemosyne. Apollo's new life is obscurely connected not to the disavowal of the past but to its conservation. At the moment that

Apollo passes from a twilight state of hiddenness into brilliant visibility, he suffers pangs that evoke childbirth even as they conjure up death— a tortured transitional moment that naturally speaks to Woodman and explains why these lines in Keats are ones to which she returns several times in her book. But what is not remembered about the Keats passage also haunts her use of it. For *Hyperion* breaks off at this point, and was abandoned by the poet, as if in writing these words down something unexpected had dawned upon him. Has Apollo and the creator-poet for which he is an idealistic figure in fact ascended to a higher mode of being? Keats is not altogether confident in the answer to that question, as ferociously pressing as it is to him on this, the eve of his own mortal illness and in the shadow of his brother's death. The poet-creator struggles to be born, and to divest himself of the dreamy naïveté of the pastoral in which he had once found comfort, however illusory; but at the point of that parturition a terrible doubt falls across his path, a sense that his own declaration of authenticity rings false, tolling him back to his sole self. What is this virile "life" into which he so grandly aspires to die? In turning to the classical language of *Hyperion* Keats exchanges the language of the pastoral for that of epic. But is this necessarily the progress towards enlightenment that it feels at that moment to be? Or has he simply moved from one mythical universe to another, exchanging abstractions but describing this exchange as the triumph of life, the violent leap *from* a dead (because lifeless) world *to* a living one that dies? The fact that the poem breaks off at this point is perhaps the most palpable answer that Keats could give—it is the way the poem abstains from answering; and in that self-fracturing gesture, *Hyperion* signals an inconclusive attachment to the world of Apollonian light towards which it turns so expectantly. As Geoffrey Hartman argues, "The very rituals that wing him into a new sphere prove too literary, too magical-archaic, and do not prevent fresh anxieties about the authenticity of his passage."[14] Keats's speaker lays claim to dying into life, but then shudders to a halt, the poem ceasing at the precise moment that it appears to begin, or rather to begin anew.

Keats is a crucial part of the secular scripture informing Woodman's thinking; along with Shakespeare and the Bible, it is his work that she carries with her into the inferno of the radiation chamber. In what ways does *Bone: Dying into Life*, whose title points us to this crisis point in Keats's life and work, also register a similar crisis—but protect itself from this crisis by remembering it in the form of someone else's words? For I do think that a part of Woodman is wary of the claims made for this life into which she dies, especially insofar as that life demands an ascesis that is structurally indistinguishable from the anorexia of her earlier self, a life which imagines itself as having purged from its subtle body the "last remnant." What Balachandra Rajan says of the fate of Apollo in *Hyperion* could be said of *Bone*: "If the basis is supersession by a superior state, the state must be shown and not claimed to be superior. Apollo's dying into life is named rather than lived through. ... It breaks off poised upon Apollo's shriek, the significantly inarticulate boundary between a superceded past and a future which cannot yet be brought into being, which the imagination can direct itself towards but is unable to occupy."[15]

More than any other Romantic poet, perhaps, Keats resisted the tendency to be blinded by his idealisms, including those most tempting of idealisms—the ones that appear to offer a foolproof escape from idealism. Woodman's allegiance to Keats is, I think, a secret fealty to that insight, even if she appears to take the poet's faith in a wrenching transformation without remainder at face value. Elsewhere in the book there are significant signs, however, that Woodman senses the difference between claiming and actually showing that the enlightened state of the covenant with Sophia is unquestionably superior. Wrestling with whether to take the full course of radiation therapy, for instance, Woodman resists giving herself over to "the power of that machine and the perfectionist mind that controls it" (73). Her friend Pauline objects to that objection, probing the deepest presuppositions of Woodman's stance. You see a killing perfectionism in the biomedical technology of the medical regime, Pauline points out; but isn't your faith in the healing powers of consciousness itself a perfectionism, and thus no less murderously indifferent to life? "'You know,' she said, 'idealization can be a lack of femininity. If you idealize to the point of blinding yourself to what may save your life, that is not being on the side of life, the positive side of the feminine. Blindness is negative'" (73). Woodman's response to the corrosive powers of Pauline's insight is at best noncommittal, and the conversation quickly turns from Woodman's psyche to the psyches of other unnamed "women" (74). But this deflection does nothing to reduce the significance of the

interrogation at the hands of Pauline, who is, after all, an avatar of
Woodman, an other who speaks for an alterity that thrives within
Woodman herself—and thrives to the point that she is given a role in
the narrative of *Bone*. Another way of saying this is that if the first
person voice in *Bone*—identified as Marion—speaks for an abiding
faith in the feminine, she does not and cannot speak for the book as a
whole, which, in the form of Pauline, contains a critique of itself.
Pauline models a "feminist" consciousness whose principle target is
the frightening prospect of a "feminism" that will risk death to be on
the side of life.

   That "feminism" is surely what Woodman elsewhere calls a
"projection." And as she tells us, when it comes to "muster[ing] every
ounce of Spiritual Warrior in myself to defend my feminine feelings
and values" there are "[n]o projections allowed!" (62). What is
revealing is that this declaration of the need to unburden herself of
projections—more "yearning for the lightness of bone"—is made at
the conclusion of the one journal entry in which Woodman most calls
attention not only to their operation but also to the ways in which
they pre-empt experience as much as they give shape and meaning
to it. For Woodman has here recalled a trip that Ross makes to New
York during the course of her illness; as she claims, even her loving
husband must for a time be renounced, "moved off" (62), lest she be
distracted from the true path of consciousness. The notion that Ross
could in fact be disposed of, even momentarily, seems fantastically
unlikely, a fact confirmed by Woodman's own journal entries which
re-inscribe his metaphorical presence in his literal absence. While in
New York Ross sees *Angels in America*, Tony Kushner's Pulitzer prize
winning play about HIV/AIDS—one of the few occasions in *Bone* in
which Woodman acknowledges the rich world of illness narratives that
informs her own story. Woodman does not see the play herself, and
hears of its details only second-hand, through her husband's reporting
of them. But the narrative structure of the journal entry in which
this occasion is remembered is very telling, for *before* any of Ross's
perceptions of the play are even mentioned, Woodman rewrites the
play so that it becomes an allegory of the struggle to reaffirm the
covenant with Sophia. Ross has told her that "The Great Work begins"
is the play's evocative last line, but rather than considering how, in
its own context, this turn of phrase grows out of the play for which

it effects closure, she responds to it with a surge of interpretive labor that drains Kushner's story of its own details and replaces them with a story that sounds uncannily like the story that *Bone* is telling. "The Great Work that is beginning is the realization of the feminine as the bridge between God and humankind," she writes, proceeding to give a brief but detailed analysis of the play's archetypal dimensions. *Bone* overwrites *Angels in America*, and for the moment that superimposition is given the full weight of Woodman's authority as an analyst. Only at the end of this move on the play does Woodman pause, noting— albeit tentatively—that what she has been saying with such confidence may not be fair to Kushner's vision: "But I'm not sure that's what *Angels in America* is about," she concedes.

A week later, in a different journal entry, Woodman returns to the matter of the play, where she more frankly admits that her views about its details were "straight idealization" (70). "Ross saw a Nietzschean world, a world where there is no god, no sacred book. We are on our own. We have to improvise and do what we can for ourselves. 'The Great Work' is the invention of ourselves, even as the play is an invention of ourselves. And as for the angel, she flies on pulleys that we can see, an impoverished homemade creature." "So much for that projection!," Woodman writes, but: "At least I brought to consciousness what I think 'The Great Work' is" (70). Woodman acknowledges that she has simplified and abstracted the play but recuperates her self-conscious surprise at so fundamentally mistaking its content by reassuring herself that even in error she continues on the path of consciousness. But in context, this seems like a half-hearted justification, especially when set against the more passionate account of the play that Ross provides. Whatever Woodman *says* has happened, these two journal entries tell a somewhat different story. We are most often told that grasping the archetypal dimensions of reality is a matter of holding the illuminating mirror of consciousness up to the nature of things; but here we see not a mirror at work but a lamp, and catch Woodman in the act of projecting upon reality what may be true only in her imagination. For it is Woodman who is improvising here, not the supposedly deprived characters flying about Kushner's stage, and it is Woodman who self-consciously draws our attention to it. In other words, we are afforded the opportunity to see in Woodman what she eventually sees and regrets in Kushner's play, namely the possibility that what feels like a universal truth, more evidence of how "God organizes our lives" (61), is in fact "an invention of ourselves."

For a brief moment, it is as if the curtain is raised on the work of consciousness, revealing it to be a projection—not a true account of the nature of things in their essence but a device that is "homemade" and that "flies on pulleys." Is *Bone* itself not such a device? In these journal entries about Kushner's play are we not given a chance to observe the machinery of consciousness, the push and pull of the book's own pulleys? Woodman barely contains that realization about the work of consciousness by associating it with what she dismisses as "a Nietzschean world," a world she experiences as "impoverished." Yet, in admitting that her interpretation of Kushner's play is an "idealization" and a "projection," Woodman also tacitly concedes that the myth of consciousness is not without its own impoverishment. *Angels in America*, or rather, Ross's "Nietzschean" view of it, stands as a figure for all that resists the idealizing designs that *Bone* has on reality—that is, as another instance of an irreducible remainder, a remainder, moreover, that is allowed in the second journal entry to "splutter back into life" after having been relegated to the margins by the forcefulness of Woodman's glossing powers. I am not so sure that the notion that in this world "[w]e are on our own" and that "[w]e have to improvise and do what we can for ourselves" is nearly as far from Woodman's project of soul-making as her dismissal of it as "Nietzschean" suggests. Woodman wants to dispose of that surprising connection between her book and Kushner's play by locating the latter in a universe of nihilist abstraction, but the fact that it is also a universe that is identified with and filtered through Ross—who haunts the book—reminds us that the world of *Angels* is closer to Woodman's psyche than at first might appear. The threatening, if counterintuitive, proximity of *Angels* to *Bone* would help explain the pre-emptive way in which Woodman attempts to assimilate Kushner's universe to her own, only to end up conceding the violence of that move.

What is revealing is that between the two journal entries concerning *Angels*, Woodman circles back to the question of "projections." It is as if in the days between simplifying the play and realizing the forcefulness of that simplification, Woodman is prompted to consider the role of other idealizations in her life and work. We know that the book is about to suffer a seismic shift because Woodman cites Susan Sontag's *Illness as Metaphor* in the margins: "Nothing is more punitive than to give a disease a meaning—the meaning being invariably a moralistic one. ... The disease itself becomes a metaphor" (67). In many respects *Bone* is written *against* Sontag's influential reflection on the representation of disease—particularly cancer narratives—since it is an exploration of metaphor as a source of healing rather than as a fund of stigmatization. But for a moment Woodman pauses to reconsider this faith, and to allow for the possibility that the work that she is doing in the name of consciousness (which is work whose primary goal is to give meaning to illness, her own and others') also risks moralizing it, fitting it to normative frameworks that coarsen human experience even as it claims to alleviate suffering. Woodman responds to Sontag's observation with a list of "punitive" metaphors by which her own illness has been characterized:

> 'It's the father complex, kills the mother, tears out the womb.' Or "It's the Negative Mother imprinted on your cells driving you to death.' Or 'Endometrial cancer is found to have a hereditary factor.' Or 'You never gave up your grief for Fraser. Your grief is destroying you.' Or 'Tear things to shreds. Let your rage go.' Or 'The cancer personality gives all to others and keeps nothing for itself, and when it has given all, it gives more' (68).

What is astonishing about these competing narratives of illness, these different ways of bringing cancer to the bar of consciousness, is that not one is without relevance to Woodman's own project of soul-making. Yet they are dismissed as aggressive denials of her life rather than embraced as lucid explanations of her encounter with death. "Projections! Projections!" she exclaims, in a journal entry that is remarkable for being one of the few instances in *Bone* in which Woodman allows herself outwardly to express a flash of anger. As projections, they are improvisations that say much more about the projector's "love of death" than the ill person's need to live. These are the myths and stories for which the unwell subject is cruelly "sacrificed," as Woodman says, but it seems important to say they are also idealizations that *Bone* elsewhere affirms and explores to one degree or another. All of these dismissed stories of Woodman's cancer are also stories that *Bone* tells, even if they are characterized here as explanations of her illness that have been violently imposed upon her by others: the family history of cancer, the melancholic attachment to Fraser, the depletions that she suffers for playing the maternal role with her patients and students, each of these epidemiologies Woodman must also acknowledge as her own. And as she suggests, things get complicated when the sick subject does the most embarrassing thing: rather than dying according to plan, she "splutters back into life" (68)! Woodman is herself an instance of that messy excess, inasmuch as she here denounces the very projections that she herself is responsible for putting into play in *Bone*. The projections that she decries are at once hers and not-hers, familiar and unfamiliar; this is an indeterminacy for which *Bone* seems poorly prepared, not least because it remembers that Woodman's life is larger than the designs that would explain it. In his contribution to this volume, Ross Woodman observes that "Marion's life and work resides not in the construction of a masculine system, but in the feminine deferral of it." One almost hears in this account William Blake's ambiguous declaration of independence: "I must Create a System, or be enslav'd by another Man's."[16] As Blake intuited, disavowing the chains of an authoritarian order risks creating another order that is more subtly authoritarian. For Woodman's "feminine deferral" of the masculine threatens at points to take on elements of the masculine system it would let go—especially its asceticism, and its faith in a higher orderliness. What saves it from becoming what it beholds, in the manner of Shelley's warrior Prometheus frozen in combat with the tyrant Jupiter, are these moments of self-difference, the internal margins where the book interrogates its most passionately held assumptions. Embracing the uncertainty of her own future readings by writing against herself, Woodman resists the last temptation, the temptation to be seduced by the anorexic requirements of her own system. These are the moments in which her text "splutters back into life."

We have only begun to read *Bone: Dying into Life*.

NOTES

1. Marion Woodman, *Bone: Dying into Life* (New York: Viking, 2000), xii. All further quotations will be from this edition. Page numbers will be cited parenthetically in the text.

2. In the voice of Johannes de Silentio, Kierkegaard recalls Abraham's gamble of faith: "I can make the mighty trampoline leap whereby I cross over into infinity." This jump, as it were, is compared to movement in dance (to which we might well compare Woodman's dance at the end of *Bone*): "It is supposed to be the most difficult feat for a ballet dancer to leap into a specific posture in such a way that he never once strains for the posture but in the very leap assumes the posture." See Søren Kierkegaard, *Fear and Trembling / Repetition*, trans. and ed. Howard V. Hong and Edna H. Hong (Princeton: Princeton University Press, 1983), 36 and 41.

3. Kirkegaard, 41.

4. Jacques Derrida, "Epoché and Faith: An Interview with Jacques Derrida," *Derrida and Religion: Other Testaments*, eds. Yvonne Sherwood and Kevin Hart (New York: Routledge, 2005), 31.

5. See, for example, *Bone* (70). In the Preface to *Daybreak* Nietzsche too dwells on the question of reading and speed:

> It is not for nothing that one has been a philologist, perhaps one is a philologist still, that is to say, a teacher of slow reading:—in the end one also writes slowly. Nowadays it is not only my habit, it is also to my taste—a malicious taste, perhaps?—no longer to write anything which does not reduce to despair every sort of man who is "in a hurry." For philology is that venerable art which demands of its votaries one thing above all: to go aside, to take time, to become still, to become slow—it is a goldsmith's art and connoisseurship of the word which has nothing but delicate, cautious work to do and achieves nothing if it does not achieve it *lento*. But for precisely this reason it is more necessary than ever today, by precisely this means does it entice and enchant us the most, in the midst of an age of "work," that is to say, of hurry, of indecent and perspiring haste, which wants to "get everything done" at once, including every old or new book:—this art does not so easily get anything done, it teaches to read well, that is to say, to read slowly, deeply, looking cautiously before and aft, with reservations, with doors left open, with delicate eyes and fingers. ... My patient friends, this book desires for itself only perfect readers and philologists: learn to read me well! —

See *Daybreak: Thoughts on the Prejudices of Morality*, trans. and ed. Maudemarie Clark and Brian Leiter (Cambridge: Cambridge University Press, 1997), 6.

6. In his *Jerusalem*, among other works, Blake opposes the deadening effects of what he calls the "bloated Form" of the "Moral Law" to the "vitality" of the "Minute Particular." See *Complete Writings*, ed. Geoffrey Keynes (Oxford: Oxford University Press, 1972), 738.

7. As Woodman claims, her life, seen from the perspective afforded by consciousness, is a series of detours that are always already returns: "Dear Sophia, how the cycle spirals and swings into wider spirals and how your love holds that spiral true in my heart" (21).

8. Friedrich Schelling, *Philosophical Inquiries into the Nature of Human Freedom*, trans. James Gutmann (La Salle, Illinois: Open Court, 1986), 34.

9. Quoted by Jacques Derrida, *The Gift of Death*, trans. David Wills (Chicago: University of Chicago Press, 1995), 16.

10. Gillian Rose, *Mourning Becomes the Law: Philosophy and Representation* (Cambridge: Cambridge University Press, 1996), 133.

11. See, for example, Emmanuel Levinas, *Otherwise than Being; or Beyond Essence*, trans. Alphonso Lingis (Pittsburgh: Duquesne University Press, 1998).

12. Emmanuel Levinas, *Totality and Infinity: An Essay on Exteriority*, trans. Alphonso Lingis (Pittsburgh: Duquesne University Press, 1969), 134. "*Dasein*" is the term Heidegger uses to describe the barest structure of the being of human being.

13. For useful but very different discussions of the impossibility of punctually having done with loss, and of the ways in which the economy of mourning is always already disrupted by melancholic remainders, see Jacques Derrida, "Mnemosyne," in *Memoires: For Paul de Man*, trans. Cecile Lindsay, Jonathan Culler, Eduardo Cadava, and Peggy Kamuf (New York: Columbia University Press, 1989), 1-43; and Judith Butler, "Bodies that Matter," in *Bodies that Matter: On the Discursive Limits of "Sex"* (New York: Routledge, 1993), 27-55.

14. Geoffrey H. Hartman, *Beyond Formalism: Literary Essays, 1958-1970* (New Haven: Yale University Press, 1970), 370.

15. Balachandra Rajan, *The Form of the Unfinished: English Poetics from Spenser to Pound* (Princeton: Princeton University Press, 1985), 227, 231.

16. William Blake, *Complete Writings*, 629.

MULTI-SENSORY IMAGINATION

JOAN CHODOROW

I have long been inspired by our treasured colleague Marion Woodman and her passionate engagement with the body-psyche connection. It is now a pleasure and privilege to join Nancy Cater and fellow authors in this special issue of *Spring Journal.* My task is to approach—even so briefly—the multi-sensory nature of images and imagination.

Images are experienced and expressed through any or all of the sensory modalities. According to Antonio Damasio, these include visual (sight), auditory (sound), olfactory (smell), and gustatory (taste), as well as tactile (touch), together with other somatosensory image-experiences, such as muscular, temperature, pain, visceral, and vestibular.[1] The Greek word for "body" is *soma* and the word "somatosensory" brings to mind billions of receptors located all over the body providing an ongoing stream of sensory experience from the world and the self.

Joan Chodorow, Ph.D., is an analyst member of the C. G. Jung Institute of San Francisco. Publications include *Dance Therapy and Depth Psychology, Jung on Active Imagination,* and the forthcoming *Active Imagination: Healing from Within.* She lectures and teaches internationally.

As far back as 1902, Jung recognized that images are not only visual. In his medical dissertation, "On the Psychology and Pathology of So-called Occult Phenomena," he described a series of visions or hallucinations "of a systemic nature involving all of the sense organs equally."[2] Following Charcot, Jung differentiated visual images, auditory images, and motor images.[3] In his 1904 word association studies Jung wrote: "An inner image is vivid if the associations immediately connected with it spring to mind. The nearest associations upon the image of a concrete object are the sensory aspects: the visual, the acoustic, the tactile, and the motor."[4]

Jung's early observation that inner images come to life when their sensory aspects are amplified (made ample), brings to mind a beautifully written contemporary study. In *Body and Earth: An Experiential Guide*, Andrea Olsen gives many examples of the multi-sensory nature of amplification. In the following passage, she interweaves neurological and experiential perspectives to describe the way a thought may develop into a vivid, dynamic image:

> When an image begins in the cerebral cortex as a thought (imagine a tree), it travels down to the occipital lobe to the visual buffer. As we deepen our visualization (what does the tree look like, what is its smell, what movement does it inspire?) associations surface to fill in precise details, until the image becomes quite clear. In this way, we create a visual representation of our thoughts that can seem as real as an actual memory. When we visualize, imagine or image an activity, we also stimulate neuromuscular circuitry, engaging a full body response, even when we are sitting still. (Imagine climbing the tree: where do you put your foot, where do you touch the branch?) If visualization is accompanied by actual physical practice, it is highly effective in stimulating efficient, integrated, neuromuscular circuitry.[5]

Returning to Jung's continuing interest in the multi-sensory nature of the psyche, in 1916 he wrote "The Transcendent Function," his first essay about the method he came to call active imagination. In this important early contribution, he seemed to suggest a kind of typology of the senses when he wrote that "visual types" tend to see fantasy pictures, while "audio-verbal types" are more likely to hear inner voices.[6] I imagine he may have been thinking about tactile types when he wrote: "There are others again, who neither see nor hear anything inside themselves, but whose hands have the knack of giving expression to the contents of the unconscious."[7] He goes on to say:

> Those who are able to express the unconscious by means of bodily movements are rather rare. The disadvantage that movements cannot easily be fixed in the mind must be met by making careful drawings of the movements afterwards, so that they shall not be lost to the memory.[8]

Years later, when discussing the mandala in his 1928-1930 dream seminar, he made the comment: "You can draw a mandala, you can build a mandala, or you can dance a mandala."[9] In the same seminar (about a year later), he said: "Anyone with a motor imagination could make a very beautiful dance out of that motif."[10] Marie-Louise von Franz reported that Jung once told her symbolic enactment with the body is "more efficient than 'ordinary active imagination,'" but he could not explain why."[11]

I invite you now to consider a series of multi-sensory images. I encourage the reader to engage any parts of the following reflections that might be useful, and leave the rest. Take the time you need for transitions, especially from one mode to another. Although I shall sometimes describe the sensory modes separately, in reality, the natural integrative function of imagination tends to create multi-sensory images. Speaking of perception, Andrea Olsen reminds us that it is "cumulative, generally simultaneous, and necessarily selective. Rarely does one part of the sensory system act alone."[12]

To begin: take a deep breath, close your eyes—go inside—and invite a visual image to appear. If psyche presents a particular visual image, relax, take a deep breath, and play with it by imagining its sound, smell, taste, touch, movement, and more. If it feels right, make a drawing or painting of it, and/or express it symbolically in other ways.

Again, close your eyes and go inside. This time, wait for an auditory image. You may hear or imagine or remember an inner voice, or voices, or sounds, or music from within. If you imagine an inner sound, it may be related to the visual image that came before, or it may be related to something else. If you want to amplify a particular sound, you might play with your voice, inviting the auditory image to whisper, speak, sound, or sing through your vocal apparatus. In *Memories,*

Dreams, Reflections, Jung described his experience of such images: "Sometimes it was as if I were hearing it with my ears, sometimes feeling it with my mouth, as if my tongue were formulating words; now and then I heard myself whispering aloud."[13] If you hear a rhythmic sequence, your hands may want to clap the rhythm, or use a drum or gong, or bells or piano or other musical instrument. Sometimes sounds, vibrations, and songs from within are harmonious and beautiful. Other times, there may be terrible inner sounds that play unbidden, repeatedly. Alfred Wolfsohn, a "shell shocked" veteran of the First World War, was haunted for many years by the sounds of trench warfare, especially the screams of his dying comrades. It wasn't until he found a way to express the unbearable sounds symbolically, that he could begin to find relief.[14]

If you are ready to explore another mode, close your eyes, go inside, and wait for an olfactory image. You may notice actual aromas in the world around you, or psyche may offer a particular fragrance or smell from another time and place. If you were to express an olfactory image symbolically, how would you do it? Given my own preferences, I imagine expressing a particular fragrance or smell in dance or movement, then draw or paint and perhaps develop it further in a story or poem.

Once again, close your eyes and go inside. This time, invite a gustatory image. Does a memory or fantasy come of a particular taste, or a combination of tastes? What are the associated textures, smells, temperatures, and colors? Images of sweet, sour, bitter, and salty tastes are actual flavors with corresponding receptors on the tongue, as well as symbolic experiences of life. How might the tastes of foods we accept and reject be expressed symbolically? How might the wanted and unwanted tastes of life itself be expressed?

Turning now to the world of somatosensory images, go inside and invite a tactile (touch) image. You may begin by sensing the actual contact between your skin and the clothes you are wearing. What is the difference between skin surrounded by air, and skin brushed lightly by soft fabric, or more tightly by elastic? There may also be image-experiences of light touch, firm touch, gentle stroking, deep stimulation, and more. If a particular tactile image comes, are there associations to comfort and well-being, discomfort and pain, or the dimensions of heat and cold? What are some of your other associations? If you want to express a tactile image symbolically, are you drawn to clay, movement, and sandplay? What other forms come to mind?

There is an ongoing stream of kinaesthetic (muscular) images, as we perceive the motion, weight, or position of the body. Proprioceptive nerve endings in the muscles, tendons, joints, and inner ear provide an ongoing flow of sensory experience from within. Close your eyes and discover what kind of shape your body wants to make and let yourself sense the shape from within. When you open your eyes again, as you read—even if you are sitting still—your body is likely to fluctuate between stillness and small amounts of movement. As you breathe, there is a subtle, continuous cycle of three-dimensional growing and shrinking. You may be focused on your actual body the way it is. And/or, your body may remember and imagine a world of movement experiences from long ago and far away. Is there a particular memory or fantasy of bodily position, weight, or motion? Using a particular image (or any other image-experience) as a starting point, let yourself explore and express it literally and symbolically in movement. The great gift of inner-directed movement has to do with its integrative function; the body is not only multi-sensory, it is at once actual and imaginal.

Another somatosensory image involves temperature. By attending to the world of sensations felt in your body, your attention may be drawn to the actual inner/outer temperature, and/or you may remember and imagine a particular impression of warmth, heat, fire, or coolness, cold, freezing from a symbolic perspective.

Other somatosensory images include pain, visceral, and vestibular images. Again, sensory experiences may be both literal (actual) and symbolic (imaginal). By attending inwardly, you might notice various muscular aches and pains. Or, you might remember and imagine pain images from another time and place. In addition to sensory experience from pain receptors in different parts of the body, there is also a parallel world of uncomfortable, sometimes unbearable emotional pain. Is it possible to get acquainted with pain, without getting identified with it? What might be some ways to express pain symbolically?

Visceral images involve the autonomic nervous system, including changes in heart rate, respiration, and more, together with the undulating motions and rumblings of the gut. These and other visceral experiences are often related to the felt patterns of various emotions, for example, the heavy-hearted feelings of sadness and grief, the "sick," nauseous feelings of shame and disgust, and the buoyant, light-hearted feelings of enjoyment and joy, to name a few.

Vestibular images have much to do with equilibrium. There are unwanted medical conditions that produce dizziness or vertigo. At the same time, kittens and puppies chase their own tails for the fun of it until they fall down, and children may spin voluntarily until they fall (and then watch the sky go round). Roger Caillois describes *ilinx,* a particular classification of games involving rapid whirling or falling movements that seek to "momentarily destroy the stability of perception and inflict a kind of voluptuous panic upon an otherwise lucid mind."[15]

How do we approach and explore the psychological and symbolic dimensions of these powerful somatosensory image-experiences?

The sensory modalities are intricately interwoven with emotions, symbol formation, and psychological development. Although it goes beyond the scope of this review to explore the links between emotions and the senses, it is clear that they amplify each other and from an evolutionary perspective, the senses may have been early precursors to the emotions.[16]

The living body—infused with sensory and emotional experience—is a mystery and a miracle. As Jung described it in *The Zarathustra Seminars*: "The living body contains the secret of life, it is an intelligence. It is also a plurality which is gathered up in one mind."[17] He names different parts of the body, such as toes, fingers, ears, stomach, knees, and goes on to say:

> Each part is always something in itself. The different forms and localizations are all represented in your mind as more or less different facts, so there is a plurality. What you think with your head doesn't necessarily coincide with what you feel in your heart, and what your belly thinks is not necessarily what your mind thinks. The extension in space therefore, creates a pluralistic quality in the mind. That is probably the reason consciousness is possible.[18]

NOTES

1. Antonio Damasio, *The Feeling of What Happens: Body and Emotion in the Making of Consciousness* (New York: Harcourt, Inc., 1999), 318.

2. C. G. Jung, "On the Psychology and Pathology of So-called Occult Phenomena," *Psychiatric Studies, The Collected Works of C. G. Jung, Vol. 1,* trans. R.F.C. Hull, Bollingen Series XX (Princeton: Princeton UP, 1970) § 45.

3. *Ibid.* § 86, note 35.

4. C. G. Jung, "Studies in Word Association," *Experimental Researches, Vol. 2,* trans. Leopold Stein in collaboration with Diana Riviere, Bollingen Series XX (Princeton: Princeton UP, 1973) § 472.

5. Andrea Olsen, *Body and Earth: An Experiential Guide* (Hanover: Middlebury College Press, 2002), 89.

6. C. G. Jung, "The Transcendent Function," *The Structure and Dynamics of the Psyche, Vol. 8,* trans. R.F.C. Hull, Bollingen Series XX (Princeton: Princeton UP, 1969) § 170.

7. *Ibid.* § 171.

8. *Ibid.*

9. C. G. Jung, *Dream Analysis: Notes of the Seminar Given in 1928-1930,* (Bollingen Series XCIX, (Princeton UP, 1984), p. 120.

10. *Ibid.*, p. 474.

11. Marie-Louise von Franz, "Supplement: On Active Imagination," in *Inward Journey: Art as Therapy,* by Margaret Frings Keyes (La Salle: Open Court, 1983), 126.

12. Andrea Olsen, *Body and Earth*, 57.

13. C. G. Jung, *Memories, Dreams, Reflections,* ed. Aniela Jaffe, trans., Richard and Clara Winston (New York: Vintage Books, 1961), 178.

14. Paul Newham, "Jung and Alfred Wolfsohn," *Journal of Analytical Psychology,* Vol. 37, 1992.

15. Roger Caillois, *Man, Play and Games,* trans. Meyer Barash (New York: Schocken Books, 1979), 23.

16. Louis Stewart, in Joan Chodorow, *Dance Therapy and Depth Psychology: The Moving Imagination* (London: Routledge, 1991), 84.

17. C. G. Jung, *Nietzsche's Zarathustra: Notes of the Seminar given in 1934-1939,* edited by James L. Jarrett, Vol. I (Princeton: Princeton University Press, 1988), 360.

18. *Ibid.*

Hope Versus Hopelessness in the Psychoanalytic Situation and Dante's *Divine Comedy*

DONALD E. KALSCHED

The True God transforms violence into suffering.
The False God transforms suffering into violence.
— Simone Weil

Introduction

In what follows, I will discuss the issue of hope in the psychoanalytic situation and also its opposite, hopelessness, against the backdrop of some archetypal imagery from the most "hopeless" place of all— Hell, as it is envisioned in the first book of Dante's *Divine Comedy*, the *Inferno*.[1] In this approach, hope is seen as being intimately connected with a process that Winnicott[2] called "indwelling" and Christianity calls incarnation, i.e., the descent of the spirit into the body. Dante's poem suggests that there is a "force" in the psyche that opposes

Donald Kalsched, Ph.D., is a Jungian analyst in private practice in Katonah, New York. Currently he is active with the Inter-Regional Society of Jungian Analysts and also serves as Dean of a Jungian Studies Specialty at the Westchester Institute for Training in Psychoanalysis and Psychotherapy in Bedford Hills, N. Y. His recent book, *The Inner World of Trauma*, is in its fourth printing.

indwelling and that cannot tolerate incarnational processes—a force that drives the spirit out of the body and generates hopelessness. This inner "force" constitutes a formidable archetypal defense, and I would like to show how this defense is pictured archetypally in Dante's medieval poem, and how it operates personally in the psychotherapy of a patient I will call Helen.[3] Much of my understanding of healing in psychoanalysis is informed by Marion Woodman's work, which highlights how the human body—especially the female body—often suffers under tyrannical abuse by the mind's perfectionism and violent oppression. In this paper I try to unmask the tyrant—the "false God" who perpetually transforms suffering into violence—and to show in a clinical case, how He slowly gives over his power and his prisoners to relationship.

In Dante's fourteenth-century poem, both the pilgrim and his guide, Virgil, begin their journey at the Gate of Hell, where they read the chilling inscription: "Through me the road to the city of desolation, … Abandon all hope, Ye who enter here."[4] As the poets enter the precincts of Hell, they soon realize that hope must be abandoned here because the suffering in Hell is eternal suffering—it goes on and on without relief—without hope of comfort or of liberation or release. This "eternal pain" was, for Dante, the worst imaginable punishment for a sinful life on earth. It seems that the human imagination cannot comprehend anything quite so terrible as suffering that goes on and on forever without hope. This kind of suffering is very familiar to us in the clinical situation with those patients who must defend themselves from the unbearable experience of early trauma. Their suffering never "completes" itself. It goes on and on "eternally." Why is this?

Freud and Jung called this kind of repetitive suffering "neurotic suffering," as distinguished from the authentic suffering necessary for individuation. Around this distinction most of our understanding of psychopathology revolves. It turns out that neurotic suffering never ends because it is kept alive by an inner factor, and, among other things, this inner factor will not let a normal affect-cycle complete itself. Everything stays suspended and repetitive. Both Freud and Jung were impressed with this fact. Freud said, "[T]here is no doubt that there is something in these people that sets itself against their recovery."[5] And Jung—describing his patient Sabina Spielrein—talked about a "morbid" fragment of personality or complex in her psyche, "the

"Dis," from *Images of the Journey in Dante's Divine Comedy*,
by Charles H. Taylor and Patricia Finley

inclinations, judgments, and resolutions of which move only in the direction of the will to be ill." This perverse second personality, Jung said, "devours what is left of the normal ego and forces it into the role of a secondary (oppressed) complex."[6]

Dante's fourteenth-century poem gives us a remarkable image of this "perverse second personality." Here is the "god" who turns suffering into violence and in the process, creates an inner hell of hopelessness. Dante's name for this diabolical entity, ruling Hell from the ninth circle or Pit, is not Satan or Lucifer, as we might expect, but "Dis," from the Latin, meaning to divide, split in two or negate ("*Dite*" in Italian).

Hopelessness and 'Dis'

If we look at the structure of Dante's poem we find that the work is divided into three parts, corresponding to three realms of the "afterlife." Each part is a stage in the journey Dante must make. He must make this journey because he is depressed. The poem's first lines state: "Midway through this way of life we're bound upon, I woke to find myself in a dark wood, where the right road was wholly lost and gone."[7] And for his "midlife" depression, an encounter with the "underworld" of Hell is apparently the necessary prescription—a kind of homeopathic remedy. Dante has lost hope, and in order to recover hope, he has to abandon hope as he knows it. This is Dante's paradox— one that has relevance to the clinical situation as well. Actually it might be more accurate to say that in order to recover hope, Dante must "enter the area of abandoned hope"—but he must do this voluntarily and consciously—with his guide, Virgil, as a witness. It would do Dante no good if he simply fell into the pit of Hell. One part of him has to be conscious of what he's doing ... to witness it. This part is represented by the shade of Virgil.

In the first third of the poem, Dante must descend into the Inferno through a series of stages, starting with Limbo, the outermost layer, and proceeding through nine levels down into the very center of the Earth, in order to encounter the image of absolute evil. Here is the dread seat of the ghastly "Dis" (see illustration)—a kind of netherworld trinity—a three-headed, bat-winged monster, living at the point of densest gravity and severest cold in Hades, devouring a sinner in each of his slathering mouths and freezing the Cocytus with the icy wind from his bat-like wings. I think Dante's poetic insight that the darkest force of evil we can imagine is equivalent to the life-negating, dis- integrating energies of the "under" world helps us relate the poem's medieval Christian imagery to the clinical situation, where we are very familiar with "Dis" as, for example, dis-sociation, dis-memberment, dis-integration, dis-illusionment, dis-avowal, dis-hearten, dis-grace, dis-courage, dis-ease—even dis-aster, which means losing one's connection to the stars, to one's god-given destiny and hence, to hope.

The three-headed cannibal known as "Dis" is well known to psychoanalysis, but he has a controversial pedigree. Freud thought of him as a personification of the death instinct, as did Melanie Klein. Bion[8] spoke of a malevolent destructive force in the psyche that reverses Alpha function and disintegrates everything back into "Beta" bits. Jung spoke of the archetypal shadow, and Ronald Fairbairn[9] of an "Internal Saboteur" perpetually attacking a vulnerable "libidinal ego," thus filling the inner world with "bad objects." Sandra Edelman[10] has recently shown how the archetypal affect of shame always follows attacks by this dark daimonic entity in the unconscious.

My own musings about this source of evil in the human psyche[11] have been informed by these theorists, but with the important proviso that Dis embodies an archetypal defense whose energies were originally part of the Self's wholeness, and therefore his "intention" or "telos" is equivocal, trickster-like, and hard to categorize as pure evil. As we know from mythology, Dis is a fallen Angel—Lucifer himself, the light-bearer. He is also the "agent provocateur" of consciousness in the Garden of Eden, so he can't be all bad. Although he is quintessentially the great nihilist, the splitter, the attacker of every *coniunctio* in the interest of *disiunctio*, he is also the source of dis-cernment and dis-crimination, dis-tinctions and the capacity to dis-tance and dis-identify. To honor this ambivalence, I have called him a Protector/Persecutor, the instigator in the unconscious of a "self-care system" assuring the person's survival at the expense of true-self living. He is the "god" who turns suffering into violence when suffering has been too much for the child. Dis can keep a person alive out of sheer will-power, and I have seen this happen. Some of my patients felt—as children—that they owed their very lives to the chastizing, tyrannical voice of Dis, and they are not wrong, although the life "he" gave them is not the true life they seek. What these patients experience, and what I have been forced to acknowledge with them, is *how dissociative processes provide a "daimonic" or archetypal container where human mediation has broken down.* Nobody but Jung really understood this, although he neglected terribly the interpersonal and developmental processes through which human mediation comes about.

Failed mediation between the inner and outer worlds is, by definition, *traumatic* because the raw impact of unformulated, un-symbolized experience hits the child's psyche like a bolt of lightning hits the electrical panel of a house. Without a human transformer for this high-voltage archetypal affect, all the circuits can be blown. Kohut[12] calls this experience "disintegration anxiety," which, he says, constitutes a mortal threat to the very core of personality—threatening what I have called the "imperishable personal spirit," or human soul, with destruction. This must be avoided at all costs, and so Dis arrives on the scene to prevent the overwhelming impact of affect from being *experienced.* In other words, trauma doesn't split the psyche; Dis splits the psyche and he does this to save the life of the trauma victim. Dis-

integration saves the soul from destruction, even though in the process
our suffering is turned into violence.

So Dis is the dark angel made necessary by our incapacity to process
all our experience. In his defensive function, he *dismembers* experience—
chops it to pieces and then makes sure that the pieces do not link up
again. In the process, he destroys hope—or it might be better to say
that he cannot tolerate hope; he is too "realistic." Hope is connected
to wholeness and he, after all, is "Dis." Wholeness is anathema to
him, so he keeps the parts "dis"-integrated. Affect in the body is severed
from its corresponding image in the mind and thereby an unbearably
painful meaning is obliterated. An innocent remainder of a pre-
traumatic self is split off and regresses (with Dis's help) into an autistic
enclave—a kind of limbo of lost souls in the psyche. Amnesia barriers
are erected to make sure this lost innocence does not remember what
happened to it. Meanwhile, a "progressed" part of the personality
grows up too fast, becomes self-sufficient, and goes on living in the
outer world in a secret pact with the Fallen Angel himself. Part of this
"pact" is that the now-lost innocence, encapsulated and split off, will
be forgotten. This innocent remnant is not without hope—the hope
of the prisoner for parole or release—but as the years drag on, this
wistful hope and longing rapidly turns into hopelessness and despair.
And Dis rarely commutes the sentences of his imprisoned innocents.
When Dis takes over, the flame of hope slowly goes out.

So Dis is the "engine" of hopelessness in the deep unconscious, at
least as medieval artists have imagined him—"Emperor of the Sorrowful
Realm."[13] In order to recover hope, the Pilgrim with his guide must
descend into the pit to encounter this creature—then they have to
climb down the great hairy body of Dis, right down to his groin area.
At this point, miraculously the whole armature of the poem turns 180
degrees. Their direction is reversed. Down becomes up. Instead of
climbing down, Dante and Virgil find themselves climbing up the
hair legs of the beast to emerge at the base of the seven-story mountain
of Purgatory in the southern hemisphere. Here they see the stars again
for the first time, and hope that was lost in the Inferno, is rekindled.

Suffering and Refusal

Of the three realms Dante must negotiate, both the Inferno and
the Paradiso are outside time and space—eternal—so the suffering

in Hell is eternal just as the joy and bliss of Paradise are eternal. Only the Purgatorio—an intermediate realm—is in time. It is here, between Heaven and Hell, that the sinners are slowly "working off" their sins through acts of repentance and contrition. They are moving towards the eternal and therefore they are not without hope. They have escaped the endless suffering in the prison-house of Dis. Their violence towards themselves has been turned into suffering and they are suffering towards something ... towards a hopeful end.

Thus, Hell and Purgatory define two kinds of suffering in the poem, and in Dante's vision, the central act of human consciousness that differentiates the meaningful suffering of Purgatory from the endless, eternal suffering of Hell, is an *act of repentance*. The sinners in Purgatory have repented. The sinners in Hell have refused to repent— refused to acknowledge their own brokenness, their own humanity. For this reason, their torment is eternal and real hope has been lost to them. So refusal is central to the phenomenology of the hopeless space we are exploring. Dis himself is the great refuser, as we will see in a moment. He once had a chance to be God's light-bearer on earth, but he refused to follow God's plan to create man in His own image. This was a humiliation of his splendor that he could not countenance. He refused the incarnation—and so, often, do we.

Neville Symington[14] reminds us that this refusal is a choice. Symington says there is one major choice that defines whether our lives will be hope-filled and satisfying or not—whether we choose what he calls "the Lifegiver." We have this choice before us, he says, at every moment of our lives. He does not say what the Lifegiver is—it remains a mystical idea—but he says it comes into being only when we choose it. If we refuse the Lifegiver—if we refuse the suffering that is allotted to us as the struggle to realize our true selves, then we will choose the God who turns suffering into violence—we will choose Dis, and his narcissistic pathology will follow.

I will say more about this in a moment. But first a few words about hopelessness in the clinical situation—to help us understand how a pact with this Devil gets signed in an individual's life.

Hope and Transitional Space

When a patient walks into our office seeking psychotherapy, we can be fairly sure that he or she is in psychic pain, and that associated with this pain is a sense of hopelessness. *This hopelessness—and hence the lost hope of the person's life—is located in the realm of a person's "becoming," which has been foreclosed.* When I say "realm of a person's becoming" I am using Martin Buber's[15] language to describe the intermediate realm we all know so well from Winnicott's contributions to the early development of the infant and child psyche. Hope seems to reside in a successful negotiation of this "potential space," or transitional space.

One of the reasons Hope seems to reside in this space is that in the "becoming" of potential space—in the actualization of personal potential that occurs between the baby and the mother—in this space, something *more* appears to be going on than what Winnicott[16] described as the paradoxical meeting of the baby's hallucinated need for the breast with the mother's actual breast. All true depth psychologies have a vision of what this something *more* might be. Jung's vision was that something transpersonal was happening in this space. An inner foundation of individual wholeness (the Self) was slowly precipitating itself into being as an individual ego.[17] To put it in mystical and religious terms, we might say that God is becoming man in transitional space. Something pre-existent in the field of omnipotence is being transmuted into the human personality. In the "realm of a person's becoming," a splinter of the Godhead is entering time-and-space reality and taking on flesh and becoming a human soul. This is a hopeful idea. It suggests that the human personality has a transpersonal origin and essence. Omnipotence is not just something to be purged away. Omnipotence contains a "seed" of the future and has an "intention" with respect to the core or essence of personality. It has an implicate order, if you will, that Winnicott did not consider.

Yet even Winnicott[18] cannot resist becoming mystical when he discusses that "coming into being" that happens or fails to happen in transitional space. As the mother continually introduces and re-introduces the baby's mind and body, Winnicott says, something mysterious comes to "indwell" in the body, and as Winnicott describes it, we would be hard-pressed not to think of this "something" as the human soul. Indwelling leads to "personalization," which again Winnicott does not define, but it has to do with feeling real and becoming a person. So hope has centrally to do with something ineffable—mind, psyche, spirit—taking up residence in the body and this, symbolically speaking, has always been known as the incarnation of the spirit in matter.

What happens then, we might ask, when the potential space for this incarnational process is not provided ... when the space of human becoming is foreclosed? Winnicott speaks of a "reversal" of maturational processes. Instead of indwelling, the soul cannot make it across the threshold from omnipotence to the reality principle. Instead of personalization, de-personalization results ... instead of integration, dis-integration, instead of indwelling, dis-embodiment ... the soul leaves the body and becomes a "ghost." Dis-integration, dis-embodiment, de-personalization. We see from the prefixes of these words *who* has moved in to foreclose the potential space of a child's becoming—none other than old Dis himself.

The Case of Helen

Consider the following situation. A little girl named Helen, aged 4, (later my patient) is brimming with excitement and hope as the family prepares to move into their first real home, where she has been promised her own room and a real backyard with sandbox and swing set. The family is gathered outside on a beautiful spring day, greeting the neighbors and getting acquainted as the moving van unloads its cargo. In a creative act of inspiration, little Helen picks a bouquet of flowers and enthusiastically hands them to her mother in celebration of this moment.

I would invite the reader to pause here and contemplate what is at stake in this moment ... a little girl reaching out for her mother with a handful of flowers in total exuberance. It is a moment of enthusiasm. The root of that word is "en-theos"—God or Spirit filling the person. Here is a moment saturated with what Buber[19] calls the "microcosmic richness of the possible"—hope *in potentia*. We might say that something of this child's unique, God-given personal spirit was reaching across a threshold here in a desire to incarnate. This incarnation did not happen.

The mother looked down at the flowers—then quickly at the neighbor's yard and then anxiously scolded her daughter: "No, No, Helen! What's the matter with you! How could you! You picked those flowers from Mrs. Smith's garden. Now you go and apologize to her." Dragging the little girl by the arm, she forced this apology out of her and simultaneously broke her heart, destroying the hope implicit in this creative act, foreclosing the transitional space in which Helen's personhood was coming into being.

Now occasional derailments like this in an otherwise affirming childhood atmosphere are not going to matter all that much—they will not destroy hope, because such injuries can be repaired through empathy and understanding. But with my patient Helen, this kind of shaming by the narcissistic mother was typical. The word "love" was never spoken in her family, she told me, and Helen never remembers being touched, whereas everyone touched the family dog. Instead of love there was ridicule, and at the dinner table and as the father regularly became drunk, somebody always got humiliated or shamed. She was the "stupid" or "ugly" one because she asked dumb questions and because she had an overbite and looked like a "beaver" they said. Then, after dinner, the father continued drinking, and as he became more violent, would regularly take off his belt and strap little Helen on her bare bottom. If she protested, he would slap her in the face.

After one of these humiliations, Helen remembered the experience of suddenly watching herself from another place in the room. This separation between her "watcher" and the frightened little-girl-self being hit and humiliated happened automatically at first. But as the violence increased, little Helen actually began to seek out these states of dissociation because they made her feel strangely less anxious and more calm. She found that with a certain concentration in front of the mirror, she could bring them about. She would stare at herself until she began to feel unreal, until gradually the person looking and the image in the mirror were like two different people. Here we can begin to feel the icy winds of Dis slowly insinuating themselves into Helen's life. She began to dissociate—to "watch" herself. In her "watcher" mode, she felt invulnerable—liberated from the fragile crybaby self who couldn't stop sobbing, and she began to harden herself against the mother's shaming and the father's beatings. Ironically, this was the first moment of her "self-consciousness"—her "dis-crimination" of an observing self-state from the undifferentiated oneness of childhood experience. Unfortunately, this self-division occurred for defensive purposes only, and it was too early for her emerging wholeness to be broken. Helen's God-given spirit was slowly leaving her body.

Meanwhile, in the outside world, Helen had become a behavior problem. She refused to participate with the family in activities. She refused to eat. She ran away from home. She picked fights with other kids at school. It wasn't long before she developed an eating disorder and started wishing that she were a boy. First she started bingeing and purging—later she became anorexic. In college she reverted to bulimia. She hated her fat body because of its needs and its imperfections, and she hated the little crybaby girl who lived in that body. By the time she arrived in my therapy office in her late 30s she had become a very self-sufficient, successful professional woman on the outside, a journalist and scholar, proud of her accomplishments and all the famous people she knew. But inwardly, she was in despair, and the "voice" of this despair was a relentless, chastizing voice that said, "No, no, Helen! What's the matter with you!" This voice made sure that underneath all her outward success, lay a deep sense of her inadequacy as a person. The secret world of her bingeing and vomiting was the "proof" of her failure and her worthlessness.

It was as though Helen grew into a life held together by one giant refusal. One part of her felt loathsome, fat, and undesirable, but she could not admit to these humiliating feelings. She could never let herself "fall" into this brokenness. There was too much shame in it and she was too proud. Instead, she would hold herself "above" her shameful self. She refused to be broken. She refused to be humiliated ever again. One part of her was perpetually hungry and full of longing—another part hated this weak, whiney child-self. She felt weak and needy—she felt nothing. She gave in to hunger and binged—she purged this awful weakness, vomiting until she spat blood. She needed; she did not need.

In therapy, she was equally ambivalent. One part of her had a positive transference to me as a nurturing father—the child hiding within herself, we might say—while one part sat back and vigilantly scanned me, prepared to point out my foibles, my inadequacies as an analyst, my "irresponsible vacation schedule," grudgingly acknowledging on occasion that I had a point. In my countertransference, I had a sense of what it might have been like around Helen's family's dinner table. I began to feel stupid and inadequate—like I had buck teeth and couldn't say anything right.

One day I raised my patients' fees, including Helen's. Although she insisted during the session that she had no particular reaction to this (everything was "fine"—just send her the bill, she "didn't even want to think about it"), an hour later she called me in an agitated state and cancelled her next appointment. She was furious and wanted nothing more to do with therapy and its crass "business arrangements." "Fuck you!" she screamed into the phone and hung up. I did not call her back. Later that week I received a letter in the mail full of profuse apologies for her anger on the telephone and self-recriminations about her bad temper. When I next met her in the waiting room, she asked sheepishly if I was "all right." She confessed how overwhelmed she had been by rage and anger and talked of the panic she felt at having "ruined" the relationship. Then she mentioned a dream she had the night of her "explosion" on the telephone.

In the dream, she and an unknown man are on some sort of mission. They wend their way through a thick dark woods and come eventually upon a deep cave with two stone pillars at its entrance. Just inside, on the edge of the enveloping darkness, huddled near one of the pillars, hides a little girl, tattered and dirty, like one of the "wild children" discovered in France. The dream ends as the patient wakes in fear. Helen had an instinctive sense that this dream was important. There was something haunting to her about this "wild child"— something fearful, yet compelling and attractive. She associated the unknown man in the dream to me and she thought her fear in the dream on encountering the wild girl was like her fear when all the wild anger had leaped out of her.

Interpretation

Here is a moment Ronald Fairbairn[20] would have described as a terrifying "release of bad objects" from the unconscious— something some patients dread more than anything else. Helen had never risked this amount of rage with me before. She had "Dissed" me in no uncertain terms. Yet, when old Dis was liberated from the unconscious, so was this abandoned child-self, as if the rage connected to dissociation had to be unlocked from the inner world and directed outward in an actual object-relationship before we could "see" this lost child hidden in its cave. As our work proceeded over the ensuing months, there were many other dreams in which this abandoned child appeared, and much "dissing" energy that flooded into our relationship.

These lost, innocent children in Helen's psyche were encapsulated in a part of her inner world that was inaccessible to her prideful ego, with its intolerance of vulnerability. They were somehow kept alive like hydroponic plants, feeding on the ambrosia of Helen's fantasies of liberation—hope that grew dimmer every day as Helen's life became more and more dominated by self-hatred. Finally she forgot about them altogether. They disappeared into an autistic enclave. We will see such an autistic enclave in Dante's vision of Hell. It is called Limbo and, aptly enough, it is also the place that holds Hell's innocent children.

Dante's Descent into Limbo

After Dante and his guide pass through the Gate of Hell and the Vestibule of Hell, they are ferried across the Acheron by Charon to the edge of the actual Pit of Hell. At the uppermost level inside a special walled area, they find themselves in the first circle, Limbo (from *limbus,* meaning "border" or "edge").

Limbo, to the medieval Christian imagination, was the realm of "stuck" souls, eternally suspended in an altered state, undead, but also unalive, guilty only of having lived and died before Christ's coming. The souls caught there did not merit the extreme torments of Hell's deep flames (the "pain of sense"); yet, on the other hand, they had inherited Adam's original sin and, without the benefit of the sacrament of baptism, they were obliged to suffer too, though for them was reserved a lesser pain—"pain of loss," loss of the beatific vision and of any possibility of redemption—only eternal hopelessness and alienation from God. Hence, Limbo contains only the righteous who lived before Christ—righteous pagan men and women, as well as innocent, unbaptized infants, lost children—all locked up in a kind of crypt, far away from Dis's red-hot tortures.

As the outermost layer of Hell, Limbo is forever separated from life by gates that are eternally locked and bolted. Dante asks Virgil, his guide, whether these locked gates have ever been penetrated— have these innocents ever gotten help? Virgil's reply: only once—by a man who came in great light and glory. Virgil is, of course, referring to none other than Jesus Christ, who is said to have descended into Hell following his death on the Cross. The event was known as the "harrowing of Hell": Christ descended into Hell, penetrated the crypt, broke the gates, wrestled for three days with Dis himself, vanquished him, and freed the prisoners in Limbo. It is in keeping with Dante's paradox that Jesus descended into the realm of hopelessness at his moment of greatest hopelessness.

Jung had some interesting things to say about this moment in Christ's life. In some extemporaneous remarks he made to the Analytical Psychology Club in New York in 1937, he said:

> The utter failure came at the crucifixion, in the tragic words "My God, My God, why has Thou forsaken me?" If you want to understand the full tragedy of those words you must realize that they meant that Christ saw that his whole life, sincerely devoted to the truth according to his best conviction, had really been a terrific illusion. He had lived his life absolutely devotedly to its full and had made his honest experiment, but on the cross his mission deserted him ....[21]

Jung goes on to explain that because Jesus was faithful to this process of disillusionment, surrendering his ego ("not my will but Thine be done"), letting go even to the point of bodily death, he found his way to a larger life and a larger story beyond his previous understanding. This larger story and larger life was the new life imaged as the resurrection—the resurrection of the body.

In addition to its theological significance, the resurrection represents, quintessentially, the restoration of hope. Now all the realms of the cosmos, Hell, Heaven, and the in-between world where we live, have been connected through the agency of the God-man. Body, mind, and Spirit are linked again and hope returns. The space of becoming is restored. We might think of this story of divine "intercession" by Christ, descending and ascending, as a restoration of the psyche's "transcendent function"—a restoration of that potential wholeness and symbolic capacity previously foreclosed by Dis. These are moments that bring hope.

Helen in Limbo

H elen also began to have such experiences of linking on a small scale. One in particular occurred in a session soon after her angry outburst and the dream of the lost child. She had just suffered a searing rejection by a hoped-for boyfriend and sat in the session complaining about a knot of tension in her stomach. She was afraid her childhood ulcer was coming back. I asked her to close her eyes and concentrate on this pain in her body, even intensifying it, to see what it might reveal to her. She had trouble with this, but eventually relaxed enough to focus on her stomach pain, and after a brief time suddenly "saw" her "little girl," arms extended outward, her mouth distorted in a silent scream for mother. This image brought an enormous upwelling of sadness. Helen burst into tears and sobbed uncontrollably for several minutes. This was highly unusual for her. She usually hated her "crybaby self," the "mewling, whining, puking thing," as she called her. But now she was at a different place in her process. She felt overwhelming sadness, and yet in her surrender to these affects, there was great compassion for the lost little girl in herself. Neville Symington would say that Helen made a choice in her tearful surrender. She stopped refusing and chose the Lifegiver.

In the psychoanalytic process, this is always a noteworthy moment. When Dis relaxes his guard and the child comes back, the lost wholeness comes back with it, and the realm of becoming is opened once again. Hence, the child in Limbo carries the lost hope for renewed life, and in its abandonment and return represents the "divine child," that mysterious carrier of hope in the psyche that Jung [22] described as the "urge in every being … to realize itself," being an "incarnation of the inability to do otherwise."

Descent into Nether Hell

After leaving Limbo, as Dante and his guide descend the downward spiraling path towards the pit, the poets encounter a series of increasingly horrifying apparitions that fill them with dread and growing anxiety. Finally, they approach circle nine—the level of deepest evil—and are chilled by a freezing wind, caused by the bat-like wings of Dis himself. As they stumble over the bodies of the damned, frozen into grotesque agonies underfoot, through the icy fog, they get their first glimpse of the Evil One. Dante writes:

> And when we had come so far that it seemed right
> to my dear master, he should let me see

> *that creature fairest once of the sons of light,*
> He moved himself from before me …
> And said, "Behold now Dis!"
>
> How cold I grew, [says Dante] how faint with fearfulness
> Ask me not, Reader; I shall not waste breath
> Telling what words are powerless to express;
> This was not life, and yet it was not death ….[23]

Dante's description captures exactly the death-in-life hopelessness of the sorrowful inner world over which Dis rules—"this was not life, and yet it was not death."

Archetypal Background of Dis

In the quote from Canto 34 (above) Dante describes Dis as that *"creature, fairest once of the sons of light."* This is a reference to Dis's origin as Lucifer, the light-bearer who, by some accounts, was originally God's most resplendent angel, but who fell from heaven before the creation of Adam. The story, based upon Apocryphal literature from the first and second centuries,[24] tells of how Lucifer, God's greatest angel and the bearer of light, discovered that God was planning to create man in his own image. This shocked and disturbed Lucifer because it meant that God's attention was being diverted from Lucifer's splendor and magnificence. Even worse, Lucifer saw that God was planning to come down into the world and be incarnated as a man— man with a fleshly, hairy body—almost an animal. This so outraged him, so offended his identification with the perfection of the Godhead, that he refused to surrender his pride and resolved to rebel against the humiliating plan to incarnate. Together with a group of other rebel angels, he was cast out of heaven and fell farther and farther down towards that ever-receding twilight where Being borders upon Nothing. There, he created for himself a netherworld and put himself in the service of negation rather than creation and so became the great nihilist, Dis.

This genealogy of Dis as the fallen Lucifer helps us to understand what the great refusal at the core of "eternal suffering" is about: *it is a refusal of the incarnation.* In other words, it is a refusal of embodiment, of what Winnicott calls "indwelling." I find this a telling archetypal "explanation" of why old Dis so ruthlessly attacks the links between affect in the body and imagery in the mind as he continually dismembers experience. He was born in a rebellion against the spirit's longing for the body—and so he tries to keep the spirit from embodying wherever he can. He does this because he believes that such embodiment will constitute an annihilation—of himself!

Having left his spiritual home with the Godhead to become a terrorist, he stands at the edge of an even greater hopelessness—an "unthinkable" terror—the black hole of meaninglessness and nullity, the total annihilation of the human spirit. As an archetypal defense, he throws himself into this hole, to plug it. He is the "something" in the gap of nothingness—the last visible bastion of defense against the soul's total annihilation and humiliation. He gives archetypal anxiety a face, turns suffering into violence, and keeps the fragmentation-prone ego in prideful being—ever vigilant, driven to survive, refusing to be broken in a world full of shame and humiliation.

Summary and Conclusions

So in our exploration of Hell, both clinically and archetypally, we have witnessed differing images of hope and hopelessness associated with two different kinds of suffering. There is first the kind of suffering we might call neurotic suffering, which goes on forever, following a repetition compulsion of misery, and which always follows the refusal of another kind of suffering—the suffering necessary to become real. We saw this in Lucifer, when his pride and perfectionism overcame his love for God and he refused to bow to an incarnate deity. We saw it also in Helen, as the space between her incarnating soul and the world was repeatedly foreclosed and she began to dissociate from a suffering that was unbearably traumatic. In this dissociation was a refusal—a refusal by Dis, the fallen angel—a refusal to love because loving would lead to humiliation. The dissociation initially saved her life. But once this bridge was crossed in Helen's inner life, hope was lost because the "space" of creation, symbolization, and embodiment was foreclosed. The same was true for Lucifer. By refusing the creative descent of God into limited, flawed humanity, through love, he inherited a world of a lost hope, where only the shadows of lost love can exist—trapped as the specters of innocent children imprisoned in a Limbo of the undead, where an illusory hope is kept alive through wistful longing. Hoping against hope, we might say. Hoping with only a slim chance of "realization." Realistic Hope is restored to the lost souls in this autistic enclave only when the God-man—the representative of God's love on earth—re-enacts Lucifer's fall into Hades, but voluntarily, by surrendering to human limitation, to the body, and to death, because of his faith in a larger story. In so doing, he breaks open the gates of Hell and liberates the lost souls, twice-born into life again. Here is the God—the counterpart to Dis—who transforms the violence of dissociation into a suffering that can be borne—who holds the opposites, and restores hope.

Dante follows a similar path in his recovery of hope—first down into the pit of disillusionment and hopelessness, but voluntarily and with a witness—then up again, after his encounter with Dis, into the light, where he can begin the climb through Purgatory into Paradise. Like Dante, Helen followed the path of descent into Hell and ascent into wholeness. Plunged into her own living Hell by the repeated foreclosures on her efforts to become herself, she divided into two— one part innocent but weighed down by her feelings of loathsomeness and defilement, hiding in a Limbo of lost hope, embedded in her disowned body—another part ruthlessly alive but inflated with pride and full of hatred for her embodied self. Finally, she let herself fall apart, and this is when she came together—when her lost original wholeness came back with her little girl, and with it the lost hope of her life.

In Helen's process, just as in Dante's image of Hell and Limbo, until the innocent parts of the self—encapsulated and lost—enter the space of becoming and join in the drama of self-realization, hope cannot be born, because the core of personality—the acorn, the soul-child—is kept out of the suffering necessary for humanization. As Helen Luke reminds us in her insightful essay on suffering, only when the innocent part of us begins to suffer can we find our way to the new life and hope that the Christian myth envisions as the resurrection.[25]

All in all, whether hope can be recovered in an individual's life depends to an unexpected degree on human mediation, loving containment, secure attachment, and loving attention to affects-in-the-body. Unless we are loved out of our divinity into our embodied humanity, divinity (operating as archetypal defense) will make our future descent into the body difficult, if not impossible. Winnicott would say that the infant's true-self gesture must be staged repeatedly "within the orbit of omnipotence" in order for omnipotence gradually to be given up. Another way of saying this is that only love can make us whole because only love is willing to risk the loss of perfection implied in each act of incarnation. Love mediates the gap between omnipotence and reality, between "spirit" and "matter." And for those who have had to survive without this mediation, the descent into the body will be resisted at every turn. For some, this resistance will be daimonic.

But the struggle matters profoundly, and as Jung has taught us, one of the places this great struggle is joined in the modern period is in the psychoanalytic transference. Here is one of the places where the foreclosed space of personal becoming will be opened again—or not.

I would like to end with a kind of gnostic reading of the spirit's descent as we have followed it so far. The process of "becoming the self you were intended to be" (Jung's definition of individuation) involves the materialization of something spiritual. Some seed of true selfhood needs to make a perilous journey through very dangerous territory from the world of Eternity to the world of Time, from Spirit to Matter, from Divine to Human *in order to become a human soul*. Along the way, it will face many trials and suffer great disillusionment, and it may never be able to make a full commitment to this hopeful journey if its suffering into reality is too great. It may even find itself split in two by a daimonic force it never reckoned with, part of it becoming cloistered in an autistic enclave without hope. Sometimes—not always—it will be able to return from this dissociated state and enter into life once again. And if, through all the brokenness of the human condition, it finds enough of those sunny days when life seems possible, enough of those "empathic self-objects," secure objects of attachment, and "optimal frustrations" that make love worth the sacrifice of omnipotence, if it makes it to these shores with some of its original divinity intact and not as a false self—then it will have "arrived home from where it started, recognizing it for the first time."[26] This gives us reason to hope.

NOTES

1. A slide-illustrated version of this paper was given at the Barcelona Congress of the IAAP in August, 2004. It appears here in a form modified for print.

2. D. W. Winnicott, "On the Basis for Self in Body," in *Psychoanalytic Explorations*, eds. C. Winnicott, R. Shepherd, and M. Davis (Cambridge Mass: Harvard University Press, 1989), 261-283.

3. In order to disguise the material and protect confidentiality, this case is a composite description of my work with more than one person.

4. Dante Alighieri, *The Divine Comedy, Cantica I, Hell*, trans. Dorothy L. Sayers (New York: Penguin Books, 1978), 85.

5. Sigmund Freud, "The Ego and the Id," in *Standard Edition of the Complete Psychological Works of Sigmund Freud, XIX* (London: Hogarth Press, 1966), 49.

6. C. G. Jung, "Association, dream and hysterical symptoms" (1906), quoted in Bernard Minder, "Sabina Speilrein, Jung's patient at the Burgholzli," *Journal of Analytical Psychology* 46.1 (2001): 45.

7. Dante, 71.

8. W. R. Bion, *Transformations* (London: Heinemann, 1965).

9. Ronald Fairbairn, *Psychoanalytic Studies of the Personality* (London: Routledge and Kegan Paul, 1981).

10. Sandra Edelman, *Turning the Gorgon: A Meditation on Shame* (Woodstock, CT: Spring Publications, 1998).

11. Donald Kalsched, *The Inner World of Trauma: Archetypal Defenses of the Personal Spirit* (London: Routledge, 1996)

12. Heinz Kohut, *The Restoration of the Self* (New York: International Universities Press, 1977), 104.

13. Dante, 286.

14. Neville Symington, *Narcissism: A New Theory* (London: Karnac Books, 1993).

15. Martin Buber, *The Knowledge of Man*, ed. Maurice Friedman (New York: Harper Torchbooks, 1965).

16. S. W. Winnicott, "Transitional Objects and Transitional Phenomena," in *Playing and Reality* (New York: Basic Books, 1971).

17. C. G. Jung, "The Psychology of the Child Archetype," in *The Collected Works of C. G. Jung*, tr. R. F. C. Hull (Princeton: Princeton University Press, 1953), 9 § 1.

18. S. W. Winnicott, "On the Basis for Self in Body," in *Playing and Reality* (New York: Basic Books, 1971), 271.

19. Martin Buber, *The Knowledge of Man*, ed. Maurice Friedman (New York: Harper Torchbooks, 1965).

20. Fairbairn, 59ff.

21. C. G. Jung, "A Farewell Speech," given to the Analytical Psychology Club of New York on Oct. 26, 1937 (unpublished), The Kristine Mann Library of the C. G. Jung Foundation, New York City.

22. Jung, "The Psychology of the Child Archetype," 289.

23. Dante, 285 (emphasis added).

24. See Jeffrey Burton Russell, *The Devil: Perceptions of Evil from Antiquity to Primitive Christianity* (Ithaca, NY: Cornell University Press, 1977).

25. Helen Luke, "Suffering," in *The Way of Woman* (New York: Doubleday, 1995), 56-62.

26. T. S. Eliot, *Four Quartets* (New York: Harcourt, Brace & World, 1971), 59.

Listening to the Body for the Sake of the Soul

ANITA U. GREENE

Introduction

The bare hardwood floor stretched out before me as I waited for an impulse from within to set me in motion. Out of the corner of my eye I noticed Marion Woodman waiting in another part of the room. I suspected she shared a similar anxiety around moving in the company of experienced dancers and dance therapists on that first morning of the Authentic Movement Workshop taking place at Jacob's Pillow in the Berkshires. We had been included through the invitation of Joan Chodorow, who was developing authentic movement as a form of active imagination in her analytic practice. She valued our common Jungian orientation and vision of body as a neglected but essential part of psyche.

Authentic movement encourages a letting-go of consciously planned movement, allowing internal bodily felt signals to initiate

Anita U. Greene, Ph.D., IAAP, is a graduate of the C.G. Institute of New York where she has taught and served on the Board. She is trained in the Rubenfeld Synergy Method,® which combines Alexander and Feldenkrais body techniques. Anita has a private practice in Amherst, Massachusetts, and writes and lectures widely about the integration of body and psyche.

Portions of this paper were presented at the XVI Congress of the International Association for Analytical Psychology, Barcelona, August 2004.

movement. On that first morning the initial anxiety around letting go of control and "letting it happen" turned into an opportunity to explore new ways of activating and expressing the somatic unconscious. In no time Marion and I became indistinguishable from other movers, learning to listen kinesthetically to our inner sensory receptors. Each session was securely held by several seated observers and no session ended without verbalizing what had happened from the perspective of both participants and witnesses.

The shared experience at Jacob's Pillow began a collegial friendship and collaboration that has lasted over twenty years. In 1984 the three of us presented the first workshop on *Body and Psyche* at a National Jungian Conference. In the last decade a new generation of analysts from many countries has joined us in our quest to integrate psyche and soma within the analytic framework. The 2004 Congress at Barcelona with its offerings and pre-Congress movement workshop attests to the growing awareness among Jungians of the reality of the bodily dimension of psyche.

Among modern Jungians, Marion Woodman has been the most vocal about the widespread dissociative relationship to soma in our time. Although she began her work with analysands with eating disorders, who present some of the most obvious cases of alienation from body, she soon enlarged her focus to include both women and men who have grown up in a patriarchal culture that emphasizes spirit and rational thinking over body and connected feeling. She states: "The body work I do is an effort to connect with the unconscious through the body. For me, a bodily symptom is one way of expressing the unconscious. The dream is another way of expressing it."[1] Woodman has encouraged, nay insisted, that her analysands participate in ongoing groups that use various breathing and movement techniques to facilitate a more immediate experience of psyche.

Talk and Touch

I share with Marion Woodman a profound concern for the healing of the psyche-soma split in our culture and in our analytic work. My clinical approach differs from hers in that I work directly with the body part of psyche in the analytic session. Moving from talk to gentle touch techniques in my Jungian practice has become so natural for me that I bristle somewhat at questions from colleagues who are concerned that I might be compromising verbal and symbolic process as well as encouraging enmeshment with patients and possibly jeopardizing my analytic objectivity.

Let me show you how it works with an example: A middle-aged woman, a therapist herself, who has been working with me for several years, brought in a dream about her personal mother in which she could do nothing right. She spoke of the subtle ways in which her mother shamed her around her size and her large extraverted energy. The "too-muchness" of her essential being never felt accepted and so she "dulled" herself down to fit in with what was expected, becoming sensitive to others' needs and denying her own.

Halfway through the session, we moved to the table. I suggested that my patient, who lay on her back, focus on her breathing and attend to what parts of her body responded to mother. As I reached under her shoulders she remarked how they seemed to tighten up every time she mentioned mother. I confirmed that was happening as we continued talking about the dream. I suggested she take a moment to focus on the shoulders. Then she said: "I think there is anger there around the deflating energy of my mother's need for control. But I suspect this is the tightness of my own controlling energy. Who would I be if I could not restrain my intense feelings? We had moved from the external mother to the denigrating aspects of her internalized mother complex. We spent some time discussing the ways she belittled herself over not being a more loyal daughter, loving partner or competent therapist.

I noticed that her breathing was becoming constricted and I sensed or intuited (often I cannot tease them apart) that my hands wanted to move toward her pelvic area. I placed them gently over her belly and suggested she send the breath in under my hands. "Oh, I can't," she replied. "It's solid concrete." Putting my hands alternately under her right and left sides, I waited until I could feel her body allow me to release her hip joints. "The cement's cracking," she said. "I can see a young girl's hand reaching up and the rest of her is struggling to get free. But the harder I try the more stuck she becomes." As my analysand surrendered into her breathing and stopped trying, the cement became softer, and a prepubescent girl sprang out wearing a red dress. "Oh," she declared, "she's a dancer.

No, she's an ice skater. I felt so klutzy then and ashamed of having to wear chubby-size clothes. How can I let that ugly, unwieldy body take center stage, which she clearly wants to do?"

The session was nearly over. We sat down again in our respective chairs as she spoke with some anguish about her rejected "ugly" side. After table work, I may encourage patients to move in whatever way their body-psyche directs. Or, we may sit and reflect on what happened. I always take time to reorient patients to the world to which they must return before they leave the session. Whether I am talking or touching, I work in an embodied way, aware of my subjective bodily states and somatically induced countertransference reactions. The Rubenfeld Synergy Method®, in which I am trained, teaches non–intrusive touch techniques as a tool to explore memories and emotions hidden away in the muscles and tissues of the body.[2] The fingertips, with their 700 touch receptors every 2 millimeters, are extremely sensitive instruments for non-verbal communication. Touch directly links the "cell-consciousness" of both patient and therapist.

In my experience, the greatest gift we can give to our patients is a fully incarnated psyche. A centered, grounded presence creates a neutral and safe container. The non-erotic touch (Rubenfeld calls it "Zen" hands) that I use respects boundaries and, paradoxically, allows an enabling space to develop between analyst and patient for the experiencing of past emotional events in the present moment. I am reminded of Jung's warning to those who take flight into intuitive mysteries: "whatever you experience outside of the body, in a dream, for instance, is not experienced unless you take it into the body, because the body means the here and now."[3]

Reawakening to Touch

More than forty years have passed since my first analyst took my hands and held them as I was leaving the session. During the hour, a dream had reconnected me with a despondent little girl in myself. His appropriately timed touch, expressing concern over my distressed psychic state, brought forth a flood of tears. Unable to stem the tears or the accompanying release of painful memories and emotions, I sought refuge in a nearby park. As I engaged with the four-year-old child, who refused to be stuffed back into the psychic closet, an inner voice spoke: "You have forgotten how primary touch is for experiencing your self." In that moment the imaginal, emotional and sensory dimensions of psyche came together with an alive immediacy that profoundly changed my sense of self. It became the primary motivation behind my exploration of ways to integrate psyche and soma in the context of analytic treatment.

As I became aware of how dissociated I had become from that part of psyche that operates on a somatic level, I realized that no amount of talking or dreaming about body would reunite me with my split-off body complex. In addition to my Jungian analysis, I began working with Charlotte Selver, a pioneer in the area of sensory awareness, as well as taking classes in expressive movement. At the same time I began "psychic" training at the Jung Institute in New York, I entered Ilana Rubenfeld's "somatic" training program in the same city. Body awareness cannot be taught verbally. To touch another requires a sensitive kinesthetic awareness of one's own bodily blocks and tensions in order to avoid bringing them to the patient, in much the same manner as a good analytical training exposes and neutralizes one's complexes to avoid contaminating the psychic container. Let me be clear. Analysts should not use touch techniques unless they are willing to spend several years in a body training program experiencing how their bodies mirror the psychic complexes and are conveyed through nonverbal language to others.

Jung describes the unconscious complex as having a somatic aspect that locates itself in our flesh and bones. It cannot be ignored because it irritates the tissues and pulls at the nerves. In 1936, he stated it most succinctly: "The separation of psychology from the basic assumptions of biology is purely artificial, because the human psyche lives in indissoluble union with the body."[4] When I first began integrating body and psyche in my practice, I found only one article written by a modern Jungian that seriously considered the use of touch within the analytic setting. In 1970, Camilla Bosanquet questioned whether the lack of consciousness around nonverbal communication and ambivalence toward touching on the part of analysts may deprive patients of a valuable means of communication, including all the associations attached to the act of touching and being touched.[5]

The blind spot of Jungian analysts, many of whom are both introverted and intuitive, is their tendency to attribute the highest conscious value to image and imagination, in effect, downplaying the somatic dimension of psyche. Although Jung intuitively understood that transcending the present level of consciousness involves acknowledging the body, he reveals his bias toward the ultraviolet, imagistic pole of the body-mind continuum when he argues that the "realization and assimilation of instinct" can never take place at the infrared end of the psychoid spectrum but only through the "integration of the image which signifies and at the same time evokes the instinct."[6] My clinical work demonstrates that psyche can be directly approached and assimilated through the infrared instinctual pole by an embodied processing that involves becoming aware of what the somatic unconscious is saying with its tensions, blocks, and interruptions in the flow of energy. Paying attention to an ache in the head can reveal as much about psyche as confronting a frightening figure in a dream. Both involve a dialogical and symbolic intrapsychic process that moves us beyond immediate experience to underlying meaning.

Case Example

A middle-aged woman came to work with me at a crucial transitional stage in her life. Her three children were old enough to allow her the luxury of either taking a full-time job or going back to school to train for a much desired career in the helping professions. Her husband supported her in this endeavor. She grew up in a conventional middle-class family and remembered no warm intimate moments with either parent. She was bright and capable, and had learned at an early age to hide her underlying need for dependence under a mask of achievement and an independent persona. During the first session, she wondered if her chronic migraines might thwart her plans for professional training. "They have been a painful companion since I was a small child, striking me unexpectedly about once a month and putting me out of commission for three days. I would like to do some body work with you but I don't expect anything to change." As we probed more deeply into her relationship to her mother, she recalled that those three days in a darkened room, painful though they were, were the only times she had mother all to herself. My gentle touching of her head brought forth a deep-seated sadness, but no tears, until one session, when she arrived with the remnants of a migraine, vulnerable and despairing. As I held her head (perhaps evoking the lost mother's presence), encouraging her to allow the pain to be felt, she had an image of herself at the age of four, muffling her sobs in a pillow. Then she remembered that was the time she vowed never to let her mother know what she was feeling. We discussed the possibility that her headaches might be the result of the pressure of unexpressed emotion, which could find release only in a throbbing migraine.

We returned to the four-year-old again and again. Touch grounded my patient in the present moment, providing a safe reliving of both the rage and grief around the devaluation of her intense feeling nature. The migraines lessened and gradually disappeared as my analysand allowed strong feelings to surface and be expressed before they could become caught in the head.

Body as "Doubtful Friend"

Jung called the body a "doubtful friend ... the personification of this shadow of the ego" when he described body as a repository of those aspects of oneself that the ego has rejected as negative and shameful.[6] Early in her work with analysands with eating disorders, Woodman observed how distorted such patients' images were of their bodies and how they failed to identify or accurately perceive sensory information. She writes: "Pretending there is no body, or treating it with indifference, is pretending there is no shadow."[7] Chodorow believes there is a vital link between memory and movement. "By attending to the world of bodily felt sensations, the mover recreates a situation that is in many ways similar to that of an infant who swims in a sensory-motor world."[10] Embodied sensory experience releases kinesthetically stored, often preverbal, and affect-laden memories of childhood. The immediacy of the bodily experience (the here and now) provides a secure container for accessing and handling intense affective reactions at the core of repressed complexes and permits better toleration of the inevitable frustrations inherent in ego development and differentiation. The body may be a "doubtful friend" in the way it discomforts us with primitive affect and embarrasses us with unpredictable behavior, but it can tell the truth about us more honestly and directly than the more polished and verbal rational persona often permits.

Reading the Body-Psyche

As analysts, we do not have to use movement or touch techniques to become more observant of the nonverbal language that confronts us daily in our consulting rooms. Crucial diagnostic information is conveyed by the way a patient enters the office, greets the analyst, sits in a chair, meets or avoids the eye, gestures, or changes posture. For example, one woman in her initial session tiptoed around me and sat rather tentatively in the chair as though she were trying to avoid my energy field. The undercharged nature of her energy and the lack of muscularity in her legs revealed to me that this woman had probably never experienced the ability to stand her ground vis-à-vis the other. The aura of hesitancy and weakness in her body suggested an early deprivation of maternal support, which was indeed the case. She was completely unconscious of what her body-psyche was communicating to me about the exact nature of the psychic complexes we would be confronting in the analytic work.

Dissonance between verbal and body language reveals shadow. I call them "slips of the body." After working with a dream which contained a scene with gangster types acting rather sadistically toward several women, an overly compliant male analysand straightened up in his chair, held his breath, and struggled to remain calm. Although his tone of voice was pleasant and indicated agreement with my interpretation of the dream, I noticed that his hands, palms down on the top of his thighs, began to move toward the knees and clench into fists at the end of the movement. At the same time I noticed my own jaws and shoulders tightening, an indication to me of somatically induced anger. When I asked him to exaggerate his hand motions, he looked at me in surprise. "What hand motions?" He looked down and repeated the movement. He admitted with some embarrassment that he was angry with me for "insinuating" that he could harbor such feelings toward women. He was trying to "wipe me off." The atmosphere cleared immediately and we were able to engage more directly with what was actually happening between us. Resistance palpably experienced on a bodily level cannot be so easily denied, and, in fact, is more readily acknowledged.

Another way to invoke the body-psyche is to embody characters in dreams. A male analysand in his late thirties presented a dream in which two men were fighting in hand-to-hand combat. From the image in the dream we both concurred that the "winner" of the struggle seemed to be the man standing with his hands on his hips looking down with some contempt on the "loser" who was squatting, with his feet spread apart, looking up with a slight smile on his face. When I suggested that he put his own body into each of the combatants' postures, he discovered just the opposite to be true. The "winner's" stance was actually more precarious and off-balance than the "loser's" squatting position, which was closer to the earth, well-grounded, and more powerful. Embodying the postures led my analysand into a surprisingly different way of understanding the meaning of the dream. To the "winner" he now associated verbal and intellectual arrogance; to the "loser," an animal-like shrewdness that could topple the arrogant man with one well-timed lunge. The dream offered a description of the battle within himself, couched in non-intellectual images of hand-to-hand combat. The patient's overvaluation of his intellectual prowess and rational approach to emotional issues was being challenged, up-ended, in fact, by a more instinctual, earthy shadow figure.

Needless to say, we as analysts are not exempt from unconscious body language that may speak more loudly than our words. If therapists do not live comfortably in their own bodies, they cannot help patients live comfortably in theirs. When therapists' posture, facial expressions, gestures, and voice level convey reactions dissonant with their verbal communication, they sow confusion, at the least, and alienation when the nonverbal messages are not owned. When a patient says to me, "Why are you frowning?" I take that seriously. First, I own it. Then I explore what is happening inside of me as well as what the frown is saying to the patient. Defensiveness on the part of the analyst or anxiety around what the analysand is revealing is communicated immediately through subtle body language.

Body-Mind Connection

With great prescience, Jung stated in 1912: "It seems highly probable that the psychic and physical are not two independent parallel processes, but are essentially connected through reciprocal action."[11] For several decades, disciplines in the neurosciences have been demonstrating the fundamental error of Cartesian dualism.

Jungians need to pay attention to what psychoneuroimmunologists, such as Candace Pert, have discovered in their research. She asserts that we are psychosomatic information networks. She demonstrates how the neuropeptides and their receptors, found in all systems of the body, are the biological underpinnings of our capacity for consciousness. In her book, *Molecules of Emotion,* Pert writes: "Mind doesn't dominate body, it *becomes* body—body and mind are one—Thus, it could be said that intelligence is located not only in the brain but in cells that are distributed throughout the body."[12]

The research of the neuroscientist, Antonio Damasio, on patients with frontal lobe damage alerted him to how interconnected cognitive and emotional deficits are in the behavior of such patients. In his book, *The Feeling of What Happens: Body and Emotion in the Making of Consciousness,* he demonstrates how, from a neurological point of view, the split between reason and emotion is a fallacy. Damasio declared in a recent interview: "The mind exists for the body, is engaged in telling the story of the body's multifarious events, and uses that story to optimize the life of the organism."[13]

Scientific discoveries investigating the limbic brain are revealing its crucial involvement in precognitive emotional conditioning and regulation. Our nervous systems are not self-contained, but depend on the development of these two functions through wordless interactive interplay with the nervous systems of our primary caregivers. Emotional response patterns are set long before cognitive brain functions emege. In their book, *A General Theory of Love,* three psychiatrists boldly present another paradigm of therapy. They write: "The mind-body clash has disguised the truth that psychotherapy *is* physiology. When a person starts therapy, he isn't beginning a pale conversation; he is stepping into a somatic state of relatedness."[14] Their use of such terms as "limbic resonance" and "limbic regulation" reveal their belief that transformative change in psychotherapy comes from working at this level of psyche. I believe that Jung's concept of the psychoid unconscious demonstrates his underlying assumption about the intimate interaction between psyche and soma.

Affects as a presymbolic mode of experiencing oneself and their early role in shaping psyche are being explored in psychoanalytic literature. In the light of the recent research, Jung was remarkably ahead of his time when he stated in 1907: "The essential basis of our personality is affectivity. Thought and action are, as it were, only symptoms of affectivity."[15] Jung's experiments with the Word Association Test revealed to him the interconnectedness of mind and body. He observed that when an unconscious complex was activated in a subject, the intense feeling tone at its center produced a perseverating and cumulative effect on *both* body and psyche. I am indebted to my late colleague, Lewis H. Stewart, for filling in the gaps in Jungian theory around the nature and function of specific affects. Drawing on previous research into innate affects, Stewart formulated a system of seven archetypal affects, such as anger and shame, which have universal forms of facial expression and bodily innervations.[16] They dynamically link the psychic and somatic experiencing of both analyst and analysand. Becoming aware of somatic cues, e.g., a tightness in the chest or an empty feeling in the stomach, can alert an analyst to the presence of a repressed affect operating beneath the verbal communication.

The few studies mentioned above are representative of the many hundreds of others confirming the interrelationship between body and mind. Our emotional history, our capacity to relate to others, our belief systems, our deepest sense of self (all soul concerns) are inseparable from the life of the body. Integrating some form of body awareness into the therapeutic process does not, ultimately, have to do with learning touch or movement skills, nor is it about whether to hug patients or hold their hands; it is about analysts becoming attuned to their own and their patients' somatic communications. Both can remain firmly seated in their own chairs. Tension in the spine, a tight pelvis, cramped breathing, a stiff neck inhibit somatic processing, as I discovered when I became aware I was sitting in the wrong type of chair. After many tries, I located a chair that supported the underside of the thighs at the height of the knees with a back that held rather than enveloped my lower back. Sitting more comfortably in the cradle of my pelvis, legs uncrossed, feet resting securely on the floor, I noted that I felt more grounded and present to myself. Tightness in the jaw and eye muscles indicated to me how I had correlated those tensions with paying attention. I noticed how eyes resting easily in their sockets have a more inclusive and integrative vision than eyes with a forced focus.

To sharpen my perceptual awareness of the body-psyche of analysands, I ask such questions as: Are they living comfortably in their bodily home? Do they allow the earth to support them or do they hold parts of themselves up? How flexible or rigid are they around head and neck, shoulders and arms, upper and lower torso, pelvis and legs, ankles and feet? Do the body parts fit together in a coordinated way? Do imbalances occur between the right and left, the top and bottom, the front and back parts of the body?[17]

Is the breathing pattern free or constricted? The way we breathe is directly related to available energy to live life fully. So close is the connection between breathing and the quality of one's psychic state that it can be used as a tool for helping analysands focus on their immediate physical and emotional reality.

Breathing and Soul State

I n yogic traditions, the air we breathe contains not just the oxygen we need to sustain physiological life but a life force vital to our sense of wellbeing. Except during vigorous exercise, most of us breathe with much less than our full capacity. We all have experienced how breathing reflects our emotional condition. Breathing becomes agitated when we are angry, stilled when fearful, heaving when grieving, held when shamed, accelerated when joyful. Any experience of anxiety inhibits deep inhalation and exhalation. One woman patient who spoke with a rapid, breathless pace, refused to slow down when I suggested she pause to take a deep breath. After several such suggestions, she yelled at me. "I don't want to breathe. There are certain things I don't want to feel!" Shallow breathing protects us from a chance meeting with disturbing emotional content.

Breathing is closely linked to two different kinds of nervous systems: the autonomic system, which allows us to breathe spontaneously without conscious planning, and the voluntary system, which gives us intentional control over breathing. This interrelationship makes breath a kind of gateway between conscious and unconscious processes. Madelene Proskauer, a breath therapist with a Jungian background, uses breath as a tool in raising somatic consciousness. She remarks that focusing on breath is a way of doing active imagination in the body.[18] Inner images and disquieting feelings, held in by constrained breathing, will often arise spontaneously to consciousness when one's breath can flow in a more natural rhythm.

Case Examples

As I observed the expanded and rigid chest area of one male analysand, I realized that he was a man who could take air in but not allow the muscles around the rib cage to relax in full exhalation. I experienced his resistance to exhaling fully in my own breathing, which became tight and constricted, a somatically induced countertransference, which alerted me to the control he needed to exert over every aspect of his life. He had rebelled against an oppressive family, created a successful business, and prided himself on his aggressive managerial style. He had sought therapeutic help rather reluctantly when his wife threatened to leave him if he did not find a way to relate more empathically to her and the children. When some trust had been established, I asked him what might happen if he put his hand on his chest and breathed out slowly. He experienced such extreme anxiety that we had to proceed very slowly over several sessions. The sensation, he said, as he exhaled, was one of falling into a black void with no bottom. Compulsive doing had given this particular man a sense of purpose and accomplishment. Letting go of his breath corresponded to letting go of his controlled sense of self. He did reach bottom and discovered a needy and angry two-year-old boy partly buried under a pile of debris.

A middle-aged woman let her body sink back into the chair. Her sunken chest and slow belly breathing revealed a woman who seemed to remain in a constant state of exhalation. She came to me because she could not pull herself out of a deep depression. Her inabililty to breathe in and expand her chest accurately reflected her deflated sense of self that could not mobilize the self-assertive energies necessary to move her life in a more creative and focused direction. At times I noticed that my own inbreath became shallow, as though my body-psyche were mirroring her condition. As each session began, she collapsed in the chair and continued her dreary tale of a critical mother and a father who forced her to massage his head and feet. When I suggested she try sitting up and breathing in, she replied somewhat testily, "Oh, I can't. That would take too much effort." I replied: "Can you exaggerate your present posture and tell me what it is saying?" Reluctantly, she admitted: "I want you to do all the work. Don't expect me to take any active part in the therapy." As my jaw tightened I sensed the repressed rage underneath her slumped posture. I anticipated, correctly, that until she could own, feel, and express this anger, she would not be able to take a full breath or mobilize her energy to move forward.

Working with breath often brings up childhood memories. As he began to inhale more deeply, a young male analysand remembered how long he could hold his breath under water. "I feel strong when I can hold on to myself." As he exhaled, he observed how his chest softened and his center of gravity moved down into the pelvis where he encountered a ten-year-old boy who was trying not to cry. He remembered being called a "crybaby" by his father during a particularly traumatic move to another part of the country. "I feel weak when I'm down in my belly." The patient wondered if the upper half of his body had matured into adulthood while the lower half was still stuck in the shameful "sissy" feelings of his ten-year-old self. Acknowledging his emotionally wounded little boy was the beginning of some fruitful analytic work. Learning to reparent his genuine, but repressed, feeling side provided this young man with a more secure sense of his masculine identity and potency, which he sorely needed in his workplace and in his relationship to women.

Conclusion

Imaginal processing works with the images and affects that arise spontaneously out of patients' dreams, fantasies, and artistic products during the course of analysis. It can release emotions but tends to ignore body-based reactions. Embodied processing involves awareness of what the somatic unconscious is saying with its tensions, blocks, and interruptions in the flow of energy. Although it begins with a physical sensation, it often transforms that sensation into a feeling or image so that the border between imaginal and embodied modes of experience is blurred, at which point their reciprocal relationship becomes apparent. *Both* are symbolic ways of working. Each mode complements the other. The imaginal approach to psyche needs the grounding effect of embodied awareness to bring the intuitive insight into the present moment of actual experience. The embodied approach to psyche needs the expansive effect of imaginal awareness to allow the sensate insight to take flight into the mythopoeic dimension of experience.

Western civilization, for much of the 20th century, seems to have forgotten what Jung recognized as a "factor ... which mediates between the apparent incommensurability of body and psyche, giving matter a kind of 'psychic' faculty and the psyche a kind of 'materiality', by means of which *one can work on the other*"[19] (emphasis added). Body that is regarded as only flesh, bone, sinew—*materia*—is still caught in the old idea of the body/mind antithesis. To introduce somatic awareness and body techniques into the analytic framework is *not* to introduce a suspect or alien element. Rather, it is to heal a split that has haunted the analytic process for generations.

NOTES

1. Marion Woodman, "An Interview with Marion Woodman," *The Round Table Review* 2.5 (1995).

2. Ilana Rubenfeld, *The Listening Hand: Self-Healing Through the Rubenfeld Synergy Method of Talk and Touch* (New York: Bantam Books, 2000).

3. C. G. Jung (1934), *The Visions Seminars*, Vol. 2 (Zurich: Spring Publications, 1976), 475.

4. C. G. Jung (1936), "Psychological Factors Determining Human Behavior," *Collected Works* 8 § 232 (Princeton: Princeton University Press).

5. Camilla Bosanquet, "Getting in Touch," *Journal of Analytical Psychology* 15.1 (1970): 56.

6. C. G. Jung (1946), "On the Nature of the Psyche," *Collected Works* 8 § 414.

7. C. G. Jung (1935), "The Tavistock Lectures," *Collected Works* 18 § 40.

8. Marion Woodman, *Addiction to Perfection: The Still Unravished Bride—A Psychological Study* (Toronto: Inner City Books, 1982), 78.

9. Joan Chodorow, "The Body as Symbol: Dance/Movement in Analysis," in *The Body in Analysis*, eds. N. Schwartz-Salant and M. Stein (Wilmette, Illinois: Chiron Publications, 1986), 97.

10. C. G. Jung, (1912), "On Psychic Energy," *Collected Works* 8 § 33.

11. Candace B. Pert, *Molecules of Emotion: The Science Behind Mind-Body Medicine* (New York: Scribner, 1997), 187.

12. Antonio Damasio, "I feel, therefore I am: a thinker reunites mind and body," E. Eakin (interviewer), *New York Times*, April 19, 2003.

13. Thomas Lewis, Fari Amini, and Richard Lannon, *A General Theory of Love* (New York: Vintage Books, 2000).

14. C. G. Jung (1907), "The Psychology of Dementia Praecox," *Collected Works* 3 § 78.

15. Lewis H. Stewart, "Affect and archetype in analysis," in *Archetypal Processes in Psychotherapy*, eds., N. Schwartz-Salant and M. Stein (Illinois: Chiron Publications, 1987), 131-162.

16. Anita U. Greene, "Conscious Mind—Conscious Body," *Journal of Analytical Psychology* 46 (2001): 575.

17. Madeline Proskauer, "The Relationship Between Body and Psyche as it Manifests in My Work," *The Journal of Biological Experience: Studies in the Life of the Body* 2 (1980): 56-62.

18. C. G. Jung (1959), "Flying Saucers in Modern Myth," *Collected Works* 10 § 780.

Wounded Instincts, Weeping Soul:
Working with Embodied
Countertransference

JACQUELINE GERSON

In the course of my clinical work, beginning as a therapist employing movement, music, and art, and later learning to incorporate these elements into verbal analytical psychotherapy, I came to encounter, in a number of female patients, a series of anguished voices that sounded in my mind like one collage of feminine cries. This sound, accumulated in the bodies of the women I was attending to, carried the symptoms of lifetime stories of ongoing deep wounding, and I felt confronted by a similar desolate voice in myself. This was a strong countertransference experience that made my body feel burdened. Moving was difficult, and added to that was a lack of vision that was foreign to my intuitive soul. Instead of the guiding images I was used to, questions took my mind. I started thinking: how severe can the damage to the feminine be? How deep is the sort of wound that I find my mind feeling into, as I participate in the mysterious realms of interrupted life, survival, and

Jacqueline Gerson is a Jungian analyst with a private practice in Mexico City. She is a Founding Member of the Asociación Mexicana de Analistas Junguianos. She has previously been published in *The San Francisco Jung Institute Library Journal* and with Daimon Verlag.

death that my women patients regularly traverse. Why is it necessary for women who individuate to come so close to the problem of death?

I re-read Mexican writer Jaime Sabines's beautiful poem about death to see if I could draw some inspiration from it:

> What a savage custom this is—burying the dead! Killing them, annihilating them, wiping them off the face of earth! It treats them treacherously, denies them the possibility of reviving.
>
> I am always waiting for the dead to rise, to break open the coffin and say with joy: Why are you crying?
>
> ...
>
> I laugh—at the wreaths, the flowers, the weeping, the profusion of kisses. It's a jest: Why did you bury it? Why didn't you leave it outside until its body dried up, until its bones started speaking to us about the death? Why not burn it, or give it to the animals, or throw it into a river?
>
> We should have a rest house for the dead, ventilated, clean, with music and running water. Each day, at least two or three would come back to life.[1] (My translation.)

Sabines's poem re-kindled my hope. It enabled me to feel in myself the faith that for years only my analyst could carry for me, finally bringing me to where I am, a Jungian analyst myself, bearing witness to her own "dead" aspects, "standing up and coming back to life," and working out of my own wound as a woman. I have become someone who can offer a "rest house for the dead," someone charged with sealing the container in which people can "revive" their sense of meaning in life. I often see them do this. But in my analytic office I also am forced to observe the "savage custom of burying the dead" and of trying "to wipe them from the face of the earth." I observe this whenever archetypal defenses of the Self arise in someone filled with fear, for whom "each new life opportunity is mistakenly seen as a dangerous threat of re-traumatization and is therefore attacked."[2] "In this way," Kalsched tells us, "the archaic defenses become anti-life forces which Freud understandably thought of as part of the death instinct."[3]

As an example of the kind of death process that I have had to learn to carry as a woman analyst in an embodied way, let me describe the case of a forty-five-year-old woman whom I will call Ruth. She has been in analysis for seven years and has "brought to life" many different aspects of herself. Often she has presented to me a life that seemed to be flowing. She has described reading a lot, taking interesting courses, traveling, attaining a stable and comfortable financial position, developing warmer relationships with her children, and even taking pleasure in encounters with friends, although these occur only seldom. A lot of work had been done to bring Ruth to this amount of bloom, and she is very committed to her individuation process. Nevertheless, not long ago, one day near the end of a session, I heard her say in an obscure but authoritative tone of voice: "You know Jackie, after all, I feel no joy."

In this remark, I heard once more the despair so many of my female patients have voiced at one time or another, to the point that I now experience it as their common complaint: How much more? How long will it take? Knowing that these questions are really manifesting my client's deep pain in the face of persisting archaic defenses that have become hardened anti-life (and therefore anti-feminine) forces, and that she has been unable to find an answer in herself as to how to soften them, I experience a strong countertransferential feeling of deep sadness. I reply, as if to her and all her sisters, in a voice that is also not just my own: "I don't know how long, but I do believe that it is possible, and I will be with you for as long as it takes. You are not alone."

Following this session, I searched for the meaning of Joy and read in Stewart's helpful essay on "Affect and Archetype in Analysis" that "... the affects of Joy-Ecstasy (representing Eros) and Interest-Excitement (representing Logos), function as twin dynamisms of the life instinct, making it certain that newborn mammals, and particularly humans, will enter the world with joie de vivre and divine curiosity. This assures an active engagement with the world through which the fundamentals for survival are acquired."[4]

It was this "joie de vivre" that Ruth was telling me she lacked when she said: "After all, I feel no joy."

Her confession of a lack of connection to the life instinct was, for me, a shocking outcome of our years together. Working with Ruth has been an exciting intellectual adventure. She is a bright and very spirited woman with whom talking has been a profoundly interesting experience. She often shares her readings of different books, giving me generous selections of the author's ideas, which she can quote by heart. She often questions me as to whether I have already read this and that, making me feel too slow and dull for her enquiring and restless mind, which has always seemed to me, if anything, too alive. Just keeping up with her has been a challenging experience. This "Athenian aspect"[5] in Ruth has at times seduced my own mind with fascinating recountings of her interests that have kept us both engaged. Nevertheless, when I heard from Ruth about the actual lack of joy in her life, even though it took my mind by surprise, I recognized that I had already felt just this in my own body over the years of working with her.

It was really through embodied countertransference feelings that I was able to accept Ruth's communication that there is a profound lack of joy in her life. I particularly remember coming to the end of one of our earlier sessions and feeling my body go completely numb. There was just no feeling, no flowing of affect; it seemed as though my blood could have stopped running and no matter how active my mind continued to be, my body would remain profoundly asleep, to the point of death. I realized then that I would have to recuperate my body myself. I had to find a way of connecting with some source of vitality in order for my blood to start flowing enough again just to be able to stand up and walk, and I knew that that source was not to be found in Ruth. In fact, Ruth had mentioned numbness in her own body, for which she seemed to be turning to me for release. I was thus in a kind of "*participation mystique*" with her disconnection from the vitality affects.

I wondered: What happened in Ruth's life to make archaic defenses of the self arise and become anti-life forces with the power to suppress her "joie de vivre"? And what did it mean that in the countertransference I was able to feel this problem only in my body, without the capacity to reflect on this important lack in a cognitive, thinking way?

The second question is perhaps the easier one to answer. Caroline Myss, in *Anatomy of the Spirit*, says: "Sometimes the body responds emotionally and manufactures emotional chemicals (neuropeptides) even before the brain has registered a problem."[6] Analytical psychology needs to take seriously the fact that the capacity to think is a later developmental achievement, appearing long after the first awareness of embodied feelings.

Similarly, Damasio, inquiring into the purpose of feelings, in *Looking for Spinoza: Joy, Sorrow, and the Feeling Brain,* writes:

> ... [F]eelings can be mental sensors of the organism's interior, witnesses of life. ... [T]hey let our fleeting and narrow conscious self know about the current state of life in the organism for a brief period. ... [They refer] to the harmony or discord deep in the flesh. Joy and sorrow and other feelings are largely ideas of the body in the process of maneuvering itself into states of optimal survival. Joy and sorrow are mental revelations of the state of the life process.[7]

So, too, embodied countertransferential feelings reflect the state of the life process in an analysand as evoked in the body of the analyst. They arise as a compensatory response to the devouring Logos of a neurotic state of mind. It was only in my body that the problem of vitality at the core of Ruth's animus possession *could* exist. In the mind she was sharing with me, life data were entirely overridden by her most inquiring intellect, with its superb logic and its corollary requirement that her life justify the theory, which left no room for her simply to be. According to Ruth, her life had to become reasonable[8] at whatever cost: it had to become knowledge—of herself, of the psychological aspects of her mind, and of life itself. So her actual, non-theoretical experiential process was kept in *my* body. There, and there only, was it able to go on existing. Not through words, that is, not by using any Logos of my own would I have been able to grasp that I was containing something so precious and so much at risk. Critical to the success of the therapy was that it not be a theory I had, but her own individual and unique process, located for safekeeping in me, that would guide us to create her real "opus" in analysis. There had, thus, for a time, to be a split—really a division of labor, in which she was carrying the mind, while I carried the body. This was so that eventually there could be "a reciprocity in which conscious and unconscious, mind and matter, [could be] joined to produce a third. That third [was] the meeting of body and spirit bringing with it an act of joyous recognition."[9]

It was only after seven years, which both of us had to survive—Ruth enduring the frustration of my "slow" mind and process and I enduring the perplexing numbness of my body whenever I was with her—that she was able to make her all-important confession: "You

know Jackie, after all I feel no joy." This admission that our work
had not connected her with her vitality was less a signal to me that
we had failed than an announcement of Ruth's capacity for trusting,
and I was ready to embrace it. She then proceeded to share with me
for the first time a very old image that went back to her childhood,
one that she had never previously told anyone, not her previous
therapists and not even her remarkable professors. This image belongs
to a deep fantasy that had taken root in her psyche very early. Though
it is unlikely that the events of the fantasy happened literally, she
remembers them as very real, and so they were to me when she
recounted them:

> *When I was a small girl, I was taken to a place where North Americans
> lived, a place where industrial residues were also processed. I was going
> there to visit a friend, and other girls were there too, maybe for a party or to
> camp out together. I, instead of blending into the group, separated from the
> gathering and wandered to a place farther away, where there was a lake, a
> big lake. I wanted to throw myself into the water to swim. On the other side
> of the lake, there was a small dog barking happily. Though I had the
> impulse to do so, the dog was the one that actually threw himself into the
> water. I then saw him frantically trying to get away from the water, but
> instead, before my eyes, he dissolved and died, because it was poisonous
> water. It had residues from manufactured materials and so ended up being
> very dangerous. When I saw the dog die, I felt sad, but at the same time, I
> was relieved that I was not the one that died and that he had been sacrificed
> for me. To this day it feels strange that there was no protection around the
> lake, since it obviously contained toxic water.*

I believe this memory, which a psychoanalyst might call a screen
memory, encapsulates a great deal of Ruth's psychological history. Since
she was very young, Ruth has felt a strong impulse towards
individuation, so in the remembered incident, she separates from the
crowd. This is an authentic movement of detachment into an individual
journey of consciousness to be lived. She does not settle for blind
conformity and collective participation, as would have been enough
for many another girl invited to a party with her friends. Even after
seven years of analytic work with me, Ruth often feels a restlessness to
go beyond what meeting with me can naturally provide. She has a
constant striving to know and understand more, which is what I believe

brought her to analysis in the first place. Her need to separate from what is happening around her in order to keep her striving stance has an individualistic tone, one that leaves her feeling, and actually being, quite lonely. This is and is not the same as the suffering that goes with individuation. As Ulanov has said, "In Jung's thought, individuation contrasts sharply with individualism—the realization of self at the expense of others. Becoming all of oneself (individuation), with all the parts, ugly, underdeveloped, as well as superior and skilled, can only occur in relation to each other and to the collective, which is to say to the group, to society, to the human family."[10]

Ruth's memory is thus in a sense a screen for the entire journey that Ruth has been on since her early childhood. In the course of it, like other Mexican people I have analyzed, she has often had to consider the shadow side of the cultures surrounding her. We Mexicans are frequently forced to absorb all kinds of carelessly handled unprocessed cultural "residues" from our neighbors to the north and south, residues that then ferment in us to produce acidic, toxic material in our unconscious. Even more broadly, many women in our time have become witness to a global degradation of the feminine, which is also toxic in its consequences. Represented by the lake, this is the fresh water bounded by earth, water that has become acidic and poisoned, no longer the water of life. We can speak of this toxic water that destroys rather than sustains as representing a negative form of the father's *anima,*[11] a caustic patriarchal anima in which life can only dissolve.

In listening to Ruth's unique story, I learned that throughout his life, her father had consistently brought a characteristic approach to life events, particularly to family crises: far from attending to and caring for life's movements, he refused to process them, preferring, instead, to vanish—often for months at a time—until the crisis had "dissolved and died." He simply abandoned the family affects ("residues"), leaving behind a toxic anima for someone else to deal with. It was in this noxious environment that Ruth grew up, an environment in which Eros and trust are destroyed in a most undermining way.

On a practical level, it was Ruth, as the eldest of five children, who was left to take care of the conscious situation in the home. She had to take over not only for her father but for her mother as well. Ruth's mother, who was eventually diagnosed with severe borderline personality disorder, was so narcissistically vulnerable that when faced with abandonment, real or perceived, she would be plunged into disastrous confusion, which she would compensate for with ruthless aggression and profound contempt, usually directed physically or verbally at one of her children. Ruth, ever forward thinking, took it on herself to protect her siblings by taking the load off their mother. In this way, Ruth's strong connection with the Great Mother became established vis-à-vis the Witch aspect of the same archetype, even as her unreflected trust and faith in life were being dissolved in the acidic waters of her father's abandoned, fermenting anima. In consequence, Ruth's attitude towards the world itself became corrosive, even though she positioned herself as its rescuer. Hers was an heroic version of the negative mother complex.[12] Woodman writes that

> the negative mother does not want the individual to develop personally, she doesn't want joy, creative excitement, or freedom around her …. The possibility of enjoying oneself—in work or play—is a dangerous zone that has to be foreseen and dealt with consciously; otherwise the complex takes over with its dark pall of duty.[13]

A person with a negative mother complex like Ruth's has an animus that insists she override her instincts to ensure a safe outcome. What arose in Ruth was a suspicious attitude toward the world, which led her to question everything intellectually. Her capacity to be playful, smiling, "wagging her tail" with trust in the environment around her to more or less take care of her as she did so, simply dissolved. At the same time, she would go right on being the dutiful dog that would swim right into the toxic family environment, suffering and complaining bitterly as she did so.

There is a religious problem at the core of such a constellation of internalized negativity. Von Franz writes that

> the mother goddess who has been ignored appears as a personification of hurt feelings, vanity, or resentment. She is the personification of feelings which have turned sour—milk which has turned sour ….
>
> The source of things going wrong, and of evil in women … is that archetypal reaction of not getting over a hurt, or resentment, or a bad mood, through being disappointed in the feeling realm, and then being overpowered by the animus.[14]

I have many times heard from Ruth her very profound longing to be able to relate in a loving way to her parents. By now, they have already become old, but she still has not been able to appreciate how she has channeled her loving response to them entirely into dutiful action. Ruth tells me she loves them even as they are, but Ruth's is a Logos mode of love. The Eros in her extraverted thinking, which would be the other basic dynamism of the life instinct, is too severely wounded in her to function in a way that could give her and her parents simple pleasures of daily interactions of the kind that other families can often enjoy in the midst of difficulties.

The parents seem to be seeking some of this when they make requests of Ruth, which they do constantly. But she responds to their dependency and bids for attention entirely in a concrete, duty-bound, direct problem-solving way. Ruth has told me, "You know me Jackie. It only has to be said, and I will do it." And I think to myself: if there could only be some joy, she would also discover the love that can accompany one's doing. Often, I have observed that Ruth "does" what is not even asked for by anyone. Naturally enough, when she has actively and committedly done whatever she imagines will take care of different situations (and she is often helpful, with an impeccable logic based on a well defined strategy), Ruth is left with resentful feelings. She will speak to me bitterly about "having to solve something because I know how to do it."

Outside the family, Ruth has a reputation for being resourceful and efficient. Within her family, however, she is many times confronted with the impossibility of proceeding with what she reasonably believes has to be done. That is hard for her. It awakens the impotent and hurt little girl stuck with having to take care of a chronically dysfunctional household while processing emotionally contaminated residues that were never taken care of, usually an impossible task. Trying to cope with that task tends to constellate the unsatisfactory inner parental figures—the father who disappears and the mother who is too ambivalent to relate to what's been left for her to solve. When the inner figures take possession of Ruth, she abandons and refuses the world around her and becomes filled with contempt for herself for not finding any joy in her life.

Recently, Ruth told me about a situation that came up in relation to caring for her father. He had been turning to her brothers and sisters to assist him in a very complicated business matter. Instead of acknowledging Ruth's skills and asking her for help, or at least including her in the discussions around what to do, he strikingly avoided consulting her. That was an important narcissistic blow, and I felt in the following sessions with Ruth that we had now arrived at the bones, and, to use the imagery of the poet Sabines, her bones were ready to start talking about her dead. Ruth had become transparent to me in her pain and her grief. She started crying, a very rare behavior for her. It was the weeping, the moistness of her tears, that was finally able actually to soften the defensive armor that had been built up over so many years, character armor that I had come to regard as impregnable. With her body finally expressing itself through crying, I was privileged to observe the healthy dissolution of caretaking mechanisms that had become the persecutors of Ruth's aliveness, leaving her numb, without space for enjoyment. Woodman says, "So long as we are petrified in a static world there is no danger of us opening ourselves to weeping our own tears or singing our own song."[15] But now Ruth was weeping at last.

As I heard Ruth sobbing, knowing that it was for a lifelong pain that had been frozen, I could feel in my own body that Ruth was, in Marion Woodman's phrase, "dying into life."[16] I felt profound compassion for her. I remembered our long and exciting intellectual conversations in which I had listened to Ruth talking brilliantly, and I returned to the woman in front of me who could only cry. And in myself, I started feeling my body. It was back! It belonged to me! It was awake! For the first time in all the years of working with Ruth, something felt born and alive in me. When the session was over, I stood up and I realized how light my body felt. Standing up, walking, moving! It was possible.

Deeply moved by our session, I remembered, later that day, how many times Ruth has quoted passages to me from biographies of women and described theories and authors talking about the possibility of transforming women's lives, often linking this hopeful material to her own painful question: "Why isn't it happening for me?" In the past, I would feel a heavy load of sadness when she addressed this question to me. Today, I felt light because it *was* happening for Ruth. Of course I don't know what will come next in her analysis, but I do know this: in my body, something has begun to flow, and I deeply trust that authentic movement.

Let us remember Marion Woodman's words when in prayer she asks:

> Please God, let me live the Spiritual Warrior, fighting for the
> new order. Dear Sophia, let your radiance release me into
> Virgin/Crone. Masculine and feminine together, we may make
> the transition.[17]

As I hope the case of Ruth illustrates, I have discovered in my
work as an analyst that when I join my patients in their personal
journeys, a process in which I am called to merge, or better, submerge,
with each one of them, my body is a fundamental instrument. This
body of mine, that has given me, and still does, so much pleasure, and
yet has caused me so many tears, is always there for me in the
commitment I make with each one of my clients. As an instrument,
the body needs to be tuned regularly. A cello professor at the
Conservatory of Music in Mexico once told me, "One cannot just grab
the cello, open one's legs and expect it to sound!" This professor, a
wonderful teacher, liked to say that one must develop a relationship
with one's instrument: one has to embrace it, caress it, and allow it to
say what it feels needs to be said. As he put it, "if you try only to order
what you want out of it, your instrument will only make noise. It may
cry out, but you won't be able to bring out, and get to know, the
music that it contains. And you, when faced with this lack of
relationship, will abandon it. It will abandon you too." Just so, the
body, our inherent instrument, deserves to be treated with love. Its
unique "music" is neither pre-verbal nor post-verbal; rather, it
accompanies the words we say and that we hear our patients saying to
us. The body receives and responds; hears and needs to be heard; feels
and wants to be felt; knows and must be known.

Embodied countertransference is not about thoughts that appear
in relation to our patient, nor about feelings that arise when we are
with the patient. It is about hearing our own instrument, which is
always telling us about how we are holding our patient's lived
experience. Put even more broadly, the body's story as we feel it in
analysis is about the mystery of the psyche as perceived by matter, our
bodies being the matter where one can find psyche. The body is often
about perceiving life when threatened by death, but it is equally about
honoring the process of dying when that is threatened by life. The
body is about knowing in the flesh, feeling in the blood, sustaining in

the bones, and containing in the skin. The body's story is about soul in the body, yes, but it is even more about *embodied* soul; as such, it is about a dance between perilous opposites in which I have been able to find meaning in my work and moments of joy in my life.

NOTES

1. Jaime Sabines, "Que costumbre tan salvaje," in *Yuria* (Mexico: Joaqun Mortiz, 1967), 27.

2. Donald Kalsched, *The Inner World of Trauma: Archetypal Defenses of the Personal Spirit* (London: Routledge, 1996), 5.

3. *Ibid.*

4. Louis H. Stewart, *Affect and Archetype in Analysis* (Wilmette, Illinois: Chiron Publications, 1987), 135.

5. Jean Shinoda Bolen, *Goddesses in Older Women* (New York: HarperCollins Publishers, 2001).

6. Caroline Myss, *Anatomy of the Spirit* (New York: Three Rivers Press, 1986), 35.

7. Antonio Damasio, *Looking for Spinoza: Joy, Sorrow and the Feeling Brain* (Florida: Harcourt, 2003), 139-140.

8. Louis H. Stewart, *Affect and Archetype in Analysis* (Wilmette, Illinois: Chiron Publications, 1987).

9. Marion Woodman, *Addiction to Perfection: The Still Unravished Bride* (Toronto: Inner City Books, 1982), 57.

10. Ann Belford Ulanov, *Attacked by Poison Ivy: A Psychological Understanding* (York Beach, ME: Nicolas Hays, 2001), 114.

11. John Beebe, "The Father's Anima," in *The Father,* ed. Andrew Samuels (New York: New York University Press, 1985).

12. C. G. Jung, "Psychological Aspects of the Mother Archetype," *The Archetypes and the Collective Unconscious,* trans. R. F. C. Hull, *Collected Works,* vol. 9i (Princeton: Princeton University Press, 1959).

13. Woodman, *Addiction to Perfection*, 66.

14. Marie Louise von Franz, *The Feminine in Fairy Tales* (Boston: Shambhala Publications, 1972), 31.

15. Marion Woodman, *Addiction to Perfection,* 68.

16. Marion Woodman, *Bone: Dying into Life* (New York: Viking, 2000), xi.

17. Woodman, *Bone*, 24-25.

WHEN A BODY MEETS A BODY

ROBIN VAN LÖBEN SELS

Generally speaking, psychotherapists acknowledge that a therapist's personality and style of working influence the context of work with patients. Just as infants are in-formed by information pouring into them from their environment and social surroundings, so psyche and soul[1] are influenced by methods of investigation and the participating personalities. While implicit transference and countertransference issues are active in any therapeutic endeavor, these factors may not become the center of therapeutic attention, however, for transferential language is not the only way to describe transitional ligaments between two personalities. Jung once remarked that "it is not transference that enables the patient to bring out his material: you get all the material you could wish for from dreams."[2] Dreams or no dreams, and no matter what descriptive language we choose, the unconscious remains unconscious and we never come to the end of it, even with dreams, if only because it presents itself to us in a body—our own, and those of our patients.

Robin van Löben Sels is a Jungian analyst in private practice and the author of *A Dream in the World: Poetics of Soul in Two Women, Modern and Medieval* (Routledge, 2003) and *Wanting a Country for This Weather and Other Poems* (Mellen, 2003).

"If a body meet a body, coming through the rye ...." So goes the old Scottish folk song based on the poem by Robert Burns, and this refrain came to mind when I looked for a title for this article. I cannot begin to describe my experience of participating in psychotherapeutic work without grounding it first and foremost in the phenomenon of body and what happens when "a body" meets "a body" in the therapeutic relationship—meaning, when I meet someone in my consulting room. So let me try to embody descriptively here my imaginative vision of the binocular, psycho-religious attitude with which I engage in psychotherapeutic work with another person.

Most times, my attitude consists of a kind of ambivalent, open unknowing which values both psychological and religious experience but does not seek one over the other. I value the pains and puzzles, the processes and price of depth therapeutic work. In terms of time, attention, energy, and money, a therapeutic relationship makes great demands upon two persons, yet the rigors of the therapeutic work are most worthwhile. The transformation and healing to which the process leads can mean the world to a patient with an injured self-integrity. When I bring this attitude to an in-depth therapeutic relationship, I gain access to a capacity for a particular kind of experiencing, which I will describe in greater detail in what follows—a capacity for experience that embraces one's whole being, "with all one's heart, with all one's soul, and with all one's might": a full, embodied consciousness of human being.

This attitude helps me to imagine my therapeutic work in terms of three interpenetrating modes of therapeutic practice, which I call body awareness, a capacity for primary experience, and participating consciousness. I employ these modes simply by virtue of who I am, my predisposition to 'be them' (I use them spontaneously), and their use enriches the texture of my experiences with patients. Let me state from the outset, however, that I regard these modes as my own, and I keep my idiosyncrasies to myself, seldom, if ever, discussing or describing them to patients. Nevertheless, my attention to the psychological terrain they encompass intensifies our emotional intimacy, and my sensitivity to the power of these modes at the outset of the therapy helps my patients to establish self-integrity, which becomes a shared point of reference for the rest of the therapeutic relationship.

When discussing my practice with my colleagues, I use my psychoanalytic background to conceptualize and put into words what I do with my patients. Concepts such as the Oedipus Complex and the pre-Oedipal stage, transference and countertransference, archetype and image, neurosis and psychosis, complex and introject, projection and regression, interpersonal, intrapsychic, and intrapersonal—these and other words come and go, quickly to mind and easily to tongue. Outside the consulting room, we psychotherapists are a talky lot. However, this is not a true reflection of what actually happens in my consulting room. During a therapy session, I tend to think very little and rely primarily on sensing. I listen, but not with Freud's evenly hovering attention, or Bion's freedom from memory and desire. While my attitude resonates with Jung's advice to "throw away the books" and pay attention to what happens, my attention veers toward what Christopher Bollas[3] calls the "unthought known," though I welcome the "unfelt feeling" even more. After providing some background, I will describe in greater detail the modes through which I practice therapy, musing on my perceptions and the implications of each mode, explaining how each mode includes, interpenetrates, and overlaps the other two, and I will end with thoughts, and ideas to which I think each mode refers me in the therapeutic situation.

I consider my initial therapeutic activity to be one of 'beholding,' rather than 'looking at' the person across from me, whether I focus on the person, the relationship, or dreams. Before sight[4] begins to dominate the relationship and subject-object differentiation sets in, the act of beholding helps me to experience feelings of emotional communion with the other person. Beholding gives priority to the tactile, kinesthetic, rhythmic, and musical dimensions of personal interaction rather than to verbal and visual stimuli, as is the case in Western culture in general, and even in some psychotherapeutic practice.

While I listen for divisions and conflict in fantasy and perception, I also listen for personal access to a depth of affect which can safely ease a way below and beyond obstructions posed by mental oppositions. Are emotionally-paired 'opposites' ready to hand? Love and hate, fear and courage, jealousy and envy, as well as goodwill and anger, sadness and joy, pain and pleasure, guilt and forgiveness, judgment and mercy, curiosity and prudence, spontaneity and self-reflection?

I listen, envision, and imagine. I also breath and move and speak, and my occasional 'interventions' (interpretations, analyses, comments, and questions) tend to be more imaginative than conceptual, more emotionally linking than analytic. I use a method of psychological and emotional assemblage, a clinical method of employing the three modes of attending the psyche listed above. Apprehending the appearances of another person's reality involves all my senses, not just the aural and visual ones. The sheer presence of another person constellates sensate bodily impressions on conscious and unconscious levels of my awareness. A kinesthetic sensibility may emerge, as if the therapeutic relationship were dancing over time.

Initially, I 'feel' for what seems like the right emotional distance for me to both behold and observe the other. The asymmetry of my being the analyst and the other being my patient, or my being older and the other being younger holds an obvious power differential. To find the right position I often feel I must leave behind my interpretive tools and culturally determined preconceptions, a process I cannot engage in abstractly beforehand. I rely upon an ongoing internal process of opening to difference and change between the other and myself. Establishing the right distance involves not so much an active 'positioning' as it does a floating, listening attention (participating consciousness) and an ensuing continuous process of emotional adaptation (a capacity for primary experience). Only within these modes can I adjust my perceptivity so that eventually I use my eyes as well as my wits to see more, and better.

As far as I can tell, in the interaction of a therapeutic hour I dwell in an imaginative sensing of the three overlapping modes of apprehension described earlier: body awareness, a capacity for primary experience, and participating consciousness, perspectives emerging from my own embodied experience. I do not imagine these as archetypal personifications of agents within the psyche, nor do I consider them to be depersonalized agencies of the mind. Nor are they internal objects. I do not imagine them as ways of understanding, either. As modes of figurative comprehension, they point *toward* understanding by way of imagery, imagination and feeling,[5] but they make no claim to understand. Jung[6] once observed that "understanding is a binding power, at times a veritable murder of the soul, as it flattens out vitally important differences." Jung goes on to say that "the core of the individual is a mystery of life, which is snuffed out when it is 'grasped.'" I agree with Jung, and much about the psyche and the therapeutic process lies beyond my understanding.

Because these modes do not refer to ego-endeavor, they are oblique. Being figurative, each mode figures strongly in the comprehension of the other two, so that no one has a single source or only one effect. In both source and effect, bodily awareness, a capacity for primary experience, and participating consciousness continuously overlap. Taken together, they form an organic model of an embodied way of being in the world which, while I may intentionally cultivate them as modes of therapeutic being, open me in general to qualities of consciously lived experience.

Emerging as they do from my bodily self, these are my access to dreams, creative imagination, and the collective unconscious.[7] Objectively, all three modes connect me to collective aspects of my life: body awareness connects me to my personal, bodily reality; participating consciousness connects me to a social, communal life by way of the collective (both conscious and unconscious); and a capacity for primary experience relates me to the world around me and my kinship with all living creatures. All three direct me toward what scientist Carl Sagan[8] called a "fundamental unit of primary identification" with the planet earth and the human species, for which I feel we have a desperate need.

I see the collective aspects of life to which my modes refer nested together, like the layers of an onion or a set of Russian dolls. Each expresses an important, generalized area of human reality and embodies some way that my ego-consciousness links with unconsciousness. For example, body awareness links me with the unconscious by way of my senses and my bodily experience of dream; a capacity for primary experience links me with the unconscious by way of an unfettered access to a range of emotional experience responding to a shared heart of human life; and participating consciousness links me to the unconscious by way of my imagination, dreams themselves, and my encounter within the imaginal world. Although they are intertwined, from time to time one mode is more helpful than the others in thinking about discrete areas of psychological and religious experience. Each mode is best referred to using both clinical and imaginative language, for each partakes in depth and clusters around a consciousness of what it is like to be a wholly embodied human being.

In ancient Greece, a *therapeutes* was a companion, an attendant with healing or curative powers. These modes have become my therapeutic companions. They make up a trinity of ways of attending not only the psyche, but also both participants in the therapeutic setting: process as well as relationship. They are lenses of a kind, aids that compensate, complement, and parallel all that emerges into consciousness. Each implies a relatedness essential to being. Interrelated and overlapping, they form not a triad or a trio of modes, but a three-oneness, a tri-unity of ways of attending, linking, and gaining access to something else. Each mode joins the other two as an aspect of the oneness to which they refer, an envisioning backed by my therapeutic attitude. Taken together, they allow for what I imagine to be a full expression of personality—mine and the other person, body, psyche and soul.

At the same time, these modes represent an expansion of the oneness of a sense of personal self into three. Without the oneness to which each mode points, disconnection of each from the other would result in an assortment of perspectives rather than a tri-unity. Body awareness, a capacity for primary experience and participating consciousness form a trinity in the way that Jung defines trinity: not as a matter of tri-psychological coexistence, but as a unity effected through reflection from internal and reciprocal relationships.[9]

To see these modes as Trinity, however, implies that a particular dimension of consciousness is at work. To understand 'three-ness' as Trinity is to proceed from a secular consciousness of three-ness (a trio, a triad, three modes, three persons), wherein we relate to three-ness as a dimension of being outside ourselves, a dimension to be used on occasion or called upon, *through* the symbolic consciousness that is woven into the fabric of our existence.[10]

Where Jung defined three-ness as Trinity and the perception of symbolic consciousness, educator and mathematician Michael Schneider tells us that a third dimension of consciousness—of three-ness, for example—indicates the presence of the sacred.[11] A sacred dimension of consciousness points toward a more subtle center, touching upon the power that motivates our actions and emotions, our thoughts and desires. The witness of this center of gravity is not in space but in pure, imageless awareness, the place in the reader which is now aware of these words. "This is the motivating power-with-which-we-are-conscious," says Schneider, "identical to the heart of every natural form and symbolized by the center of the circle. It is the seed of our mysterious ability to be aware."[12] To bring consciousness to this seed of our mysterious ability to be aware is to penetrate to the sacred dimension of Being and to seek the center's correspondence with oneself.

The sacred dimension has a particular significance involving consciousness and the profound *mystery of awareness,* not only the awareness of mystery. Here it is not what I do with my three modes, for example, but what the three-ness of my modes does to me, to my consciousness.

> Sacred space is within us, not in body or brain, but in the volume of our consciousness. Wherever we go, we bring the sacred within us to the sacred around us. We consecrate locations and studies by the presence of this awareness, not just the other way around. ... Awareness is the ultimate sacred wonder, though we tend to endow objects outside ourselves as sacred while ignoring the same source within us. The timeless, symbolic patterns of the world's religions, art and architecture remain symbolic of our own sacred inner realm. To find this space within us, we pay attention to paying attention, in imageless awareness, directing sustained attention to that which the symbols and images refer within us.[13]

When I refer to my three modes as a Trinity, I am pointing to an arch of personal experience which, in turn, I think, points to the therapeutic process of creating a self-supporting personality structure capable of resolving opposing tensions into a solid, stable whole, which eventually no longer needs support from without (i.e., no longer needs a therapist). Every arch has a keystone. One patient, for example, found her keystone experience in an experience of soul, initiated by the presence of the Holy Spirit.[14] Another experienced the keystone alchemically, as the Stone became alive.

However the keystone experience appears, an experience of Trinity (as opposed to *thinking about Trinity*) shows us that we are not separate from the universe but braided into it, complete wholes living in a greater whole. My three modes are attentive 'presences' in which I become immersed. Often I experience them as 'standing by,' like the watchful presence of the three angelic beings in Andre Rublev's fifteenth-century icon of the Trinity.

A Xhosa proverb says, "*Ubuntu ungamntu ngabanye abantu*" ("A person is a person through other persons"). Expanding on the meaning of this proverb, Archbishop Desmond Tutu writes:

> Ubuntu is very difficult to render into a Western language. It speaks of the very essence of being human. ... It is to say, "My humanity is caught up, is inextricably bound up, in yours." We belong in a bundle of life. We say, "A person is a person through other persons." It is not, "I think therefore I am." It says rather: "I am human because I belong. I participate, I share." A person with ubuntu is open and available to others, affirming of others, does not feel threatened that others are able and good, for he or she belongs in a greater whole and is diminished when others are humiliated or diminished, when others are tortured or oppressed, or treated as if they were less than who they are.[15]

These words could inspire all object-relations theory as well as thoughts about the Trinity. My underlying understanding of personhood symbolized by Rublev's Angels and my three modes resonates with D. W. Winnicott's ideas of personalization and indwelling, for example. Winnicott's notion of personalization counters what he calls depersonalization, an indication of a lack of the kind of tri-unity of body, psyche, and soul that I refer to here. Winnicott says,

> I adopted the term 'personalisation' as a kind of positive form of depersonalisation ... various meanings are given to depersonalisation, but on the whole they involve ... loss of contact with the body and body functioning, and this implies the existence of some other aspect of the personality (e.g., psyche, spirit, primitive or archetypal defenses).[16]

In religious terms, the three modes and three aspects of collective living to which they link me (personal, social, and ecological) return me (*relegere, religio*) to the possibility of a Trinitarian experience of reality, where, despite my analogies, I am simply suggesting that something of the Trinity may be found in human life. And the presence of these modes in the therapeutic hour can allow for places in human experience where meaning becomes God-shaped and the roots of Being may open and fill.

Psychologically, my trinity of modes informs my therapeutic attitude and provides the physical, psychological, and emotional breadth necessary for experiencing the emergence of personhood. Envisioning these modes of attending the psyche constellates their presence into the texture of a therapeutic relationship. As a patient's personality undergoes transformation, these modes strengthen and deepen, enabling a stressed ego (mine gets stressed, as well) to withstand the potentially enormous impact of activated archetypal energy. In effect, each mode helps contain an influx of impersonal libido as the energy is freed from complex entanglement and becomes available for possible personalization in the world.

I like to imagine that my 'holding' to these ways of attending the psyche expands my therapeutic stance so that the collective arenas within therapy open wide. My cultivation of their presence opens me to depths and reaches of the psyche, permeates my work with patients, and informs my life. While the modes 'attend' the psyche, their presence frees my patients and me to relate. Simultaneously, they anchor our work in the here and now.

Body Awareness

Our culture's massive collective preoccupation with body is evident in our concern with body-image, appearance, and body development. It shows in the proliferation of new approaches to "working on the body." But an attitude that "uses" the body often precludes the kind of awareness to which this mode alludes. Outwardly, an athlete or dancer may epitomize embodied living; inwardly, however, he or she may be as unrelated—or as destructively related—to psychologically informed embodiment as, for example, any outwardly mild-mannered man with psychosomatic headaches, or competent woman with an eating disorder. "Training" the body does not entail psychological or emotional relatedness, both of which are necessary for what I mean by body awareness.[17]

The substantial form of the human body provides us with an intimate and universal way to understand reality. Curmudgeon or not, St. Paul had it right when he made the distinction between body (soma) and flesh (sarx). Flesh refers to our outward, visible, mortal condition— to the solidarity of our dismemberment, pain, and solitude, connoting human beings in their distance and difference, their isolation. Using the term 'body' collectively as well as individually, Paul directs us to where wholeness becomes the essence of what a body is, where body means what is essentially whole or has become so. The body, not the flesh, is the Temple of the Holy Spirit. In Paul's understanding, body comes to connote what we have in common, irrespective of individual differences, connecting us to each other and to the universe. Mystically, the consubstantiality of the body refers to human nature as a whole. Whereas 'flesh' establishes our solitude and otherness, the 'body' is the bearer of resurrection. There is no resurrection of the flesh. In Christian understanding, "it is the body that is for the Lord, and the Lord that is for the body."[18]

I see the body as our primary metaphor for the structure of Being. All three modes of attending the psyche relate to body as an original template, even though how and why the body is gendered and valued and how we personally experience embodiment differs from culture to culture and according to individual circumstances. For a psychoanalytic thinker like Winnicott, for example, authenticity of being means *body* authenticity. It means experiencing one's true self in body tissues which actively explore one's environment, rather than feeling impinged upon by it.

Shadowed by death, the body holds neither inherent evil nor inherent threat. What the dancer Martha Graham meant when she spoke of the house of pelvic truth is that the body is a landscape of truth-telling. It is as if an ancient, undivided world lies curled inside us with an ancestral memory of wilderness. It offers us a vast, all-embracing harmony, as rhythmic as the lion-colored flanks of the California foothills, as majestic as a valley in the great Northwest. Our true experience of the wild is inside us, beyond our ego or mental control, with rules and laws that do not obey our human will. Inherent to the body is a kind of primordial force, in which experience and consciousness are earthed and contained by our desirous, mortal, flesh-and-blood awareness. Just as we can relate to three-ness from a secular, symbolic, or sacred consciousness, so we can relate to the body as a sign, a symbol, or a site—a home. Without the quality of body awareness, neither the capacity for primary experience nor participating consciousness is realizable, for both of these modes presuppose inner and outer recognition of personal, bodily reality.

Whole-hearted acceptance of body's concrete existence is essential, of our essence. We cannot individuate without it. When bodies are unloved, whether by ourselves or others, hatred flows in, or intense neglect ensues. More than symbol, more even than the bread and wine of the Last Supper, each body is a knowing connection, a telling thing, a medium of experience, of expression and being. The body navigates us to where it wants us to go from an inner map not available to consciousness. Developing a sense of body awareness requires that we become aware of what the body wants, and how the body feels emotionally, and that we integrate all of this with personal consciousness. In Jungian language, integration of the body entails integration of the Shadow, i.e., making conscious all that has been given away for the sake of an adequate, socially acceptable public mask. Untouched pain, grief, shame, and fear create unconscious ecologies of mind and body—both.

> You do not have to be good.
> You do not have to walk on your knees
> for a hundred miles through the desert, repenting.
> You only have to let the soft animal of your body
> love what it loves ....

These words of poet Mary Oliver[19] tell us how to enter the body, how to touch an unconscious ecology of mind. When we hear the voice of nature, we may enter the metaphysical world. We must listen to the animal, must become the animal we are. We need to believe in what we do not have to invent. Elizabeth Costello, novelist Coetzee's sixty-seven-year-old writer, thinks of her body thus: "a dumb, faithful body that accompanies us every step of the way; a gentle, lumbering monster given to us to look after; a shadow turned to flesh that stands on two feet like a bear, laving itself continuously from the inside with blood."[20] Using animal terms rather than an appeal to ideas (reason) or the divine (religion), Coetzee unveils the process by which Costello's revelation of her body disabuses her of the fantasies devised by her mind. Her body's truth, humble, modest, and tethered to the earth, tells her that there is no rescue from this life with all its suffering; there can be only fitful respite from it, and acceptance, however tentative, of what nature puts before her. This truth lies beyond the pale of language. Our problem is that we feel we both are and are not our bodies. We may feel that we are more than our bodies—but not in the sense of being something different from them.

Integration of the Shadow on a bodily level relates to an achievement of self-other awareness and differentiation. "Acceptance of the shadow is the essential basis for the actual achievement of an ethical attitude towards the "Thou" who is outside me," writes Erich Neumann,[21] whether that "thou" be person, place, or world. Native American writer Linda Hogan suggests that in order to restore power and integrity to the inner world, we must befriend what is wild: "The body, made of earth's mud and breathed into, is the temple, and we need to learn to worship it as such, to move slowly within it, respecting it, loving it, treating ourselves and all our loved ones with tenderness … love for the body and for the earth are the same love."[22]

Nothing in a body's life goes unregistered, so wholeness enters through the body's door. The threshold of consciousness is a bodily threshold, even for dreams. Without body we cannot bring our psycho-physiological experience to an emotional level of *felt psychic experience*, which can bridge inevitable gaps in being. Any experience of *enantiodromia* occurs in the body. And William Blake declares that body is a part of soul: Man has no Body distinct from his Soul; for that called Body is a portion of the Soul discerned by the five Senses. The importance of having an embodied source of feeling, soul and transformative experience cannot be overstressed.

So, housing a sense of being that is both in the world and of the world, the body anchors our waking and sleeping mind. Dreaming is as physical as breathing: scientists can trace the brain waves and eye movements that occur during dreaming; breathing quickly or more slowly, we move, or cry out in our sleep. To conceive of dreams as autonomous is to imply that they happen independently of the body. When we do not acknowledge that the body dreams, we are prone to see dreaming as the activity of the disembodied soul.

Yet dreams are in the world because body is in the world. And dreams are of the world because body is of the world. Metaphor may be the spirit's rhetoric, but body is the spirit's chemistry: psyche and soul together work through matter, and even our consciousness is the earth's odd bloom. Symbolic mother, matrix, and ground of being, the body is our first house—our first environment, the residence into which we incarnate and our most personal experience of earth. The space where the body is is the most intimate space we know, a place of joy and fear, love and hate, anger and courage and illness. When we feel pain, sickness, and loss, we enter the body as the Valley of the Shadow of Death; when we feel joy, inspiration, and sanctification, we experience the body transfigured, the Body Blessed.

Jung once likened entering the archetypal world to entering the primitive depths of the human brain stem. Body awareness is particularly important for those of us who work with the emotional realities of others because it is easy to forget the embodied nature of dream, or how linked to body our language and memory are. A felt integrity of bodily existence can re-balance a "mind-body split," in which we live in our heads or out of ego-consciousness alone. Body awareness counters the tendency to experience one's own mind as an object.[23]

A conscious emphasis upon bodily being, body awareness, and an imaginatively embodied life helps to dissolve the character structures formed in response to early traumatic or emotionally unbearable experiences. It allows us to re-experience the imprints of archetypal blows in our lives, emotional repercussions locked in gut and stomach, lung and muscle, sinew and bone.[24]

Within the body's realm, when the magical levels of the psyche are activated, whatever discipline the ego pursues, one experiences illumination or confronts the numinous. If one has been practicing yoga, one reaches enlightenment; if one has been sitting Zen, one has the experience in the language (or non-language) of Zen. If one has been working in Reichian therapy, one experiences the body's armor melting. If one has been in Jungian psychotherapy, one experiences synchronicity, or individuation, perhaps, or healing. Yet all these expressions translate the transformation of consciousness and the transformation of the ego's powers of conceptualization, striving, will, and agency, into deeper dimensions of reality—into process, incarnation and into a *wholeness of experience*, from head to heart and body, inclusively.

Usually something is left out of these equations. That missing 'something' points to a religious reality, which is always new, a part of experience which does not translate easily into anything else. Religious reality, although it emerges from the psyche and is pointed to by the archetype—is neither psyche nor archetype, but truly Other. If religious reality has any direction at all, it points to the future, toward a new creation. Religious experience claims the body boldly.[25]

Of the role of the body in spiritual reintegration, Rumi tells us that "the physical form is of great importance: nothing can be done without the consociation of the form and the essence. However often you may sow a seed, stripped of the pod, it will not grow. Sow it with the pod, it will become a great tree. From this point of view, the body is fundamental and necessary for the realization of the Divine intention."[26] For the person to whom such a revelation is given, a trusting capacity for bodily expression—for creating, enacting, speaking, writing—must be engaged if the experience is to be communicated to others. Revelatory experience proceeds out of a body and into discourse and communication with other bodies in the world.[27]

In the spiritual domain, a revelatory event breaks the normal continuity of life, and although it is considered to be 'supernatural' because it is divine, it is nevertheless a 'natural,' rather than a psychological event. Events in the sensory domain, although they too are natural, also break the body's sense of normal continuity and function like images of revelation: lightning splits the heavens, or snow falls during the night, transfiguring the world by covering its impurity, expressing not so much inspiration (or intellectualization) as a state of sanctity.[28]

Jung honors the body not only as the vessel in which psyche appears, but as the vessel in which *reality* appears "all the way down" into matter itself:

> The symbols of the self arise in the depths of the body and they express its materiality every bit as much as the structure of the perceiving consciousness. The symbol is thus a living body, *corpus et anima*; hence the 'child' is such an apt formula for the symbol. The uniqueness of the psyche can never enter wholly into reality, it can only be realized approximately, though it still remains the absolute basis of all consciousness. The deeper 'layers' of the psyche lose their individual uniqueness as they retreat farther and farther into darkness. 'Lower down,' that is to say as they approach the autonomous functional systems, they become increasingly collective until they are universalized and extinguished in the body's materiality, i.e., into chemical substances. The body's carbon is simply carbon. Hence 'at bottom' the psyche is simply 'world.' In this sense I hold Kerenyi to be absolutely right when he says that in the symbol the world itself is speaking. The more archaic and 'deeper,' that is the more

physiological the symbol is, the more collective and universal, the more 'material' it is.[29]

That religious experience may be more transformative of the body than psychological experience can ever be is a continuing revelation to me. For a long time I had thought (with early Jung) that the psyche housed almost everything, but it does not house the body, and the soul lives in the body, even as it speaks through psyche. The importance of the body for the life of the soul has become central to my thinking. Under the auspices of body awareness go all my more psychoanalytically thought-out concerns about mind-body splits and separations and about true and false selves; about body and character armor; about birth-trauma and psychosomatic symptoms; about instinctive sexuality; about post-traumatic stress disorder and behaved or unconsciously enacted attitudes toward life in the body, including eating disorders and addictive behavior. All of these disorders we act out in the world, affecting other persons and society as a whole in addition to ourselves. By such extension we generate great suffering and distress, bad dreams from which our shuddering world is struggling to emerge.

A Capacity for Primary Experience

Two definitions of secondary experience clarify what I mean by "capacity for primary experience." Psychologist Edward Reed[30] tells us that secondary experience is second-hand, indirect knowledge gained from information which has been packaged and presented to us by others. Poet David Whyte[31] suggests that secondary experience is ego-experience used defensively. We need what we acquire from secondary experience—a sense of identity—even when our need for corroboration from outer sources defends us against primary experience. And we are most defended against ourselves when we are afraid of fear. A primary experience of the mind's loose moorings fills us with terror: that way madness lies, and fragmentation.

Yet living by secondary experience alone sets up a tremendous drain on the world, because we are never satisfied. Only when we set aside the mind's dichotomies and settle into the body, putting ourselves squarely into the world, can we ask ourselves, "What is my own first-hand, primary experience of being alive?" In answer to this question, primary experience draws upon a great quarry of emotion, a shared heart of experience which, in turn, draws upon our human embodiment. Where primary experience is, we have no defense, for it cannot be argued against. Here body awareness and a capacity for primary experience merge.

In a formal discipline like Zen sitting, we intentionally take a stand within formlessness, within primary experience.[32] There we discover that experience is our own but at such a depth that it calls upon our common humanity. In primary experience we contact imagination so deep that it becomes a way of paying attention to the world instead of ourselves, an *attention which takes into account the attention the world pays back to us*. There is an exchange of attention between outer and inner, self and other, and soul comes alive where these attentions meet.

When we establish rapport with the emotional experience ceaselessly taking place in our bodies, we do not need to think as much, or in the same way. Thinking is useful when there is something to ponder, but defensive thinking (as in second-hand experience) cuts us off from relating to the world around us. When experienced in their entirety rather than as fleeting shadows in the recesses of the mind, emotional states can prevent us from misusing the capacity to think. "In tracing thoughts back to their roots, back to the original feeling states" says psychiatrist Mark Epstein,

> we get out of our heads and return to our senses. A different experience of mind is then possible ... something closer to the Western notion of the psyche. Psyche ... [is] the container in which thoughts and feelings happen. It is like the underlying nervous system that connects the mind-body process. In Buddhism it is compared to clear space—the big blue sky of mind.[33]

The Judaeo-Christian tradition sometimes calls this kind of imaginative activity contemplation. Comparing it to a strain of music, theologian Douglas Steere[34] imagines contemplation as a simple, unimpeded, penetrating gaze on truth, a self-justifying activity in which we become awake, reflect on the Sources of Being, and are drawn back to the One. No matter who we are or what we are doing, there can be contemplation, says Steere. Anyone can do it, anywhere. Entering primary experience by way of the body, we find ourselves rooted in the body and ensouled, having no other form in which to be.

Far from causing us to lose touch with body or world, then, a capacity for primary experience makes it possible for us to keep two attentions running simultaneously, outer and inner, self and other, body and world, all the way down, without shutting off when we come to previously disowned emotions such as grief and shame. Winnicott suggests that in some ways the unconscious functions as a dark storehouse of moments of non-being, containing aspects of the self which could not metabolize trauma emotionally. There these moments lie, unconscious and refusing to grow older until they are resolved or rediscovered. For an ongoing capacity for primary experience to become real, several primary defenses (e.g., denial, repression, and the habitual grip of identification with old and new feeling states) need to loosen. Intense, internal dialogue with personal and collectively-sanctioned attitudes and convictions can begin to undo the "hardening of the heart." Often body armor loosens, too. Whether of mind or body, defenses hinder our capacity for primary experience. Until we unearth them so that we can confront them consciously, we (and those around us) invariably suffer their side-effects.

What most characterizes the mode of primary experience is the ability to belong to opposing worlds simultaneously. Dream and dreamer, outer and inner, body and mind meet. "Things without hands take hands," says poet Theodore Roethke. When we embody a capacity for primary experience we are initiated into participating consciousness and linked with the correspondences of outer and inner worlds. Collective images commonly associated with transformation and initiation—forests and deserts, darkness or the mountain top— correspond with our primary experience of the outer world—'mountains become mountains, rivers become rivers again.' Embodying primary experience means that we have begun to form an experiential continuum between conscious and unconscious life within, individual and communal life without, and a subjective and objective participation in the natural, psychological, and spiritual ecology of the world.

Under the auspices of a capacity for primary experience reside all my musings about dissociation and depersonalization; about mind-as-object; about ranges of emotion, emotional expression, and emotional receptivity; about split or multiple personality manifestations; about dreamed or behavioral access to archetypal energy; about imagery, whether created, dreamed, or seen, imagined or encountered; about creativity and art; about memory and will, willfulness and willingness, and a capacity to acknowledge the reality of the psyche; about narcissism and the ability to form attachments and bonds; about madness and ecstasy and passion and love; and about the capacity for an all-out, no-holds-barred way of experiencing life. Absence of the capacity for primary experience affects not only the individual, but those around him or her and the world at large, especially the world of collective consciousness.

Participating Consciousness

The general idea of participating consciousness is familiar under other names.[35] Some refer to it as 'feminine consciousness,' or consciousness of interrelatedness. In an imaginative East-West geography, participating consciousness is explored in Eastern traditions as Buddha-like mindfulness or awareness of 'mutual arising' (Tao Te Ching).

Participating consciousness functions internally within the dimensions of a single personality, and externally between persons and between person and world. Initially, participating consciousness registers experience without prejudice and participates without prejudgment in whatever is presented to it from without or within. This is not to say that participating consciousness lacks judgment, but rather that underlying this mode is an acceptance of the human condition which precedes any psychological, emotional, aesthetic, or ethical transformation. Participating consciousness participates in all that is accessible to a sensibility that is alive and in the moment, here and now.

As a mode of attending the psyche, participating consciousness is exactly what it sounds like: the capacity to participate as consciously and as deeply as possible in imaginative, emotional, psychological, physiological, and spiritual reality. Through participating consciousness, we become aware of our capacity for primary experience. When otherness is registered by the body, participating consciousness joins in. This is why participating consciousness is not the same as *participation mystique*.[36] If it has a bias, participating consciousness works against unconscious identification with transcendence, especially when the transcendent soars beyond emotionally embodied participation. It resists easy identification with 'transcendent' spiritual development and practices that proceed at the expense of soul and body, or nature and being in the world.

Nor is the capacity for participating consciousness evidence of *'abaissement.'*[37] In contrast to ordinary consciousness, in a state of *abaissement* (whether the influx of unconscious material is triggered by an archetype or unconscious complex or appears in the form of a dream), participating consciousness stands sufficiently apart to take in the activated psyche, thereby participating in the wider field of cognition, which opens when ordinary ego-consciousness is 'lowered.' Participating consciousness takes advantage of 'extrane knowledge' (Neumann's term), which is otherwise inaccessible, especially to ordinary ego-consciousness.

Nor is participating consciousness matriarchal consciousness. Neumann defines matriarchal consciousness as an original form of consciousness in which the ego's lack of development keeps it open to processes of the psyche. In matriarchal consciousness, the spontaneity of the unconscious and the receptivity of consciousness are greater than in the relatively detached patriarchal consciousness typical of Western ego-development. Participating consciousness may edge its way back from ordinary consciousness toward the receptivity inherent in matriarchal consciousness, but it does not go all the way. Participating consciousness emerges from a process of having related to the spontaneity of the unconscious already, so that unconscious spontaneity is less marked. To participating consciousness, the world appears diaphanous. Aware of two worlds at once, participating consciousness reaches to name the texture of Being, the nub and feel of it, out of a sense of commingled existence. Participating consciousness reaches to encounter the unconscious with a kind of psychological "second naiveté" to use Paul Ricoeur's term.[38]

Insofar as it is body-based, participating consciousness participates in both masculine and feminine modes of being. Overall, it participates in Being to the extent that it registers primary experience in dream and body, in vision and life. Straddling self-centeredness and non-self-centeredness at the moment of experience, participating consciousness can use the fact of unconscious projection as a means of finding out more about what is truly out there, down there, or within. When we are able to employ "projection as perception," Ann Ulanov[39] suggests, our consciousness has been softened and enlarged by an ability to withdraw originally unconscious projections. Then attention can be directed to the mystery of that person, place, or thing 'out there' which evoked the projection. With participating consciousness, the withdrawal of projection becomes more than a process of important self-discovery because it reaches beyond concern with self to include eager attention to the other, holder of the 'hook' which drew the projection forth. In Jung's special terminology, the withdrawal of projection changes from an offering of self-discovery to an offering of discovery of the Self. For participating consciousness, psychological projection becomes a tool for exploring both self and other, a means of reaching out toward the world.

Participating consciousness encompasses at once all three of the suggested derivations for the word "religion": *relegere*—to treat or consider carefully (Cicero); *religare*—to bind or tie back (Lactantius, Augustine); and *religere*—to gather again, to recover what is lost (Augustine). It addresses a particularly contemporary form of collective illness that manifests itself as 'dis-eased' states of attention, a form of spiritual illness in which one's capacity for attention itself suffers an addictive 'spaced-outness.' So weakened that it cannot coalesce into anything even remotely resembling a 'position' from which it might investigate the inner world, dis-eased attention neglects the background of life (Edinger), does not gives careful scrutiny either to inner or outer worlds (Cicero, Jung), does not feel bound to or reunited with any source of Being beyond itself (Lactantius, Augustine), and seems to be without sense of 'space' (body) or form (soul) in which the unconscious exists as anything other than an abstraction. To me this phenomenon indicates collective damage to the religious instinct. A collectively-damaged religious instinct tends to ignore soul, relegate spirit to matter, treat the psyche as either nothing or everything, and equate the Self with God. These states of being stand among us as states of fragmentation, meaninglessness, brittleness, alienation, malice, and spite.

Because it includes bodily being, participating consciousness is sensuous. Although it can be intellectually rejected or repressed, it has an immediate, visceral quality which is not easily disputed or intellectually dismissed. *Participating consciousness willingly mediates a bodily sensibility that has been renewed in the heart.* We can think of it as a lunar consciousness, or a refined shamanic consciousness, or even a quantum consciousness, which works with and expresses evidence of the creatively embodied nature of the world. With a foot on either side, bridging the gap between consciousness and unconsciousness, participating consciousness balances oppositions in a tension of polarity instead of treating them as static contradiction or attempting to turn one pole of the opposition into the other. Not exactly double-sided or two-faced (like Mercurius), participating consciousness juggles.

Professor Owen Barfield is the earliest modern thinker I know of to articulate this particular kind of consciousness.[40] Barfield writes about "final participation," by which he means *awareness of the fact* that we participate in phenomena with the unconscious part of ourselves. Barfield reminds us that although we may convince ourselves of the fact of this kind of participation in our world, this fact has epistemological significance only to the extent that we experience final participation consciously—a final participation raised from potentiality to act. This, I think, is what happens in religious experience, in an experience of soul. It does not happen in psychological experience alone.

Participating consciousness expresses self-other awareness as such, but it also implies a capacity for intersubjectivity, that is, an ability to grant that the 'object' of one's subjectivity is a subject within a world of its own, to use Jessica Benjamin's words.[41] Thus it includes an *awareness of intention*, whether of behavior or experience, feelings or text, or dreams. Stretching toward an object, conscious intentionality is conscious of *something*. Ewart Cousins[42] reminds us that intention is an especially good tool for understanding and interpreting mystical experience precisely because it plunges us into participation in such apparently separate realms as mind and body, psyche and soul, ourselves and our environment. Furrowing the earth of body, plowing the ground of sensibility, participating consciousness lays the foundation for fully-human consciousness. In a comprehensively embodied experience of participating consciousness, consciousness and unconsciousness (and by extension, ourselves and our milieu) are no longer perceived as fundamentally separate. We are given a unitive, numinous experience in which God's gift of the world may become the gift of God's presence in the world, as well.

The receptivity that accompanies participating consciousness resembles the openness to 'not shutting off' necessary to a capacity for primary experience. From the perspective of both modes, although such openness develops in most depth psychotherapeutic relationships, it is not subjectively experienced as a conscious achievement by either participant. Rather, it is experienced as a gift. The knowledge gained by such openness is not knowledge gained by adding on information and skill, and the experience of it sometimes involves the loss of both information and skill. Linking with meaning, participating consciousness accrues a kind of knowledge that bears little resemblance to becoming smart or intelligent. Like the naive capacity for primary experience, participating consciousness relates us to something that we feel we have lost and need to find again. Accruing this kind of knowledge often involves not more consciousness but a recognition of foolishness and ignorance. Rather than struggling to accumulate experience or achieve a particular state or activity, body and mind can fall into a natural coordination out of which participating consciousness precipitates and participates in inner and outer reality naturally.[43]

Inwardly, participating consciousness participates in shifting changes of self-identity, self-states, and changing modes of being. Despite its linking nature, it does not always bridge, for it also participates in internal and external emptiness, in unbridged gaps, where it makes room for what mystical writers refer to as "infusion."[44] What, then, differentiates participating consciousness from Jung's symbolic consciousness? I would say that symbolic consciousness is less aware of its roots in primordial being. I would say that participating consciousness is more body-based. It has more to do with voice than with vision, with listening than with hearing. Relating to an encounter with presence more than to a perception of symbols, participating consciousness resonates with a personalized and indwelling soul more than with the psyche's personification of the archetypes. Where symbolic consciousness points to an 'image of God,' an embodied participating consciousness empties itself in order to serve human life. Thus, it is more on the side of an embodied ego than on the side of the Self. It is closer to the linking and holding nature of the feminine principle of Being than it is to the thinking and interactive masculine principle of Doing.

Inclusive of darkness and smallness (think of the *I Ching*'s "Taming Power of the Small"), participating consciousness tends toward conservation, containing rather than claiming space. It is embedded more in time than in timelessness. Relative to symbolic consciousness, participating consciousness leans more toward life than toward spirit; broods more on earth than on heaven; stands more on the side of the human than the divine, and is mindful of mortality.

It is easy to imagine that every gain in self-knowledge represents an ascent or increase in consciousness. But the knowledge that arrives with the advent of participating consciousness is of another kind, qualitatively different but equal in value. Participating consciousness implies a simultaneous awareness of all that lies hidden when mental life is dominant. It links personal and collective life, the personal unconscious and the collective dream. Thomas Berry[45] imagines that the place where these dimensions mingle, merge and differentiate is the Earth's dream, known in former times as the idea, the image, the feeling and the experience of what Plato called the World-Soul or the *Anima Mundi*.[46] When this place emerges in an individual life, I call it the site of a dream-in-the-world.

In the ways they interconnect, each with the others, these three modes of attending the psyche tend toward a wider self-knowledge rather than an encapsulated individualism, but perhaps participating consciousness leads the way. At the end of the twentieth century, when we could weep for a necessary rejoining, revaluing, rejuvenating reconciliation and return to self, other, and God, perhaps we *and* the earth dream of healing in the *religious* sense of that word. Ecological, communal, and individual issues cry out for lost, needed attention. Weaving itself in and out, up and down, over and under, participating consciousness senses the possible presence of One World in the midst of so many. To participating consciousness, soul need not remain unconscious in being, or be blurred with the reality of the psyche.

Plotinus gives a maternal significance to the Holy Spirit as the World Soul, or moon, and suggests that although the world-soul has a tendency towards separation and divisibility, it is the *sine qua non* of all change, creation, and reproduction. Here is the feminine principle writ large. In contrast, Jung, speculating on an earth spirit, imagines that the spirit that 'penetrates all things' or shapes all things is the world-soul.[47] But it seems to me that by naming a spirit, Jung's speculations too easily collapse an experiential reality (i.e., experience of soul) into the old dichotomy of consciousness versus unconsciousness, collective or otherwise, as if the *anima mundi* were an image to be thought about rather than an entity to be encountered. Defining the world-soul as 'an unending All of life' and wholly energy, a living organism of ideas which become effective and concrete or incarnate only in life, Jung goes on to suggest that the intellect is its progenitor and father: "what the intellect conceives the world-soul brings to birth in reality."[48] My point of view accords more with that of Plotinus: given the experiential nature of the soul, I suggest that the body's life-mystery is the progenitor of the world-soul, not intellect, or mind, or spirit.

Under the aegis of participating consciousness come all my wonderings about intelligence and Intelligences; about psycho-spiritual senses and an imaginal world; about personalization and indwelling, and self-other awareness; about meditation and contemplation; about spirituality; about sleep, and dreaming, and dying; about synchronicity and transformations of consciousness, and transformations *in* consciousness; about quantities and qualities of consciousness; and about the interrelatedness of all things.

These are my three modes, three ways of attending the psyche, defining broad areas of concern united in my practice. Like incense, or premonitions, they hover behind the nitty-gritty dailyness of personal interaction, accompanying my psychotherapeutic work. Sultan Valad,[49] Rumi's son, tells us that we must be born twice, once from a mother and again from our own body and existence. The body is like an egg, says Valad, in which our essence becomes a bird through the warmth of love, and then we go beyond body to fly in the eternal world of soul. I offer these elaborations for us to ponder over as we think about what goes on in our consulting rooms, hourly, daily, yearly, person by person, perhaps saying softly to ourselves (surely you know the words—this song is not THAT old!), "If a body meet a body, coming through the rye ...."

NOTES

1. For an in-depth explanation of the distinction I make between psyche and soul, see my recent book, *A Dream in the World: Poetics of Soul in Two Women, Modern and Medieval* (Hove, Brunner-Routledge, 2003). See also, Maureen Murdock's review of this book in this issue of *Spring*.

2. C. G. Jung, *Collected Works* 18 § 351.

3. Christopher Bollas, *The Shadow of the Object* (New York: Columbia University Press, 1987).

4. Vision is the sense most closely associated with awareness of separateness. Thus, vision reinforces a sense of differentiation and the feeling of individual identity. "Looking at" implies a distance necessary for sight to become meaningful.

5. What Owen Barfield in *Saving the Appearances: A Study in Idolatry* (New York: Harcourt, Brace and World, 1965) calls "original participation," meaning knowledge by way of imagery rather than concepts, survived in the West down to the Scientific Revolution. Throughout the Middle Ages, men and women continued to see the world primarily as a garment rather than as a collection of discrete objects they confronted. Likewise, Hermetic wisdom was (and remains) based on a belief that real knowledge occurs only by way of a union of subject and object in a psychic-emotional identification with images, rather than through a purely intellectual examination of concepts.

6. C. G. Jung, "Letter to Hans Schmid," in *Letters, 1960-1950, Vol. 1*, trans. R. F. C. Hull, ed. G. Adler (London: Routledge and Kegan Paul, 1973), 30-32.

7. "The collective unconscious ... is the mighty deposit of ancestral experience accumulated over millions of years, the echo of prehistoric happenings ... in the last analysis, a deposit of world-processes embedded in the structure of the brain and sympathetic nervous system ...." (Jung, *Collected Works* 12 § 299, 8 § 380).

8. A million years ago, when there were no nations on the planet, humans lived in small families of a few dozen people each. As wandering hunter-gatherers, we identified with nothing beyond the limited horizons of our immediate family group. As our horizons expanded, so did our identification, from family group, to tribe, to horde, to city-state, to nation, to empire, to today's 'superpower.' "The average person on the Earth today owes primary allegiance to a group of something like one hundred million people," says Sagan. "It seems very clear that if we do not destroy ourselves first, the unit of primary identification of most human beings will before long be the planet Earth and the human species. To my mind, this raises the key question: whether the fundamental unit of identification will expand to embrace the planet and the species, or whether we will destroy ourselves first. I'm afraid it's going to be very close." Carl Sagan, *Billions and Billions:*

Thoughts on Life and Death at the Brink of the Millenium (New York: Ballantine, 1997), 240.

9. C. G. Jung, "On the Psychological Concept of the Trinity," trans. Gary Hartmann, *Quadrant* XXVIII:1 (Winter 1998): 7-29. Although "Trinity" is a Christian term for the community of God as Father, Son, and Holy Spirit, one God fully present in three divine "Persons," this notion is not articulated as such in either the Old Testament or the New. Perhaps its objective roots lie in the narratives of Jesus praying to God as his Father and being led by the divine Spirit. Over time, traditional ideas about the concept of Trinity provided a relevant psycho-theological structure through which an entire community of persons experienced the Three Persons of the Godhead. Today, as dogma and idea, the concept of the Trinity continues to be a collective experience through which God continues to manifest presence in individuals and groups. As such, the Trinity functions as a collective lens through which to view experience or a collective container in which to contain experience, by means of which both individuals and worshipping communities can have personal experience of the "God of the mystics," regardless of their religious background.

10. We 'use' numbers; we 'count' three. Symbolic consciousness recognizes the pattern of three-ness as representative of far-reaching principles, guides to a cosmic canon of design, whose clearest text is what has been called the Book of Nature. For me, living in this world without insight into the hidden laws of Nature is like not knowing the language of the country of my birth.

11. Michael Schneider, *A Beginner's Guide to Constructing the Universe: The Mathematical Archetypes of Nature, Art and Science—A Voyage from One to Ten* (New York: Harper Perennial, 1995).

12. *Ibid.*, 9.

13. *Ibid.*, xxii-xxiiii.

14. See my recent book *A Dream in the World.*

15. Desmond Tutu, *No Future without Forgiveness* (New York: Doubleday, 1999), 31.

16. D. W. Winnicott, "On the Basis for Self in Body," in *Psychoanalytic Explorations*, eds. Clare Winnicott, Ray Shepherd and Madeleine Davis (Cambridge, Mass: Harvard University Press, 1989), 261.

17. Religious disciplines offer a variety of techniques to suppress, modify, or purify the body in order to attain a state of perfection,

happiness, purity, or to acquire supernatural power. In such disciplines, the body may be used, subjected, transformed, or improved, every bit as much as in modern sports training. The Christian ritual of the Eucharist differs from some of these disciplines entirely, in that it accomplishes a state of communion with the deity by infusing something pure into the body. Buddhist disciplines seem to loosen the grip of ego identification. In Soto Zen, the body's breathing is the prototype of *wu-wei* or Chin, that is, "non-action." In Judaism and Islam, the act of portraying the Creator as embodied in image is expressly forbidden since the Almighty is believed to be devoid of any representable content. In Hinduism, where embodiment is not the determining factor in the difference between gods and humans, incarnations abound. The Taoist body is a microcosm of the geographical country, the social and administrative state, ultimately of the whole cosmos. In Taoist thought and practice the body becomes a central symbol, the focus of ritual, rooted in the older traditions of spirit possession, alchemy, and the search for longevity and immortality.

In Christianity, the Body of Christ incorporates three major loci of religious significance: the human body of Jesus transformed at the resurrection; the consecrated bread, whose Eucharistic reception ritualizes a form of symbolic cannibalism; and the church as the People of God, the community that is the vehicle of God's redemptive activity on earth. "Because there is one loaf of bread, we, who are many, are one body; for we all partake of the one loaf of bread" (1 Corinthians 10: 17, World English Bible).

18. Christopher Bamford, "Washing the Feet," in *An Endless Trace: The Passionate Pursuit of Wisdom in the West* (New Paltz, New York: Codhill Press, 2003), 287-88.

19. Mary Oliver, "Wild Geese," in *Dream Work* (New York: The Atlantic Monthly Press, 1986), 14.

20. J. M. Coetzee, *Elizabeth Costello* (New York: Viking, 2003).

21. Erich Neumann, *Depth Psychology and a New Ethic*, trans. Eugene Rolfe (New York: Harper & Row, 1969), 8.

22. Linda Hogan, "Department of the Interior," in *Minding the Body: Women Writers on Body and Soul*, ed. Patricia Foster (New York: Bantam Doubleday Dell, 1994), 12-13.

23. Edward G. Corrigan and Pearl-Ellen Gordon, eds., *The Mind Object: Precocity and Pathology of Self-Sufficiency* (Northvale, New Jersey:

Jason Aronson, Inc., 1995). Put simply, a too-early identification with our mind's capacity to organize and conceptualize experience, to understand and verbalize it, leads to denigration and denial of the pleasures and sufferings of bodily existence. Life becomes obscured by our unconscious reliance upon a state of knowledge.

24. Theologian Sallie McFague suggests that Jesus' healing miracles, which focus attention on bodily pain and bodily relief, are to be understood as religious statements of how much the body matters in Christian thought, that the healing metaphor for salvation "does not suggest ecstatic fulfillment of all desires but rather preservation from destruction or, at most, the restoration to adequate bodily functioning ... [to] what in ecological terms is called "sustainability," the ability to function in terms of bodily needs." Sallie McFague, *The Body of God: An Ecological Theology* (Minneapolis: Fortress Press, 1993), 167-68.

25. Less vulnerable than dreams to our habits of mind, direct religious experience is embodied in a person or a people. The Jews crossed the Red Sea and spent forty years wandering in the desert. Mary conceived and bore a son. Jesus was born of a woman, grew up, ate and drank, walked and preached, and died on a cross. Saul was thrown from his horse and blinded on the road to Damascus. My patient Maire felt light coursing along her spine, autonomous orgasm, and the Presence of the Holy Spirit. While practicing Hatha Yoga, Maire felt herself led to what felt like the heart of religious reality, an enormous infusion of energy and light emanating from within her body and the body of the world. This substantive experience led Maire to feel, not less embodied, but more, and accepting of her mortality. "I've gone from being in a 'morality play' to being in a 'mortality plan,'" she said. Instead of an experience of Nothing or the 'empty center' of Jung's imaginative vision of the Self, Maire experienced Something which gave her a new life and a Second Chance. Instead of falling endlessly, Maire found herself securely "held" (in Winnicott's terms), not in a mother's arms, nor in the arms of an archetype, but in her own body—not by the archetypal world, but by that to which the archetype points, and from which archetypal energy emerges.

26. Laleh Bakhtiar, *Sufi: Expressions of the Mystic Quest* (London: Thames and Hudson, 1976), 21.

27. In Christianity, Judaism, and Islam, the transmission of wisdom is held to originate with the divinity. Descending during the 'night of predestination' as a whole, undifferentiated state of Divine knowledge, the Quran was fixed not in the mind of the Prophet (who could not read), but in his body, in what was understood to be an undifferentiated mode of consciousness which related to pure cosmic potentiality. See Titus Burckhardt, *Introduction to Sufism*, trans. D. M. Matheson (San Francisco: Harper Collins, 1995), 45. R. Guenon (Burckhardt, 43, n. 5) writes that the "night of predestination" is identified with the very body of the Prophet. What needs noting here is that the revelation was received in the body of the being entrusted with the mission of expressing the Principle. Likewise, the Gospel of John says: *Et verbum caro factum est* ("And the Word was made flesh"—*caro*, not *mens*: mind, thought, intellect). This is an exact expression in a form proper to the Christian tradition of what the "night of predestination" represents in the Islamic tradition.

The understanding of revelation as outlined in the Quran is similar to that found in the Vedas of the Hindu tradition. Like the Quran, the Vedas are understood to subsist from all eternity in the Divine Intellect. Its "descent" is brought about by virtue of the primordial nature of sound. The *rishis*, like the prophets, are said to have received it by inspiration (visual and auditory), and transmitted it just as they saw and heard it without any mental discrimination on their part (Burckhardt, 44-45). Here what is traditionally called cosmic does not imply the unconscious as we know it. Islam's emphasis upon the primacy of the body has little connection with psychology's speculations about an unconscious from which psychic impulses arise, for in Islam, a principle (spirit) is known to have brought about such a descent.

28. In all three "religions of the book" (Judaism, Christianity, Islam), received teachings are continually renewed by contact with a source which lies outside time. Although the formulation of traditional doctrine is immutable in essence, it must be renewed within the framework of given conceptual styles in relation to different possible modes of intuition and experience, and according to human circumstances. Occasionally, some saint or mystic is gifted with an experience that is deemed worthy by tradition of inclusion. When this happens, the body of religious tradition changes organically, out

of the depths of the human soul. Psychologically speaking, religious traditions contain "footprints" of individual religious experience which have been gathered together and painstakingly formulated by a body of practitioners and believers over time. Jung reminds us that "Creeds are codified and dogmatized forms of original religious experience ... every creed is originally based on the one hand on the experience of the numinosum and on the other hand upon *pistis*, that is to say trust or loyalty, faith and confidence in a certain experience of a numinous nature and the change of consciousness that ensues ...." (*Collected Works* 11 § 9-10.) But all religious experience, as well as the painstaking gathering and formulating of religious experience, happens in bodies and by means of bodies, individually and communally.

29. *Collected Works* 9i § 291.

30. Edward S. Reed, *The Necessity of Experience* (New Haven: Yale University Press, 1996).

31. David Whyte, *The Heart Aroused: Poetry and the Preservation of the Soul in Corporate America* (New York: Currency and Doubleday, Bantam Doubleday Dell, 1994).

32. When asked by Frederick Franck, "What is Zen?" Daisetz Teitaro Suzuki replied, "I would say Zen is that which makes you ask that question. When you ask 'What is Zen?' you are asking 'Who am I' and when you ask 'Who am I?' you are asking 'What is it to be human?' It is the existential question, the primal riddle we bring along into the world when we are born and must answer before we leave it, on penalty of having gone through life in vain. ... Zen is not a religion, it is the profoundly religious ingredient in the world religions." Quoted in Frederick Franck, "On Being Human Against All Odds," in *Annals of Earth* , IX.2: 11.

33. Mark Epstein, *Going to Pieces without Falling Apart: A Buddhist Perspective on Wholeness: Lessons from Meditation and Psychotherapy* (New York: Broadway Books, 1998), 112-13.

34. Douglas Steere, *Together in Solitude* (New York: The Crossroad Publishing Company, 1985), 105-27.

35. I first came across the idea of participating consciousness in Owen Barfield's *Saving the Appearances: A Study in Idolatry* (New York: Harcourt, Brace and World, 1965). Gregory Bateson and Morris Berman, among others, also use this phrase. See Gregory Bateson, *Steps to an Ecology of Mind* (New York: Ballantine, 1972), and Morris

Berman, *The Reenchantment of the World* (New York: Bantam New Age, 1989) and *Coming To Our Senses: Body and Spirit in the Hidden History of the West* (New York: Bantam Books, 1990).

36. *Participation mystique* (after Levy-Bruhl) indicates an unconscious merger with one's people, surroundings, or world; it indicates unconscious identification with what Neumann called "cosmic anonymity" or the uroboric self—the enclosed, yet world-encompassing cosmos of the newborn. As a substrate of primary process material which underlies everything, *participation mystique* is originative, not developmental. Unlike development of the ego, *participation mystique* does not need cultural factors to trigger it, nor does any amount of civilization eradicate it. *Participation mystique* remains the basis of perception throughout life, surpassable but not done away with.

For the sake of psychic structure, separation and differentiation of the psyche precede integration and reunion within a personality. Often therapists find that *participation mystique* is something to be analyzed for the sake of emerging ego consciousness and eventual individuation.

37. *'Abaissement du niveau mental'* means a lowering of the threshold of ego-consciousness, a term Jung borrowed from Janet. With activation of a complex the ego becomes relatively unconscious under an influx of psychic material. But Neumann reminds us that as ego-intelligence dims, the field of cognition widens considerably.

38. A call for a return to and recovery of what participating consciousness implies comes from many quarters. Both quantum physics and philosophy remind us that impersonal or objective knowledge is a contradiction in terms. Paul Ricoeur, in *Freud and Philosophy: An Essay on Interpretation* (New Haven: Yale University Press, 1977), calls for a 'second naiveté.' Morris Berman (1989, 1990) finds a need for 're-enchantment.' Earlier, Michael Polyani, in *Personal Knowledge* (Chicago: University of Chicago Press, 1962), implicated us as knowers in everything we know, arguing that all our knowing is not really what we think of as 'knowing' but takes place in terms of meaning.

39. Ann Ulanov, *Receiving Woman: Studies in the Psychology and Theology of the Feminine* (Philadelphia: The Westminster Press, 1981), 61-63.

40. Barfield, 137.

41. Jessica Benjamin, "Recognition and Destruction: An Outline

of Intersubjectivity," in *Relational Perspectives in Psychoanalysis*, ed. Neil J. Skolnick and Susan C. Warshaw (New York: The Analytic Press, 1992).

42. Ewart J. Cousins, *Christ of the Twenty-First Century* (Rockport, Mass: Element Books, Continuum, 1992), 121.

43. Most contemplative traditions agree that the point of meditative practice is not to develop virtuoso skill in acquiring what we think of as knowledge (and further self-deception), but to make space for unlearning, for a letting-go of habits of mindlessness. The training and effort this requires differs from the efforts necessary to acquire something new, even if extrane.

44. James Arraj, *St. John of the Cross and Dr. C. G. Jung: Christian Mysticism in the Light of Jungian Psychology* (Chiloquin, Oregon: Tools for Inner Growth, 1986).

45. Thomas Berry, *The Dream of the Earth* (San Francisco: Sierra Club Books, 1988).

46. Plato (*Timaeus*) formulates what is probably our earliest concept of the World Soul. Jung (*Collected Works* 8 § 931) found that the alchemists related their concept of the *anima mundi* on the one hand to Plato's World Soul, and on the other to the Holy Spirit, present at the Creation, who as procreator, impregnates the waters with the seed of life. Later the Holy Spirit plays a similar role in the *obumbratio* (overshadowing) of Mary. Jung (*Collected Works* 13 § 236) also traces the *anima mundi* to Mercurius, as did the earlier Islamic writer Avicenna, whom Jung cites as saying: "... [T]he spirit of the Lord which fills the whole world and in the beginning swam upon the waters ... they call (him) the spirit of Truth, which is hidden from the world ...."

47. Jung, *Collected Works* 8 § 195.

48. Jung, *Collected Works* 5 § 198.

49. Andrew Harvey, *The Essential Mystics: Selections from the World's Great Wisdom Traditions,* ed. Andrew Harvey (San Francisco: HarperSanFrancisco, 1996), xi.

FROM SEEING TO KNOWING

JANET ADLER

I offer these words to you, dear Marion, in gratitude for the honor of participating in this special issue. When we met in 1982 at Jacob's Pillow in Lee, Massachusetts, at the first Authentic Movement conference, you and I took a long walk. Walking next to you through the forest, I am looking down at your feet and mine, as each one seems to step out of nowhere into the space directly in front of us. I hear your words and mine as we share our stories of energetic phenomena, our direct experience of the numinous. This precious walk, this gift held dear in memory, becomes a vessel which carries to you now some of my more recent thoughts and experiences reflecting my continuing inquiry into the mysteries of direct experience.

I witness a mover with eyes closed sitting on the floor, cross-legged. I see this woman lifting one foot up onto her other thigh. As it rests there, she brings the fingers of one hand to the underside of this foot, pressing the skin gently. I see her other hand scooping under her foot and, with those fingers, delicately caressing her toes. Tears are

Janet Adler has a Ph.D. in mystical studies and teaches the discipline of Authentic Movement internationally. In 1981, she founded and directed the Mary Starks Whitehouse Institute, the first school for Authentic Movement studies. She appears in two films, *Looking for Me* (1968) and *Still Looking* (1988), and is the author of *Arching Backward: The Mystical Initiation of a Contemporary Woman* (1995) and *Offering from the Conscious Body: The Discipline of Authentic Movement* (2002).

This article was originally presented as a paper to the C. G. Jung Institute of Santa Fe, New Mexico, in the Spring of 2003.

falling down her cheeks as she sits, one woman, one form, in the midst of our universe, simply holding her foot. As witness, I too, become riveted to her foot, and my own heart aches with such tenderness as I see, as though I am feeling, the tears streaming down her face. Soon, when she returns to her cushion, with eyes open, to speak her experience and to listen to mine, I hear the voice of her inner witness as she speaks of a "rush" of feeling, of love for her foot. I hear her words and know the silence around them. I see her lift her foot and know the stillness around her.

The discipline of Authentic Movement concerns a mover's longing to be seen by an outer witness, and the longing of a witness to see a mover. Most of us know a great longing for both within our nature, to see ourselves and to see and be seen by an other. How simple this can sound; how complex, incomplete, and mysterious this is! I once heard a mover say to her witness: "When I see you seeing me, I stay nearer to myself."

The core of this work is the evolution of the inner witness manifesting within the development of mover consciousness and the development of witness consciousness. The mover begins, safely in the presence of an outer witness, by learning to become aware of her impulses to move, which ones she chooses to follow into movement, and the accompanying felt density in her body, which can be experienced as sensations, emotions, or thoughts. This process of an emerging inner witness invites a clearing of the inner chambers, the places imbued with personal and collective memory, often trauma and suffering, places created through the presence and the absence of love. Such work, so many years and years of work, though in direct service of the soul, is usually compelled by the personality, the incomprehensible but vivid combination of genetic coding and personal history. Such work becomes a necessary blessing as ground for other ways of embodied knowing.

Through this process of clearing toward presence, veils lift. I love the following poem by Mary Oliver because it reflects the full range of my experiences of movers and witnesses, our commitment, our growing compassion for ourselves and for one other, our developing acceptance of what we know to be true from moment to moment. I am especially grateful for her stunning words reminding us that always and always, no matter how much inner work we do, there can remain places of density and darkness that cannot, will not, open, no matter the greatness of our desire for light.

I will sing for the veil that never lifts
I will sing for the veil that begins, once in a lifetime,
    maybe, to lift
I will sing for the rent in the veil
I will sing for what is in front of the veil, the
    floating light
I will sing for what is behind the veil-
    light, light, and more light.
This is the world, and this is the work of the world.[1]

Because the strengthening inner witness clarifies and expands, the individual becomes more able consciously to recognize, honor, and trust the body knowing, an intuitive wisdom occurring as veils lift. In the discipline of Authentic Movement, I find the term 'direct experience,' which originates within the mystical traditions of monotheistic religions, to best describe moments of purely embodied awareness for movers and for witnesses. This term is proving helpful as we attempt to bridge such experience as it moves from body, through language, toward consciousness. The studio work increasingly demonstrates qualities of a mystical practice.

What occurs in this practice has occurred similarly in different ancient and contemporary mystical traditions. There is a call toward entering emptiness. With eyes closed and with focus inward, there is an intention toward staying present, toward practicing the art of concentration. There is practice toward the rigor of impeccability in tracking inner experience. There is a longing for a language that could describe direct experience, that which is indescribable. Ritual occurs, becomes necessary. The blessing of clear silent awareness can become known. There is deep desire for daily life to manifest such a blessing, such awareness.[2]

The privilege of growing such an inner witness demands hard work as well as awareness of the blessing of such grace. Growing such an inner witness directly creates opportunity for transformation from the most delicately woven, poignant personal story, a narrative that feels completely unique, into a boundaryless space where the thirst, the longing for healing, ceases as the awareness of the experience becomes universal. What follows are words from a mover as she tracks a visual image created by embodied experience of both "the mass" and "the stem," a developmental journey in which she discovers presence in "the direct stream."

I know that the 'mass' has been something that I have felt to be a part of my body for years. It is a hunger that isn't for food. It is shrouded in wads of gauze, dampening and muffling its cry. I keep moving so I don't have to answer, because somehow in moving it is quieted.

Recently while moving, it announces itself as a 'mass of desire'. I hear very distinctly the cry for recognition, for filling and it has to do with being enough, being worthy, being okay to ask for something, anything that I want and to act on that need, desire, request.

Today actual movement into and out of the area brings sensation to it that is new, more web-like, maybe tingling. The 'stem' under the mass appears and has to do with something else … something that seems like a very mysterious thing. I am standing there and all of my being knows that a particular alignment of my spine allows me to be a part of the energy matrix that creates our manifest world rather than slightly out of the path of it. This sensation is a radical shift in consciousness or being. It's a little like feeling my body as a tuning fork in some way and when I can receive clearly through my body, my ego kind of goes away and yet I still am.

Somehow I have stepped into 'the direct stream' and it can just pass through me. I haven't dissolved, but I am a part of … and the great hunger is gone! This picture helps me understand the quantum level shift of experience that I sense when my 'stem' gets lined up with my 'mass'. Oh brother. I do feel like this is a huge opening for me into what I can now believe in as my understanding of Spirit and the Trinity. I feel like I just got baptized or something. Or maybe it's communion, because I have responsibility to act on this knowledge.

As this mover works with "the mass," she is not merged with her experience because she is tracking sensation, emotion, and thought that are occurring directly in her body, creating a dialogic awareness. When she is in the "direct stream," she enters a unitive state for what she later describes as an eternal moment. In moments of such grace, as has just been described by this mover, the inner witness is fully present as awareness and yet such presence in no way divides or complicates knowing—knowing becomes intuitive. Here there is an experience of non-duality, in which there is no separation between the moving self and the inner witness, and yet it is the development of the inner witness that makes such an experience possible. In this practice, we are moving from embodied relationship with associative phenomena toward direct experience of energetic phenomena.

As egoic layers of the mover and the witness become consciously embodied enough, spaciousness becomes palpable and seeing becomes so much more than looking with the eyes. Seeing oneself, seeing another become synonymous with knowing oneself, knowing another. Direct experience creates intuitive knowing. Robin van Löben Sels writes: "the process of seeing represents a spiritual act. ... Here, intelligence does not mean reason or discursive thought as we think of it but intelligence as an organ of direct knowledge or certainty, a pure light of intelligence that goes beyond the limits of reason alone."[3]

Such a particular kind of intelligence, clarified by van Löben Sels, is certainly germane to the phenomenon of awareness. I often return to Arthur Deikman's clear discussion about such experience within his inquiry into what he calls the observing self. He insists that we cannot observe the observing self, that we must experience it directly. He names the absence of any defining qualities, boundaries, and dimensions. "Awareness is the ground of conscious life, the background or field in which all elements exist ... behind your thoughts and images is awareness, and that is where you are."[4]

Where you are, where I am, here you are, here I am ... these words can reflect a developing intimacy with our bodies, our temples. Dilip Roy, a disciple of Sri Aurobindo and The Mother, writes of tantriks as yogis who accept life in its entirety, including the body, which they call the temple of God. His description of direct experience is refreshing:

> I found myself ensconced in a blind darkness. All of a sudden, there was a great stir above my head. I could see nothing in the gloom, but heard a voice distinctly say: 'Direct hit, direct hit, direct hit.'[5]

This direct hit is different from the experience of the moving self and inner witness being merged or in a dialogic relationship. Direct experience is synonymous with surrendering images of self, of an identity of self as one has known it. In such moments, some movers and witnesses speak of moving into and through the archetype of God, or the symbolic nature of God, into a clear silent awareness, an infinite emptiness. This emptiness is named by mystics, by Buddhists, by shamans, by human beings who have wandered and who do wander through our world inquiring into the mystery of our presence here, into the nature of fear and its relationship to awe within the exquisite and inherently ordered reality of our lives cycling.

Rabbi Akiva describes man's desire to "dispense with the mental *idea* or image of God, and by transforming himself, *experience* Him."[6] Meister Eckhart writes of wanting "to penetrate the simple core, the still desert into which no distinction ever crept, neither the Father, the Son nor the Holy Spirit."[7] He encourages a detachment from self, from the image of self so that one can unite with the formless being. Thomas Merton explains a Zen perspective: "… [O]ne is Buddha and that Buddha is not what the images in the temple had led one to expect, for there is no longer any image and consequently nothing to see, no one to see it, and a Void in which no image is even conceivable."[8]

A contemporary scholar of mysticism, Richard Smoley, speaks about direct experience from the perspective of the esoteric traditions. He discusses higher realms that have an objective existence, that can be known and experienced. "Some say these levels are more real than the one we experience in ordinary life."[9]

How do these places feel more real? They are known to be completely so in the body.

In the discipline of Authentic Movement we intend toward practicing an awareness of embodied detail, felt by the senses one by one, sequentially marked, regardless of the content or the source of what is becoming manifest. A mover speaks:

> I know God only because of this body that I am in. This knowing occurs HERE as I stand and open my hands, tilt my head back, bend my knees. I hear a soft but high-pitched sound, not vacillating, but consistent and strong, as my skin becomes porous. My boundaries evaporate as I notice a quickening, now a pulsation, now a subtle vibration traveling from my heels upward, through my yoni, my throat and out the top of my head. I am upward—no downward—I am everywhere and nowhere.

Antonio de Nicholas, another contemporary scholar of mysticism, writes: "The mystic is not stopped from practicing religion in a different way, by the use of faculties other than the cognitive. …

The primary text of a mystic … is his human body."[10] And here are the words of James Hillman, referring to Gopi Krishna and his experiences of kundalini:

> … [D]id these events actually take place in his body, in his cells, nerves, organs? Or did they take place in the yogic body? … The chakra system of the yogic body is not supposed to have any objective existence in physical space. Yet the psyche insists on this body language and body experience so that what is logically impossible is indeed psychologically not only possible but felt to be true … his physical body was for him the material place of projection of immaterial events and there in the 'body' they were experienced by the senses and felt to be 'real'.[11]

But how to speak, adequately enough, these ineffable experiences that are called many different names in different cultures, each with profound similarities and astonishing uniqueness? Speaking what is ineffable creates an instant contradiction. Though it can feel impossible to speak these 'direct hits,' these moments of unity consciousness, the human psyche longs to, and even feels it must, especially when such experiences are new to the nervous system, new to developing consciousness. But speech and language are primarily symbolic phenomena.

In the discipline of Authentic Movement it is the intention of the mover when returning after the moving experience to speak with the witness, to practice toward speaking the experience, not speaking about it. We attempt to offer the words in such a way that there can be a felt shift from the words carrying symbolic meaning or narration, toward the words energetically becoming the vibrations that they are and thus directly being the meaning themselves. Practicing in this way opens pathways for a natural process of integration, which reduces the tremendous intensity of the longing to speak such unnameable forces as they become directly embodied.

I hear a witness speak these words: "I see you turn and I feel compassion." As I listen to this particular witness speak in this moment, the word 'compassion' is compassion itself, not a symbol for it. I intuitively, directly receive the compassion. My experience here as a listener is distinctly different from what it is at other times when I hear someone say he or she feels compassion and I am brought into an experience of the meaning of the word instead of knowing a direct experience of the word.

Until recently, it has been mostly mystics who have felt challenged and yet compelled to try to speak and write such experiences. Now as these experiences are occurring more often in our culture, we are receiving words from people who do not necessarily think of themselves as mystics. Within the process of finding words, of bridging body to consciousness, it is completely natural to wonder: what does this mean? How can I understand it? A mover speaks:

> When I find myself bringing too much effort toward meaning, 'she' is trapped, the feminine is trapped. I am trapped. This is not about meaning. This is about trust. I want to stay with the contextual rather than the conceptual. I want to stay in my body.

In the discipline, we are studying the distinction between symbolic experience and direct experience. Direct experience evolves without a particular philosophy, without analytic inquiry, without narrative language. We are practicing awareness of the grace of direct experience when it occurs. The meaning, if any occurs beyond the experience itself, cannot be known until after the experience of conscious embodiment. We are trusting that insight will appear within an inherent, synchronistic order of inner process, developed within the intuitive realms. In the meantime, we are intending toward practicing the cultivation of embodied presence. When this can happen, conceptual or symbolic ways of knowing float back into the wings of our consciousness, there to support, confirm, and enrich the intuitive knowing. The following words have lived inside my desk on a faded yellow card for twenty-five years. They clarify and sustain my developing questions concerning the ways in which imaginal or conceptual experience differs from intuitive knowing:

> Intuition provides the insight that sees through the filtering screen of thoughts, images and feelings to the formless content of experience. Once you recognize the permeable and transitory nature of this screen, you can subjectively differentiate between intuition and imagination.
>
> The distinction between intuition and imagination is precisely this: pure intuition is knowledge that comes out of the formless silence, whereas imagination gives form to the formless and is conceptual in nature. When one imagines something, one is conceiving of it, no matter how abstractly. Thus, imagination is the vehicle by which intuition finds expression in life.[12]

The utter force of imagination is of course ancient, boundless, and one of our greatest and most mysterious inner resources. At times, while moving or witnessing, when the fullness of a gesture is apparent and the heart—oh, the heart—wants to break, the mind craves meaning. In such moments, imagination can erupt. The visual image can seduce, persuade one into associative phenomena. Such images can be experienced as limitless in quality, texture, context, content, light, color, sound, movement—limitless in possible meaning.

Here the mover or the witness can consciously choose to commit to the image itself, riding it into the deep nature of the conceptual mind, or choose to stay specifically with the embodied experience, aware of the image but not engaging with it. In the studio now, more and more individuals are choosing the latter, staying true first to the experience of conscious embodiment. When the body can be trusted enough because of the presence of a strong inner witness, and when the heart can be allowed to break, it becomes possible to open into another way of knowing, of being released directly into the core or formless source of the gesture.

The philosopher, Henri Bergson, offers this perspective:

> ... [P]hilosophers agree in making a deep distinction between two ways of knowing a thing. The first implies going all around it, the second entering into it. The first depends on the viewpoint chosen and the symbols employed, while the second is taken from no viewpoint and rests on no symbols. The second can attain the absolute ... an absolute can only be given in an intuition, while all the rest has to do with analysis. We call intuition here the sympathy by which one is transported into the interior of an object in order to coincide with what there is unique and consequently inexpressible in it.[13]

How can the mover find his or her way into the direct, inexpressible nature of a gesture? What does it mean to enter a thing, to enter an experience without the trusted accompaniment of the conceptual mind, yet with conscious presence? I do not know explicitly how to answer this question, but I have been studying it deeply for many years now. Just as the Zen masters can move us closer to what a thing is by telling us what it is not, I can say that to enter a thing, in this context, is not to merge with it, not to be in a dialogic relationship to it, for example, as in wondering about it from a place of curiosity, but to somehow become one with it, because of it.

I do know that a particular hue of vulnerability is necessary, a readiness to open into the completeness of not knowing, into true surrender. I know that a mover feeling intuitively that he or she must enter a specific moment "now" tells us that timing has to be related to such a choice. I also know that when such choices are made—and I believe that to enter a thing or an experience truly, one has to make a conscious choice—one is initiated into a new way of knowing, and in such a moment, consciousness changes. These realities have everything to do with the practiced attunement of an inner witness. The body is the direct route to the kind of consciousness that knows a formless silence, the consciousness that quivers at the core of all form and all space.

In this particular inquiry, I have, somewhat simplistically, isolated four ways a mover can experience a visual image from an intention to remain embodied. Of course, the subtle nuances of similarity and difference between and among them all characterize more closely the true spectrum of the developing inner witness. Though it is equally engaging to follow these journeys of image within the experience of an outer witness, I am choosing here to focus on the mover. From my perspective as both a mover and an outer witness, the content is secondary, no matter how remarkable, archetypal, or unusual the implied meaning, to the felt, embodied experience as the image is being "seen." It is the energy that is moving within the body, the energy that creates the image, that concerns authentic change, not the story that the image implies.

The first two ways occur when the mover is either moving or still. In the first way, the mover is seeing an image outside of herself, an image that is not experienced in her body. To return to the woman holding her foot, as she sits on the floor filling with emotion and gratitude, she now becomes aware of a visual image. This image has a two-dimensional quality and exists over there away from the mover, perhaps a picture of the mover. There is no felt connection between the image and the mover's awareness of her body. When such a picture appears, it is natural to wonder: What does this mean? Here the mover is reminded to try to stay within her body sensation while simultaneously being aware of the image.

> As I hold my foot in my hands, I see myself sitting in a cave
> by the sea.

In the second way, the visual image that becomes apparent also begins over there, outside of the body. If awareness of it persists, the mover might notice that it is infused with perhaps texture or movement and might choose to make the image part of her embodied experience as she begins to feel the multi-dimensional, alive qualities which resonate now inside of her. The mover learns to discern whether she is experiencing the image as it enters her body from the outside and she begins moving it or she is consciously going toward the image that she sees, entering it, now moving it ... bringing her conscious body to the image that she sees:

> I see my hands leaving my foot. My right hand reaches forward, grabbing a stone ledge that is appearing just above the surface of what looks like ocean water. I am pulling myself up, climbing into a sea cave. I sit inside this cave.

As the body and the image meet, there can naturally be even more interest in the personal meaning of a sea cave, the mover's history with such an image, the relationship history with this image between the mover and the witness, the mover's family history with this image, and so on. Here the mover's mind becomes curious, and because of the vividness of the light, the colors of the water and stone, the weight of the body changing planes, she would like to know more about this spontaneous series of sensations, perhaps emotions, and thoughts. This mover has many choices, one of which is to just stay with the embodied experience as she consciously moves into the image or the image consciously moves into her and trust that meaning, if any, can appear as intuitive knowing when the gestalt of her entire being is ready.

The third way in which an image can enter the work of a mover is for the movement itself to create the image or series of images. The body actually spontaneously forms or shapes the sensations arising within the image. The person is moving with focus, with presence and trust, when suddenly she is not seeing an image but she is inside it. The mover is directly knowing the image, becoming it. This mover has many choices, one of which is to just stay with the embodied experience and trust that if there is meaning, it will appear as intuitive knowing when the gestalt of her entire being is ready:

> I am sitting, holding my foot. My hands leave my foot and I reach forward in a certain light, like dusk. My hand touches

stone, cold and wet. I can feel it and it is as though I see it, because it is gray in color, kind of striped, but I don't see it with my inner eyes.

I know it because I am here, in it. I pull my weight up onto the stone ledge, lifting each leg, kneeling into a smooth place, wet, but just on the surface. I am turning my body around and sit with my legs crossed inside a sea cave. The curved wall behind me comes around to its edges. I can see the ocean beyond me, wide, becoming vibrant, but again not with my inner eyes. The light is dusk light, dusk light and I am here, opening, opening my arms round in front of my torso. Here I am.

This experience is very different from choosing to enter or be entered by an image outside of the self. This is not an experience guided by visual stimuli but instead by intuitive knowing. The mover does not "see" the cave by the sea yet she knows it in vivid detail. When this kind of experience happens for a mover, she is most likely shifting from a personal toward a transpersonal experience. The content of the images is not personal. There are no emotions here, as is often the case for movers when the experience is sourced in the uniqueness of personality. The centrality of egoic and associative material begins to diminish.

In the fourth way, the mover is inside the embodied image, moving the shapes of it in a manner similar to the way discussed above. But in this way, the mover follows the body as it forms the images, moving in and through them into an experience in which there is no longer any form, into no self, no thing, into a direct experience of emptiness:

I am inside a sea cave on the edge of a tidal flat. I am sitting on stone. The walls are smooth stone, curving, shaping a space, an empty space, a space of light. My arms round in front of my torso. I am holding emptiness; I am holding light. I am becoming emptiness … emptiness and now light.

There is another way, this one dependent on an absence of image from the beginning. In such an experience, there is a vivid awareness of the body within an elegant sense of placement in space, yet no guidance from body shape or image. It is the body knowing without any symbolic reference, narrative language, or egoic perception that direct experience is manifest. If any words are uttered after such an experience, they seem, especially in this situation, to be shaped by intuitive knowing, not symbolic formation.

In these last two examples, the image of the cave as well as all associated sensations integrates. The known image of the self dissolves through a felt permeability of all membranes. The inner witness becomes clear, silent, only aware as the mover awakens into a unitive state, into an experience that is known by the mover to be sacred. Time and space are perceived as infinite. One person in such a moment weeps and knows the word 'gratitude,' another 'awe,' another 'humility.' One begins spinning in silence. One speaks of union with the indwelling God, one says he is being nothing. Another simply sits without words, without desire, need, or impulse. There is no meaning in these direct experiences of emptiness. The meaning is the experience itself.

And there is still one more way I want to name, a way of knowing image that can accompany movers and witnesses, that of visions. Visions may or may not create experience of literal emptiness. They inevitably leave the mover or witness in a particular inner place in which the sense of personhood is expanded. They can occur out there, away from the personal body, or here, fully within. They can be created by the movement, with the mover inside them, or they can evolve outside the moving body. What distinguishes visions from the other ways named above is primarily the stuff of which they seem to be made.

Vision imagery is made of a quality of light, sensed as though the forms, the colors, the movement are forged by an electrical energy. For many this energy can be experienced as sensations of burning, burning line and color, movement and sound, directly into the body. The intensity of the burning can range from terribly painful physically to completely painless, as though there were no physical body to feel the burning. And lastly, the content of the images as well as the thematic development, when there is a series of them, reflects an absence of the laws of gravity, logic, form and shape, time, velocity of travel, as such qualities can be known in or near the earth realm. Here again, the content, no matter what it is, is secondary to the literal changes in body consciousness, in the way of knowing intuitively what is true.

Visions can be experienced as direct manifestations of the formless source, the eternal force, the 'no thing'. Daniel Matt's words, in a paper that means so much to me, are appropriate here:

The word *nothingness*, of course, connotes negativity and non being, but divine nothingness is a positive quality. God is greater than any *thing* one can imagine, like no thing. Since God's being is incomprehensible and ineffable the least offensive and most accurate description one can offer is, paradoxically, *nothing*.[14]

In closing, I return to the patient of Robin van Löben Sels's, who refers to what I understand to be her inner witness, that completely mysterious yet essential inner force which can be known as one of the greatest blessings of all:

> ... [S]ome place else in me kept witnessing all this because I could not, I was ended, what I used to know as 'me' had cracked wide open. I let go, but the witness held it all, unmoved and unmoving, something attending nothing and everything, I felt the force of its attention: clear, open all the way through, always."[15]

All such experiences of intuitive knowing emerging from conscious embodiment can bring some new sense of responsibility, as the woman moving from "the mass" to "the stem" to finding herself in the "direct stream" tells us. True commitment to a parent or to parenting, to a partner, to a work, to our earth body or to our own bodies, is an experience of love. It is love that explodes silently or brilliantly, wildly or sweetly from the source of direct experience. We know love when we directly experience the seer and the seen as one, the knower and the known as one and we are whole. And it is such love that permeates, hones, and makes genuine our responsibility to such a blessing.

NOTES

1. Mary Oliver, *The Leaf and the Cloud* (DaCapo Press, 2000), 15.
2. Janet Adler, *Offering from the Conscious Body: The Discipline of Authentic Movement* (Rochester, VT: Inner Traditions, 2002), xix.
3. Robin van Löben Sels, *A Dream in the World: Poetics of Soul in Two Women, Modern and Medieval* (Hove and New York: Brunner-Routledge, 2003), 85.
4. Arthur Deikman, *The Observing Self: Mysticism and Psychotherapy* (Boston: Beacon Press, 1982), 10-11.

5. Dilip Roy and Indira Devi, *Pilgrims of the Stars* (New York: Macmillan Publishing, 1973), 170.

6. Perle Epstein, *Kabbalah: The Way of the Jewish Mystic* (Boston: Shambhala, 1988), 36.

7. Meister Eckhart, *Meister Eckhart: A Modern Translation*, trans. R. B. Blakney (New York: Harper & Row, 1941), 247.

8. Thomas Merton, *Zen and the Birds of Appetite* (New York: A New Directions Book, 1968), 5.

9. Patrick D. Miller, "What Was Hidden: Looking Deeper into Christianity," An Interview with Richard Smoley, *The Sun*, 333 (September 2003), 7.

10. Antonio de Nicolas, *St. John of the Cross: Alchemist of the Soul* (New York: Paragon House, 1989), 8, 52.

11. Gopi Krishna, *Kundalini: The Evolutionary Energy in Man* (Boulder: Shambhala, 1971), 179.

12. F. E. Vaughan, *Awakening Intuition* (New York: Anchor Books, 1979), 185.

13. W. Barrett and H. Aiken, *Philosophy in the Twentieth Century: An Anthology, Vol. 3* (New York: Random House, 1962), 303, 305.

14. Daniel C. Matt, "Varieties of Mystical Nothingness: Jewish, Christian, and Buddhist Perspectives," in *Wisdom and Logos: Studies in Jewish Thought in Honor of David Winston,* ed. D. T. Runia and G. E. Sterling (The Studia Philonica Annual, Studies in Hellenistic Judaism, Vol. 9, 1997), 314.

15. Van Löben Sels, 22.

Growing a Mind:
The Evolution of Thinking Out of Bodily Experience

WENDY WYMAN-McGINTY

On an archetypal level, the trauma of rape can feel like a loss of soul. To a person struggling for physical survival in the midst of terror, rape represents a loss of innocence and one's sense of physical integrity. In her book *Trauma and Recovery*, Judith Herman notes that during a rape, women frequently cry out for their mothers or for God, and that when their cries go unanswered, their sense of basic trust is shattered.[1] In terms of their relationship to the collective, Herman suggests that "[t]raumatized people feel utterly abandoned, utterly alone, cast out of the divine systems of care and protection that sustain life. When trust is lost, traumatized people feel that they belong more to the dead than to the living."[2]

Wendy Wyman-McGinty, Ph.D., is a Jungian analyst, licensed clinical psychologist, and registered dance therapist. She has presented her work in the U.S., Europe, and Australia, and currently serves on the faculty at the C. G. Jung Institute of Los Angeles.

This paper was presented at the pre-congress day workshop entitled "Edges of Embodied Experience: The Moving Imagination," at the XVI Congress of the International Association for Analytical Psychology, Barcelona, 29 August 2004. An 800-word abstract will be published in the XVI IAAP Barcelona Congress Proceedings.

During the recovery process, patients may report feelings of dissociation and depersonalization as they begin to make contact with the depth of the trauma. Often patients may be flooded with feelings, but feel unable to think, to even put words to their experience, while others report a sense of numbness and lack of feeling. In my own practice, I have found that authentic movement, which focuses on the physical expression of inner experience, can lead to an increased ability to think and feel, particularly about feelings that have been split off, because they are experienced as potentially too disintegrating for the ego to bear.

When trauma occurs, the natural response of the psyche is to withdraw from the scene of the injury.[3] Donald Kalsched notes that when this is not possible, then the otherwise integrated ego must split into fragments, or dissociate, in order to tolerate the potentially damaging impact of the trauma. Dissociation then functions as a protective mechanism, by allowing unbearable experiences to be divided up and distributed to different parts of the mind and body, especially the parts that are unconscious. When this occurs, aspects of consciousness, such as cognitive awareness, affect, sensation, and imagery cannot be integrated. When thoughts and feelings cannot become linked,[4] patients suffer from what Joyce McDougall[5] referred to as "alexithymia," having no words for feelings. The affects which are felt to be unbearable are thus not able to acquire symbolic mental representation. Instead of being shared with another, these painful states of being often go into the body, where they exist as physical symptoms, anxiety, depersonalization, derealization, and dissociation. In bringing these split-off parts of the personality to consciousness, it is important to include both somatic experience as well as the mental aspects of thought and language.

Authentic movement is a form of active imagination in which attention is given to the somatic unconscious, the unconscious as it is experienced and expressed in the body. The patient is encouraged to focus inward, to note carefully any bodily sensations, images, and feelings, which are then utilized as the impetus for self-directed movement. Generally, the patient will close his or her eyes in order to support a more inner-directed expression of unconscious material. The analyst serves as a silent witness to the patient's exploration. In general, the analyst waits for the patient to speak about her experience, before making any reflections or interpretations. Introducing authentic movement in this way can be beneficial in helping patients make contact with certain painful states of mind that might otherwise be kept out of consciousness. Thus, movement can serve an integrating function.[6]

In this paper I would like to describe some of the ways in which a movement sequence evolves, and what this might teach us about the development of thought as it relates to somatic experience. Authentic movement, with its emphasis on the physical expression of unconscious material, allows the mover to express feelings as they are in the process of becoming known. For the witness, there is an opportunity to observe the formation of a symbolic representation before it is verbally articulated. In the process, the words themselves become the movements. As witnesses, we are in the position of observing the subtle evolution of how fragments of somatic experience emerge on the analytic stage, where they may be discarded or integrated depending on the ego's growing capacity to tolerate the accompanying affective dimension. In my own practice, I have frequently had the experience that the body has saved up an experience until there was an opportunity to tell the story "in its own words." Perhaps by evoking somatic memory, authentic movement offers an opportunity to re-experience and sort out previously undifferentiated feeling states into a more coherent narrative. There is an opportunity to re-distribute the feeling into manageable bits, which are then available to be integrated a piece at a time.

The purpose of the witness is to create a sense of trust, of emotional attunement such that early states of mind can emerge and become known in the context of a relationship between two people. Research in attachment[7] suggests that symbolic representation is achieved when there is adequate mirroring, attunement, and a sense of containment on the part of the caregiver (or analyst in this case). This is especially important when working with patients in whom the attachment relationship has been damaged. This may occur when patients identify all too willingly with what they perceive to be the therapist's state of mind (because they can't feel their own), or are too defensive (because it is too difficult for them to take in someone else. The former is characterized by the idealizing transference, while in the latter, the therapist is often kept at bay for fear that he or she will end up "taking over" the patient's experience. Authentic movement, with its focus on amplifying the internal state of the mover, can be helpful in re-directing patients to focus more directly on their own experience as primary.

Clinical Example

E liana, a professional woman in her fifties, came to see me after attending a movement workshop I had given, entitled "Loss of the Mother." Her own mother had died of breast cancer, and Eliana felt there were issues that she wanted to work on. She told me that she felt she was having trouble concentrating, and was experiencing a lack of energy for her work and an increasing sense of fragmentation. My sense was that her fragmentation was not only attributable to her depression, but also the result of some innner attack, which was undermining her ability to think—what Wilfred Bion referred to as "attacks on linking."[8]

Eliana, an exceptionally creative and intuitive woman, had been raped by an intruder some twenty years prior to our work together. Although she reported the rape to the police and confided in her closest friends, she kept the experience a secret from her family, at great cost to herself. Six months after the rape, Eliana suffered a breakdown and was hospitalized for a brief time. She received treatment after her hospitalization and thought she had "put all this behind her."

As we worked together, I observed that Eliana seemed to alternate between being cut off from her feelings and being flooded with affect to the extent that she was unable to link her thoughts together. She would report that she felt numb, stupid, unable to articulate her feelings. At times she would lapse into a narrative, after which she would be left feeling restless, confused, and disconnected. I suggested she give authentic movement a try.

Initially Eliana's movement was full of starts and stops. She would twist her face, get angry, and shake her fist at me. In general, as soon as she started to feel anything, she would stop to tell me how much she hated me, then return to her movement. She would move for a while, then stop, turn towards me and remind me, "I hate you, you know," or declare: "I feel things when I'm in the room with you. I don't like that." She would stomp around the room, pushing at the space around her with her hands. Gradually she began to take on a fighting stance, pushing something away.

Over a period of several months, Eliana relived many aspects of the rape. Unable to breathe, see, or protest verbally, Eliana had condensed herself into a hard object in order to her survive feelings of fragmentation and abandonment. In movement, she showed me in minute detail what her body remembered: the initial surprise and shock, trying to fight off the rapist, keeping her eyes shut so that she couldn't identify him, and the moment when she felt herself leave her body. As she was able to tolerate staying with the feelings for longer periods of time, Eliana experimented with fighting back, allowing her rage to explode. I think we each experienced a sense of relief when this occurred. At other times she would be flooded with feeling, unable to think. In terms of my countertransference, I was aware of feeling drawn to join her in a mindless, numbed-out state. It was only by silently reflecting on my own feelings of helplessness, rage, terror, and grief that I could begin to make a place inside to reflect on her experience.

At times she would relate this disturbing material without much affect, then recognize the impact her words were having on me as she opened her eyes and saw the expression of sadness on my face. It was only then that she would begin to cry. She told me frequently, "I don't want to look at you, because then I know my own feelings are real. I don't feel sad until I see that you are sad for me. When I look into your eyes, I can stand to feel my own pain." The sense of kinesthetic and emotional attunement that she experienced in our mutual gaze went beyond any words or interpretations I could give at that moment. I felt hopeful when she consciously began to choose feeling over disassociating, even though it was so painful.

The more she was able to tolerate the intense affects that the movement evoked, the more she was able to experience her own mind. She told me, "My thinking is different since I have been doing this work. My thoughts are connecting differently. I used to think about being afraid. I tried to change my thoughts. Now it as if my body is informing my thoughts. It feels as though my mind is on the receiving end from my body. Before my body was the last place I wanted to be. With your support I can go there even in my fear. When you are with me in witnessing, and I feel the connection between us, I am also aware that I can let God absorb some of this fear." Eliana, who is deeply immersed in her Jewish faith, felt that God had deserted her during the rape. She told me, "When God left, I did too. It took me a long time to find my relationship to God again." It was only after many months of working together that Eliana was able to articulate her sense that God was also a witness to her rape, and that perhaps God also wept with her. The idea that God somehow shared her grief meant that she was no longer so alone. Some years later, while in the process of preparing this paper, I asked my patient if there was a particular name she would like me to use for her. She chose Eliana, which means "God answered" in Hebrew. My sense was that she finally felt heard, both in terms of our relationship and in her relationship with God. The following session, she reported a dream in which I gave her a loose diamond in the shape of a diamond, which she though represented our work together. Her association was that the clarity of the diamond represented being able to see things more clearly, that it had been given to her, and that it was valuable.

In our next session, Eliana commented on some of the changes she had observed in herself. In this example, the movement served as a linking mechanism between her affective state and the emergence of somatic memory. She began by stating, "I'm noticing some new behavior. I'm into fixing things and following through. I usually give up and wait for someone else, like a man, to do them." Eliana then described, with a sense of pride and accomplishment, some of the things she had repaired in her home. This sense of moving forward was quickly followed by a remark which let me know how difficult it was for her to hold onto these new feelings, and which I think reflected her ambivalence about change and growth. Seemingly out of the blue, she mentioned her birth, telling me, "Did you know that when I was born, I just managed to avoid a C-section. I really took my time to enter the world. It was like I couldn't decide: in or out." I commented on how hard she had been working to birth herself, both in our work and in her outer world. I also suggested that perhaps she was letting me know that just as in her birth process, she didn't want the doctor to rush her process. "That's right," she replied.

Eliana then indicated that she wanted to try movement, and began by closing her eyes and quietly focusing her attention inward. Slowly she bent over at the waist. She told me, "I feel heavy and earthy. My heart is so heavy." She began to cry softly. "It's like I weigh hundreds of pounds. I feel a thick band [around me], almost like stone—so much pressure, I can't breathe. It's so difficult. I feel like there is a stone in my heart." Although she wasn't yet aware of what she was grieving, the sadness in the room was palpable. As she spoke, I became aware that I felt increasingly weighed down, almost as if I were going into a trance. Eliana began to sob as she told me that she felt completely alone during the rape. I reflected back how difficult it must have been to have felt so completely alone, and how hard she must have had to work to hold herself together without knowing what the outcome would be. She responded by putting her hand over heart to hold it. Then haltingly, she relayed how angry and powerless she felt when her brother had molested her. She next told me that she was having trouble holding onto this feeling, and before I could make an interpretation, she continued, saying she had recently lost some weight and had bought some new clothing. She commented on how new this was and that she was trying to hold onto the good feelings. I replied by saying that perhaps there could be room for both kinds of feelings. Then, closing her eyes, she said she was remembering her parents fighting, and that she went to stay with a family friend after her brother exposed himself to her. She told me, "I wish he could have been confronted in front of me. We never worked through the problem." The grief was pervasive.

We sat quietly for a few minutes. Then Eliana opened her eyes and began to speak about our relationship. She said, "You want me to feel safe. I didn't realize how valuable you are. It's so subtle. I always think that you won't be able to contain me. Then you come in from underneath, or something shifts. You surprise me each time. I always think you won't be there. Your process is so different from mine. You have a woman's femininity and I have a man's femininity. This is your home field. I have thought a lot about our relationship. You are sensing me from an inner place. You stay who you are [the constancy of the parent]. You don't jump out of your own skin. I'm constantly disappearing, going into someone else to see what feeling is needed."

In this session, Eliana was beginning to articulate her growing sense of me as a different kind of container, one that was interested and stayed with her, even when things were difficult. Rather than being reactive, which is how she experienced herself, she felt me more as a steady presence. This is very similar to Winnicott's concept of the "holding environment," which gives the child a "continuity of being."[9] Equally important was the recognition of a sense of safety and trust in our relationship. Although I wasn't perfect, she realized that I was doing my best to track her and that her states of mind were important to me. Her comment that I was sensing her from an inner place seems to reflect a lived experience of attunement. Eliana was increasingly aware of and able to articulate the ways in which she would adapt to what she perceived were the needs of others in order to maintain a connection with them, a trait that is characteristic of an anxious attachment style. She was pleased that I did not let this happen in my relationship with her and that she could count on my steadiness, even when she became frustrated or angry with me. She frequently told me that she didn't like to look at me after she had moved, because she could see that I was affected by her. She told me, "When I look at you and your expression, I realize that what I am feeling is real—it affects another person." Her growing ability to bear the tension between not looking at me and the desire to be seen and felt paralleled her movement from an anxious/avoidant form of attachment to a more secure attachment position.

Over time, as Eliana became more conscious of her tendency to dissociate when things were painful, a gradual shift began to take place. Instead of "spacing out," she was able to bring difficult feelings to our sessions and work with them. She would still tell me she hated me when she began to move, but the difference was that she could laugh about it, as if it were our private joke. Intuitively, she understood that hating also meant loving, and that we could talk about it. She was also able to feel my caring for her, even when she hated me. Since I survived her hatred, hate and love could now be joined. There was a quality of affection that underlay the fact that she could have loving and hating feelings towards me, that of course one could feel both gratitude and hate towards a mom who "made" her feel things. Her sense of humor was evidenced in other ways. She once made a card for me that said: "If inquiring minds want to know why you became a therapist, you can tell them, 'I put the fun back in dysfunctional.'" Eliana's sense of humor reminded me of the importance of psychological play in psychotherapy as a necessary part of psychological growth.[10] In terms of the transference, it now felt as if Eliana was freer to use the play space between us.

A few weeks later, Eliana came in, telling me she had a writing block. As an English and drama teacher, she often writes poetry, plays, and prose. She went on, "I ask my students questions, but never think about why I am asking them. I think I get rid of feelings associated with ideas. I have some kind of gap." We talked about what things she didn't want to think about, such as the rape and sexual abuse, and also about how easily she dismisses her distress because it is so hard to hold a space in her mind in which to reflect about herself. She then volunteered, "I loved my mother, but I didn't respect her. She didn't have any power. My mother didn't teach me any skills. I grew up in a very chaotic house. With you, it's all about, 'let's open it up,' 'let's explore it.' I remember my parents arguing." She was quiet, then said softly, "My mother had depth. I do too, and I love that about myself." She began to talk about her hospitalization six months after the rape. She said she remembered the exact moment when she began to dissociate, to feel like she was coming apart. At that time, she wasn't aware that the rape had evoked the earlier traumas of molestation by an uncle as well as by her older brother, who had exposed himself to her. She whispered, "I didn't want to feel."

For many years following her hospitalization, Eliana believed that she was schizophrenic. She felt she had had some kind of breakdown and had briefly lost touch with reality. This was particularly frightening, as she has a younger brother who is a chronic schizophrenic, who alternates between living in a board-and-care facility with intermittent hospitalizations. Although logically she realized that she was able to function in the world, there were times when she felt disconnected and withdrawn, and worried that she was like her younger brother. My sense of her was that she had dissociative episodes, but that she did not have a psychotic core. I wondered out loud whether she would like to learn more about her diagnosis. She said she would, and together we read through the criteria. Eliana sat quietly, tears rolling down her cheeks. Quietly, she began to speak. "This is the first time I have been able to think about what happened to me in the hospital. I see that I am not like my brother." What she found so moving was that she could finally think and feel about what had happened to her after the rape. She recognized that her internal structures had not been strong enough to withstand the trauma, and that there was a name and a description for what had happened to her which was congruent with her experience. As she left, she said, "You have no idea what this session has meant to me. All these years I thought there was this terrible thing inside that was wrong with me. Now I know differently."

One of the most significant things about this session was Eliana's growing ability to use her mind in a reflective way while processing very difficult and painful material. She was able to think about what had happened to her without blocking out how terrifying it had been. I believe that working with the rape over several months made it possible for her to begin to process this material in a new way. First, because of its physicality, the movement allowed her to recover traumatic material experientially.[11] Second, she was able to tell me the story without having to use words. She could show me before she was able to tell me. Third, she was able to go as slowly as she needed to, taking her time to work through the images over and over until they could begin to be talked about and eventually integrated. Finally, the creative aspect of the movement process allowed her to experiment at a bodily level with different responses: her memory of the actual event, the opportunity to respond differently in movement (e.g. fighting back), and finally the grieving process for what had been lost.

Some months later, Eliana came into a session feeling distraught and agitated. A neighbor had parked his car in a way that blocked the entrance to her condominium. She felt dismissed, that it didn't matter to him whether or not she could get in and out of her home at will. She made the connection to how bad she had been feeling about herself. She said, "I want to be isolated and safe. I feel like a dot, a shadow with feelings I want to run away from. I want to be autistic, like a detached retina." I felt she was describing the relief of withdrawing into the autistic shell, as described by Frances Tustin.[12] Eliana closed her eyes, a signal that she wanted to move. As she began to walk, moving her arms out into space, carving a place for herself, she told me, "I need to come into being in order to have a border, but it means risking exposure. Almost immediately, she told me, "I hate you" (her way of letting me know that she was beginning to feel something more intensely). "I don't want to get hurt, so I get empty. Instead of staying with my own feelings, I'll say, 'I'll go along with that.'" As she continued to move, her associations were to her schizophrenic brother. She told me she felt she was beginning to dissociate as she felt what his sense of emptiness must be like. When I asked her what was scary to think about, her immediate association was to her older brother, who had exposed himself to her when she was twelve and he was eighteen. "My father didn't stand up for me with my brother and he didn't stand up for me with my uncle." She mentioned the film *Monsoon Wedding*, in which many members of an extended Indian family stand up to a wealthy uncle who had molested one of his nieces. She wondered what that might have been like, instead of having a family doctor who advised the parents to have Eliana move out for a while, adding, "Imagine, I was supposed to give up my parents and my home because my brother couldn't control himself." As Eliana was able to hold her rage more actively in her own mind, she realized she needed an edge, a boundary, if she was to exist as a separate person. Inside the boundary, feelings that had previously threatened her sense of psychological integrity and caused her to dissociate could now emerge in the context of a relationship with another person, experienced in her body, and consciously held in her mind.

Conclusion

Bion believed that thinking is dependent first on the development of thought(s) followed by the apparatus to cope with them. He conceived of this as a dynamic process in which "thinking has to be called into existence to cope with thoughts."[13] Thoughts are seen as evolving along a continuum, beginning with pre-conceptions. Developmentally, the ability to reflect about one's internal world is linked to being able to stay in contact with feelings without dissociating or splitting off from them. In analysis, particularly in working with primitive mental states, we must find ways of creating a safe enough container or *temenos* in which these fragments of psychological experience can emerge and begin to be linked. It is in the transference relationship that we may first become aware of our patient's relationship to these more fragile states of mind, as well as our own. Numerous authors have suggested that painful states of mind are often relegated to the body, where they exist in mute form as physical symptoms.[14] Similarly, trauma may leave an individual with an experience that cannot yet be mentalized, because it is felt to be potentially too disintegrating to allow into ego consciousness.[15]

The function of the witness is to provide a holding environment in which patients can begin to link up feelings that are difficult to hold onto because they are felt to be potentially too disintegrating to the ego. Without someone to mirror, contain, and help to metabolize the intensity of the affects and manage the psychic pain (what Bion referred to as the alpha function[16]), they go into the body[17] where they remain in the form of physical symptoms, including anxiety, depersonalization, and derealization. Authentic movement allows the individual to experience and express these painful states of mind in such a way that encourages the linking of thinking and feeling. The purpose of the witnessing relationship is to support the development of a reflective function,[18] which enables the individual to contemplate states of mind in himself and others, and this in turn can lead to an integration of the personality.

Whether or not we use movement in our work with our patients, it is my hope that by becoming more sensitive to the ways in which the body holds what the mind cannot, we can help to create a space in which these previously unintegrated parts of the psyche can begin to emerge and become known.

NOTES

1. J. Herman, *Trauma and Recovery: The Aftermath of Violence— From Domestic Abuse to Political Terror* (New York: Basic Books, 1997).

2. *Ibid.,* 52.

3. D. Kalsched, *The Inner World of Trauma* (London & New York: Other Press, 1996).

4. W. R. Bion, "Attacks on Linking," *Second Thoughts* (London: Maresfield Library, 1959): 93-109; J. McDougall, *Theaters of the Body: A Psychoanalytic Approach to Psychosomatic Illness* (New York: W. W. Norton, 1989); Kalsched, *Trauma.*

5. McDougall, *Theaters.*

6. W. Wyman-McGinty, "The body in analysis: Authentic movement and witnessing in analytic practice," *Journal of Analytical Psychology* 43 (1998): 239-260; W. Wyman-McGinty, "Development of a self," in *Authentic Movement, Volume 2,* ed. P. Pallaro (London: Jessica Kingsley Publishers, in press).

7. P. Fonagy, *Attachment Theory and Psychoanalysis* (New York: Other Press, 2001).

8. Bion, "Attacks."

9. D. W. Winnicott, "The theory of the parent-infant relationship," *The Maturational Process and the Facilitating Environment* (Madison: International Universities Press, 1965), 47.

10. D. W. Winnicott, "Playing," *Playing and Reality* (New York: Basic Books, 1971), 37-55; J. Sanville, *The Playground of Psychoanalytic Therapy*, (Hillsdale, N.J. & London: The Analytic Press, 1991).

11. Kalsched, *Trauma*.

12. F. Tustin, *Autistic Barriers in Neurotic Patients* (New Haven & London: Yale University Press, 1986).

13. W. R. Bion, "A theory of thinking," *Second Thoughts* (London: Maresfield Library, 1962), 110-119.

14. J. Chodorow, *Dance Therapy and Depth Psychology* (London & New York: Routledge, 1991); McDougall, *Theaters*; M. Woodman, *The Owl Was a Baker's Daughter: Obesity, Anorexia Nervosa, and the Repressed Feminine—A Psychological Study* (Toronto: Inner City Books, 1980); M. Woodman, *The Pregnant Virgin: A Process of Psychological Transformation* (Toronto: Inner City Books, 1985); M. Woodman, *The Ravaged Bridegroom: Masculinity in Women* (Toronto: Inner City Books, 1990), Kalsched, *Trauma*; Wyman-McGinty, "The body in analysis."

15. McDougall, *Theaters*; Kalsched, *Trauma*; J. Mitrani, *A Framework for the Imaginary: Clinical Explorations in Primitive States of Being* (Northvale & London: Jason Aaronson Inc., 1996).

16. Bion, "A theory of thinking."

17. Mitrani, *Framework*; Woodman, *Owl*; Woodman, *Pregnant Virgin*; Woodman, *Ravaged Bridegroom*; Wyman-McGinty, "The body in analysis."

18. J. Knox, *Archetype, Attachment, Analysis: Jungian Psychology and the Emergent Mind* (Hove & New York: Brunner-Routledge, 2003).

BELLEZZA ORSINI AND CREATIVITY:
IMAGES OF BODY AND SOUL FROM A
SIXTEENTH-CENTURY PRISON

ANTONELLA ADORISIO

(Translated from Italian by Robert Mercurio)

With a different set of images, everything can still be changed.
—Ilio Adorisio

Around 1528-1529, word reached the episcopal vicar of Fiano Romano that various acts of sorcery and witchcraft had been committed by a woman named Bellezza Orsini. After hearing the testimony of three witnesses, the local judge ordered the vicar to arrest her. She was then taken to a castle in the town and imprisoned.

Bellezza Orsini had married at a very young age and was widowed shortly thereafter. She then cared for one of the daughters of the Orsini counts for a while, spent some years in the monasteries of San

Antonella Adorisio is a registered psychologist and psychotherapist in Italy, a dance-movement therapist (Diploma A.T.I.- Supervisor A.P.I.D.), an art psychotherapist (Diploma Goldsmith College-University of London), and a Jungian candidate (C.I.P.A. Rome), who previously served as an historical researcher at a private university in Rome (L.U.I.S.S.). In addition, she has worked as a professional dancer, has taught contemporary dance, and is an Authentic Movement teacher, who trained with Janet Adler and Joan Chodorow.

Paolo at Nazzano and at Civitella San Paolo (as a prisoner according to some witnesses, as a "guest" according to the testimony of Bellezza), and joined the Franciscan order.

Shortly before her imprisonment for witchcraft, Bellezza had been banned from the town of Filacciano, where she was well known as a healer and midwife; indeed, all of the witnesses who later levelled accusations against her came from this small town nestled on the banks of the Tiber in the Sabina region. All of the charges were related to deaths and illnesses that the accusers perceived to result from unsuccessful cures, and were thus linked to Bellezza's role as a healer. As a healer, it was believed, she could not only cure illnesses, but also cause them.

In the legal proceedings against Bellezza, all the witnesses testified that she was widely known to be a witch. However, if she was feared and avoided, she was also respected and sought after in cases of illness and disease, since the victims themselves, believing that they were under her spell, were convinced that only she could heal them. The witnesses made no accusations that Bellezza attended nocturnal Sabbaths or had sworn an oath of submission or loyalty to Satan. Yet she finally confessed, after being subjected to the *spaccada,* a form of torture in which the accused's hands were tied behind his or her back and attached to a rope and pulley, which were then used to hoist the person off the ground and thus dislocate the arm joints. Weakened by this process and exhausted from her imprisonment, Bellezza told the judges everything they wanted to hear, going well beyond what she was formally accused of, admitting to diabolical heresy, and affirming the existence of a fearful society of witches.

Bellezza's confession opened the doors to the secret world of witchcraft with all its typical practices: the smearing of bodies with oil and nocturnal flights to secret distant places, banquets, dancing and the celebration of anti-Christian rites, and wicked acts of sorcery performed together in groups. What Bellezza revealed was a carefully organized network of women spreading over central Italy, with mistresses and commanders, broken down into ranks, all headed by Queen Befania. The headquarters of this society was the city of Rieti, but the favorite site for its nocturnal assemblies was the famous nut tree at Benevento.

All the diabolical implications of witchcraft were thus confirmed. When Bellezza confessed and pleaded for mercy, she validated the accusations of her prosecutors.[1] In the end, she took her own life, and even as she was about to die, she confirmed her belief in the existence of Satan with these words: "Tempted by the diabolical spirit, I decided to kill myself and thought of nothing else than abandoning this world ...."[2]

Circularity

I was a young university student when I first started rummaging through the dusty papers in the Rome State Archives and the Vatican Library. I can still recall the welcoming atmosphere and the smell of the wooden furnishings, just as I remember the feeling of trepidation, reverence, and fear as I leafed through pages written many centuries earlier. I had read up thoroughly on the question of witchcraft, and I knew that there were no traces left of Bellezza's trial proceedings held in Rome, since they had probably disappeared along with parts of the secret archives of the Inquisition. In a booklet published in 1883 (and cited by later historians), Antonino Bertolotti had examined the various trials in and around Rome, but had not given any indication as to where records of these proceedings could be found. If they in fact existed, might there be others too? I was determined to persist in my search, despite the discouraging views of the experts that the material had been destroyed. A deep inner conviction and an impulse to follow my intuition kept me going; I was convinced that sooner or later I would find the proceedings of those trials.

I began going through the listings of all the trials held in Rome in the sixteenth century. These were contained in huge leather-bound parchment tomes. At the same time, I was also reading the *Avvisi di Roma,* a sort of daily journal or newspaper of city life describing the events of that time, from famines and plagues to the finding of abandoned babies, from arrests and the flooding of the Tiber to sightings of comets and the births of monstrosities. It was a truly powerful experience for me! Seated there in the silent, protected atmosphere of the Vatican Library, I was continually catapulted into the streets of sixteenth-century Rome. I "witnessed" the waters of the Tiber overflow their banks and carry off the stores of grain, wine, and oil. I could sense the feelings of precariousness and fear that natural

calamities brought upon the people, and I was touched by the
spontaneity with which the *Avvisi di Roma* described these sentiments.
One entry from 1517 reads as follows: "[A]nd in the evening, at about
one thirty at night, there was a great storm with hail, thunder, and
lightning bolts ... which frightened all of Rome and seemed a very
great thing indeed."[3] As in ancient times, fear was still a reality of life
and was acknowledged with rituals and sacrificial offerings. And in
this transitional period, a period in which there was not as yet a clear
distinction between the sacred and the profane, between spirit and
matter, attempts were made to placate fear by means of magical
practices. An animistic view of nature prevailed, along with a sense
that some spirit was lurking behind every natural phenomenon. In
the sixteenth century, it was considered quite normal to see ghosts
along a castle wall or elves in a tree. Magic, which existed side by side
with Christian spirituality, was part of the domestic, religious, and
moral life of most people. Through magic, the unknowable could be
revealed, the future could be mastered, and desires could be fulfilled.
Thus, a link with the beyond was created, and in some way a
relationship with unconscious energies was set up.

This period also saw the beginnings of the establishment of a
form of central authority, not only as far as the State was concerned,
but also within consciousness; this served to hold the uncontrollable
forces of nature and the psyche in check. In order to offset the
transitoriness of existence, reality was divided up into several parts,
each separate and ever more isolated from the others; in this way it
could be more easily controlled. Little by little, fear itself was banished
from the list of legitimate human emotions. Descartes, for example,
says explicitly that fear is not a specific passion but, being the opposite
of daring, owes its origins to the element of surprise; hence the best
way to avoid it is to use the art of premeditation so as to be adequately
prepared for events.[4]

Since then, fear of the unknown, which is often accompanied by a
sense of shame, has been the object of a powerful form of collective
repression, which has reinforced the tendency to identify everything
that is different as deserving of persecution. James Hillman reminds
us that fear, as well as love, can be a significant stimulus for
consciousness; by remaining in contact with fear, we encounter the
unconscious, the unknown, the bright as well as the uncontrollable in

life.[5] We also know that "startle is the affect of centering, orientation, and re-orientation; it is our response to the unexpected. On the instinctive body level, the kinaesthetic and proprioceptive senses keep us centered and oriented."[6] This element of surprise (which the rationalistic mentality tries to avoid at all costs) enables us to recognize the messages that come from the unconscious and to subsequently enter into dialogue with them so as to re-orientate our consciousness.

It was indeed a happy surprise for me to discover one day, while paging through the tomes of trial proceedings in the State Archives of Rome, a text without a name, recounting the trial of Bellezza Orsini, or more precisely, of Bellezze, daughter of Pier Angelo Ursini of Collevecchio. I don't think I have ever delved so passionately into a text as when I set out to decipher these difficult notes. I succeeded in completing my thesis on witchcraft trials for my university degree, and later published an article on the same topic. I subsequently changed professions, taking up psychotherapy and dance therapy, and forgot all about witches.

More than fifteen years later, I had a particularly powerful dream. I saw a young woman dressed in white come running towards me asking for help. Large amounts of blood, along with a white foam, oozed out of her breast and her right arm. She told me that these were the signs left on her body by the whippings she had received at the institute where she had been kept prisoner and from which she had managed to escape. I felt a connection between the dream and a physical symptom of my own: two months earlier I had dislocated my right shoulder, something that had happened to me before and was to happen again in the future. I thought back to the dislocated joints of all the people who had been subjected to the *spaccada*. Could it be that the cells of our bodies hold the memory of wounds from the past, which are not only individual but also collective?

A few months later, a very old woman began to appear in my experiences of active imagination through movement and/or writing. She was a very, very old woman, bent over, with her grey hair gathered up on her head. This woman, who spontaneously took form in my body, was not only very old, but was also bound in chains. I let myself go with the kinaesthetic impulse of the moment and found myself in that very position. I moved forward slowly with my head bent down and my wrists tied behind my back. I dragged my feet heavily as my toenails scraped along the floor. I felt immense pain, tension, and an enormous weight on my shoulders.

I had accepted, into my own body, the image of the woman prisoner, and I felt the full weight of her condemnation and a sense of ineluctability. Her path could only be one of hopelessness. I stretched out my arms in an attempt to loosen the ties that bound me, but despite the great effort I made, my hands remained as if stuck together. I was pulled by two opposing forces: one directed by the ego, the other by the unconscious. I could do no more than let myself be taken over by what was happening and, with the aid of my will power, try to bear the tremendous strain that all this tension entailed. At other moments, I found that my arms were tangled around my chest. I felt the desperation of this woman who, with all her might, wanted to free herself, but who was no match for the forces that kept her imprisoned. A kinaesthetic impulse led me to arch my back, and as I bent it backwards, I broke out in a sweat and trembled. I tried to free my arms, but to no avail, and I continued to feel tremendous tension. The effort I was making was such that my muscles trembled, and with my feet anchored to the floor, my back arched backwards while my arms stayed tangled around my chest, pressing down on it and on my heart. The image of this woman, which had come to life in my body, enabled me to feel the full force of her desire to live and the full impact of her imprisonment.

I gradually got to know her. In the various dialogues I held with her, I asked her name and why she had appeared to me; her answer was: "I feel alone, closed, helpless. I wish I could be part of the current that carries everything away. I want to enter into Nothingness and into Nature." Sometimes, throwing her arms up towards the sky and holding them there, tense and spread apart, she would shout, "Why? Why? Why?"[7]

Time: The beginning of the sixteenth century.

Place: A prison with massive walls, built within a castle in the countryside, north of Rome.

Two historical characters: A man who interrogates, investigates, and threatens to use the *spaccada*, demanding a confession so as to be able pass judgement. An old woman, a healer, obliged to defend herself against accusations of witchcraft.

Legal necessity: A confession that gives legitimacy to the conviction. No sentence could be passed without a confession of an alliance with Satan. Likewise, without a confession, the existence of a fearful secret society that posed a threat to the existing order (which was consolidating its power) would not have been confirmed. Prior to the fourteenth century, iconographic images of witches contained no allusions to the demonic, and neither ecclesiastical nor civil law made mention of alliances with Satan. Furthermore, ecclesiastical courts were not empowered to pass death sentences. In such cases, after ascertaining the crime of heresy, the church courts were obliged to hand the accused over to the secular courts, which had, only a short time before, been empowered to condemn heretics to be burnt at the stake. In order to eradicate the ancient magical practices and polytheistic pagan cults, state and ecclesiastical authorities needed to place witchcraft and heresy on the same plane, portraying the former as the most heinous form of the latter on the grounds that it implied a pact of association with diabolic forces. In 1326, Pope John XXII issued a papal bull entitled *Super illius specula*, which officially equated witchcraft with heresy, thus sanctioning legal prosecution of this practice. From that time on, the legal procedures surrounding charges of witchcraft became more and more intricate until a specific investigational procedure finally gave rise to the famous tract entitled *Malleus Maleficarum,* written by H. Institor and J. Sprenger in 1486.[8] This tract was widely circulated and immediately became a point of reference for judges and theologians engaged in the battle against heresy. Through this text, a new image of witchcraft began to spread throughout Europe, an image that included oaths of submission to the devil, participation in aerial flight and nocturnal Sabbaths, apostasy, the eating of babies, human procreation through diabolic intervention, and a close, indissoluble connection between women and demonic powers.

Volumes have been written on witches and witchcraft and we needn't go into the topic any further. What is important to note at this point is the systematic way in which imaginative activity was demonized and thus damaged. Institor and Sprenger went so far as to decree that the main vehicle by which witches carried out their work was the imagination, which managed to trick the organs of sense perception; it was in this way, they explained, that the devil was able to penetrate the human mind and create perceptual aberrations, which in turn led to uncontrollable actions. The deception was thus perpetrated not on reality itself, but rather, on the organs of sense perception. Thus, everything that was the product of the senses, of perception and physical sensations united with the imagination, was no more than the fruit of some diabolical illusion.

Institor and Sprenger further held that by means of the imagination of persons stricken by forms of witchcraft, diabolic forces could actually transport bodies from one place to another, make the male genitalia disappear, or turn a young person into an old one, a human being into an animal, or an ugly woman into a beautiful one. Witches, who were the human agents of the devils, could unleash rain and hailstorms at a glance, thus ruining crops; they could, likewise, bring about male impotence, sterility, miscarriages, illnesses, madness, and even death, in addition to changing love into hate and solidarity into envy. In the view of Institor and Sprenger, devils exercised power over the soul only indirectly, accessing it only through the body, over which they held the power to act in every imaginable way. By 'body' and the senses connected with it Institor and Sprenger meant the five external senses (sight, smell, hearing, taste, and touch) and the four internal senses, i.e., imagination or fantasy, common sense, judgment, and memory. Thus, by disrupting and deceiving the intellect and the senses through the illusory phantasms of the imagination, the diabolical powers were indirectly able to reach and disturb the soul.

A Change in the Attitude of the Defendant

At first, the defendant is bold, proud, and confident of her role as a healer and is convinced of her innocence; she counters every accusation, recounting her version of the facts. The sixty-year-old Bellezza comes across as a woman who is in touch with her own sense of power, active, astute, creative, and imaginative in the way she describes not only her work as a healer but also her role as a go-between in matters of love. She appears to be relatively free of stereotyping and social conditioning.

But the pressure of the continual questioning and the torture inflicted on her take their toll, and Bellezza eventually admits to everything her accusers want her to. Her independence gives way to a willing form of collaboration, but she still manages to retain the freedom of her imagination. By confronting and surviving her own fear, she is able to express her creativity while operating within the framework of the judicial authorities. Not only does she admit to being a witch and an ally of Satan, but she goes so far as to provide a long, detailed description of the organization of a female society of witches, with all of the heinous acts and anti-Christian rituals they were said to perform. She takes onto herself and incarnates the monstrous image of the old sorceress who devours children, and, as she does so, produces tales of amazing creativity, conjuring up a world where everything is turned on its head. As Ann and Barry Ulanov remind us in their fascinating book, the witch, from her realm outside of the human community, brings with her the opposite of all we know, thus overturning the order of things.[9]

During her questioning, Bellezza is repeatedly traumatized by those interrogating her and by the torture which she is threatened with and subjected to. The abuse heaped on her and the hope that she might be spared if she capitulates bring forth a demon (whether good or bad) that convinces her of her guilt and even compels her to commit suicide, the ultimate act of self-condemnation. From this point of view, what happens to Bellezza confirms the typical pattern of abuse. Her confession is the expression of all the things that most frighten her accusers; but in the end she does not give them the satisfaction of burning her at the stake. Bellezza allows herself to be turned into a monster; she accepts the masculine projection of the wild woman in the grip of instinct and the devouring mother who eats her own children. Before the final sentence can be pronounced, she succeeds in her third suicide attempt. If, on the one hand, she willingly collaborates with her prosecutors, on the other, she reserves the right to determine her own death. In her mind, her destiny could not have been clearer: she takes her death into her own hands, rather than let others determine that she should be burnt at the stake. This choice of hers can be seen both as a last desperate act of defiance and as a liberation of the soul.

Inverting the Inverse

Tempted by the diabolic spirit, I decided to kill myself, with no other thought than to abandon this world. These are Bellezza's final words. "When innocence has been deprived of its entitlement, it becomes a diabolical spirit." Donald Kalsched quotes these words of J. Grotstein[10] at the beginning of his interesting book. In Kalsched's

view, the archaic and dissociative defences of the psyche which emerge
as a result of traumatic events are the personification of the ambivalent
archetypal figure of a demon who is both protector and persecutor.
The demon, in order to avoid further trauma, protects the personal
spirit from the possibilities of change and, in an effort to block any
sort of change to the existing order of things, can become a fierce
persecutor. For Kalsched, the archetypal defences can even lead to the
death of the guest personality (suicide) as a means of protecting its
personal spirit from being violated. From this perspective, the urge to
suicide emerges as the work of a diabolical spirit, which, in an attempt
to protect the personal spirit, the true Self, from further instances of
trauma, chooses death rather than life. From the point of view of the
soul, the urge to suicide appears as the profound desire for the
transformation of pain into peace, of imprisonment into freedom. For
Hillman, the urge to suicide is often linked to a deep need for
transformation in that the transformative force kills as it produces
something new.[11] From a symbolic point of view, might the desire for
suicide on the part of a psychic figure subjected to torture not be the
urge towards birth springing from a profound need for renewal and
regeneration of the soul?

The story of Bellezza Orsini is a true story and is paralleled by
other equally true stories. The theme of the victim and his or her
persecutor continues to be a timely one, a theme that transcends the
boundaries of culture and gender. If we try to imagine these figures
and the psychic dynamics at work within them, both from the male
and the female point of view, we might well ask how many of them are
alive and present in each of us in the world today. To what extent is
there an innovative and creative side (male and/or female) which falls
prey to an inner persecutor (male and/or female), who will go to any
lengths to preserve the status quo? With the help of the imagination,
finally freed from the demonic projections it has been subjected to,
we can bridge the gap between body and spirit and see the story of the
imprisoned woman and her accuser as archetypal aspects in our bodies
and in our psyches, without forgetting that nowadays "she" could also
be a "he" and vice versa.

Time: Our own days.
Place: A prison. A confined and confining space, which also

protects—a container, an alchemical vessel. The uterus is such a place. The prison also contains creativity and is a place of initiation, where one is enabled to open up to transpersonal energies.

Two characters as intrapsychic figures: An imprisoned woman and her persecutor. The first contains the threatening side of the feminine, the side which devours and leads to perdition. The second holds the threatening side of the masculine, which dominates and represses. The masculine and feminine elements are in the prison together; both are strong, both are active, both are threatening, yet both are frightened, weak, and capable of being creative. The meeting of the two can indeed lead to the birth of something new.

Psychic necessity: The freeing of the imagination, which makes the creation of bridges possible. The essence of psychic wellbeing lies in circularity, a sense of connection, relationship, and in the communication between opposites, not in splitting. Psychic balance calls for the creation of symbols capable of holding opposites together, and thus enabling us to be open to new prospects.

With the demonization of the imagination, the vital bridge between body and soul was lost, and it has taken centuries to recover a sense of trust in our senses, in the intuitive capabilities of the body, and in feeling in general. The shadow of diabolic trickery is ever ready to threaten the ego's rationality and to block the flexibility, the widening, and the deepening of our consciousness. I am particularly interested in examining the historical dimensions of this demonization of the body and the imagination (a legacy which we carry with us in our blood and in every cell of our bodies) in the light of the great developments in the fields of creative art therapies. My own personal experience has brought me into close contact with C. G. Jung's practice of active imagination and with authentic movement as developed through the invaluable insights of Mary S. Whitehouse, Joan Chodorow, and Janet Adler.[12]

Dance/movement as active imagination makes it possible to perceive psyche and body as a unity within which a series of bridges allow for passage and communication between one and the other. When moving and being moved we sense the connection between images and sensations felt in the body. The imagination, the emotions, and the proprioceptive sense (the bridges which lead us to a sense of unity) are just those elements which for centuries were considered fertile ground for the agents of the devil. By trusting in the power of the imagination and in the body's intuitive wisdom, we can re-establish contact with the roots of our humanity, explore the world in a creative way, and be open to the new possibilities it offers us.

At the outset of an experience of active imagination through movement, the dialectical tension between the ego and the unconscious is expressed in the relationship between moving consciously and being moved by the unknown. "There are also times when the images themselves seem to want to be embodied as if the image could make itself better known by entering the body of the mover. When this occurs the experience shifts from *dancing with* a particular image to allowing oneself to *be danced by* it."[13] Soon after the initial surprise, the ego can choose to actively explore these forms. The situation which results is a paradoxical one in that ego and image are present together within the same body, without identification. The body becomes the means of manifestation for the image while the ego holds a position of observation and interaction, maintaining just the right intrapsychic distance. An event such as this can be experienced as understandable only if we accept the paradoxical nature of it; psyche and matter, body and soul are actually perceived as a unity and the embodied imagination carries out its function as bridge between the two.[14]

The Transformation of the Ego Through Meeting the Old Imprisoned Woman and Her Persecutor

Just how can we invert the inverse and allow for the negative experience of the imprisoned witch to become a positive experience? As the Ulanovs emphasize in their book, the hag personifies the archetypal image of a primordial, autonomous feminine force, in touch with its creative, spiritual, and intellectual powers. She brings the urge to be oneself and she gives value to the unique nature of the individual, to its resources and to the treasures that need to be brought to the surface. She is the guardian of unexpected, unconscious potentialities which can unfold before the familiar world of consciousness. The hag carries within herself the wise, healing woman who intercedes and has the power to plumb the depths, to open up new horizons, and to bring new truths to light. In some fairy tales it is she who is able to instill trust and to point out the way to safety and salvation. In the view of A. and B. Ulanov, the hag can fulfill her positive function when, thanks to the right attitude of consciousness, both the *animus* and the *anima* act as bridges between the ego and the unconscious.

Kalsched as well sees the old crone as a form of the ancient wisdom of the psyche, which is familiar with the positive, integrating potentialities of the Self, hidden within its own dark side. The old crone guards the personal inviolate spirit and, in Kalsched's view, seeks to find a home for that spirit in the lives of those whose suffering and desperation finally land them in her lair.[15] This is just what happens to the shepherd's daughter in the tale of Prince Lindworm, which Kalsched mentions; the den of the old crone can be found only by running through the woods, allowing oneself to be scratched by thorny branches, and abandoning oneself to a sense of desperation. What the witch helps us to do is to face up to the shadow and to the dark side of the Self, a confrontation which implies a voluntary sacrifice and an active choice which, in turn, make the experience sacred and allow the link between the human and the divine to deepen.

I believe that the archetypal image of the old woman contains imprisoned creativity as well as lost, unknown truth. She lives in the unexplored depths of the forest, a place with no beaten paths, nor maps to find one's way. We can choose to go into the forest in search of the witch; in the thick of the woods we risk stumbling along in darkness without a compass or torch, or going round in circles among the prickly thorns, without meeting anyone who could point out the path. We might catch a glimpse of a light, run after it only to see it go out, and lose all sense of bearing once again. But all at once, the path might just appear, right under our feet, to make us realize that the right way is the one we were already on. Marion Woodman reminds us that the creative process really consists in the ego's abandoning of its own known boundaries so as to touch the unknown possibilities of the unconscious; thus, the personal steps back and makes way for the transpersonal.[16]

By instilling in us trust in the unknown, the old woman instills trust in the creative process. She can lead us down into the depths just as she can accompany us in a sort of pioneering discovery of new horizons. But, in order to undertake this journey, it just might be necessary to give up the luxury of certainty. A true initiatory journey involves setting out empty-handed, with a willingness to leave behind all that we had, as well as a willingness to deal with that inner persecutory side of ourselves that wants to leave everything just as it is.

The first place we come upon may well be a prison, the place where we find ourselves confined within four walls; and perhaps we will discover that we have always been there, without realizing it. Naturally, we try to escape, but each unsuccessful attempt to get away ends up with the protector/prosecutor dragging the ego back into isolation once again. "You escape ... and I strike you down once again," says the persecutor; but each time it is struck, the ego is just a little freer. This is the great paradox: the persecutor, like the old witch and like Bellezza in the face of her accusers, becomes "the 'wounding healer' or the 'healing wounder.'"[17]

If we refuse to be devoured by the negative experience with the inner persecutor, this experience can become a positive one for the death of our old identity, brought about through voluntary sacrifice; this then allows for a new form of creative identity to emerge. "Care of the soul demands acceptance of all this dying."[18] We might experience the opposite of what happened to Bellezza: our well-adapted and pleasingly conventional identity may make way for one that is more individuated, independent, and in touch with the transpersonal and spiritual aspects of reality. This is part of the great process of individuation, a process which entails the ability to stay in relationship with the unconscious even as we emerge out of its undifferentiated aspects. Transformation comes about through an endless series of deaths and rebirths. The torment and laceration we feel in body and soul when a psychic function or habitual stance of consciousness is about to die can be compared to labor pains. And the more the prison door swings open, the greater the pain. But little by little, a light grows out of the darkness.

Connections

Today more than ever before it is necessary for the life of the psyche that the masculine and feminine polarities exist side by side in a reciprocal, respectful, and harmonious form of cooperation. Marion Woodman points out that by integrating body and soul we can go beyond the split between the masculine and the feminine, thus allowing for a true inner marriage. This new consciousness, in which masculine and feminine are no longer separated, is aware of its dependence on a higher, greater transpersonal force.[19] When the archetypal figures of the victim and the persecutor can move closer together, thanks to the mediation of the ego, then the creative principle can truly come to life, both in men and in women.

I have met the old woman again in my experiences of active imagination through movement and/or writing. At times she lay on a bed of straw, overwhelmed by melancholy and regret at having grown old before she had had a chance to really live. On other occasions I saw her wandering about in the Land of the Unknown, bent over and dragging along a heavy sack. She humbly stretched out her hands, asking for forgiveness, saying that her name was "Poverty." This old woman was also the thousand-year-old crone who, clad in nothing but rags, and with straggly grey hair and shining eyes, once encouraged me by handing me a set of keys which would allow me to open a door and finally find my true path. Then one night the prison doors were flung open and a sea of fire washed in over the four walls. Together with the old woman, I had to learn to confront the persecutor by walking on burning coals.

Then one day, the old imprisoned woman left me. I watched her go off and knew it was indeed her with her grey hair gathered up on her head. She wept at having to bid farewell to all the beloved things that surrounded her. I watched and said goodbye as she walked freely up over a hill. She carried a basket in one hand, and at one point she turned and smiled at me, only to then change instantly into a little girl, still clutching the same basket, now filled with flowers and fruit.

If we can manage to welcome the passive, chained old woman when she comes to call, then we will be able to encounter the free, active, creative woman hidden within her. It is essential that the ego try to keep alive its relationship both with the image of the old woman and with the image of the persecutor, avoiding any form of identification with either of these. In order to liberate the woman from prison, the ego must stand up to the guardian of the status quo, and at times this means going through the fire of purification. The walls of our inner prison are not made of something foreign to the psyche; those walls are within the psyche, they are the psyche itself. Opening a space in those walls may entail the need to set them on fire and to experience the suffering of the burning chains which bind the enflamed soul.

Is the witch in the darkest depths of the forest the one who lies hidden in the image of the old imprisoned woman? Is she the one who holds the secret of integrated knowing, of holistic knowledge, which includes spirit, instinct, thinking, feeling, movement, and image? The ego's encounter with the archetypal figure of the protector/persecutor and the image of the old imprisoned woman allows the creativity holds to spring forth. The ancient spirit that dwells in her brings with it the wisdom of the unknown, the wisdom of mystery, and trust in the prospect of new life.

What do you say? Shall we go and meet her?

NOTES

1. Antonella Adorisio, "Stregoneria e vita religiosa tra città e campagna nel cinquecento romano," *Sociologia* (1983): 167-212.

2. Archivio di Stato di Roma, *Tribunale del Governatore, Processi criminali del secolo XVI, vol. 6, processo n. 1, fol. 474 v°.*

3. Adorisio, "Stregoneria e vita religiosa," 171.

4. Jean Delumeau, *La paura in occidente* (Turin: Sei, 1979), 19.

5. James Hillman, "An Essay on Pan," *Pan and the Nightmare* (Dallas, Zurich: Spring, 1972).

6. Joan Chodorow, *Dance Therapy & Depth Psychology: The Moving Imagination* (London, New York: Routledge, 1991), 84.

7. Antonella Adorisio, "La danza e il movimento," *L'immaginazione attiva: teoria e pratica nella psicologia di C. G. Jung,* eds. F. de Luca Comandini and R. Mercurio (Milan: Vivarium, 2002), 218-219.

8. Heinrich Institor and Jacob Sprenger, *Malleus Maleficarum* (Strasburg, 1486-87).

9. Ann and Barry Ulanov, *The Witch and the Clown: Two Archetypes of Human Sexuality* (Wilmette, IL: Chiron, 1987).

10. Donald Kalsched, *The Inner World of Trauma: Archetypal Defences of the Personal Spirit* (London, New York: Routledge, 1996), 11.

11. James Hillman, *Suicide and the Soul* (New York: Harper and Row, 1964).

12. Joan Chodorow, *C. G. Jung on Active Imagination* (New York, London: Routledge, 1997); Patrizia Pallaro, *Authentic Movement: Essays by Mary Starks Whitehouse, Janet Adler and Joan Chodorow* (London:

Jessica Kingsley Publishers, 1999).

13. Chodorow, *Dance Therapy*, 126.

14. Antonella Adorisio, "Il corpo e l'immaginazione attiva," *Rivista di Psicologia Analitica* 51 (1995): 161-180.

15. Kalsched, 211.

16. Marion Woodman, *The Pregnant Virgin: A Process of Psychological Transformation* (Toronto: Inner City Books, 1985).

17. Thomas Moore, *Care of the Soul* (New York: Harper and Row, 1992), 112.

18. Moore, 142.

19. Marion Woodman, *The Ravaged Bridegroom: Masculinity in Women* (Toronto: Inner City Books, 1990).

Bi-Directional Healing:
The Biology of the Psyche Soma Dance
In the Work of Marion Woodman

ELISABETH BAERG HALL

> Oh body swayed to music, oh brightening glance
> How can we know the dancer from the dance?
>
> —W. B. Yeats

It was a numinous moment in my life. I had just received a diagnosis of lymphoma, and confirmatory surgery was five days away. Numbed by fear and finding it hard to concentrate, I had a serendipitous opportunity to meet Marion Woodman, who I knew had faced similar challenges. That meeting in 1996 marked an important step in what became for me a mythic journey of psyche and soma grounded in the landscape of my own body. In the BodySoul Rhythms workshops developed by Marion Woodman and her colleagues, Ann Skinner and Mary Hamilton, I came to learn a method

Elisabeth Baerg Hall, M.D., has a psychiatric practice at BC Children's Hospital in Vancouver, B.C., specializing in psychotherapy with adolescents. In workshops together with Barbara Hort and Candice Everett, Elisabeth enjoys building bridges between her medical knowledge and our inner experience of body and soul. (www.theater-of-the-soul.com)

of healing that employs a unique and dynamic integration of body and soul. Those workshops were integral to my own physical healing, for which I will always be deeply grateful.

There is another dimension to this story. I am a physician, trained as both a psychiatrist and family practitioner. My love of the body's biology led me to study the mechanisms of my own healing, as well as that of my patients and of participants in Marion's workshops.

In this paper, I will describe some healing elements of Marion Woodman's work, speaking primarily of the destabilization induced by excessive stress, and of the healing role played by cytokines—a spunky little group of chemical messengers in the body. Many dedicated researchers are mapping what clinicians have known to be true for years: psyche and soma perform an intimate dance in physical and psychological healing.[1] My goal is not to provide a comprehensive analysis of the body's dance, but rather to excite you with new possibilities. Mind-body medicine has advanced by leaps and bounds, and we are ready now to make some compelling new hypotheses and to take great joy in the wonders of the psyche-soma connection.

It would be a year after my first meeting with Marion before I could work with her and her colleagues in a more intensive way. During that year, I explored the terrifying realm of the unknown in my own body. After nine months of enlarged abdominal lymph nodes and almost daily fevers of 104 degrees or higher, the pre-operative diagnosis of Non-Hodgkin's Lymphoma was virtually assured. Postoperatively, however, the pathology was unclear and the diagnosis disturbingly uncertain. In the months following my surgery, I visited numerous specialist physicians, including those at Rochester's Mayo Clinic, but the disease managed to elude a clinical diagnosis. With every medical encounter reiterating the unknown nature of this disease, I was challenged to drop deeper into my own healing work. It had to be an organic process. It eluded all attempts at conceptualization, structure, or planning.

I dreamed:

I am teaching about conducting (psychotherapy) groups with some others who are very oriented to processing dynamics. I want them to get together to discuss an overview of what we are doing. They keep saying 'yes' but never follow through. One night they say they'll meet me. I go to the designated hotel room. While leaving to get my baby ready, I hear my colleagues engaged in loud and happy singing. I go back to the room, which is now full of dark tribespeople preparing bodies for burial. They are making beautiful painted masks.

Challenged by this scenario of mystery and ritual, which is rooted in the full circle of life, I realized I was trying to articulate the unknowable, and discovered a new level of trust in my own process. Until then I had practiced medicine and lived my life believing that modern medicine was an exact science. With that belief altered, I met the Unknown anew as my friend. I began a formal Jungian analysis. I started working with hypnosis targeted at the problematic areas in my surgical pathology report ... liver, lymph nodes, spleen, blood. I read Rilke. I built a garden. I walked by the ocean.

Playing with physiologic metaphors, I came to perceive my Type B body as allergic to my Type A brain. The harshness of the illness ensured I had no choice but to honor this slower Type B style. With every recurrence of the symptoms, I came into contact with a new level of fear, and was called to a new level of surrender. Given the severity of these symptoms, my physicians worried that a life-threatening illness may have been missed, but they were eventually convinced to resist their urges to order more tests and consultations. Together, we adopted a phenomenological approach to my symptoms and let go of the quest for a diagnosis.

After a year in the terrifying but often playful sanctuary of the Unknown, I finally had an opportunity to attend a BodySoul Intensive. As I had done when creating my own garden sanctuary in the year before I met them, Marion, Ann, and Mary pay careful attention to laying a rich groundwork for the integration of spirit and matter (*mater*) that they encourage in their work. They consciously create a container for the garden of the workshop group using images of the positive feminine. As the participants enter the space for the first time, there is a sense of a new possibility of being. Women who have attended several intensives assist in this process by bringing their embodied experience of BodySoul to the circle. The result is a supportive group culture in both spirit and matter.

In the same way, the individual container of the body is prepared for integrative work gradually over the span of seven days. Every morning of an intensive is devoted to dream work in the group. In the afternoon, the participants are invited to move, dance, and voice in an embodied way. Physical stamina develops effortlessly. The cells of the body are oxygenated with the awareness of voice and vibration. In the initial stages of the seven days, the focus is on balancing and caring for body and soul.

In the body, this process of balance and care is known as homeostasis. To maintain equilibrium, many systems in the body function via an intricate web of feedback response loops. For example, an increase in corticotrophin releasing hormone (CRH) secreted from the hypothalamus in response to messages of stress leads to an elegant up-and-down regulation of other hormone systems. This responsiveness exists on every level of the body. On an anatomical level, the phenomenon of neuronal plasticity shows us that the body can compensate for the loss of some functional areas of the brain with enhanced function and size of other brain areas. This responsiveness is also evident in biochemical interactions on the cellular level, where constant fluctuation and movement maintain a steady state of physical well-being. And this steady state of homeostasis is itself continual movement. To describe the psychological aspects of this state, Marion quotes T. S. Eliot: "Except for the point, the still point, there would be no dance, and there is only the dance ...."[2] In our bodies, homeostasis is both the stillness and the dance where hormones, neurotransmitters, and tiny particulate matter seek a healthy equilibrium as they continually vibrate and flow, both to their own rhythms and in loving response to one another.

This is how the body dances homeostasis in a healthy state. By contrast, in a stress-induced disease state, the body has been called to adapt beyond her capacity. The concepts of "allostasis" and "allostatic load" offer a refined understanding of the impact that stress can have on body physiology. "Allostasis" means (literally) "maintaining stability (or homeostasis) through change."[3] "Allostatic load" refers to the cumulative physiological wear and tear borne by the body from her attempts to adapt to stress.[4] Allostatic load is the best adaptation the sweet body can muster under duress. It describes the changes in physical phenomena like blood pressure, heart rate, and insulin levels which occur in response to stress: the mechanisms of her natural tendency toward wholeness. The body will always do her best to adapt, but when her systems are unbalanced under the cumulative load of stress, disease may be the result. Marion's focus on the psyche-soma dialogue contributes to healing by offering an opportunity to recalibrate allostatic load in the body.

One exercise developed by Marion and her colleagues is an excellent illustration of the mechanisms that might underlie this recalibration of the stress-induced allostatic load. In the BodySoul intensives, Marion and her colleagues integrate a variety of activities from the disciplines of psychology, dance, and theatre to introduce possibilities for psyche-soma healing. As the week goes on, these activities are woven together with a focus on increased integration.

In one of the final exercises of the week, participants are encouraged to choose a pleasant or positive image (that is not a human being) from one of their own dreams. The collective space is then prepared and, with conscious witnessing, the participant metaphorically invites the positive image to enter her body. The initial exploration of the image may involve responding to its entirety, color, shape, sound, or scent. It is important to note that the exercise does not ask the participant to identify with the image. Participants maintain an observational state of wonder, curiosity, and exploration. (This is similar to the state of playful curiosity employed in hypnosis techniques to increase communication between right and left brain hemispheres.) Each participant is encouraged to follow the aspect of the image that interests her, activating even more curiosity and wonder. When the image is invited into a healthy area of the body, it becomes infused with breath and is alive in the body. All the while, psyche stands by, observing this process with no judgment or expectation. The image enters the body with its own unique associations from the dream. It is allowed to transform with the body, moving and giving itself voice as a means of expressing the experience and then responding to it. The image affects the body and the body responds with new sensations and images. Brain synapses respond to these new visual or thought cues. In this moment the whole body is changed.

After more than twenty years' experience using exercises like this one, Marion and her colleagues began inviting women to apprentice with them, opening the door for novel applications in different venues. Two colleagues and I are now conducting our own workshops as Theater of the Soul, which we have based closely on these training experiences with Marion, Mary, and Ann.

In one of these workshops, we had the privilege of meeting a courageous 60-something woman (I will call her Rose), who had struggled for years with childhood-onset diabetes. Rose resented the need to control her insulin levels. She suffered excruciating neuropathic pain in her hands and feet. This type of pain is caused by a combination of factors resulting from poorly controlled blood sugars, including hardening of the arteries or atherosclerosis, which leads to reduced blood flow and decreased cellular feeding. Before our workshop, Rose had a dream image of a new shoot of fresh green vine growing through a concrete sidewalk. During the workshop, when we introduced the exercise described above, Rose took this image into her body, inhaling it like oxygen. She let herself be danced by the image. She drew it. She was compelled by it. She talked later of feeling revitalized—newly alive. Months later, we learned that Rose had made huge changes in her life, not the least of which was a decision to take insulin and monitor her sugar levels. Her neuropathic pain was blunted. For Rose, the dream image taken into her body in this way seemed to have given her far more than an impetus for psychological healing and behavioral change. Her chemistry itself seemed to have been transformed at a cellular level. The new green vine eased through the concrete—the atherosclerotic plaque that lined her arteries—bringing oxygen and nutrients to her cells. At the level of her cellular metabolism, hope flowed in. And hope is a physical thing.

The healing I have personally experienced and the healing I have observed in others through BodySoul exercises like this one has led me to study what is actually happening on a cellular level in these moments of grace. While there are many hypothesized mechanisms of healing at work here, I would like to focus on the unique contribution of cytokines.

Cytokines are a key component of a relatively new discipline, psychoneuroimmunology (PNI), which integrates previously separate areas of medicine and has changed our understanding of the immune system's functioning. Rather than being understood only as a defence system that fights intruders and infection, the immune system is now seen as a whole-body sensory organ. In this important new role as a sensory organ, the immune system is now understood to be capable of bringing subtle messages to and from areas of the body not previously thought capable of giving or receiving feedback.[5] This revolution in our understanding of the immune system's sensory role is in part due to the identification of cytokines, the tiny protein messengers that do the actual communicating among the body's various systems. Their extraordinary responsiveness has led some researchers to refer to them as the hormones of the immune system.

Cytokines have many unique functions in addition to their traditional role of calling in cellular defenders, like white blood cells, against known and unknown threats in the body. They can carry messages from one area of the body to another. Once they arrive at their destination, their messages can stimulate a cascade of reactions that alter the physiology in that area. There is an intricate network of cytokine mediated communication between cytokines and other cells. Whether or not more cytokines are created depends in part on that cell's previous exposure to a cytokine. They can be created locally in the body by cells that are not part of the immune system. For example, in the gastrointestinal tract, cytokines can be created by endothelial cells that line the stomach or by smooth muscle in the bowel.

This is not to say that cytokines have a universal passport to all areas in the body. They cannot easily pass through the filter into the brain, for example. The body's unique solution to this challenge is to carry the cytokines' immunologic messages to the brain by an important nerve of the central nervous system—the vagus nerve. The vagus nerve, which means the "wandering nerve," literally wanders through the body helping to regulate a number of centrally important body functions like respiration, heart rate, swallowing, and digestion. It uses the impulses of the neurological system to send messages, generated by cytokine transmitters of a completely different system, to the brain. In the brain, powerful neurotransmitters like endorphins and noradrenalin of the neurological system are stimulated to translate these messages, leading to the production of more cytokines in the brain!

This unusual ability to communicate between the neurologic and immunologic systems works in either direction or bi-directionally, lending a physiologic basis to Marion's metaphor of the interwoven back-and-forth of the psyche-soma dance. Messages from the brain can be sent by the vagus nerve to stimulate immune system activity at local sites in the body, as well as transmitting the body's messages to the brain. Unique and previously unimaginable communication is happening from the body to the brain and back again. The dance has begun.

There is something quite feminine about how cytokines dance this message in the body and brain. Defying linear classification, they respond to feedback loops that involve other body systems and can communicate between systems not previously understood to send messages in this way. This unique essence is also revealed in the paradoxical way that cytokines function. For example, some cytokines bring about inflammation, and some decrease it. Some cytokines bring about a natural and health-restoring set of 'sickness' behaviours, where we are slowed down with fevers and sleepiness to maintain a resting state when fighting an infection.[6] In the case of autoimmune disorders, these same cytokines can produce sleepiness and fevers, which are problematic and impair functioning even in the absence of infections.

We have discussed the wonders of the bi-directional circuit that talks between the body's systems. We have learned that messages sent by the neurological system can trigger the production of the immune system's cytokine messengers in both the body and the brain. This is thought to be a key means by which cytokines communicate messages of stress in the body. Some scientists believe the body deals with messages of psychological distress in the same way as it deals with physical stressors. From this perspective, communication between the body and brain regarding a stressor, whether physical or psychological, can occur in both directions and by the same cytokine-propelled circuitry that is the pathway between the immune system and the brain.[7] Because this circuitry is bi-directional, and the brain is just as involved as the body, the hypothesis is that the activation of the cytokine messenger system can occur either as a result of physical stressors (i.e., events occurring in the body) and then be communicated to the brain, or as a result of psychological stressors (i.e., thoughts, perceptions, or emotional events occurring initially in the brain) and then be communicated to the body.[8]

Cytokines, then, play an important role in communicating messages of physical and psychological distress in the body and in the development of the diseases that result from this allostatic load. As we consider the healing aspects of Marion's work, and the contribution of cytokines to the biological underpinnings of these changes, I would argue that the style, environment, and delivery of Marion's work is stressful in a positive way. It is precisely this quality of being stressful that brings the capacity to send new messages where previously the communication was shut down. From the moment the positively evocative group experience of the Feminine is called forth, a pathway is set in the brain and body to communicate new messages with the clarity of the stress-driven message in the body and brain. Throughout the week's intensive with Marion and her colleagues, each new experience serves to ensure that the new pathway is easier to access, bringing in new hope and possibility on the cellular level. Positively stressful experiences are understood to have a significant impact in the body.

In the stress literature, both the positive and negative forms of this phenomenon are considered. For example, the Holmes and Rahe Social Readjustment Rating Scale, which is commonly used to predict a person's health status following major life events, includes happy events such as marriage, birth, and positive changes in money or work, as well as unhappy events such as divorce, illness, and the death of a loved one.[9] From this perspective, positive stressors can be just as problematic as negative ones. It is also likely that the mechanism involved in the body's response to a positive stressor holds within it other possibilities. For example, if cytokines are capable of carrying messages of both psychological and physical distress from brain to body and body to brain, and since the body is tuned to do its very best to deal with allostatic load in an adaptive and rebalancing way, cytokines are likely capable of carrying these new messages within the body-brain. If the trigger or starting point for these positive messages is new, emotionally charged, or "stressed," these messages will be dispatched through the powerful cytokine system. In this way, a positive event in the brain, with a valence of positive emotional stress, may be experienced as a moment of "ah-ha" in the body, triggering a cascade of new energetic potential.

When we consider the biological basis of the psychological and physical healing that occurs in the exercises developed by Marion and her colleagues, we must examine the role played by positive stressful emotional and physical experiences. Returning to the case of Rose, who experienced improved physical symptoms related to her diabetes, the intentional act of inviting her own positively charged dream image into her body and exploring that image in a physical way, with movement and voicing, precipitated psychological changes. The psychological changes led to behavioral changes, which are again interwoven with and responsive to the physical ones. Rose's own dream image of the vine growing through cement may have been experienced literally in her body as a blood-borne, life-giving vine bringing oxygen and nutrients to the nerve cells in the farthest reaches of her body.

Embracing the integration and bi-directionality of the psyche-soma and mind-body connection, my colleagues and I have begun to work directly with participants' challenging physical symptoms. From these women, whose ages range from 25 to 80, we have heard of physical challenges ranging from disabling bunions, accidental fractures, and hiatus hernias to complex syndromes of malignant cancers, autoimmune diseases, and rare genetic disorders. We encourage participants, within the safety of the group container and their own cherished bodies, to work with their body symptoms in the same way they might work with their dream images. Lovingly held in the open-minded curiosity of the workshop environment, participants sometimes find themselves able to step back from the fear associated with these symptoms. Together, we then interweave physiologic facts and subjective experiences related to their symptoms, in order to identify the metaphors that can help them derive meaning from these challenges.

Using this approach, we worked with a poet (I will call her Annie), who was perimenopausal and had been suffering from chronic and severe uterine cramping for the past eighteen months. She was afraid that her doctor would recommend a hysterectomy but Annie, unlike every woman in preceding generations of her family, was determined not to undergo this procedure. The severe and chronic nature of her pain was becoming so debilitating, however, that she was having trouble functioning in daily life, and her poetry had dwindled to a virtual trickle.

In the workshop, we explored Annie's physical symptoms as if they were a dream. We recalled the essential role of uterine cramping in childbirth, which Annie had experienced. She clenched her fists while describing the intensity of the pain, and the other women clenched their fists in response. Annie then entered into a relationship with her uterine pain, assuring her body there was no further need to be productive in this manner. She was able to describe and challenge her family pattern of removing a useless uterus, and in its place, she considered celebrating the continued presence of her own uterus in her body.

When we reached the point in the workshop where participants were asked to invite a positive dream image into the body, Annie chose a dream in which she had found a huge diamond wrapped in burlap in the backyard. As she explored this image in the beginning of the exercise, Annie first hefted it in her hands, and then she unwrapped the burlap around it and found that it was a black diamond and then she felt it moving into her body, changing itself and her body as it moved. Annie sensed that her uterus assumed a new energetic form as she worked with the image. Immediately after the exercise, she wrote her experiences onto a white mask. Here is Annie's experience, as she wrote it onto the mask, in line after line of words:

> uncut diamond (daimon)
> world's largest (largesse)
> wrapped in burlap (sackcloth) (and ashes)
> out in the backyard (the garden)
> sitting on the green grass (wet and fragrant)
> right in the open (vulnerable)
> someone could take it
> but it is mine from my family—
> how did they get it,
> did they steal it, are they thieves
> am I descended from thieves (probably)
> but I have decided to bring it in
> (right into my body).
>
> First I feel the burlap covering
> and find (realize) it keeps
> the many rough edges from cutting me
> as I try to handle and heft it.
>
> Then I want to look at it
> so I peel back the burlap and work it off
> and find the diamond material is all
> black and glassy—a big chunk
> of black diamond (obsidian).
>
> I recover it in the burlap in preparation
> to take it in (reverse birth).
>
> Then I find my left hand
> will receive its black energy

into my arm, up around my neck
to my right jaw, across my jaw up
my left ear to my left brain then
down to my third eye, resting there,
down to my throat chakra, pausing there,
on down to my pelvic bowl (chalice)
which fills with this black energy.

Ink.

The burlap comes in too (afterbirth?).
Black and brown. Ink and paper.
I curl into fetal position for
some rest and gestation.
It is okay in there.
I am positively impregnated.

More than two years later Annie remains pain free, and her poetry is flowing freely again.

It is important to say that Annie had spent a considerable amount of time in Jungian and body-oriented therapy, preparing the physical and psychological ground for these healing changes. What's more, she believed in the power of this work, and her belief undoubtedly activated many different healing systems in her body. So it was that, compelled by grace and synchronicity, and operating in the ground of a well-prepared psyche and soma, Annie's cytokines danced their messages through her body in a healing way.

Are specific details about the biological underpinnings of these experiences necessary for healing to occur? I think not. But the body has an intelligence that is often underrated. If understood within the context of what we know about the ever-increasing artificiality of the split, there is much to be gained by attending to the images and symptoms that hold the energetic charge whether dream- or body-based. I would propose that rather than seeing symptoms in the body as an indication of pathological shadow material, any symptom should be welcomed as a precious message to psyche and soma. The gift of Marion Woodman and her colleagues is a method by which we can dance and explore this mystery in our own psyche-somas.

Long after I had embarked on the study of psychoneuro-immunology, and had fallen in love with cytokines, I learned that my undiagnosed illness, now much resolved, was best understood as a cytokine regulatory disorder. Although my health is much improved, I continue to experience this mysterious illness as a teacher with unusual and non-negotiable expectations. As I have recovered, dreams have come to me, telling me to cross over borders, to bridge the experience of the known and the unknown in my own body, and then to talk about it. Here is my offering.

NOTES

1. For example, Candace B. Pert, *Molecules of Emotion* (New York: Touchstone, 1999).

2. T. S. Eliot, *Four Quartets* (New York: Harcourt, Brace and Co., 1943).

3. Peter Sterling and Joseph Eyer, "Allostasis: A New Paradigm to Explain Arousal Pathology," in *Handbook of Life Stress, Cognition and Health*, ed. S. Fisher and J. Reason (New York: J. Wiley and Sons, 1988), 629-649.

4. Bruce McEwen and Eliot Stellar, "Stress and the Individual," *Archives of Internal Medicine* 153 (1993): 2093-2101.

5. For example, J. Edwin Blalock, Eric M Smith, and Walter J. Meyer, "The Pituitary-Adrenocortical Axis and the Immune System," in *Clinics in Endocrinology and Metabolism* 14 (1985): 1021-1038.

6. For example, Keith W. Kelly, Rose-Marie Bluthe, Robert Dantzer, *et al.*, "Cytokine-induced Sickness Behavior," *Brain, Behavior and Immunity* 17 (2003): S112-S118.

7. Steven Maier, "Bi-directional Immune-brain Communication: Implications for Understanding Stress, Pain and Cognition," *Brain, Behavior and Immunity* 17 (2003): 69-85.

8. Steven F. Maier and Linda R. Watkins "Cytokines for Psychologists: Implications of Bi-directional Immune Brain Communication for Understanding Behavior, Mood, and Cognition," *Psychological Review* 105.1 (1998): 83-107.

9. T. H. Holmes and R. H. Rahe, "The Social Readjustment Rating Scale," *Journal of Psychosomatic Research* 11.2 (1967): 213-218.

CREATIVITY AND THE NATURE OF THE NUMINOSUM:
THE PSYCHOSOCIAL GENOMICS OF JUNG'S TRANSCENDENT FUNCTION IN ART, SCIENCE, SPIRIT, AND PSYCHOTHERAPY[1]

All psychological theoreticians in this field run the same risk, for they are playing with something that directly affects all that is uncontrolled in man—the numinosum, to use an apt expression of Rudolph Otto's. ... Every time the researcher succeeds in advancing a little further towards the psychic tremendum, then, as before, reactions are let loose in the public ....

— Carl Jung, *The Structure and Dynamics of the Psyche*, 1934, pp. 103-104

There is nothing mysterious or metaphysical about the term "transcendent function." It means a psychological function comparable in its way to a mathematical function of the same name,

---

[1]This paper is dedicated to Marion Woodman's teaching and inspired writings, which have kindled our generation's quest for healing in mind, body, and soul.

Ernest Lawrence Rossi is a Jungian Analyst, the Science Editor of *Psychological Perspectives* and the author, co-author and editor of 23 professional books and approximately 140 papers on psychotherapy, dreams, psychobiology and therapeutic hypnosis.

which is a function of real and imaginary numbers. The psychological "transcendent function" arises from a union of conscious and unconscious contents.

— Carl Jung, "The Transcendent Function,"
1916, p. 67

In the beginning of his essay on psychology and religion Jung (1937/1958) outlined the relationship between religion, the numinosum, and the transformations of consciousness.

I want to make clear that by the term "religion" I do not mean a creed. It is, however, true that every creed is originally based on the one hand upon the experience of the *numinosum* and on the other hand ... trust or loyalty, faith and confidence in certain experience of a numinous nature and in the change of consciousness that ensues. The conversion of Paul is a striking example of this. We might say, then, that the term "religion" designates the attitude particular to a consciousness which has been changed by experience of the *numinosum*. (p. 8)

The modern molecular biologist does not speak of religion but investigates the empirical basis of consciousness and the numinosum as states of psychobiological arousal that turn on gene expression and brain plasticity—the growth and transformations of neural networks throughout our lifetime (Cohen-Cory, 2002). Bentivoglio & Grassi-Zucconi (1999), for example, ask questions about the biological nature of consciousness, dreaming, behavior, memory, learning, and gene expression that are fundamental for updating our understanding of creativity and the nature of the numinosum.

The study of Immediate Early Genes (IEGs) indicates that sleep and wake, as well as [REM or dream sleep], are characterized by different genomic expressions, the level of IEGs being high during wake and low during sleep. ... *IEG induction [within seconds] may reveal the activation of neural networks in different behavioral states.* Although stimulating, these findings leave unanswered a number of questions. Do the areas in which IEGs oscillate during sleep and wake subserve specific roles in the regulation of these physiological states and in a general 'resetting' of behavioral states? Is gene induction a clue to understanding the alternation of sleep and wake, and REM and non-REM sleep? ... *Does this explain the molecular and cellular correlates of arousal, alertness, and, more in general, of consciousness?* (p. 249, italics added)

These questions bridge the "Cartesian gap" between mind and body by using the concept of biological information (von Baeyer, 2004). The modern concept of biological information was originally formulated as "the dogma of molecular biology" by Watson and Crick (1953a & b), for which they received the Nobel Prize. I expanded their original dogma of molecular biology, now known as "bioinformatics" (Figure 1a), to include "psychological experience" in a circular loop as illustrated in Figure 1b (Rossi, 2002, 2003a-c, 2004a-d).

The original dogma of molecular biology illustrated in Figure 1a proposes how (1) the linear *sequence* of nucleotides in our genes is a code of biological information that (2) generates the three-dimensional *structure* of the proteins, which (3) *function* as the *physiological* molecular machines of the brain and body. That is as far as Watson and Crick were willing to go in 1953—there was no place for the psyche, consciousness, and psychological experience in their original dogma of molecular biology. Since that time, however, neuroscience research has documented how the psychological experiences of *novelty* (Eriksson *et al.*, 1998), *psychosocial enrichment* (Kempermann *et al.*, 1997), and mental and physical *exercise* (Van Praag *et al.*, 1999) can evoke gene expression (genomics), protein synthesis (proteomics), and the physiological functions of the brain and body. Such research is the empirical basis for my adding the dimension of psychological experience to the diagram of Watson and Crick's linear dogma of molecular biology in Figure 1a to construct the circular mind-body loop of psychosocial genomics in Figure 1b, which illustrates how *psychological experiences* of psyche, mind, and consciousness can modulate gene expression and brain plasticity. The most profound implication of this mind-body

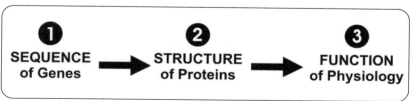

Figure 1a: Watson & Crick's Linear Dogma of Molecular Biology of 1953 (with no explicit role for consciousness and psychological experience)

loop is that heightened experiences of consciousness, which characterize the *numinosum,* can evoke gene expression, brain plasticity, and mind-body healing in the complex computations (iterations and recursions) of psychophysiology, psychosomatic medicine, and psychotherapy. The natural bioinformatic translations between mental experience (psyche) and biological information (soma) shown in Figure 1b provide us with the possibility of understanding how Jung apparently was able to cure cancer, psoriasis (molecular-genomic diseases), and other body dysfunctions with his purely psychological approach to the numinous experiences of the psyche (1937/1958, pp. 13-14).

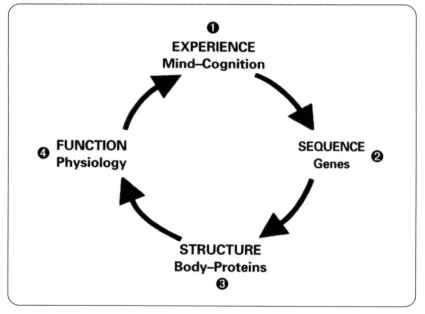

Figure 1b: Rossi's Bioinformatics Cycle of Psychosocial and Cultural Genomics.
(1) Psychosocial stress and the psychological experiences of psyche and mind can modulate (2) the alternative splicing of the sequence of gene expression (genomics), (3) protein synthesis and structure (proteomics), and (4) the physiological functions of the brain and body. This psychosocial genomics "top-down" approach to Jung's synthetic or constructive method illustrated on the right side of this mind-body circle of information transduction is balanced by the more usual "bottom-up" approach of molecular biology, behavioral genetics, evolutionary psychology, and sociobiology illustrated on the left side of the mind-body circle.

Let us now review some of the conceptual details of this new bridge between psyche and soma to close the so-called "Cartesian gap" between mind and body and update Jung's (1918/1966) "Synthetic or Constructive Method" of healing. The new discipline of *psychosocial and cultural genomics explores how psychological experiences modulate gene expression, protein synthesis, brain plasticity, and the physiology of the body* as illustrated in Figure 1b (Rossi, 2002, 2004). Notice that psychosocial and cultural genomics is a "top-down" synthetic approach, which emphasizes how the mind modulates biology. This is the opposite of the scientifically more popular "bottom-up" approach of molecular biology, behavioral genetics, evolutionary psychology, and sociobiology, which emphasize how biology modulates the mind and behavior via evolutionary selection over many generations. Psychosocial genomics, by contrast, is concerned with how psychological experiences and behavioral states in the here-and-now of this moment (e.g. during psychotherapy, dreaming, and numinous experiences in the creative arts and sciences) can modulate gene expression, brain plasticity, and mind-body healing—as we shall soon describe in greater detail.

The Psychosocial Genomics of Jung's Synthetic or Constructive Method

Jung (1918/1966) introduced his synthetic or constructive method of working with the transcendent function as follows:

> *The process of coming to terms with the unconscious is a true labour, a work which involves both action and suffering.* It has been named the "transcendent function" because it represents a function based on real and "imaginary," or rational and irrational data, thus bridging the yawning gulf between conscious and unconscious. *It is a natural process, a manifestation of the energy that springs from the tension of opposites, and it consists in a series of fantasy-occurrences which appear spontaneously in dreams and visions.* ... The natural process by which the opposites unite came to serve me as the model and basis for a method consisting essentially in this: everything that happens at the behest of nature, unconsciously and spontaneously, is deliberately summoned forth and integrated into the conscious mind and its outlook. *Failure in many cases is due precisely to the fact that they lack the mental and spiritual equipment to master the events taking place in them.*

Here medical help must intervene in the form of a special method of treatment. (p. 80, italics added)

How would current neuroscience update Jung's constructive method of *"coming to terms with the unconscious [as] a true labour, a work which involves both action and suffering"*? What is this *"true labour"*? What is the *"natural process, a manifestation of the energy that springs from the tension of opposites"* in terms of psychosocial and cultural genomics? How shall we interpret Jung's words *"Failure in many cases is due precisely to the fact that they lack the mental and spiritual equipment to master the events taking place in them"*? Figure 2 is an empirical map of the nature of the numinosum and the bioinformatic transformations of the transcendent function for answering these questions.

Figure 2 illustrates the new psychosocial genomics perspective on the nature of the numinosum as the psychobiological arousal of consciousness via a wide variety of experiences such as pain, stress, trauma, novelty, dreaming (REM sleep), creative moments, and the normal Basic Rest-Activity Cycle (BRAC) on all levels from mind to gene. We now know that any experience of psychological arousal or behavioral activity stimulates sensory and neural action, which within seconds evokes (1) immediate early gene expression (IEGs as described above by Bentivoglio & Grassi-Zucconi, 1999) that turn on (2) target gene transcription providing the DNA code for (3) the new protein synthesis of the molecular machines (growth factors, hormones, neurotransmitters, etc.) that generate (4) brain plasticity, mind-body healing, and the further transformations of consciousness.

This bioinformatics model of the nature of the numinosum answers another mind-body question: how do we account for the difference in consciousness between humans and non-human primates when they both have about the same number of genes (approximately 30,000) which are more than 99.6% alike? Cáceres *et al.* (2003) summarize their research in this area as follows:

> Little is known about how the human brain differs from that of our closest relatives. To investigate the genetic basis of human specializations in brain organization and cognition, we compared gene expression profiles for the cerebral cortex of humans, chimpanzees, and rhesus macaques by using several

independent techniques. We identified 169 genes that exhibited expression differences between human and chimpanzee cortex, and 91 were ascribed to the human lineage by using macaques as an outgroup. Surprisingly, most differences between the brains of humans and non-human

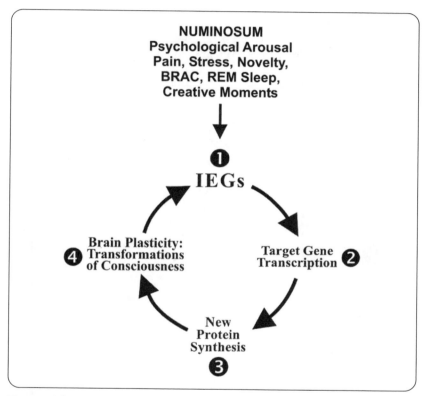

NUMINOSUM
Psychological Arousal
Pain, Stress, Novelty,
BRAC, REM Sleep,
Creative Moments

❶
IEGs

❹ Brain Plasticity:
Transformations
of Consciousness

Target Gene
Transcription ❷

New
Protein
Synthesis
❸

Figure 2: The Numinosum as a Special State of Psychobiological Arousal Activating the Gene Expression and Protein Synthesis Cycle in Jung's Transcendent Function. A major implication of current neuroscience research is that the numinosum is an unusually heightened state of psychobiological arousal via a wide variety of experiences [such as pain, stress, trauma, novelty, dreaming (REM sleep), creative moments and the normal 90-120 minute Basic Rest-Activity Cycle (BRAC)], which can turn on (1) immediate early genes (IEGs) within seconds, which (2) promote target gene expression (transcription) that (3) code for the synthesis of proteins that are the molecular machines of life regulating (4) brain plasticity in the transformations of consciousness via Jung's transcendent function, memory, and learning.

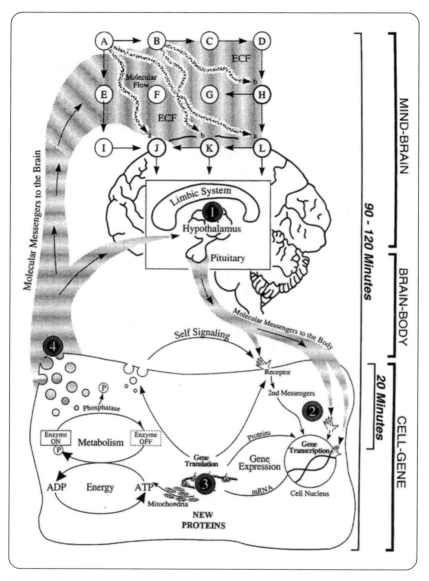

Figure 3: Psychosocial and Cultural Genomics Illustrated as a Four-Stage Model of the Complex Adaptive System of Mind-Body Communication and Healing. This circular loop of information transduction between mind and gene emphasizes the flow of hormones (messenger molecules) between the mind-

continued on next page

primates involved up-regulation, with ~90% of the genes being more highly expressed in humans. By contrast, in the comparison of human and chimpanzee heart and liver, the numbers of up- and down-regulated genes were nearly identical. *Our results indicate that the human brain displays a distinctive pattern of gene expression relative to non-human primates, with higher expression levels for many genes belonging to a wide variety of functional classes. The increased expression of these genes could provide the basis for extensive modifications of cerebral physiology and function in humans and suggests that the human brain is characterized by elevated levels of neuronal activity.* (pp. 13030, italics added)

In other words, it is the higher activation of consciousness, what Carl Jung and Rudolph Otto (1923/1950) would call "the numinosum," generated by elevated gene expression levels that distinguishes between the performance of human and non-human primate brains. These elevated gene expression levels can be detected with the new DNA microarray technology, which can assess the entire human genome in a single sample of blood (Rossi, 2000, 2002, 2004 a-c). Figure 3 is an illustration of these communication pathways via the blood—the molecular messengers (i.e., hormones, neurotransmitters of the nervous system, cytokines and interleukins of the psychoneuroimmune system,

---

continued from previous page

brain, brain-body, and cellular level of gene expression via the blood stream that normally takes place every 90-120 minutes in Kleitman's Basic Rest-Activity Cycle. The brain's neural networks at the top, represented by the rectangle of neural units, A through L, which receive molecular signaling through the extra cellular fluid [ECF] from the blood, are regarded as a complex adaptive system: a field of self-organizing communication processes that are the psychobiological basis of mind, memory, learning, and psychosomatic medicine. (1) The Limbic-Hypothalamic-Pituitary bioinformatic system between mind and brain; (2) molecular messengers evoked by sensations and psychosocial cues turn on gene transcription (expression) within minutes; (3) messenger RNA (mRNA) from gene expression codes for new protein synthesis within minutes to hours; (4) many of these proteins are the basis for enzymatic activity generating the energy of metabolism and other messenger molecules (e. g. hormones, neurotransmitters, cytokines) that return via the blood to the brain to modulate consciousness, memory, and learning to complete the circle of information transduction between mind and brain.

etc.) between mind, brain, and the genome of every cell of the body (Rossi, 2002, 2004 a-c).

Whitney *et al.* (2003) documented how individuality and variation in gene expression patterns in human blood can be assessed with DNA microarray (gene chip) technology to investigate these questions about varying states of health and illness.

> The extent, nature, and sources of variation in gene expression among healthy individuals are a fundamental, yet largely unexplored, aspect of human biology. *Future investigations of human gene expression programs associated with disease, and their potential application to detection and diagnosis, will depend upon an understanding of normal variation within and between individuals, over time, and with age, gender, and other aspects of the human condition.* (p. 1896, italics added)

This implies that DNA microarrays are a more sensitive, comprehensive, and reliable measure of psychological states of consciousness, emotions, behavior, brain plasticity, and mind-body healing. From the psychosocial genomics perspective, cultivating this inner garden of our archetypal genomic resources is the ultimate task of Jung's "coming to terms with the unconscious ... a labour, a work which involves both action and suffering" in the process of individuation (Rossi, 1972/2000, 2004 a-c). Table 1 lists a brief sampling of gene candidates for the DNA microarray technology assessment of the role of Otto's numinosum and Jung's transcendent function, active imagination, and constructive method in modulating gene expression, brain plasticity, and mind-body healing. A few quotations from the technical literature cited in Table 1 provide a quick survey of the implications of this data for understanding the nature of the numinosum and the psychosocial genomics of Jung's synthetic or constructive method.

The Numinosum as Heightened Gene Expression in the Human Cortex

Cáceres *et al.* (2003) do not use the word "numinosum" in their empirical paper on the elevated gene expression levels that distinguish human from non-human primate brains, but their molecular-genomic outline of heightened neuronal activity in human consciousness

Table 1: A brief sampling of gene candidates for the DNA microarray technology assessment of the dynamics of Otto's numinosum and Jung's transcendent function in modulating gene expression, brain plasticity and mind-body healing (From Rossi, 2002, 2004 a-c).

The Numinosum as Heightened Gene Expression in the Human Cortex

SYN47	DCTN1	Cáceres *et al.* 2003
CAMK2A	MAP1B	
IMPA1	RAB3GAP	
CDS2	ATP2B1	
KIF3A	USP14	

Brain Plasticity in Consciousness, Memory, Learning, and Behavior Change

c-fos, c-jun, krox, NGFI-A & B	Bentivoglio & Grassi-Zucconi, 1999
CREB	Kandel 1998
BDNF	Russo-Neustadt *et al.*, 2001
CYP-17	Ridley, 1999
~ 100 Immediate Early Genes	Rossi, 2002, 2004a

Dreaming and Replay in the Reconstruction of Fear, Stress, and Trauma

Zif-268	Ribeiro *et al.*, 2002, 2004
	Nader *et al.*, 2000

Chronic Psychosocial Stress and Alternative Gene Expression

Acetylcholinesterase (AChE-S & AChE-R)	Sternfield, *et al.*, 2000; Perry, *et al.*, 2004
Nerve Growth Factor (NGF)	Alfonso *et al.*, 2004
Membrane Glycoprotein 6a (M6a)	
CDC-like Kinase 1 (CLK-1)	
G-protein alpha q (GNAQ)	
CRE- dependent reporter gene	Alejel, 2001

Psychoneuroimmunology

Interleukin 1, 2, 1ß, Cox-2	Castes *et al.*, 1999; Glaser *et al.*, 1993

Clock Genes & Behavior State-Related Genes

About 100 sleep related genes	Cirelli *et al.*, 2004
Clock, Period 1, BMAL	Rossi, 2004d
Period 2	Rosbash & Takahashi, 2002

Maternal Behavior and Therapeutic Touch

ODC gene	Schanberg, 1995
Opioid Receptor Gene	Moles *et al.*, 2004

is of profound significance for understanding the nature of the numinosum and the transcendent function in Jungian psychology.

> The identification of the genes that exhibit regulatory changes in adult human cortex provides clues to the biochemical pathways and cell-biological processes that were modified during evolution. *The apparent up-regulation of so many different genes suggests, among other things, that the general level of neuronal activity and the metabolic processes that support it may be unusually high in human cortex.* Consistent with this is the up-regulation of genes involved in synaptic transmission, including the control of glutamatergic excitability (*SYN47*, also known as Homer 1b), plasticity at glutamatergic synapses (*CAMK2A*), phosphatidylinositol signaling (*IMPA1, CDS2*), synaptic vesicle release (*RAB3GAP, ATP2B1*), axonal transport along microtubules (*KIF3A, DCTN1*), microtubule assembly (*MAP1B*), and targeting of proteins to postsynaptic densities (*USP14*). *We have also found expression changes related to energy metabolism.* For example, *CA2*, which is expressed in glia, has been related to the generation and transport of lactate by astrocytes for use by neurons as an energy source. To our knowledge, the possibility that the human brain has an unusually high metabolism has not been previously considered. Typically, larger brains have lower metabolic rates (per unit of tissue) than smaller brains. Nevertheless, recent studies with imaging techniques to measure cerebral glucose metabolism in the conscious state suggest that metabolic rates are as high or even higher in humans than in macaques. *Higher levels of neuronal activity are likely to have important consequences in cognitive and behavioral capacities,* and of the genes up-regulated in humans, *CAMK2A* is involved in learning and memory, and mutations of *GTF2I* (Williams syndrome), *CA2* (marble brain disease), and *SC5DL* (lathosterolosis) have been linked to mental retardation. (p. 13034)

Brain Plasticity in Consciousness, Memory, Learning, and Behavior Change

Eric Kandel (1998), who received the Nobel Prize for Physiology or Medicine in 2000, describe the relationship between gene expression, brain plasticity, and mind-body healing via psychotherapy and counseling, a relationship that is essential for understanding the psychosocial genomics of Jung's constructive method, in these words:

Insofar as psychotherapy or counseling is effective and produces long-term changes in behavior, it presumably does so through learning, by producing *changes in gene expression that alter the strength of synaptic connections and structural changes that alter the anatomical pattern of interconnections between nerve cells of the brain.* As the resolution of brain imaging increases, it should eventually permit quantitative evaluation of the outcome of psychotherapy .... Stated simply, *the regulation of gene expression by social factors makes all bodily functions, including all functions of the brain, susceptible to social influences. These social influences will be biologically incorporated in the altered expressions of specific genes in specific nerve cells of specific regions of the brain.* These socially influenced alterations are transmitted culturally. They are not incorporated in the sperm and egg and therefore are not transmitted genetically. (p. 140, italics added)

Dreaming and Creative Replay in the Reconstruction of Fear, Stress and Traumatic Memories

Recent neuroscience research has found that when experimental animals experience significant *novelty, environmental enrichment, and exercise* during their waking state, the *zif-268 gene* is expressed during their REM sleep (Ribeiro *et al.*, 2002, 2004). *Zif-268* is an *immediate-early gene* and *behavioral-state related gene* that is associated with the generation of proteins and growth factors that facilitate brain plasticity. Ribeiro *et al.* (2004) summarize their results as follows:

The discovery of experience-dependent brain reactivation during both slow-wave (SW) and rapid eye-movement (REM, dream) sleep led to the notion *that the consolidation of recently acquired memory traces requires neural replay during sleep.* ... Based on our current and previous results, we propose that the 2 major periods of sleep play distinct and complementary roles in memory consolidation: pretranscriptional recall during SW sleep and transcriptional storage during REM sleep. ... In conclusion, *sustained neuronal reverberation during SW sleep, immediately followed by plasticity-related gene expression during REM [dreaming] sleep, may be sufficient to explain the beneficial role of sleep* on the consolidation of new memories. (p. 126-135, italics added.)

I have hypothesized that what the neuroscientist calls *"novelty, enrichment, and exercise"* in the evocation of gene expression and brain plasticity is on the same continuum of psychobiological states that Rudolph Otto (1923/1950) describes as *"fascination, mysteriousness, and tremendousness"*—the essence of the numinosum in spiritual experience. *This "novelty-numinosum-neurogenesis-effect" implies that gene expression and creative "neural replay" during dreaming and active imagination are the psychosocial genomic essence of Jung's constructive method and psychotherapy in general* (Rossi, 2002, 2004 a-c).

The genes listed in Table 1 are, in principle, all accessible via the creative replay dynamics in the arts, the sciences, spiritual rituals, and psychotherapy. It is the mission of the psychosocial genomics of Jung's constructive method to explore the conditions that make this possible. The genes listed in Table 1 are only a very tiny fraction of the approximately 30,000 genes in the human genome and an even smaller percentage of the 1.2 million genes now estimated to exist in nature as a whole (Venter *et al.*, 2004). This list is certain to grow with further research in the psychosocial genomics of the transcendent function.

Acute and Chronic Stress Evokes Alternative Gene Expression: The Cancer Connection

Chronic psychosocial stress associated with disturbed circadian rhythms in everyday life has been associated with cancer (Rosbash & Takahashi, 2002). Acute stress can induce a series of dramatic changes in cholinergic gene expression (or "splicing"), changes that alter the normal balance of acetylcholine and acetylcholinesterase metabolism associated with the posttraumatic stress disorders (PTSD) and many related mind-body dysfunctions, which are well summarized by Sternfeld *et al.* (2000).

> ... [U]*p to 30% of individuals exposed to an acute traumatic experience develop posttraumatic stress disorder, a syndrome characterized by progressively worsening personality disturbances and cognitive impairments. ... The accepted notion is that physiological stress responses are beneficial in the short run but detrimental if over-activated or prolonged. ...* We recently reported massive induction of a unique mRNA species encoding the rare "read-through" variant of acetylcholinesterase (AChE-R) in brains of mice

subjected to forced swimming stress. AChE-R differs from the dominant "synaptic" variant, AChE-S, in the composition of its C-terminal sequence. … In hippocampal brain slices, *induced AChE-R seemed to play a role in delimiting a state of enhanced neuronal excitation observed after acute cholinergic stimulation. This observation suggested that AChE-R acts as a stress modulator in [the] mammalian brain.* (p. 8647)

 … Our current findings therefore demonstrate that *AChE-R, most likely with another modulator or modulators, may be beneficial in the response to acute stress at two levels: (i) by dampening the acute cholinergic hyperactivation that accompanies stress and (ii) by protecting the brain from entering a downward spiral into progressive neurodegeneration through an as-yet unidentified mechanism, which could involve noncatalytic activities and/or direct competition with AChE-S.* In that case, the *diversion of up-regulated AChE expression after insults to the central nervous system from production of the usual AChE-S to the unusual AChE-R isoform [by stress-induced alternative gene expression or splicing] would reflect an elegant evolutionary mechanism to avoid the dangers of over-expressed AChE-S.* These findings imply that mutations conferring heritable up-regulation of AChE-R would protect the mammalian central nervous system from some age-dependent neuropathologies. (p. 8652, italics added)

While such up-regulation of AChE-R has a protective effect in acute stress, the most recent findings in this area suggest that chronic over-production of AChE-R can lead to over-proliferation of cells that can lead to cancer, as noted by Perry *et al.* (2004).

In conclusion, our findings are compatible with the hypothesis that CREB's basal levels are insufficient to block the AChE-R proliferative effect in cells with extreme excess of AChE-R compared to CREB. … *This may increase the risk for glial tumor growth in individuals exposed to anticholinesterases or head trauma, both shown to induce massive AChE-R overexpression.* (p. 7, italics added)

CREB is a transcription factor that turns on gene expression related to brain plasticity in consciousness, memory, learning, and behavior change (see Table 1), which are vital to the creative process, the numinosum, and Jung's transcendent function.

The Nature of the Numinosum: The Psychosocial Genomics
of the Four-Stage Creative Process in Jung's
Transcendent Function

Figure 4 outlines the classical four-stage process of creativity that relates Jung's four psychological functions (sensation, feeling, intuition, and thinking) as they emerge from the psychosocial genomics of the transcendent function in the arts, sciences, and psychotherapy as well as numinous experiences in spiritual practices.

The lower diagram in Figure 4 summarizes, in a simplified manner, the normal circadian (24-hour) profile of alternating 90–120 minute rhythms of waking and sleeping characteristic of Kleitman's Basic Rest-Activity Cycle (BRAC). The ascending peaks of rapid eye movement (REM) sleep typical of nightly dreams every 90–120 minutes or so are illustrated along with the more variable ultradian rhythms of activity, adaptation, and rest in the daytime. This lower figure also illustrates how many hormonal messenger molecules of the endocrine system, such as *growth hormone*, the activating and stress hormone *cortisol,* and the sex hormone *testosterone,* have typical circadian peaks at different times of the 24-hour cycle. The upper portion of Figure 4 outlines how a psychotherapy session is the creative utilization of one natural 90–120 minute BRAC rhythm of arousal and relaxation. I have outlined research that suggests how the classical four stages of the creative process (data collection, incubation, illumination, and verification) utilize Jung's four basic psychological functions (sensations, feeling, intuition, and thinking) (Rossi, 2002, 2004a).

Figure 4 illustrates how the psychological experience of the four-stage creative process (upper curve) emerges from the proteomic (protein) level (middle curve) depicting the energy landscape for protein folding into the correct structures needed for psychobiological functioning (adapted and redrawn from Cheung *et al.*, 2004). This proteomic level, in turn, emerges from the genomic level illustrated by the curve below it (adapted from Levsky *et al.*, 2002). This genomics curve represents the actual gene expression profiles of the immediate-early gene *c-fos* and 10 other genes (alleles) over the typical Basic Rest-Activity (BRAC) period of 90-120 minutes.

This set of curves illustrates our basic psychosocial genomics hypothesis: gene expression (genomics) and the dynamics of proteins (proteomics) are the ultimate bioinformatics foundation of the classical four-stage creative process in psychotherapy and mind-body medicine. These biological transformations at the genomic and proteomic levels are typically experienced as Kleitman's 90-120 minute Basic Rest-Activity Cycle in normal human psychophysiological rhythms. The basic psychosocial genomics hypothesis implies that these psychobiological rhythms can be trained and utilized to modulate the genomic and proteomic levels for therapeutic purposes by many of the diverse and seemingly unrelated approaches of mind-body medicine (Rossi, 2002, 2004 a-c; Rossi and Nimmons, 1991).

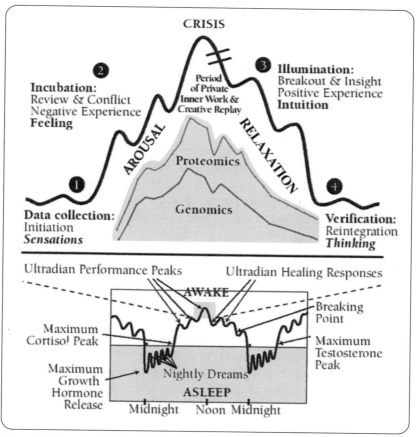

Figure 4: The Four-Stage Creative Process of the Transcendent Function Emerging from Genomic and Proteomic Levels in Everyday Life as Well as the Arts, Sciences, and Psychotherapy.

*The Psychosocial Genomics of the Four-Stage Creative
Process in the Transcendent Function*

We are now in a position to gain a better understanding of the bioinformatics of Jung's view that failure in coping adequately with the transcendent function in many cases is due precisely to the fact that people lack the mental and spiritual equipment to master the events taking place within them. From the perspective of psychosocial genomics, Jung's comment on failure in *"coming to terms with the unconscious [as] a true labour, a work which involves both action and suffering"* could refer to a breakdown in any of the four stages of the creative process, each of which requires a specific type of therapeutic intervention by Jung's constructive method as outlined below.

Stage 1: Preparation, Data Gathering: Intense and deeply meaningful psychological states of arousal—such as trauma, pain, stress, novelty, dreaming (REM sleep), and creative moments in everyday life as well as in the arts and sciences can initiate the activity of Immediate-Early Genes, Activity (or Experience) Dependent, and Behavior-State Related Genes in our brain and body. Our genes are not always in an active state; genes have to be stimulated in everyday life by internal and external environmental and psychosocial signals to generate the proteins that are the molecular machines of life that do creative work. Stage 1 of the creative process includes a search for the problem the mind-body is attempting to solve on an unconscious or implicit level, and often begins with Jung's sensation function. Sensations stimulate neural activity and curiosity, the desire to learn more, which sets us forth on deeply motivating outer and inner journeys of discovery and self-creation on all levels from mind to gene expression.

A natural initiation into mind-body healing begins with the typical history taking at the beginning of any form of psychotherapy. The typical tears and distress in an initial interview, for example, indicate that the person is already accessing state-dependent memory and emotional arousal, which evoke gene expression and new protein synthesis—a potentially healing venture. *The therapist's main job at this point is to recognize that therapy has already begun and to simply facilitate it by letting people tell their own story.*

Stage 2: Incubation, The Dark Night of the Soul: This is the valley of shadow, doubt, and depression that leads many people to psychotherapy. This is "the storm before the light" portrayed in drama, poetry, myth, and song in many cultures. Stage 2 is the crux of the transcendent function, and is frequently manifested as emotional conflict, crisis, and psychosomatic symptoms. *Stress-induced alternative pathways of gene expression and protein synthesis often generate conflict in the period of private inner work and creative replay* of Jung's feeling function at this stage. I hypothesize that in the natural processes of growth and the transformations of consciousness during life transitions, one invariably falls into anxiety (Sklan *et al.*, 2004), conflict (Birikh *et al.*, 2003), and the reconstruction of memory and learning (Cohen *et al.*, 2003) on all levels from mind to gene, which some molecular biologists describe in terms of the genomic shift from AChE-S (Stimulation) to AChE-R (Relaxation). *This is the struggle stage of the hero's journey, when many people experience a failure in their mental or spiritual equipment, which Jung described as occurring during the process of individuation.*

The therapist's *main job in Stage 2 is (1) to offer open-ended therapeutic questions designed to access the emotional complexes and archetypal patterns encoding symptoms and (2) to support the person through the sometimes painful arousal that makes him or her abort his or her natural cycle of creativity, problem solving, and healing in everyday life.* After a painful emotional crisis and catharsis, some people experience a private period of creative inner work that should not be intruded upon by the therapist. Less is often more at this delicate stage of the transcendent function, when respectful listening and emotional support *to encourage the person to reengage his or her numinous dream dramas with the creative replays of active imagination to facilitate development and healing on all levels from mind to gene is required* (Rossi, 2004a-c).

Stage 3: Illumination, Numinosum, Creative Insight, Problem Solving, and Healing: This is the famous "Ah-ha" or "Eureka" experience celebrated in ancient and modern literature when Jung's intuitive function is manifest in the arts, sciences, and creative moments of everyday life. People are surprised when they receive a creative thought and automatically dismiss their originality as worthless, since it has never been reinforced in their early life experience. *I hypothesize that gene expression and new protein synthesis at this numinous stage generates brain plasticity—the making and breaking of brain connections—the actual synthesis of new synapses and connections between brain cells that encode new human experience and the creative transformations of consciousness via the transcendent function.* It is imperative that people learn how to recognize and support these new developments in their consciousness, which are often heralded by little smiles and joy that breaks through the clouds of previous conflict. Psychosomatic symptoms tend to disappear dramatically as personal problems are resolved with the new perspectives that develop. *The therapist's main job at this stage is to help the subject recognize and appreciate the value of the "new," which often appears to emerge spontaneously and unheralded.* Often the subject may have already thought of the options that come up for problem solving at this stage but dismissed them since they have never been validated.

Stage 4: Verification and Reality Replays: In this final stage of the creative cycle the person needs to verify the value of the new experiences of Stage 3 by exercising them with creative replays in the real world as well as in dreams and active imagination. New experiences and insights are often fragile and can be easily lost. It is ironic that our family and friends, who wish us well, often do not recognize the new that develops within us. Because of this, the people who are closest to us often do not know how to support us in the realization of our new reality. Thus, adolescents experience the generation gap when they have difficulties with their family and friends. Falling in love can be fragile and fickle. Innovators and creative workers have been perpetually misunderstood and persecuted throughout history for daring to assert their new consciousness. *The therapist's job in this stage is to (1) facilitate a follow-up discussion to validate the value of the psychotherapeutic process, (2) reframe symptoms into signals and psychological problems into inner resources,* and *(3) prescribe further "reality homework" to test, extend, and reinforce the new neural connections being synthesized. Evidence suggests that 4 weeks to 4 months are required to stabilize these new neural networks* (Van Pragg *et al.*, 2002).

Summary and Implications

Current neuroscience research implies that psychobiological arousal during creative experiences in psychotherapy as well as the arts, sciences, and spiritual practices can modulate gene expression, protein synthesis, and brain plasticity. We have traced the source of Jung's "failure in ... the *mental and spiritual equipment to master the events taking place*" within the individual to the genomic level during

Stage 2 of the creative process. We do not, however, know the extent and limitations of this new "top-down" psychosocial genomic perspective on Jung's synthetic or constructive method for the "true labour" of optimizing our archetypal genomic resources. This suggests that Jung's (1918/1966, p. 5) call for a "return of the individual to the ground of human nature, to his own deepest being with its individual and social destiny" can be taken literally. We need to support psychosocial and cultural genomics research with the new DNA microarrays (gene chips) for exploring our relationship to the genomic ground of our creative being, the transcendent function, and the nature of the numinosum.

REFERENCES

Alejel, T. (2001). Effect of antidepressives and psychosocial stress on the Expression of a CRE dependent reporter gene in the brain of transgener mice. Philipps University Theisi, Marburg. http://archiv.ub.uni-marburg.de/diss/z2002/0040.

Alfonso, J., Pollevick, G., van der Hart, M., Flügge, G., Fuchs, E., Frasch, A. (2004). Identification of genes regulated by chronic psychosocial stress and antidepressant treatment in the hippocampus. *European Journal of Neuroscience,* 19:3, 659-666.

Birikh, K., Sklan, E., Shoham, S., & Soreq, H. (2003). Interaction of "readthrough" acetylcholinesterase with RACK1 and PKCßll correlates with intensified fear-induced conflict behavior. *Proceedings of the National Academy of Scientists,* 100:1, 283-288.

Bentivoglio, M. and Grassi-Zucconi, G. (1999). Immediate early gene expression in sleep and wakefulness. In Lydic, R. and Baghdoyan, H. (1999). *Handbook of Behavioral State Control: Cellular and Molecular Mechanisms.* New York: CRC Press, 235-253.

Cáceres, M., Lachuer, J., Zapala, M., Redmond, J., Kudo, L., Geschwind, D., Lockhart, D., Preuss, T., and Barlow, C. (2003). Elevated gene expression levels distinguish human from non-human primate brains. *Proceedings of the National Academy of Scientists,* 100, 13030-13035.

Castes, M., Hagel, I., Palenque, M., Canelones, P., Corano, A., & Lynch, N. (1999). Immunological changes associated with clinical improvement of asthmatic children subjected to psychosocial intervention. *Brain & Behavioral Immunology,* 13(1), 1-13.

Cheung, M., Chavez, L., and Onuchic, J. (2004). The energy landscape for protein folding and possible connections to function. *Polymer,* 45, 547-555.

Cirelli, C., Gutierrez, C., & Tononi, G. (2004). Extensive and divergent effects of sleep and wakefulness on brain gene expression. *Neuron,* 41, 35-43.

Cohen-Cory, S. (2002). *The Developing Synapse: Construction and Modulation of Synaptic Structures and Circuits. Science* 298: 770-776.

Cohen, O., Reichenberg, A., Perry, C., Ginzberg, D., Pollmächer, T., Soreq, H. and Yirmiya, R. (2003). Endotoxin-induced changes in human working and declarative memory are associated with cleavage of plasma "readthrough" acetylcholinesterase. *J. Molec. Neurosci.,* 21, 199-212.

Eriksson, P., Perfilieva, E., Björk-Ericksson, T., Alborn, A., Nordborg, C., Peterson, D., & Gage, F. (1998). Neurogenesis in the adult human hippocampus. *Nature Medicine,* 4, 1313-1317.

Glaser, R., Lafuse, W., Bonneau, R., Atkinson, C., & Kiecolt-Glaser, J, (1993). Stress-associated modulation of proto-oncogene expression in human peripheral blood leukocytes. *Behavioral Neuroscience,* 107, 525-529.

Hoffman, K. & McNaughton, B. (2002). Coordinated reactivation of distributed memory traces in primate cortex. *Science,* 297, 2070-2073.

Jung, C. (1916/1960). The Transcendent Function. In *The Structure and Dynamics of the Psyche.* Bollingen Series XX, Volume 8. *The Collected Works of C. G. Jung.* (R. F. C. Hull, Trans.). New York: Pantheon Books, pp. 67-91.

Jung, C. (1918/1966). The Synthetic or Constructive method. In *Two Essays on Analytical Psychology.* Bollingen Series XX, Volume 7. 2ed edition. *The Collected Works of C. G. Jung.* (R. F. C. Hull, Trans.). New York: Pantheon Books, pp. 80-89.

Jung, C. (1937/1958). *Psychology and Religion.* In *Psychology and Religion* Bollingen Series XX, Volume 11. *The Collected Works of C. G. Jung.* (R. F. C. Hull, Trans.). New York: Pantheon Books, p. 8.

Kandel, E. (1998). A new intellectual framework for psychiatry. *The American Journal of Psychiatry,* 155, 457-469.

Kempermann, G., Kuhn, G. & Gage, F. (1997). More hippocampal neurons in adult mice living in an enriched environment. *Nature,* 386, 493-495.

Levsky, J., Shenoy, S., Pezo, C., & Singer, R. (2002). Single-Cell Gene Expression Profiling. *Science,* 297, 836-840.

Moles, A., Kieffer, B. & D'Amato, F. (2004). Deficit attachment behavior in mice lacking the u-opioid receptor gene. *Science,* 304, 1983-1986.

Nader, K.. Schafe, G., & Le Doux, J. (2000). Fear memories require protein synthesis in the amygdala for reconsolidation after retrieval. *Nature,* 406, 722-726.

Otto, R. (1923/1950). *The Idea of the Holy.* NY: Oxford University Press.

Perry, C., Sklan, E., & Soreq, H., (2004). CREB regulates AchE-R - induced proliferation of human glioblastoma cells, *Neoplasia,* 6:2, 1-8.

Ribeiro, S., Mello, C., Velho, T., Gardner, T., Jarvis, E., & Pavlides, C. (2002). Induction of hippocampal long-term potentiation during waking leads to increased extrahippocampal zif-268 expression during ensuing rapid-eye-movement sleep. *Journal of Neuroscience,* 22(24), 10914-10923.

Ribeiro, S., Gervasoni, D., Soares, E., Zhou, Y., Lin, S., Pantoja, J., Lavine, M., & Nicolelis, M. (2004). Long-lasting novelty-induced neuronal reverberation during slow-wave sleep in multiple forebrain areas. *Public Library of Science, Biology. (PLoS),* 2 (1), 126-137.

Ridley, M. (1999). *Genome: The Autobiography of a Species in 23 Chapters.* N.Y.: HarperCollins.

Rosbash, M., & Takahashi, J. (2002). Circadian rhythms: the cancer connection. *Nature,* 420, 373-374.

Rossi, E. (2000). Exploring gene expression in sleep, dreams and hypnosis with the new DNA microarray technology: A call for clinical-experimental research. *Sleep and Hypnosis: An International Journal of Sleep, Dream, and Hypnosis.* 2:1, 40-46.

Rossi, E. (1972/2000). *Dreams and the Growth of Personality: Expanding Awareness in Psychotherapy.* New York: Pergamon Press. Updated in the 3ed edition as *Dreams, Consciousness, and Spirit.* Phoenix, Arizona: Zeig, Tucker, Theisen.

Rossi, E. (2002). *The Psychobiology of Gene Expression: Neuroscience and Neurogenesis in Therapeutic Hypnosis and the Healing Arts.* NY: W. W. Norton Professional Books.

Rossi, E. (2003a). Gene Expression, Neurogenesis, and Healing: Psychosocial Genomics of Therapeutic Hypnosis. *American Journal of Clinical Hypnosis.* 45:3, 197-216.

Rossi, E. (2003b). Can We Really Talk to Our Genes? Psychosocial Genomics. *Hypnos: The Journal of European Society of Hypnosis in Psychotherapy and Psychosomatic Medicine*, Vol. 30, 1, 6-15.

Rossi, E. (2003c). The Bioinformatics of Psychosocial Genomics in Alternative and Complementary Medicine. *Forschende Komplementarmedizine und Klassische Naturheilkunde*, 10, 143-150.

Rossi, E. (2004a). *A Discourse with Our Genes: The Neuroscience of Therapeutic Hypnosis and Psychotherapy.* Editris: Benevento, Italy.

Rossi, E. (2004b). Gene expression and brain plasticity in stroke rehabilitation: A personal memoir of mind-body healing dreams. *American Journal of Clinical Hypnosis,* 46:3, 215-227.

Rossi, E. (2004c). Sacred spaces and places in healing dreams: Gene expression and brain growth in rehabilitation: *Psychological Perspectives,* 47, 49-62.

Rossi, E. (2004d). A Bioinformatics Approach to the Psychosocial Genomics of Therapeutic Hypnosis. *Hypnos,* 31:1, 15-21.

Rossi, E. & Nimmons, D. (1991). *The Twenty-Minute Break: The Ultradian Healing Response.* Los Angeles: Jeremy Tarcher; New York: Zeig,Tucker, Theisen.

Russo-Neustadt A., Ha T., Ramirez R., Kesslak J. (2001). Physical activity-antidepressant treatment combination: impact on brain-derived neurotrophic factor and behavior in an animal model *Behavioral Brain Research,* 120, 87-95.

Schanberg, S. (1995). The genetic basis for touch effects. Field, T. (Ed.) *Touch in Early Development.* N.Y.: Lawrence Erlbaum, 67-79.

Sklan, E., Lowenthal, A., Korner, M., Ritov, Y., Landers, D., Rankinen, T., Bouchard, C., Leon, A., Rice, T., Rao, D., Wilmore, J., Skinner, J., & Soreq, H. (2004). Acetylcholinesterase/paraoxonase genotype and expression predict anxiety scores in health, risk factors, exercise training, and genetics study. *Proceedings of the National Academy of Scientists,* 101:15, 5512-5517.

Sternfeld, M., Shoham, S., Klein, O., Flores-Flores, C., Evron, T., Idelson, G., Kitsberg, D., Patrick, J., & Soreq, H. (2000). Excess "read-through" acetylcholinesterase attenuates but the "synaptic" variant intensifies neurodeterioration correlates. *Proceedings of the National Academy of Sciences,* 97, 8647-8652.

Van Praag, H., Kempermann, G., and Gage, F. (1999). Running increases cell proliferation and neurogenesis in the adult mouse dentate gyrus. *Nature Neuroscience,* 2, 266-270.

Van Praag, H., Schinder, A., Christie, B., Toni, N., Palmer, T. and Gage, F. (2002). Functional neurogenesis in the adult hippocampus. *Nature,* 415, 1030-1034.

Venter, J. *et al.* (2004). Environmental Genome Shotgun Sequencing of the Sargasso Sea. *Science,* 304, 66-74.

Von Baeyer, H. (2004). *Information :The New Language of Science.* Harvard University Press: Cambridge: Massachusetts

Watson, J. & Crick, F. (1953a). A structure for deoxyribose nucleic acid, *Nature,* 171, 737-738.

Watson, J. & Crick, F. (1953b). Genetical implications of the structure of deoxyribonucleic acid. *Nature,* 171, 964-967.

Whitney, A., Diehn, M., Popper, S., Alizadeh, A., Boldrick, J., Relman, D. & Brown, P. (2003) Individuality and variation in gene expression patterns in human blood. *Proceedings of the National Academy of Sciences,* 100, 1896-1901.

BOOK REVIEWS

ROBIN VAN LÖBEN SELS. *A Dream in the World: Poetics of Soul in Two Women, Modern and Medieval.* Brunner-Routledge, 2003.

REVIEWED BY MAUREEN MURDOCK

I n *A Dream in the World*, Robin van Löben Sels compares the spiritual breakthroughs of two women, one a thirteenth-century mystic named Hadewijch of Brabant, and the other, a contemporary patient, whom she calls Mairi. She concludes that if we are to experience soul at all, we must acknowledge that soul is embodied. Soul lives in the body, even as it speaks through the psyche.

A central concern of Sels's book is to reveal that in some cases of depth psychological therapy, religious experience takes precedence over psychological experience in the transformation of the patient. When psychological transformation is explicitly described in religious language and concerned with a religious referent, i.e., the soul in relationship to God, rather than to the known ego world, the patient experiences a

Maureen Murdock, M.A., MFT, is a psychotherapist in Sausalito, California and the author of several books including *The Heroine's Journey; Fathers' Daughters* and *Unreliable Truth.*

new awareness of consciousness in relation to herself and her place in the cosmos. The patient is penetrated by something "beyond the psyche whether it comes from within as soul or from without as world." Such a penetration was experienced by Sels's patient Mairi.

Over a period of five years, Sels worked with Mairi's dreams, paying particular attention to what Sels calls her Self-directive dreams. In contrast to dreams that include mythological symbols, these dreams contain no dream ego and no persons. Mairi's Self-directive dreams often included such images as an artichoke, an enormous red rose, a bird with jeweled wings. Because of a lack of "personal access," it is difficult for the patient to come up with personal associations. Self-directive dreams can therefore feel to the dreamer as if they are being dreamed for someone other than herself, perhaps for the world—what Sels calls "a dream-in-the-world."

Mairi's experience of working with these dreams eventually made it possible for her to experience an embodied sense of soul, which became the guiding experience of her life. This experience of soul gave her a sense of an embodied self, filling a hole she had felt from early life resulting from emotional deprivation and a pre-birth trauma. So great was her experience of embodied soul that she felt completely rearranged in relation to herself, to others, and to God. She felt her consciousness change and expand. In explaining this, Sels quotes von Franz: "The ego frees itself from thought of gain and achievement in order to get nearer to true and deeper being by giving itself over, 'free of all purpose' to an inner need to grow."

Mairi and the thirteenth-century mystic Hadewijch had spiritual breakthroughs within very different historical and cultural contexts, but both women spoke of experiencing a feminine Presence. From the age of 10, Hadewijch was overcome by an intense Love, which she called Lady Love (Minne). Her religious instinct had an appropriate "object" which made sense within her life context. Mairi lives in a more psychological context, which does not acknowledge the pre-eminence of the spiritual experience. Jung has written that we are not well or whole until we have satisfied the longing that is inherent in the religious instinct. However, because we live in a culture and time that is so narcissistic, we resist acknowledging our own inferiority and limitations by loving a greater or higher reality (god). Yet there remains a god-shaped longing in the human heart that cannot be satisfied by any manmade thing.

Hadewijch describes this longing in her texts, which have come down to us from the thirteenth century. She writes that "love for God is increased by a constantly unfulfilled and unfulfillable *longing* for God and this longing is the locus of union with the love that *is* god." Hadewijch made a commitment to living her love. Sometime during the thirteenth century, she either founded or joined the Beguines, a lay women's movement that advocated alternative ways of living one's faith outside a religious order. The Beguines came into being among women of educated and noble families who rejected both the narrow life of the castle as well as the restricted life of the cloister. The Beguines lived their faith as a way of life. They were eventually suppressed by order of the Church, which was opposed to the idea of groups living under the cloak of religion without a definite Rule.

The writings of Hadewijch were lost for six centuries. She wrote that spiritual union with God consisted not in the ecstasies and visions she had experienced early in her psycho-religious development, but in serving her fellow human beings. She embraced the paradox and pain of suffering her Love for God in order to "grow up." She discovered that soul is a state of being, deeper than and prior to self-feeling and projection. Hadewijch's inner movement was from soul to psyche, whereas Mairi's inner movement went from psyche to soul.

After her last Self-directive dream, Mairi began to have an "experience of soul." She had an experience of being "lit up" from within and felt kundalini energies moving throughout her body for three days. During this time, she had a sense of a holy, feminine, abiding Presence beyond herself that "knew" her and "saw" her. She kept saying, "She cares about me. I feel it, through and through. It is the Holy Spirit, but feminine. She is with me and I'll never be the same. I feel as if I have died and been reborn. At first I felt as if a floor had fallen out from under me, but somehow the free-fall was a threshold, disguised. I crossed—or It—or She—crossed to reach me. There is no going back. I will serve Her the rest of my life."

She later described this revelation as her experience of soul. She felt this as a penetration by an "Otherness," something beyond her psyche. This experience originated in her body. Mairi described what many women have expressed before her, that her experience of feminine spirituality came from deep within her body, not from a celestial enlightenment of the mind.

Mairi was indeed fortunate to work with a therapist who was curious and knowledgeable about the religious dimension experienced in the body. Sels has what she calls a "psycho-religious attitude." Many individuals who went through what was called a "spiritual emergency" in the 1960s and 1970s did not have such a wise midwife to hold their experience of kundalini in their bodies as they broke through to a spiritual consciousness. Instead, their encounter with penetrating a perceptual barrier to a spiritual consciousness was diagnosed as psychosis. Sels held a container large enough for Mairi to give witness to her evolving awareness of the Presence beyond herself. She had a vision of the Holy Spirit as a feminine presence which, up until this time, she had never known. Others before her have called this Presence Sophia.

Sels's book makes an enormous contribution in its emphasis on the value of body awareness in psychotherapy. Sels helped her patient Mairi bring back into collective consciousness the importance and feeling value of the soul. She writes: "Soul was something different from all the psychological material we had processed together—her dreams, her feelings, her self-representations as she interacted with others. Soul was concrete, an undeniable *something real* into which Mairi felt herself fall, and out of which Mairi felt herself become. As if the inner light of embodied Being, soul was something that Mairi *was not*, but that contained her; she *experienced* soul; she did not think about it."

Through her research into the writings of Hadewijch, Sels also brings back into collective consciousness what was known, written about, and eventually suppressed about embodied Soul in the thirteenth century. Sels makes clear that we have to invite the body into the consulting room: we interfere with the evolution of our patients' psycho-spiritual consciousness if we imagine there is a separation between body and soul.

BOOK REVIEWS

MARGARET JACOBY LOPEZ. *Sing Past Winter: A Modern Psalter.* Blue Fire Books, 2003.

REVIEWED BY MAGGIE MACARY

Singing to Unknown Gods

> You are pain. I am not.
> I am pain. You are not.
> You are Christ. I am not.
> I am Christ. You are not,
> and when I am not
> I lose my mind,
> And when I lose my mind
> I go looking for yours. (29)

I t is not easy to approach a book like Margaret Jacoby Lopez's *Sing Past Winter*. Words and images weave in and out in complex patterns, until I, too, feel lost in the author's pain. Yet I am continually drawn to the book by the sense of mystery embedded in its words and its beautifully crafted images.

Maggie Macary is completing her Ph.D. at Pacifica Graduate Institute in mythological studies. Her dissertation is on myths of the fat body. She blogs daily about mythology and culture on her website, http://www.mythandculture.com, and teaches personal mythology online.

The publisher tells us outright that the book originated in the author's personal experience of chronic, debilitating pain, an experience the author manages to transcend in creating the book. A transcended experience is not easy to comprehend, especially by an outsider. One looks for clues as to how to approach such an experience with reverence for the intensely personal journey being revealed and still find a universality that makes the experience accessible to others. Like many complex works of psyche, this mystery is not easy to untangle. I, particularly, do not wish to deconstruct another's experience, unraveling the mystery so that it is no longer mysterious. Instead, I can only relate my experience of this work, and I can do that only through the Greco-Roman framing that has become my particular lens.

The subtitle indicates that this book is a *Psalter*, a book of songs to a divinity, and this tells me that a god (or gods) hides within the words and images. I ask myself: what divinity does one call on in this wilderness of pain, what god is Lopez singing to? Interestingly, I find numerous gods—Christian, Native American, Greco-Roman, Buddhist, the author mentions them all, either explicitly in verse or implicitly through her images. And yet, I sense these are not the gods she continually addresses as "You." Who is the "You" with the capital *Y* that Lopez addresses in this book?

For a clue, I look to my own body's reactions to this work about a shattered body. I feel a great beauty here in the artfully poised bodies and body parts, each one lovingly photographed and transformed by collage, charcoal, and paint. The images show great tension through the body, a tension that shakes the limbs and shatters the flesh. Lopez opens her volume with the following verse:

> Is it the rip in my heart that accepts my longing
> and grants me hope to stretch further than my reach,
> or is it creation's hand stretching the hymen of God's nature
> for me to claim my divinity's weakness?
> A confession of silent thoughts that shocks my desire
> to touch the place where eruptions start to confound my love. (15)

I immediately sense the Eros in this verse and compare it to Sappho's cry: "Love, the loosener of limbs, now shakes me again, Bitter-sweet and untameable beast."[1] I begin to investigate the notion that the god Lopez is addressing is Eros, the beastly body shaker and limb loosener.

We tend to think of Eros as incorporating both desire and pleasure, but this is not so in Greek thought. Eros rarely appears alone, but is often seen as a companion (along with Himeros) to Aphrodite. Himeros or desire, is a *drawing out* of the soul for something it sees, *"dia ten esin tes roes"* according to Plato. Eros, on the other hand, is an influx, *a flooding into* the body.[2] Aphrodite is the foam, the resulting release of the flooding into the body. Thus, the three elements—desire, act, pleasure—are an ensemble which, accordingly, are closely bound and yet distinguishable from one other.[3] It is the distinguishability that interests me here.

In Greek myth, Eros represents a limb-shivering chaotic experience felt throughout the tissues of the body. With his penetrating arrows, Eros creates an involuntary, often chaotic piercing of the flesh. To have the body opened by such an arrow signifies loss of control. The body shakes and falls apart. This is not merely a sexual experience but also a death experience. Eros is a psychopomp, a "face of Thanatos," which leads the soul into an experience of death (76).[4] It is this raw, limb-shaking, body-shivering experience of death that Lopez reveals when she writes:

> Our bones are hot, melting our marrow.
> There is nothing left to risk.
> We are finished in this place.
> Night burns and brands me a new creature
> Dying means living through the pain of birth
> And I was the only one who could tell what it was like. (47)

I cannot ignore the Eros present in Lopez's experience of pain as she photographs and paints and mythopoetizes herself beyond suffering. Almost half-way through the book, Lopez speaks directly to Eros:

> I saw the blade raised in air.
> Eros kill me with mercy
> kill all of me; leave only my tongue
> for in my tongue all desires are satisfied.
> I sing and curse my maker.
> I commit myself to you and savor your lips
> open to me (only the tiniest crack). (65)

I realize that Eros is not the "You" that Lopez is singing to. The psalm is not to this god. I remember that the gods never exist alone, that their true experience can be appreciated only through their relationships to each other. I continue to wander lost in the images and the poetry of the book, puzzling over this unseen but spoken-to god. Then two revelations give me further insight.

The first is a notation from the author about her process in creating the artwork. A crafting of photographs into collage, each image is framed and scrubbed to "emphasize the outermost bounds" of the image. Then Lopez completes each image by rubbing it with body ash, the remains of cremation. This final moment represents for Lopez the moment in which the "sacred elements of remembrance" transform from one reality to another (158). The notion of completing each image with the remains of cremation stops me short. I think of offerings to the Underworld and imagine the charred remains burnt on the portable altar known as the *escharra*. I remember that the word scar is derived from the Greek word *escharra*.

This book is a funeral rite, an offering to the divinities of the Underworld. Could it be, I think, that the "You" Lopez is addressing is simply the god of the Underworld himself? Is Lopez singing to Hades? With that revelation, I suddenly begin to see the book through the myths of descent, with the author becoming none other than Persephone herself.

The second revelation confirms my insight. After the images and the poems were put together, Lopez went back and wrote her psalm, sprinkling the lines mysteriously around images in the book. She finally reveals the psalm at the end in its entirety. Its images astound me:

> I did my best not to yield before the crescent moon
> but my body had gone too far.
> The hawk showed me his nest.
> It was close to where we slept.
> I felt your weight beside me pressing wildflowers:
> You touched me awake.
> When did you leave?

Suddenly, I catch the scent of wildflowers falling from the sky as an unwilling virgin is captured by a dark lord and transformed into a queen. When I read these lines, I imagine the author and all of us who at one time or another face unbearable pain, as Persephone with her lover Hades, the invisible one. Lopez confirms this notion when she writes of slipping "pain-free into the world of poetry, the bedchamber of an invisible lover made visible through words" (157).

Lopez creates images and poetry of love to sing to her deity-lover, Hades himself. And I understand. Eros leads the body-shaken soul into a dark place of transformation where one must confront the realities of pain and birth, life and death. But the love is for Hades, the invisible lord whose realm also holds riches. It is this Underworld realm that Margaret Jacoby Lopez surrenders to in pain, and finds herself within that pain.[5]

This book represents a profound journey of transformation that is as old as the stories of descent themselves. And yet it has been made anew by Lopez's experience of a body in pain, crying out in confusion, only to find the answer within death. Lopez has found this place where death and pain are lost in themselves, a place that is not merely transcendent, but also radically immanent, where one disappears into (rather than moves out of) the body and experiences. It is a powerful testament.

NOTES

1. Sappho, *Sappho*, trans. Robert Chandler (London: Everyman: 1998), Fragment 130.

2. C. D. C. Reeve, "Cratylus," *Plato: Complete Works*, ed. John M. Cooper (Indianapolis: Hackett, 1997), 420a.

3. Michel Foucault, *The Use of Pleasure: The History of Sexuality Volume 2*, trans. Robert Hurley (New York: Vintage Books, 1990), 42.

4. James Hillman, *The Myth of Analysis: Three Essays in Archetypal Psychology.* (New York: Harper, 1972), 76.

5. I am reminded of Gilles Deleuze, who writes about radical immanence: "... this is the point at which death turns against death; where dying is the negation of death, and the impersonality of dying no longer indicates only the moment when I disappear outside of myself, but rather the moment when death loses itself in itself ...." *The Logic of Sense*, trans. Mark Lester with Charles Stivale, ed. Constantin V. Boundas (New York: Columbia University Press, 1990), 153.

BOOK REVIEWS

MARC LAPPE. *The Body's Edge: Our Cultural Obsession With Skin.* Henry Holt, 1996.

ROY PORTER. *Flesh in the Age of Reason: The Modern Foundations of Body and Soul.* Foreword Simon Schama. W.W. Norton, 2003.

REVIEWED BY DENNIS PATRICK SLATTERY

Our language is loaded with skin metaphors: "to get under one's skin," to be "thin-skinned," to escape "by the skin of one's teeth," "to get the skinny on someone," to dismiss beauty as being only "skin-deep." Readers interested in the body as metaphor and as the locale of myth, as Joseph Campbell believed, will find Marc Lappe's book of great interest despite, its few aging wrinkles (it was published in 1996). His introduction entices: "Our skin serves as a real and metaphoric boundary between ourselves and others, between health and disease" (1).

Ever since the body was rediscovered in the 1960s through the phenomenology of Maurice Merleau Ponty (*Phenomenology of*

Dennis Patrick Slattery is a member of the core faculty in mythological studies at Pacifica Graduate Institute. His books include *The Wounded Body: Remembering the Markings of Flesh* (2000) and *Just Below the Water Line: Selected Poems* (2004).

Perception), followed by an explosion of interest in the 1980s with Elaine Scarry's *The Body in Pain*, David Michael Levin's *The Body's Recollection of Being*, and Robert Romanyshyn's *Psychological Life* and *Technology as Symptom and Dream*, the skin, the body's largest organ, has received elaborate cosmetic attention. Its multibillion dollar industry in creams, coverings, and camouflages attests to something below the surface. Skin and self-identity mirror one another through surface and depth. The skin is the slate on which many of our most painful stories are grafted, outlined, and sketched. Our skin, he reveals, gives an edge to our narratives, our imperfections, and our deeper health or disease.

Lappe's title chapters announce the range of his concerns: "At the Boundary of the Self "; "Barrier or Sieve?"; "The Silicone Story"; "The Future." Lappe, while not a psychologist or mythologist, does touch on those areas where psyche and skin find a porous route to one another; skin is less a wrap than a permeable membrane. He reveals, through a history of the science of skin exploration, that far from being a defensive wall to the world, the skin is a corridor between external influences and interior conditions. He also convincingly outlines the constant battle between the discoveries of science regarding disease and the cosmetic industry's pressure to bury those findings beneath the skin of society in order to promote their products. His notes and further readings are excellent, and open up the full range of our skin's complexity.

Roy Porter's more recent study of flesh follows on an earlier epic work, *The Greatest Benefit to Mankind: A Medical History of Humanity* (1998), which outlines in considerable depth the rise of medicine as it tracks world diseases through many civilizations. Porter writes big books—568 and 830 pages respectively. His style is quirky, clear, and complex. *Flesh in the Age of Reason* is divided into four large sections: "Souls and Bodies"; "Men of Letters"; "The Frailty of the Flesh"; and "The Science of Man for a New Society." His study is as much philosophical and psychological as it is medical. His focus on Enlightenment thought reveals the rise of the man of progress, the secular individual; autonomy and anatomy develop simultaneously to invent an individual who is serialized, discrete, autonomous, and self-determined, an end product of the thought of many philosophers, most notably John Locke (1690).

Porter's study is a model of research and a gift of continuity; to enter it is to track the persuasive thought in the West of Rene Descartes, Francis Bacon, J. J. Rousseau, Adam Smith, John Keats, Georg Hegel, and others. Fundamentally, Porter is a social constructionist who contends that each epoch reinvents humanity anew according to the prevailing ideas that propel it forward. His primary intention is to show how "the demise of the soul" (27) evolved through the Enlightenment's intent to disenchant the world "from a time when everything was ensouled ..." (27), to the present day, in which the soul is not seen fit for investigation.

Porter's vision is grand and particular at the same time. As he investigates the shifting sands of interpreting disease and health from an increasingly mechanical perspective in history, he delineates with great subtlety the rise of the medical model and the moral management of health. *Flesh* contains a bibliography, in small type, that runs 80 pages. His study should be of great interest to students of literature, psychology, philosophy, and mythology.

It's really important that you have done this extraordinary thing. This real world needs to thank you and realize what an extraordinary thing has happened here, what you have been able to bring together, to present, and to make enjoyable. Thank you.

— *James Hillman, June 6, 2004 from the stage at Mythic Journeys*

Save The Date: June 7-11, 2006

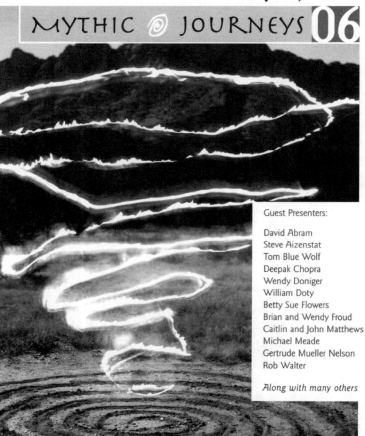

MYTHIC @ JOURNEYS 06

Guest Presenters:

David Abram
Steve Aizenstat
Tom Blue Wolf
Deepak Chopra
Wendy Doniger
William Doty
Betty Sue Flowers
Brian and Wendy Froud
Caitlin and John Matthews
Michael Meade
Gertrude Mueller Nelson
Rob Walter

Along with many others

In association with Pacifica Graduate Institute,
The Joseph Campbell Foundation,
and PARABOLA Magazine

Find us on the web at
www.mythicimagination.org
or call (404) 832-4127

The Foundation for Mythological Studies (FMS)
www.mythology.org

FMS is a California nonprofit organization, created to support and encourage the study of mythology and depth psychology in order to expand our understanding of such archetypal patterns of human behavior.

FMS has created a series of summer workshops, involving scholars in the field of Mythological Studies and Depth Psychology. Our goal is to provide affordable intimate workshops that cover a variety of specialized topics geared toward the continuing growth and education of the participants.

The first in our *Summer Workshop Series* is *From Dissertation to Publication* and will be led by noted author **Ginette Paris, Ph.D., Research Coordinator** at Pacifica Graduate Institute and **Druscilla French, Ph.D., President** of FMS.
Nancy Cater, Ph.D., Publisher, SPRING JOURNAL BOOKS will join the Workshop team as well to discuss publishing options.

Workshop Date: August 5-7, 2005
Workshop Fee: $225
Location: Evergreen, CO.
CONTACT: lori@mythology.org for more information.

FMS Board of Directors:
Ginette Paris, Ph.D., Druscilla French, Ph.D.,
Dianne Skafte, Ph.D., Peggy Olson, MA.

NEW FROM SPRING JOURNAL BOOKS

FOLLOWING THE REINDEER WOMAN
Path of Peace and Harmony
Linda Schierse Leonard
ISBN 1-882670-95-7
Price $20.00 (USD)
229 pages

Drawing upon myths, dreams, stories, and film, best-selling author Linda Leonard explores the reindeer as an archetype of feminine energy and as a symbol that can inspire both men and women in their spiritual development and serve as an image of hope, peace and harmony in the ecological dark times in which we now live.

TEACHERS OF MYTH
Interviews on Educational and Psychological Uses of Myth with Adolescents
Maren Hansen
ISBN 1-882670-89-2
Price $15.95 (USD)
73 pages

Maren Hansen conducts interviews with three master teachers of myth and explores:

◆ Why do you teach myth to adolescents?

◆ How is the study of myth related to human psychological development?

◆ What teaching methods do you use to help your students connect to the psychological dimension in myth?

◆ Which myths most effectively address the developmental stage of adolescence?

NEW FROM SPRING JOURNAL BOOKS
DAVID L. MILLER TRILOGY

THREE FACES OF GOD
Traces of the Trinity in
Literature and Life
Price: $20.00 (USD)
ISBN 1-882670-94-9
197 pages

An exploration of the concept
of the Trinity as it appears in
Christian theology, in the
psychology of Freud and Jung,
and in modern secular
literature.

CHRISTS
Meditations on
Archetypal Images in
Christian Theology
Price: $20.00 (USD)
ISBN 1-882670-93-0
249 pages

An analysis of the archetypal
images from mythology that
underlie the figure of Christ
and a study of comtemporary
imaginal versions of them.

HELLS & HOLY GHOSTS
A Theopoetics of
Christian Belief
Price: $20.00 (USD)
ISBN 1-882670-97-3
238 pages

Miller utilizes insights from
theology, mythology, literature,
and history to explore the
present meaning of the Holy
Ghost and the motif "life after
death".

ABOUT THE AUTHOR

David L. Miller, Ph.D., is Watson-Ledden Professor of Religion Emeritus at Syracuse
University and is a retired Core Faculty Member at Pacifica Graduate Institute in Santa
Barbara. He was a member of the Eranos circle from1975 until 1988, and has lectured
widely in Europe, America, and Japan for the past forty years. He is also an honorary
member of the Inter-Regional Society of Jungian Analysts and the International
Association of Analytical Psychology. His other books include *Gods and Games: Toward
a Theology of Play* and *The New Polytheism: Rebirth of the Gods and Goddesses.* For more
information about Dr. Miller's work and his writings, see his website at
http://web.syr.edu/~dlmiller.

To order, please visit our online store at:
www.springjournalandbooks.com or call *504.524.5117*

NEW FROM SPRING JOURNAL BOOKS
STUDIES IN ARCHETYPAL PSYCHOLOGY SERIES
SERIES EDITOR: GREG MOGENSON

DIALECTICS & ANALYTICAL PSYCHOLOGY
The El Capitan Canyon Seminar
Wolfgang Giegerich ♦ David L. Miller ♦ Greg Mogenson
Price: $20.00 (USD) ♦ ISBN 1-882670-92-2 ♦ 136 pages

What is dialectical thinking and why do we need it in
psychology? Conceived to meet "the call for more" that followed
the publication of Jungian analyst Wolfgang Giegerich's
landmark book, *The Soul's Logical Life*, this volume serves as the
most accessible introduction to Giegerich's provocative approach
to psychology. It is a valuable resource for students of fairy tale,
myth, and depth psychology and includes a complete
bibliography of Geigerich's writings in all languages.

RAIDS ON THE UNTHINKABLE:
Freudian *and* Jungian Psychoanalyses
Paul Kugler
Price: $20.00 (USD) ♦ ISBN 1-882670-91-4 ♦ 160 pages

Paul Kugler critically rethinks the pivotal concepts of
psychoanalysis and, in the process, makes evident what the
theoretical differences between Freud and Jung have to offer
contemporary depth psychology. Through a constructive
'dialogue' between Freudian and Jungian psychoanalysis, Kugler
demonstrates that such a project is not only theoretically
possible, but clinically valuable.

NORTHERN GNOSIS
Thor, Baldr, and the Volsungs in the
Thought of Freud and Jung
Greg Mogenson
Price: $20.00 (USD) ♦ ISBN 1-882670-90-6 ♦ 140 pages

This imaginative and scholarly work uses stories from Norse
mythology to understand major concepts from Freud and Jung.
Jung's theory of the archetype is seen as a variant of Thor's
encounters with the giants. Freud's death instinct is envisioned as
a variant of Baldr's death, and the relations of Freud, Jung and
Sabina Speilrein are reflected in the saga of the Volsungs.

To order, please visit our online store at
www.springjournalandbooks.com or call **504.524.5117**

Spring Journal

Archetypal Psychology ◆ Mythology ◆ Jungian Psychology

Spring Journal is the oldest Jungian psychology journal in the world.

Published twice a year, each issue is organized around a theme and offers articles and book reviews in the areas of archetypal psychology, mythology, and Jungian psychology.

Future Issues of Spring Journal

CINEMA AND PSYCHE (Fall 2005) *Articles by John Beebe, Michael Conforti, Linda S. Leonard, Christopher Hauke, Don Fredericksen, Glen Slater, Luke Hockley and more!*

ALCHEMY (Spring 2006) *Articles by Stan Marlan, David L. Miller, Murray Stein, Beverley Zabriskie, Susan Rowland, Dyane Sherwood, Ronald Schenk, Gus Cwik, Sherry Salman and more!*

PSYCHE and NATURE (Fall 2006)

PHILOSOPHY and PSYCHOLOGY (Spring 2007) *Guest Editors: Edward Casey and David L. Miller.*

To subscribe, please visit our online store at *www.springjournalandbooks.com*, call *504.524.5117*, or fill out the order form below:

- - ✂ - ✂ - -

Subscribe to Spring Journal and Save!

Published twice a year, a one-year subscription costs $32.00, and a two-year subscription is just $58.00. Postage within the continental U.S. is free. Please add the following postage for international orders: International Surface: $5.00 International Airmail: $15.00

Name: _____   City: _____

Address: _____   State/Zip/Country: _____

_____   Telephone: _____

_____   Email: _____

Check Enclosed*☐   Visa/MC/Amex ☐   Card Number: _____

Expiration Date: _____

* Checks should be made payable to Spring Journal, Inc. and
sent to Spring Journal, 627 Ursulines Street, #7, New Orleans, LA 70116